Communications in Computer and Information Science

2876

Series Editors

Gang Li , *School of Information Technology, Deakin University, Burwood, VIC, Australia*

Joaquim Filipe, *Polytechnic Institute of Setúbal, Setúbal, Portugal*

Zhiwei Xu, *Chinese Academy of Sciences, Beijing, China*

Rationale

The CCIS series is devoted to the publication of proceedings of computer science conferences. Its aim is to efficiently disseminate original research results in informatics in printed and electronic form. While the focus is on publication of peer-reviewed full papers presenting mature work, inclusion of reviewed short papers reporting on work in progress is welcome, too. Besides globally relevant meetings with internationally representative program committees guaranteeing a strict peer-reviewing and paper selection process, conferences run by societies or of high regional or national relevance are also considered for publication.

Topics

The topical scope of CCIS spans the entire spectrum of informatics ranging from foundational topics in the theory of computing to information and communications science and technology and a broad variety of interdisciplinary application fields.

Information for Volume Editors and Authors

Publication in CCIS is free of charge. No royalties are paid, however, we offer registered conference participants temporary free access to the online version of the conference proceedings on SpringerLink (http://link.springer.com) by means of an http referrer from the conference website and/or a number of complimentary printed copies, as specified in the official acceptance email of the event.

CCIS proceedings can be published in time for distribution at conferences or as post-proceedings, and delivered in the form of printed books and/or electronically as USBs and/or e-content licenses for accessing proceedings at SpringerLink. Furthermore, CCIS proceedings are included in the CCIS electronic book series hosted in the SpringerLink digital library at http://link.springer.com/bookseries/7899. Conferences publishing in CCIS are allowed to use our online conference service (Meteor) for managing the whole proceedings lifecycle (from submission and reviewing to preparing for publication) free of charge.

Publication process

The language of publication is exclusively English. Authors publishing in CCIS have to sign the Springer CCIS copyright transfer form, however, they are free to use their material published in CCIS for substantially changed, more elaborate subsequent publications elsewhere. For the preparation of the camera-ready papers/files, authors have to strictly adhere to the Springer CCIS Authors' Instructions and are strongly encouraged to use the CCIS LaTeX style files or templates.

Abstracting/Indexing

CCIS is abstracted/indexed in DBLP, Google Scholar, EI-Compendex, Mathematical Reviews, SCImago, Scopus. CCIS volumes are also submitted for the inclusion in ISI Proceedings.

How to start

To start the evaluation of your proposal for inclusion in the CCIS series, please send an e-mail to ccis@springer.com

Abolhassan Razminia · Dinh Hoa Nguyen ·
William Holderbaum

Editors

Intelligent Technology for Future Transportation

Second International Symposium, ITFT 2025
London, UK, November 18–20, 2025
Proceedings

 Springer

Editors
Abolhassan Razminia
Persian Gulf University
Bushehr, Iran

Dinh Hoa Nguyen
Kyushu University
Fukuoka, Japan

William Holderbaum
University of Reading
Reading, UK

ISSN 1865-0929   ISSN 1865-0937 (electronic)
Communications in Computer and Information Science
ISBN 978-3-032-20591-9   ISBN 978-3-032-20592-6 (eBook)
https://doi.org/10.1007/978-3-032-20592-6

This Springer imprint is published by the registered company Springer Nature Switzerland AG
The registered company address is: Gewerbestrasse 11, 6330 Cham, Switzerland

If disposing of this product, please recycle the paper.

Preface

We are pleased to present the proceedings of the 2nd International Symposium on Intelligent Technology for Future Transportation (ITFT 2025), held in London, UK, on November 18–20, 2025. The symposium served as a distinguished forum for scholars, researchers, and practitioners from around the world to share and discuss innovative solutions, emerging trends, and the challenges facing the development of intelligent transportation technologies.

The program featured keynote speeches, invited talks, and technical paper presentations covering a wide range of topics including autonomous driving, smart transportation infrastructure, real-time traffic management, and sustainable transportation solutions. The symposium highlighted both theoretical and applied research, fostering interdisciplinary collaboration and knowledge exchange in the rapidly evolving field of intelligent transportation.

All papers included in the ITFT 2025 conference proceedings underwent a rigorous single-blind peer-review process, each evaluated by at least three experts. A total of 67 manuscripts were submitted, of which 26 high-quality papers were accepted for presentation and publication. These contributions reflect a broad spectrum of research and provide valuable insights into current trends and future directions in intelligent transportation technologies.

We sincerely thank all authors for their insightful contributions, the reviewers for their professional dedication, and the organizing committee for their tireless efforts in making ITFT 2025 a success. We hope that the proceedings will serve as a useful resource, inspire further research, and promote continued innovation in the field of intelligent transportation.

December 2025

Abolhassan Razminia
Dinh Hoa Nguyen
William Holderbaum

Organization

Conference Chair

Zaili Yang — Liverpool John Moores University, UK

Program Committee Chairs

Emrah Demir	Cardiff University, UK
Abolhassan Razminia	Persian Gulf University, Iran
Dinh Hoa Nguyen	Kyushu University, Japan
William Holderbaum	University of Reading, UK

Program Committee Co-Chair

Fahimeh Farahnakian — University of Turku, Finland

Technical Program Committee Chairs

Wai Lok Woo	Northumbria University, UK
Wen Xiong	Beijing University of Technology, China

Publicity Chair

Zhenyu Zhao — National University of Singapore, Singapore

Technical Program Committee

Mahdi Abbasi	Bu-Ali Sina University, Iran
Agostinho Agra	University of Lisbon, Portugal
Waqas Ahmed	Universiti Kuala Lumpur, Malaysia
Aranzazu Berbey Alvarez	Universidad Tecnológica de Panamá, Panama
Nasrine Damouche	Université de Toulouse, France
Abolfazl Dehghanmongabadi	Shahrood University of Technology, Iran

Zigang DengSouthwest	Jiaotong University, China
Ehab Diab	University of Saskatchewan, Canada
Sameer-Ud-Din	National University of Sciences & Technology, Pakistan
Boban Djordjevic	KTH Royal Institute of Technology, Sweden
Ni Dong	Southwest Jiaotong University, China
Sunil Kumar Dube	Enphase Energy Inc., USA
Javier Faulin	Public University of Navarra, Spain
Hassen Fourati	Grenoble Alpes University, France
Pak Lun Fung	University of Helsinki, Finland
Stéphane Galland	Belfort-Montbéliard University of Technology, France
Christian Velasco-Gallego	Nebrija University, Spain
Álvaro Paricio García	Universidad de Alcalá, Spain
Marinella Silvana Giunta	Università Mediterranea di Reggio Calabria, Italy
Abdul Karim Gizzini	Institut Mines-Télécom, France
Arkadiusz Gola	Lublin University of Technology, Poland
Paweł Gora	University of Warsaw, Poland
Maciej Grzenda	Warsaw University of Technology, Poland
Tomasz Hachaj	AGH University of Krakow, Poland
Ali Hajbabaie	North Carolina State University, USA
Sadeque Hamdan	University of Kent, UK
Zachary Hamida	Polytechnique Montréal, Canada
Md Mokammel Haque	Chittagong University of Engineering and Technology, Bangladesh
Tarek Hasan	University of Central Florida, USA
Sihong He	University of Connecticut, USA
Brayan González Hernández	Sapienza Università di Roma, Italy
Tran The Hoang	University of Auckland, New Zealand
Weiwei Jiang	Beijing University of Posts and Telecommunications, China
Golam Kabir	University of Regina, Canada
Arkadiusz Kampczyk	AGH University of Science and Technology, Poland
Mumtaz Karatas	Wright State University, USA
Sherzod Khalilov	ISFT Institute, Uzbekistan
Mohamed Khan Afthab Ahamed Khan	UCSI University, Malaysia
Harald Kitzmann	Narva College of the University of Tartu, Estonia
Mladen Krstić	University of Belgrade, Serbia
Rafal Kucharski	Jagiellonian University, Poland
Yifu Lan	Aalto University, Finland

Chien-Sing Lee	Sunway University, Malaysia
Xin Li	Dalian Maritime University, China
Xi Lin	Shanghai Jiao Tong University, China
Xiaoli Liu	University of Helsinki, Finland
Jane Weizhen Lu	City University of Hong Kong, China
Elżbieta Macioszek	Silesian University of Technology, Poland
Nguyen Anh Minh Mai	Valeo, France
Edgar Emanuel González Malla	Universitat Politècnica de València, Spain
Mohamed Amine Masmoudi	Rabat Business School, Morocco
Saleh Mobayen	National Yunlin University of Science & Technology
Faiz Ul Muram	Linnaeus University, Sweden
Husam Muslim	Japan Automobile Research Institution, Japan
Khoa Nguyen	Carleton University, Canada
Thi Thuy Hanh Nguyen	Vietnam National University, Vietnam
Mona Faraji Niri	University of Warwick, UK
Ankit R. Patel	University of Minho, Portugal
Narong Pleerux	Burapha University, Thailand
Waishan Qiu	McKinsey & Company (Shanghai), China
Ikjot Saini	University of Windsor, Canada
Bdereddin Abdul Samad	Higher Institute of Sciences and Technique Al Zahra, Libya
Hadi Sarvari	Hong Kong Polytechnic University, China
Qing Shen	University of Washington, USA
Haotian Shi	University of Wisconsin–Madison, USA
Natalya Shramenko	Hochschule Karlsruhe, Germany
Dragan Simić	University of Novi Sad, Serbia
Željko Stević	University of East Sarajevo, Bosnia and Herzegovina
Burak Taşci	Firat University, Turkey
Burcu Tekeş	Başkent University, Turkey
Ashim Kumar Thapa	George Mason University, USA
Irfan Ullah	Dalian Maritime University, China
Shian Wang	University of Kansas, USA
Yacan Wang	Beijing Jiaotong University, China
Zhiwei Wang	Southwest Jiaotong University, China
Pak Kin Wong	University of Macau, China
Lingxiao Wu	Hong Kong Polytechnic University, China
Yushu Yu	Beijing Institute of Technology, China
Noor Zaman	Taylor's University, Malaysia
Jun Zheng	Southwest Jiaotong University, China

Contents

Transportation Electrification, Energy Systems, and Grid Integration

Intelligent Transportation Systems and Data-Driven Modeling & Optimization

Construction of Smart Highway Knowledge Graph Based on BERT-BGRU Enhanced Model

Rende Cheng[1], Shun Yu[1], Dandan Zhang[2], Quan Yu[3]($\boxtimes$), Huihui Guo[3], and Li Wang[3]

[1] Henan Zhongyuan High-Speed Zhengluo Construction Co., Ltd., Henan 450000, China
[2] Henan Transportation Planning and Design Institute Co., Ltd., Henan 450003, China
[3] North China University of Technology, Beijing 100144, China
YQ973@outlook.com

Abstract. This study has conducted research on entity extraction and relationship extraction for intelligent highways using an enhanced BERT model along with the BGRU model and has integrated knowledge representation methods to fundamentally complete the construction of a knowledge graph in the intelligent highway domain. Initially, by developing the schema layer of the intelligent highway knowledge graph, entities were classified into demand entities, service entities, functional entities, technological entities, and facility entities, and the primary relationships among them were established, including driving, undertaking, providing, and other relationships. The enhanced BERT model was used to extract entities from intelligent highway-related articles, achieving an F1 score of 86.8%, while the relationship extraction model reached an F1 score of 88.3%, both showing a certain degree of improvement over traditional models for entity and relationship extraction. Building on this foundation, through a process of filtering and refining, knowledge representation was ultimately completed in Neo4j, resulting in the construction of a comprehensive intelligent highway knowledge graph.

Keywords: Intelligent High-speed · Knowledge Graph · BERT Enhanced Model · BGRU Enhanced Model · Entity Extraction · Relationship Extraction

1 Introduction

Intelligent highways, leveraging technologies such as digital twins and the Internet of Vehicles (IoV), utilize real-time data and cognitive analytics to enhance safety, efficiency, and sustainability. Despite significant advancements, integrating heterogeneous components and defining their interrelations remain key challenges. Knowledge graphs (KGs) offer a promising solution by providing a structured framework to semantically interconnect heterogeneous data (e.g., services, technologies, infrastructure), thereby enabling intelligent decision-making. The construction of domain-specific KGs typically involves stages like knowledge acquisition, fusion, and storage [1, 2], among which knowledge extraction—encompassing entity and relation extraction—is paramount.

Using an improved BERT-BGRU model, this work suggests an integrated approach for building a knowledge graph customized for intelligent highways. The method

A. Razminia et al. (Eds.): ITFT 2025, CCIS 2876, pp. 3–12, 2026.
https://doi.org/10.1007/978-3-032-20592-6_1

improves entity and relationship extraction by utilizing Bidirectional Gated Recurrent Units (BGRU) for sequence modeling and BERT for contextualized representation learning. The model creates a logical knowledge structure by mapping the links between things and classifying them into groups like demand, service, function, technology, and facility. The success of the suggested approach is demonstrated by the experimental findings, which show an F1 score of 88.3% in relationship extraction and 86.8% in entity extraction.

This paper's remaining sections are organized as follows: Sect. 3 outlines the suggested structure and methods, whereas Sect. 2 examines relevant work.

2 Related Work

The construction of knowledge graphs typically begins with knowledge extraction, which includes entity recognition and relation extraction. Early named entity recognition (NER) systems relied on rule-based and feature-based machine learning methods [1]. With advances in deep learning, neural architectures have significantly improved extraction performance.

For entity extraction, Sherstinsky [2] applied RNNs to extract entities from sequential data but encountered issues such as gradient explosion and limited context integration. Lample et al. [3] used LSTMs to encode text and dynamically select relevant historical information, improving local word associations—though global context remained underutilized. Huang et al. [4] introduced BiLSTM and BiLSTM-CRF models, using bidirectional contextual encoding and conditional random fields for sequence labeling. Devlin et al. [5] proposed BERT, which greatly advanced numerous NLP tasks through pre-trained bidirectional representations. For Chinese NER, Zhang and Yang [6] designed Lattice-LSTM to incorporate character-word interactions, improving boundary detection. Wu et al. [7] later proposed MECT, integrating radical-level features via cross-transformers to further enhance recognition.

In relation extraction, CNNs [8] captured local spatial features, RNNs [9] learned sentence-level representations, and GNNs [10] modeled structural dependencies. Recent trends involve adapting pre-trained models like BERT to specialized domains. Bidirectional Gated Recurrent Units (BGRUs) have also proven effective for capturing sequential patterns in relation extraction [10].

Building upon these foundations, our work integrates BERT and BGRU to enhance both entity and relation extraction for intelligent highways, aiming for superior performance through effective context modeling and semantic integration.

Beyond technical algorithms, knowledge graphs (KGs) are applied in transportation in two primary ways: for macro-analysis of research landscapes using tools like CiteSpace [11], and for micro-analysis of specific events, such as traffic cases, to extract structured details like time and location [12]. The former offers broad field-level insights with simple technology, while the latter provides deep, applicable insights for specific scenarios with more sophisticated models.

3   Knowledge Graph Construction Method

3.1   Construction Process

This study constructs a knowledge graph for intelligent highways using the K-BERT-BGRU model. The process includes entity extraction, relationship extraction, and knowledge representation.

3.2   Entity Extraction

Entity extraction is performed using the K-BERT model. K-BERT integrates domain-specific knowledge, improving entity recognition for intelligent highway data. The model identifies key entities from the textual data related to intelligent highways, such as traffic signals, road types, and vehicle categories.

3.3   Relation Extraction

The BGRU model is used for extracting relationships between entities. It processes the identified entities and determines how they are related within the context of the intelligent highway system.

Table 1. The key advantages of each model

Model	Entity Extraction	Relationship Extraction	Key Advantages
K-BERT	High	High	Integrates knowledge graph, enhances domain-specific entity recognition
BERT	Moderate	High	Strong performance in general NER tasks, lacks domain adaptation
BiLSTM	High	Moderate	Effective in capturing context with sequential data
CNN	Moderate	Moderate	Good for spatial feature extraction but lacks deep context understanding
BGRU	Moderate	High	Efficient in handling sequential dependencies, great for relation extraction

3.4   Knowledge Representation

The extracted entities and relationships are represented as triples (subject, predicate, object) in Neo4j, facilitating efficient querying and managing of the knowledge graph.

3.5 Model Comparison

To evaluate the effectiveness of the K-BERT and BGRU models, we compare them with other state-of-the-art models such as BERT, BiLSTM, and CNN based on their ability to perform entity extraction and relationship extraction. Below is a summary of the key advantages of each model(see Table 1).

The comparison shows that K-BERT outperforms other models in both entity extraction and relationship extraction, thanks to its integration with domain-specific knowledge.

4 Construction Example of Intelligent High-Speed Knowledge Graph

4.1 Pattern Layer Establishment

A knowledge graph is composed of two levels: the schema layer and the data layer. The data layer stores factual information, while the schema layer organizes it. Ontology libraries are used to structure the schema, ensuring hierarchy and minimizing redundancy.

There are two main approaches for constructing the schema:

- Top-down approach: Starts by defining the ontology and schema, then adds entities. This approach uses existing structured knowledge bases, such as Freebase.
- Bottom-up approach: Extracts entities from open linked data and incorporates them into the schema. This is commonly used in projects like Google's Knowledge Vault.

Once constructed, the schema layer consists of the following components:

1. **Requirements**: These are user demands aimed at achieving goals like safety, efficiency, and sustainability. For example, providing information on road conditions or temperature.
2. **Services**: Independent activities that meet intelligent highway needs, such as travel information, traffic control, and data security.
3. **Functions**: Modules that perform specific roles within the system, like perception, service, and management functions.
4. **Technologies**: These support autonomous driving and the overall operation of intelligent highway systems, divided into logic, physical, and innovative technologies.
5. **Facilities**: Physical elements involved in transportation, like vehicles, roads, and infrastructure components.
6. **Relationships**: These define the connections between entities, categorized into **demand-driven** and **technology-driven** scenarios. In demand-driven relationships, services are propelled by demand, while in technology-driven relationships, technology stimulates functions and services.

4.2 Model Set Introduction

(1) Dataset Construction

   The dataset is split into two parts:

- Smart Highway Construction Outlines from 14 provinces (up to 2023).
- Literature dataset from the CNKI database, covering 3,122 articles from 2014 to 2023 related to "smart" and "highway."

40% of the outline dataset is manually annotated, categorizing entities into six groups. A 5% validation set is used for evaluation, and the remaining 55% serves as the test set. BIO annotation format is used:

- **B-X** for the beginning of entities,
- **I-X** for intermediate/ending parts,
- for non-entities.

(2) Dictionary Modification

The K-BERT-BiLSTM model uses google_vocab for entity extraction, but this vocabulary is more suited to general language. To improve domain relevance, an external dictionary based on smart highway-related keywords is introduced, derived from Citespace research. This dictionary is used to enhance the model's domain accuracy.

(3) Entity Extraction

Entity extraction is performed using the K-BERT-BiLSTM model. Key parameters include a sequence length of 256, dropout rate of 0.1, and a batch size of 16. The learning rate is set to 2E-5, and training is conducted for 30 epochs. A comparison is made between K-BERT and BERT-BiLSTM to evaluate the entity recognition performance.

(4) Relationship Extraction

A BGRU-based model is applied for relationship extraction. It processes sentences to identify relationships between entities. Nine types of relationships are considered, with an emphasis on how indicator entities relate to other types of entities.

4.3 Model Run Result

The model's performance is evaluated using traditional deep learning metrics: Precision (P), Recall (R), and F1 score, which is the harmonic mean of precision and recall. The performance metrics are calculated as:

$$P = \frac{T_P}{T_P + F_P} \tag{1}$$

$$R = \frac{T_P}{T_P + F_N} \tag{2}$$

$$F1 = \frac{P + R}{2} \tag{3}$$

where:

- T_P is the number of correct predictions,
- F_P is the number of false positives,
- F_N is the number of false negatives.

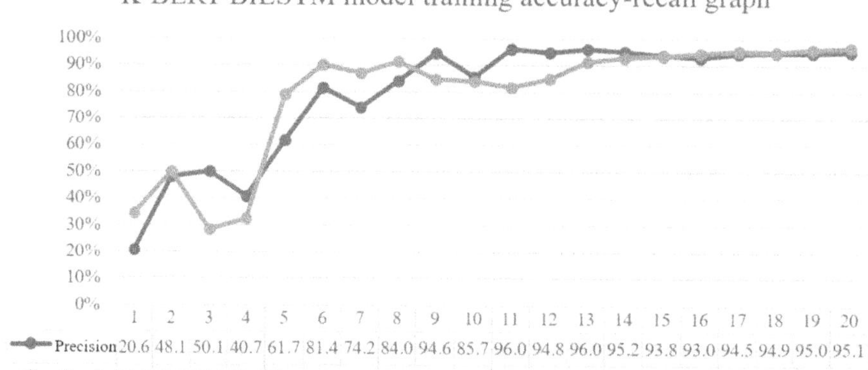

Fig. 1. K-BERT-BILSTM model training process diagram

During training, the model's accuracy and recall initially ranged between 20% and 60% in the first few epochs. After the fifth epoch, the accuracy improved and stabilized by the 13th epoch, achieving 95.1% accuracy and 96.6% recall(see Fig. 1).

The table below compares the performance of different models in terms of **Precision** and **Recall** for entity extraction (see Table 2):

Table 2. Entity recognition effect comparison table

Model	Precision (%)	Recall (%)
K- BERT-LSTM	89.0	94.5
BERT-BiLSTM	90.5	96.2
K- BERT-BiLSTM	95.1	96.6

K-BERT-BiLSTM outperforms other models in both accuracy and recall, largely due to its integration with the K-BERT knowledge graph, enhancing contextual understanding.

In relation extraction, the BGRU model is evaluated against traditional models like LSTM and CNN. The configuration uses 256-dimensional word vectors and 128 hidden units. A summary of performance is shown in the table below (see Table 3):

Table 3. Comparison table of relation extraction effect

Model	Precision (%)	Recall (%)
BGRU	89.2	87.5
LSTM	85.7	84.0
CNN	82.3	81.5

The Bi-GRU model outperforms LSTM and CNN in all metrics, excelling at handling sequential data and long-term dependencies, while also being computationally efficient. The Bi-GRU's gating mechanism ensures it selectively focuses on important features, improving performance while reducing complexity.

4.4   Construction of Knowledge Graph for Smart Highways

Fig. 2. Knowledge Graph excerpt Picture 1

This section of the knowledge graph highlights two central nodes: "Vehicle-road collaboration" and "Cloud Control Platform". These nodes connect to several related sub-nodes, demonstrating the collaboration of components in the intelligent highway system. The "Vehicle-road collaboration" node is linked to "Video Detection," "Visibility Detection," "Weather Station," and "Vehicle Information," enabling real-time data collection and management. The "Cloud Control Platform" connects to sub-nodes such as "Network Management," "Traffic Management," and "Data Processing," focusing on the efficient management of system resources and real-time optimization (see Fig. 2).

Fig. 3. Knowledge Graph excerpt Picture 2

The "Safety Management," "Artificial Intelligence," and "Base Enhancement" nodes are crucial for the system's operational safety and optimization. "Safety Management" is connected to "Situation Awareness" and "Risk Management," ensuring risk mitigation. "Artificial Intelligence" facilitates "Automated Decision Making" and "Fault Warning," while "Base Enhancement" supports the system with "Data Acquisition" and "Remote Monitoring," crucial for maintaining operational stability (see Fig. 3).

Focusing on "5G Technology" and "5G Network," this part of the knowledge graph highlights their role in "Data Collaboration," "Accurate Positioning," and "ETC Technology. " 5G is fundamental for "Intelligent Transportation" systems, enabling real-time monitoring, "Abnormal Event Detection," and enhancing "Smart High-speed Rail" operations (see Fig. 4).

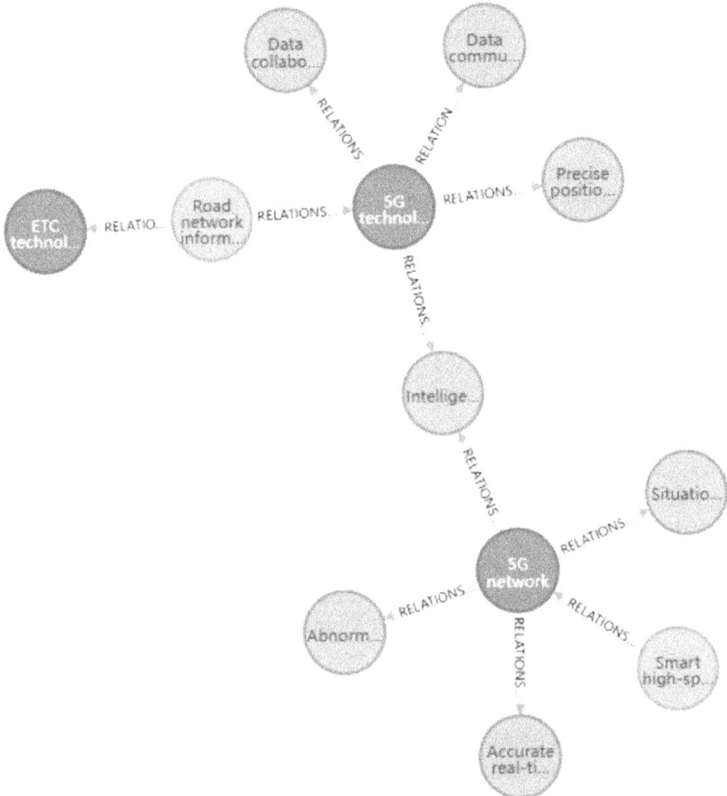

Fig. 4. Knowledge Graph excerpt Picture 3

5 Construction of Intelligent High-Speed Knowledge Graph

The knowledge graph was stored in Neo4j and visualized using different entity categories: facilities (blue), services (pink), requirements (green), functions (orange), technologies (yellow), and evaluation indicators (gray). The graph includes three primary components: perception, communication, and emergency parts.

The perception section covers services like road condition monitoring, wind direction monitoring, and temperature sensing, supported by devices such as CO detectors and video monitors. Evaluation indicators focus on visual coverage, monitoring accuracy, and perception range.

In the communication section, the communication network plays a crucial role in enabling information transmission and supporting edge computing for interaction services. Key metrics like communication range and latency are assessed.

For emergency command services, key functions include event monitoring, incident handling, and command dispatch, with performance evaluated based on metrics like false alarm rate, recognition rate, and emergency response time.

6 Conclusions

The improved BERT-BiLSTM model for entity extraction in Intelligent Highway construction documents is presented in this paper. The model identifies domain-specific entities like traffic signals, road types, and vehicle categories with high accuracy by combining knowledge graph technologies with NER techniques. The ability of K-BERT to capture contextual relationships within highway-related data is improved by the addition of soft positions and a visibility matrix. The findings show that K-BERT-BiLSTM is an effective tool for intelligent transportation systems, outperforming conventional models in entity and relationship extraction.

References

1. China Electronics Standardization Institute (CESI). (2021). White Paper on Standard Digital Knowledge Graph [EB/OL]
2. Sherstinsky, A.: Fundamentals of recurrent neural network (RNN) and long short-term memory (LSTM) network. Physica D: Nonlinear Phenomena **404**, 132306 (2020)
3. Lample, G., Ballesteros, M., Subramanian, S., Kawakami, K., Dyer, C.: Neural architectures for named entity recognition. In: Proceedings of the 2016 Conference of the North American Chapter of the Association for Computational Linguistics: Human Language Technologies, pp. 260–270 (2016)
4. Huang, Z., Xu, W., Yu, K.: Bidirectional LSTM-CRF models for sequence tagging (2015). *arXiv preprint* arXiv:1508.01991
5. Devlin, J., Chang, M. W., Lee, K., Toutanova, K.: BERT: pre-training of deep bidirectional transformers for language understanding. In: Proceedings of the 2019 Conference of the North American Chapter of the Association for Computational Linguistics: Human Language Technologies, Volume 1 (Long and Short Papers), pp. 4171–4186 (2019)
6. Zhang, Y., Yang, J.: Chinese NER using lattice LSTM. In: Proceedings of the 56th Annual Meeting of the Association for Computational Linguistics (Volume 1: Long Papers), pp. 1554–1564 (2018)
7. Wu, S., Song, X., Feng, Z.: MECT: multi-metadata embedding based cross-transformer for Chinese named entity recognition. In: Proceedings of the 59th Annual Meeting of the Association for Computational Linguistics and the 11th International Joint Conference on Natural Language Processing (Volume 1: Long Papers), pp. 1529–1539 (2021)
8. Huang, Y.Y., Wang, W.Y.: Deep residual learning for weakly-supervised relation extraction (2017). *arXiv preprint* arXiv:1707.08866
9. Miwa, M., Bansal, M.: End-to-end relation extraction using LSTMs on sequences and tree structures (2016). *arXiv preprint* arXiv:1601.00770
10. Zhu, H., Lin, Y., Liu, Z., Fu, J., Chua, T.S., Sun, M.: Graph neural networks with generated parameters for relation extraction (2019). *arXiv preprint* arXiv:1902.00756
11. Wu, Y.Q.: Cause analysis of traffic cases based on knowledge graph. China Sci. Technol. Inf. **18**, 138–140 (2023)
12. Tang, J.J., Tuo, H.N., Liu, Y., Wu, X.Y.: Identification method of participants in autonomous transportation system based on BERT-Bi-LSTM-CRF model. J. Transp. Inf. Saf. **40**(5), 80–90 (2022)

Multi-objective Route Planning for Shared Micro-circulation Transit in Future Urban Mobility: A Community-Oriented Approach

Qiming Su[1,2,3] , Xia Luo[1,2,3(✉)] , Yan Zhang[1,2,3], Hongqing Bao[1,2,3], and Hongjie Wang[1,2,3]

[1] School of Transportation and Logistics, Southwest Jiaotong University, Chengdu, People's Republic of China
`xia.luo@263.net`
[2] National Engineering Laboratory of Integrated Transportation Big Data Application Technology, Southwest Jiaotong University, Chengdu, People's Republic of China
[3] National United Engineering Laboratory of Integrated and Intelligent Transportation, Southwest Jiaotong University, Chengdu, People's Republic of China

Abstract. To enhance community-level public transit services and meet residents' mobility needs, this study proposes a bi-level multi-objective model for route and service frequency planning in shared micro-circulation transit systems. The upper-level model focuses on maximizing passenger ridership while minimizing operator costs, and the lower-level model comprehensively captures the passenger travel process through a network-based elastic demand assignment approach. A customized Non-dominated Sorting Genetic Algorithm II (NSGA-II) specifically adapted to the model is employed to generate a diverse set of Pareto-optimal solutions. A case study demonstrates the model's effectiveness and the quality of the solutions, revealing a well-distributed Pareto front with notable diversity. Analysis indicates that solutions prioritizing passenger ridership while balancing cost efficiency can lead to the most significant social and economic benefits. Visualization of the selected routes highlights that micro-circulation transit is particularly advantageous in residential and peripheral areas located farther from transit stations. For practical implementation, aligning stop locations and service sequences with actual demand patterns can significantly enhance passenger convenience and simultaneously reduce operational costs.

Keywords: Micro-Circulation Transit · Route Planning · Multi-Objective Optimization · NSGA-II

1 Introduction

Urbanization has significantly contributed to the development of communities. With the continued expansion of urban areas and the rising demand for sustainable and efficient transportation, the optimization of community-level travel modes has become a prominent focus in academic research and urban planning practice. Traditional public transit systems often fall short in addressing the "last-mile" challenge, particularly in low-density or suburban areas [1]. In response, micro-circulation buses—featuring small vehicle sizes, flexible operations, short routes, and deep community coverage—have emerged as a promising solution for future urban transport, particularly for intra-community mobility. These shared transit services bridge the gap between major transport hubs and local destinations, aligning with the shift toward smart, human-centered mobility. In recent years, several cities have introduced micro-circulation transit services linking residential communities with internal amenities and transit infrastructure [2], enhancing network integration and travel convenience. However, many current practices for route design and service frequency planning of micro-circulation buses rely heavily on manual methods, lacking a robust theoretical foundation. Consequently, these systems often face challenges in balancing passenger demand with operational efficiency and show limited adaptability to changing travel patterns.

Recent studies increasingly highlight the importance of micro-circulation transit in addressing community-level travel needs and the challenges mentioned above. Early research primarily focused on feeder services to tackle issues of community connectivity. For instance, Chien et al. developed a joint optimization model for urban rail lines and their feeder bus routes to minimize the total cost of both systems, supported by sensitivity analysis [3]. Ceder et al. proposed an index for potential demand and a model maximizing demand potential under circulating travel time constraints [4]. Sha et al. evaluated transit convenience through access and connectivity measures and proposed a mixed-integer programming model for optimizing stop locations [5]. Yu et al. optimized the circulator bus route and stopping sequence for last-mile connectivity to commuter rail by minimizing passenger and operator costs using a bi-level model and tabu search algorithm [6]. In recent years, researchers have shifted focus to micro-circulation buses as a solution for regional travel needs. Chen et al. optimized metro first/last-mile micro-circulation bus routes and schedules while considering competition from shared bikes, using a bi-level model and an enhanced genetic algorithm [1]. Du et al. designed micro-circulation buses for first/last-mile transit by clustering stations based on multimodal transportation data, constructing a spatiotemporal Origin-Destination (OD) transition network, and optimizing routes with an iterative greedy algorithm [2]. Wang et al. proposed a terminal-based zonal bus system to balance demand-responsive flexibility with operational costs, optimizing routing with a tailored heuristic algorithm that incorporates real-time adaptability and terminal constraints [7].

Most research on micro-circulation buses focuses on their role as feeders to transit stations, typically based on a "many-to-one" travel pattern where passengers board at multiple stops and alight at a single transit station [8]. However, limited attention has been given to intra-community demand. As the basic unit of urban structure, communities exhibit diverse land uses—such as residential, commercial, and service facilities—resulting in complex, "many-to-many" travel needs. To effectively serve these demands, the system must go beyond transit connectivity and address internal mobility. Moreover, prior studies often emphasize route design while neglecting operational factors, such as departure frequency. This study addresses these gaps by proposing a bi-level, multi-objective optimization model for jointly planning micro-circulation bus routes and departure schedules, using NSGA-II algorithm to identify Pareto-optimal solutions. A case study is also conducted to demonstrate the model's applicability.

2 Bi-Level Multi-objective Route Planning Model for Community Micro-circulation Buses

2.1 Problem Statement

This study focuses on the joint planning of micro-circulation bus routes and departure frequencies in communities with a single urban rail transit station. A "many-to-many" demand framework is employed to capture the complexities of mixed land use. The design features circular route that uses the rail transit station as terminal point.

The model is based on several assumptions: (1) bus routes connect exclusively to the internal rail station; (2) inter-district trips are made via either rail or conventional buses; (3) candidate bus stop locations are predefined, and the shortest paths and distances between each pair of candidate stops are known; and (4) travel demand is aggregated at the centroids of blocks.

2.2 Passenger Travel Process Network

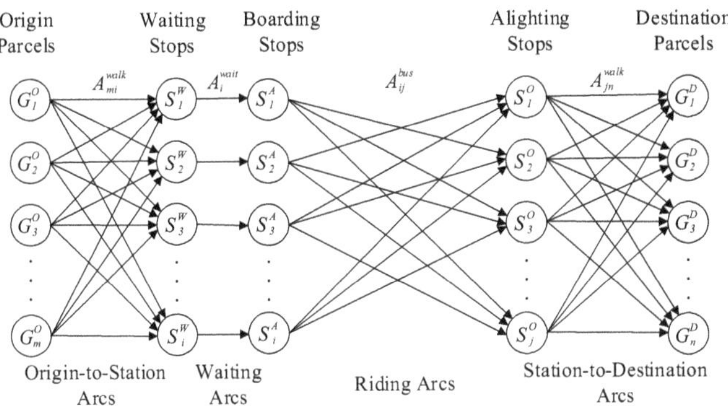

Fig. 1. Schematic diagram of bus passenger's travel process network

Based on the complete travel processes of passengers from their origin to destination, a network illustrating the processes is constructed, as shown in Fig. 1. The network is modeled as a directed graph $H = (V, A)$, let $V = G^O \cup G^D \cup S^W \cup S^A \cup S^O$ represent the set of all nodes in the network. The set of directed arcs between nodes is denoted by $A = A_{mi}^{walk} \cup A_i^{wait} \cup A_{ij}^{bus} \cup A_{jn}^{walk}$. Each arc is associated with a cost attribute, defined as the time required for the corresponding stage of the passenger's journey. Their costs can be determined using the following methods:

1) Origin-to-Station Arcs A_{mi}^{walk}: For any given pair of origin nodes and waiting stop nodes, an origin-to-station arc represents a passenger walking from origin point m to the waiting stop i via the shortest path, with the time cost calculated as:

$$T_{mi}^{walk} = \frac{d_{mi}\varphi_{mi}}{V_{walk}} \quad \forall m \in G^O, \ i \in S^W, \tag{1}$$

where d_{mi} is the shortest walking distance (km) from land parcel m to bus stop i; φ_{mi} is a binary variable, $\varphi_{mi} = 1$ if the passenger at parcel m chooses to wait at stop i, and $\varphi_{mi} = 0$ otherwise; V_{walk} is the average walking speed (km/h).

2) Waiting Arcs A_i^{wait}: For each waiting–boarding stop pair, a waiting arc represents the passenger's waiting process at stop i. Assuming passenger waiting times follow a uniform distribution $t_{wait} \sim U(0, 1/f)$, where f is the micro-circulation bus departure frequency (vehicles/hour), the expected waiting time is:

$$T_i^{wait} = \frac{1}{2f} \quad \forall i \in S^W. \tag{2}$$

3) Riding Arcs A_{ij}^{bus}: For each boarding–alighting stop pair, a riding arc represents in-vehicle travel from boarding stop i to alighting stop j. If i follows j in the circular route sequence, the passenger remains onboard until the bus completes the loop and transfers to the next vehicle. The additional waiting time equals the gap between the current bus's terminal arrival and the next departure, determined by the total route travel time l/V_{bus} and the departure interval $1/f$. The total riding time is calculated as:

$$T_{ij}^{bus} = \frac{d_{ij}}{V_{bus}} + \frac{1}{f} - \left(\frac{l}{V_{bus}} - \frac{1}{f} \left\lfloor \frac{l}{V_{bus}} f \right\rfloor \right) \xi_{ij} \quad \forall i \in S^A, \; j \in S^O, \tag{3}$$

where d_{ij} is the distance (km) along the bus route from the boarding stop i to the alighting stop j; $\lfloor \cdot \rfloor$ is the greatest integer less than or equal to the given variable; l is route length (km); V_{bus} is average travel speed of the bus (km/h); ξ_{ij} is a binary variable, $\xi_{ij} = 1$ if stop i follows stop j in the circular route sequence, and $\xi_{ij} = 0$ otherwise.

4) Station-to-Destination Arcs A_{jn}^{walk}: For any pair of alighting stop and destination node, a station-to-destination arc is constructed to represent the walking process from alighting stop j to the final destination n. The time cost is calculated as:

$$T_{jn}^{walk} = \frac{d_{jn}\varphi_{jn}}{V_{walk}} \quad \forall j \in S^O, \; n \in G^D, \tag{4}$$

where d_{jn} is the shortest walking distance (km) from bus stop j to land parcel n; φ_{jn} is a binary variable, $\varphi_{jn} = 1$ if the passenger traveling to parcel n chooses to alight at stop j, and $\varphi_{jn} = 0$ otherwise.

2.3 Elastic Passenger Demand Analysis

Service quality significantly affects passenger choice of micro-circulation buses. When competing modes remain constant, improvements in micro-circulation service can increase ridership. As route configurations influence service levels across OD pairs, demand also varies. This study optimizes route design and departure frequency to boost ridership. To quantify demand response, an elasticity coefficient λ is introduced. Based on baseline values, the elastic demand function can be constructed as follows:

$$P_{ab}^{bus} = \overline{P_{ab}^{bus}} \times e^{\lambda_{ab}\left(\frac{T_{ab}^{walk}-T_{ab}^{bus}}{T_{ab}^{walk}}-\overline{\alpha_{ab}}\right)} \quad \forall a \in G^O \cup \{r\}, b \in G^D \cup \{r\}, a \neq b, \quad (5)$$

where a represents the origin parcel $m \in G^O$ or the rail transit station r, b represents the destination parcel $n \in G^D$ or the rail transit station r. λ_{ab} denotes demand elasticity coefficient, reflecting sensitivity to service quality. Greater elasticity results in more pronounced ridership changes with service adjustments. $\overline{P_{ab}^{bus}}$ represents baseline demand, estimated from projected micro-circulation bus ridership, and $\overline{\alpha_{ab}}$ is the baseline service level, calibrated by the relative reduction in travel time that micro-circulation buses provide compared to walking.

2.4 The Bi-Level Multi-objective Optimization Model for Micro-Circulation Bus Route Planning and Departure Frequency Scheduling

This study presents a bi-level multi-objective model for optimizing micro-circulation bus routes and departure frequencies. The upper level maximizes ridership and minimizes operating costs, while the lower level simulates passenger route choices based on the travel process network to estimate demand. A feedback mechanism links the two levels: service plans influence passenger behavior, which in turn updates demand and prompts iterative refinement of upper-level decisions. The upper-level objectives are:

1) Maximizing Bus Ridership: Passenger volume serves as a critical metric for assessing the effectiveness of transit services, reflecting the extent to which established routes align with the travel demands of residents. Higher ridership also translates into greater social benefits. The objective function is defined as:

$$\max Z_1 = \sum_{i \in S^A, i \neq j} \sum_{j \in S^O} \sum_{m \in G^O, m \neq n} \sum_{n \in G^D} P_{mn}^{bus}\varphi_{mi}\varphi_{jn} + \sum_{i \in S^A} \sum_{m \in G^O} P_{mr}^{bus}\varphi_{mi} + \sum_{j \in S^O} \sum_{n \in G^D} P_{rn}^{bus}\varphi_{jn}. \quad (6)$$

2) Minimizing Operating Costs: Micro-circulation bus operating costs—including energy, depreciation, maintenance, and labor—are assumed proportional to total vehicle-kilometers traveled. Therefore, the total operating cost is formulated as:

$$\min Z_2 = fh \sum_{k \in K} q_k \delta_k, \quad (7)$$

where K denotes the set of road segments in the area; h represents the duration of the planning period (h); q_k indicates the length of segment k (km); and δ_k is a binary variable, where $\delta_k = 1$ if the bus route traverses segment k, and $\delta_k = 0$ otherwise.

The upper-level multi-objective optimization problem can be formulated as:

$$\max Z_1, \quad \min Z_2$$

$$s.t.\ l_{\min} \le l \le l_{\max}, \tag{8}$$

$$d_{\min} \le d_{ij}\theta_{ij} \le d_{\max}, \quad \forall i \in S^A,\ j \in S^O, \tag{9}$$

$$t_{\min} \le \frac{1}{f} \le t_{\max}, \tag{10}$$

$$\frac{1}{f} - \left(\frac{l}{V_{bus}} - \frac{1}{f} \left\lfloor \frac{l}{V_{bus}} f \right\rfloor \right) \le t_{\max}^{transfer}, \tag{11}$$

$$\sum_{i \in S^A, i \ne j}\ \sum_{j \in S^O} \delta_{i,j,k}\theta_{ij} + \sum_{i \in S^A} \delta_{i,r,k}\theta_{ir} + \sum_{j \in S^O} \delta_{r,j,k}\theta_{rj} = \delta_k\ k \in K, \tag{12}$$

$$\sum_{m \in G^O, m \ne n}\ \sum_{i \in S^A} \left(\sum_{n \in G^D} P_{mn}^{bus} + P_{mr}^{bus} \right)\varphi_{mi} + \sum_{n \in G^D} P_{rn}^{bus} = \sum_{n \in G^D, n \ne m}\ \sum_{j \in S^O} \left(\sum_{m \in G^O} P_{mn}^{bus} + P_{rn}^{bus} \right)\varphi_{jn} + \sum_{m \in G^O} P_{mr}^{bus}, \tag{13}$$

$$\sum_{i \in S^A, i \ne j}\ \sum_{j \in S^O} P_{ij}\delta_{i,j,k} + \sum_{i \in S^A} P_{ir}\delta_{i,r,k} + \sum_{j \in S^O} P_{rj}\delta_{r,j,k} \le P_{\max}\ \forall k \in K, \tag{14}$$

$$\varphi_{mi},\varphi_{jn} \in \{0,1\}\ \ \forall m \in G^O, n \in G^D, i \in S^W, j \in S^O, \tag{15}$$

$$\xi_{ij} \in \{0,1\}\ \forall i \in S^A, j \in S^O, \tag{16}$$

$$\delta_k \in \{0,1\}\ \forall k \in K, \tag{17}$$

$$\theta_{ij}, \theta_{ir}, \theta_{rj} \in \{0,1\}\ \forall i \in S^A, j \in S^O, \tag{18}$$

$$\delta_{i,j,k}, \delta_{i,r,k}, \delta_{r,j,k} \in \{0,1\}\ \forall i \in S^A, j \in S^O, k \in K. \tag{19}$$

Constraint (8) ensures the total route length remains within acceptable limits; constraint (9) regulates the spacing between consecutive stops; constraint (10) sets bounds on the departure headway; constraint (11) ensures adequate transfer connection time; constraint (12) prevents route overlap on the same road segments; constraint (13) maintains passenger flow balance; constraint (14) limits passenger loads according to vehicle capacity; and constraints (15) through (19) define binary decision variables to capture route structure and stop sequence logic. θ_{ij}, θ_{ir}, and θ_{rj} are binary variables. If stops i and j are consecutive in the bus route, and stop j follows i, then $\theta_{ij} = 1$; otherwise, $\theta_{ij} = 0$. The same logic applies to θ_{ir} and θ_{rj}. $\delta_{i,j,k}$, $\delta_{i,r,k}$, and $\delta_{r,j,k}$ are binary variables. If road segment k is included in the bus route between stops i and j, then $\delta_{i,j,k} = 1$, otherwise $\delta_{i,j,k} = 0$. The same logic applies to $\delta_{i,r,k}$ and $\delta_{r,j,k}$.

The lower-level model identifies passenger travel processes and evaluates passenger demand. For each OD pair, it is assumed that passengers will choose the route with the lowest time cost utilizing the travel process network. Solving the resulting shortest-path problem yields travel times, which are then used to assess service levels. These service level values are integrated into the elastic demand function introduced in Sect. 2.3 to estimate actual ridership. The calculated passenger demand is subsequently fed back to the upper-level model, enabling iterative adjustments to routing and frequency decisions based on the updated demand feedback.

3 Algorithmic Framework for Model Solution

This study presents a multi-objective optimization model to balance the often-conflicting goals of passengers and operators in micro-circulation bus systems. By exploring the Pareto front, the model identifies a range of non-dominated solutions, offering decision-makers flexible and efficient route planning schemes that capture trade-offs between objectives. The NSGA-II algorithm is employed for its effectiveness in generating high-quality Pareto-optimal sets through fast non-dominated sorting, elitism, and crowding distance preservation [9].

To reflect feedback between model levels, passenger travel behavior—modeled through the travel process network—is embedded within the NSGA-II framework. The algorithm structure is illustrated in Fig. 2, and its key components are as follows:

1) Chromosome Encoding and Decoding

This study employs a dual-chromosome structure that encodes route selection and departure frequency separately. Departure intervals are encoded as real-valued genes. Due to the complexity of bus routing constraints, directly solving the route planning problem without prior restrictions can generate numerous infeasible solutions. To mitigate this issue, a priority-based indirect encoding method is utilized for the route selection chromosomes [10]. The candidate station set C with cardinality $len(C)$ is encoded as a permutation of unique integers, representing priority levels (Fig. 3). For each station C_i, a predefined reachable set $C_i^{next} \subseteq C$ determines potential extensions, with the next stop selected from C_i^{next} based on the chromosome's priority. To avoid loops, already-included stations are excluded from future selections. If no further

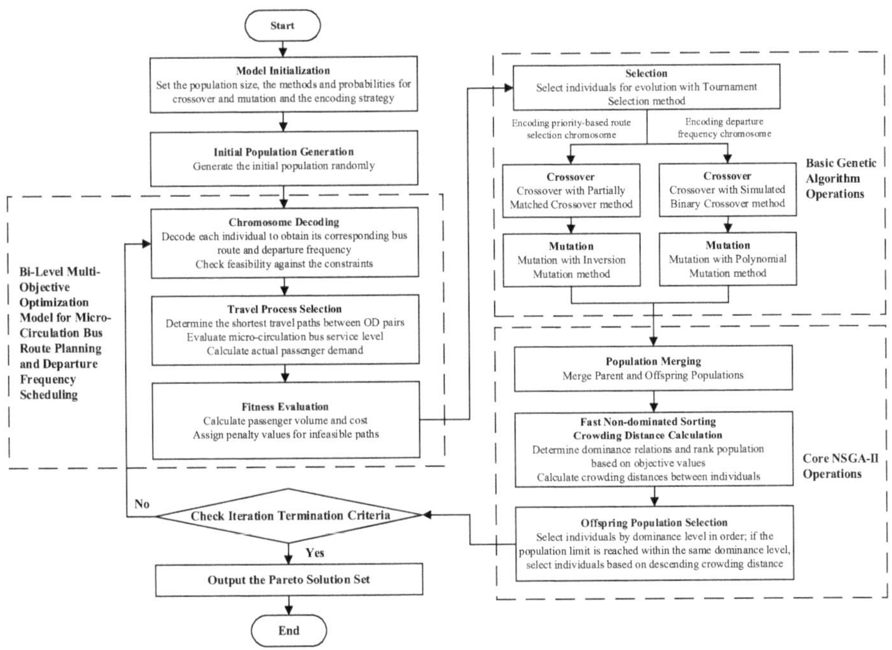

Fig. 2. Flow chart of NSGA-II algorithm

station is reachable, the route is terminated and marked infeasible. By embedding constraints into the reachability definition, the method improves the feasibility ratio during evolution.

Bus Stop Number	1	2	3	4	5	6	7	8
Priority (Encoding Object)	3	1	6	8	2	4	7	5

Fig. 3. Schematic diagram of priority-based encoding method

2) Core Procedures of NSGA-II Algorithm

NSGA-II solves multi-objective problems by ranking individuals via Pareto dominance and grouping them into non-dominated fronts. Crowding distance is computed within each front to preserve diversity. During selection, individuals from higher-ranking fronts are chosen first. If the size limit is reached within a front, those with greater crowding distance are prioritized. This approach ensures convergence toward optimal solutions while maintaining diversity, producing a well-distributed Pareto front.

4 Numerical Example Analysis

4.1 Description of Numerical Example

This study uses a planned residential community in Chengdu, China, as a case study, with the study area defined based on a 15-min radius livelihood service circle. The local road network is abstracted into a virtual network (Fig. 4), where all roads are accessible to micro-circulation buses. A north–south metro line includes a station at node 0, serving as both the origin and terminal for the micro-circulation bus. Nodes 1–27 denote candidate bus stops. The area comprises 30 land parcels (#1–#30) categorized into various land-use types, including mixed-use zones. The land-use types are classified based on both actual and planned uses as follows: Residential (#2 #4 #5 #7 #11 #12 #13 #14 #17 #18 #19 #20 #22 #24 #25 #26 #27 #28 #29); Commercial (#1 #6 #8 #9 #10 #14 #15 #16 #22 #23); Service Facilities (#3 #8 #24 #30); Primary and Secondary School (#3 #4 #21 #24 #25); Park and Green Space (#1 #26) and Social Welfare Land (#30). Analysis focuses on the morning period, defined as 6:30–9:30 AM.

The micro-circulation bus system is designed to accommodate passengers of all age groups. The average passenger walking speed V_{walk} is set at 3 km/h. Given the dense stop spacing and local road conditions, the bus travel speed V_{bus} is set at 15 km/h. Departure headways range from 3 to 10 min, while stop spacing varies between 200 and 600 m. Route lengths are constrained between 2 km and 10 km. Each bus has a maximum capacity P_{max} of 50 passengers. The baseline service level $\overline{\alpha_{ab}}$ is set at 0.75, and the demand elasticity coefficient λ_{ab} is fixed at 0.3.

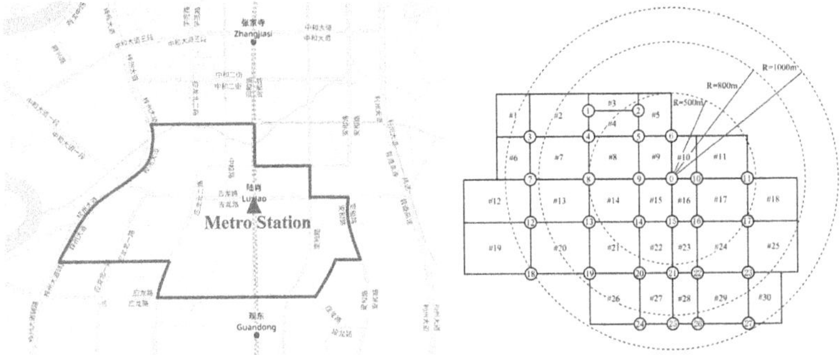

Fig. 4. Schematic diagram of road network within the research area

4.2 Results and Analysis of Case Study

These calibrated parameter values were applied to the bi-level multi-objective optimization model for micro-circulation bus routing. NSGA-II was utilized for solution, with the following settings: population size $pop\_num = 50$, crossover probability $P_c = 0.9$, mutation probability $P_m = 0.2$, and maximum number of generations max $\_gen = 500$.

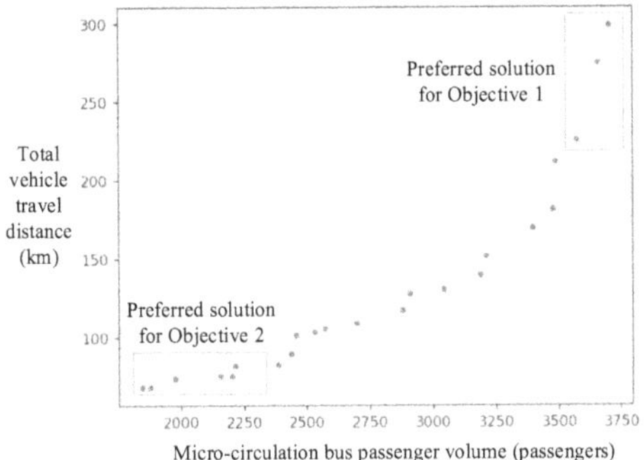

Fig. 5. Pareto Set of the multi-objective optimization model

The Pareto solution set generated by the NSGA-II algorithm is illustrated in Fig. 5. Unlike weighted-sum approaches, Pareto-based optimization provides a diverse set of non-dominated solutions, enhancing flexibility in decision-making. Each solution reflects a different trade-off between objectives; improvements in one may compromise another. Table 1 presents optimal solutions for individual objectives.

Table 1. The optimal solution of each target corresponds to the value of the objective function

	Bus Ridership (passengers)	Total vehicle travel distance (km)
Optimal Solution for Objective 1 (Maximizing Bus Ridership)	3702	298.9
Optimal Solution for Objective 2 (Minimizing Operating Costs)	1846	68.4

To maximize ridership, more stops are added to improve accessibility, attracting up to 3,702 passengers. However, this also increases route length (298.9 km) and travel time, potentially deterring some users. In contrast, minimizing operating costs favors shorter routes and lower frequencies, reducing both service quality and ridership. The cost-minimization solution serves 1,846 passengers over 68.4 km. These trade-offs emphasize the need to balance user benefits and operational efficiency.

Table 2. Some selected routes and their indicators

Path ID	Micro-circulation bus passenger volume (passengers)	Departure Interval (min)	Value of Objective 1	Value of Objective 2	Average One-way Ridership (passengers)	Peak segment load (passengers)
1	0-6-5-1-8-7-12–13-19-20-22-23-17-16-14-9-0	5	3477	181.3	97	41
2	0-6-5-2-1-8-7-12-13-19-20-22-23-17-16-15-0	6	3188	139.5	106	50
3	0-6-5-4-7-12-13-19-20-22-23-17-16-15-0	7	2697	109.2	108	44
4	0-10-22-20-19-13-12-7-4-5-9-0	8	2387	82.8	108	47

By decoding chromosomes from the Pareto set, feasible micro-circulation bus routes are obtained. The most socially and economically beneficial solutions are those that strike a balance between high ridership and operational efficiency. Several representative solutions were selected from the Pareto front and analyzed (Table 2), with corresponding routes illustrated in Fig. 6. These routes display notable diversity, reflecting the flexibility of the proposed model. In practice, selections can consider factors like road capacity and traffic management to align with real-world conditions.

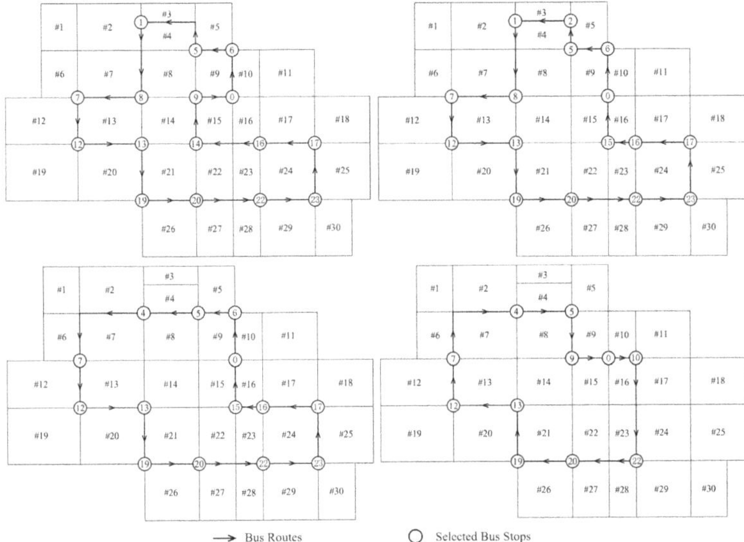

Fig. 6. Schematic diagram of some selected routes

Insights from Fig. 6 and Table 2 reveal that high-performing routes often serve both peripheral residential zones and secondary areas, highlighting the micro-circulation bus's role in enhancing connectivity for underserved locations. Additionally, not all candidate stops are used. Where stop coverage areas overlap, only one may be selected to improve travel speed and overall service efficiency.

5   Conclusion

This study addresses the integrated design of micro-circulation bus routes and service frequencies for community-based transit. A bi-level multi-objective optimization model is proposed to jointly optimize route configuration, stop selection, and departure frequency. The NSGA-II algorithm is employed to generate a diverse Pareto front of non-dominated solutions. The key conclusions are as follows:

1) At the upper level, the model aims to maximize ridership while minimizing operator costs, subject to constraints including route length, headway, stop spacing, transfer time, and vehicle capacity. The lower level simulates passenger travel behavior using a network-based travel choice model.
2) To solve the bi-level multi-objective model, the NSGA-II algorithm was utilized, employing a dual-chromosome approach to encode route selection and departure frequency separately. To enhance computational efficiency, a priority-based encoding method was applied to the route selection chromosome.
3) Numerical examples demonstrated the model's effectiveness and accuracy, resulting in a well-distributed and diverse Pareto solution set. The heterogeneous impacts of the two objectives on optimal routes are analyzed, providing valuable insights for balancing competing goals in practical applications.

4) Findings show that major demand originates from residential zones, especially those distant from rail stations. Optimizing stop placement and route sequences based on demand distribution improves both user convenience and operational efficiency.

As a vital means of addressing the travel needs of community residents, micro-circulation buses significantly enhance travel convenience and promote public transit usage. With the increasing personalization of passenger travel demands, it is imperative that micro-circulation bus route planning and operational scheduling continue to evolve to meet these new requirements.

Acknowledgments. This work was supported by the Science & Technology Project of Sichuan Province under Grant [No. 24NSFSC0356] and Program of China Scholarship Council [No. 202307000110].

Disclosure of Interests. The authors have no competing interests to declare that are relevant to the content of this article.

References

1. Chen, Y., Lai, Y., Easa, S.M., Wang, S.: Microcirculation bus routes design and coordinated schedules considering the impact of shared bicycles. J. Transp. Eng. Part A Syst. **150**, 1–11 (2024). https://doi.org/10.1061/jtepbs.teeng-8396
2. Du, B., Qiao, Y., Zhao, J., Sun, L., Lv, W., Huang, R.: Urban micro-circulation bus planning based on temporal and spatial travel demand. In: Proceedings of 2019 IEEE SmartWorld, Ubiquitous Intelligence & Computing, Advanced & Trusted Computing, Scalable Computing & Communications, Cloud & Big Data Computing, Internet of People and Smart City Innovation (SmartWorld/SCALCOM/UIC/ATC/CBDCom/IOP/SCI) 2019, pp. 982–988 (2019). https://doi.org/10.1109/SmartWorld-UIC-ATC-SCALCOM-IOP-SCI.2019.00193
3. Chien, S., Schonfeld, P.: Joint optimization of a rail transit line and its feeder bus system. J. Adv. Transp. **32**, 253–284 (1998). https://doi.org/10.1002/atr.5670320302
4. Ceder, A.: Stepwise multi-criteria and multi-strategy design ofpublic transit shuttles. **38**, 21–38 (2010). https://onlinelibrary.wiley.com/doi/10.1002/mcda.436
5. Mamun, S.A., Lownes, N.E.: Access and connectivity trade-offs in transit stop location. Transp. Res. Rec. **2466**, 1–11 (2014). https://doi.org/10.3141/2466-01
6. Yu, Y., Machemehl, R.B., Xie, C.: Demand-responsive transit circulator service network design. Transp. Res. Part E Logist. Transp. Rev. **76**, 160–175 (2015). https://doi.org/10.1016/j.tre.2015.02.009
7. Wang, Y., Chen, J., Liu, Z.: Terminal-based zonal bus: a novel flexible transit system design and implementation. Expert Syst. Appl. **238**, 121793 (2024). https://doi.org/10.1016/j.eswa.2023.121793
8. Vansteenwegen, P., Melis, L., Aktaş, D., Montenegro, B.D.G., Sartori Vieira, F., Sörensen, K.: A survey on demand-responsive public bus systems. Transp. Res. Part C Emerg. Technol. 137, 103573 (2022). https://doi.org/10.1016/j.trc.2022.103573
9. Deb, K., Pratap, A., Agarwal, S., Meyarivan, T.: A fast and elitist multiobjective genetic algorithm: NSGA-II. IEEE Trans. Evol. Comput. **6**, 182–197 (2002). https://doi.org/10.1109/4235.996017
10. Gen, M., Cheng, R., Wang, D.: Genetic algorithms for solving shortest path problems. In: Proceedings of IEEE Conference on Evolutionary Computation, ICEC, pp. 401–406 (1997). https://doi.org/10.1109/icec.1997.592343

A Graph Attention Model for the Team Orienteering Problem

Ivan Guillermo Peña-Arenas[1(✉)], Rym Nesrine Guibadj[1], Cyril Fonlupt[1], and Sohaib Afifi[2]

[1] Université du Littoral Côte d'Opale, 62228 Calais, Hauts-de-France, France
`exp684@yahoo.com`
[2] Université d'Artois, 62400 Béthune, Hauts-de-France, France

Abstract. The Team Orienteering Problem (TOP) is a combinatorial optimization problem where the objective is to determine a set of routes that maximizes the profit earned from visiting customers without exceeding a travel cost or time limit. Recent advancements have shown that combining machine learning approaches with optimization techniques can effectively tackle complex combinatorial problems. In this paper, we introduce two deep reinforcement learning methods to solve the TOP. The first framework is a Hybrid Graph Attention Model (HGAM) that integrates a deep learning neural network with dynamic programming algorithm (optimal splitting). The algorithm operates in two steps: first, a *giant tour*—a sequence of customers or locations—is generated using a deep neural network; second, this tour is evaluated through an optimal splitting algorithm. The second framework is a full-learning approach based on sampling decoding and mask mechanism to generate a feasible routes. Our experimental results demonstrate that HGAM not only outperforms a full-learning approach but also provides significantly faster results, at the cost of lower solution quality compared to specialized heuristics designed for the TOP.

Keywords: Team Orienteering Problem · Reinforcement Deep Learning · Splitting Algorithm · Heuristics

1 Introduction

The Team Orienteering Problem (TOP) extends the classical Orienteering Problem—also known as the Selective Traveling Salesman Problem—by allowing multiple tours. In this setting, a collection of candidate customers is provided, each associated with a profit that is earned upon visitation. A fleet of vehicles must serve these customers within predetermined time limits, and each customer may be visited by at most one vehicle. The objective is to choose the subset of customers that maximizes the total collected profit while ensuring that every tour respects its time constraint. The problem was originally introduced under the name Multiple Tour Maximum Collection Problem in [1], and was later formalized as the TOP and shown to be NP-hard by Chao et al. [2].

A. Razminia et al. (Eds.): ITFT 2025, CCIS 2876, pp. 25–36, 2026.
https://doi.org/10.1007/978-3-032-20592-6_3

A variety of challenging real-world problems have been formulated as orienteering problems. Examples include logistics applications, where customer delivery urgency is treated as the score, and tourist trip planning, in which the aim is to select the most attractive points of interest for visitors exploring a city or region [25].

Recent advances in deep learning—such as pointer networks, attention-based models, graph neural networks, and reinforcement learning—have shown strong capabilities in addressing combinatorial optimization problems (COPs) [3]. Deep neural networks (DNNs) are particularly appealing because they can produce high-quality solutions quickly, require limited domain-specific expertise, and benefit from parallel computation [4].

To explore alternative strategies, hybrid DNNs have been developed, often integrating optimization algorithms with machine learning models to enhance performance across various contexts, including exact and heuristic methods. In line with this idea, we propose a distinct perspective: instead of using a DNN to support an optimization algorithm, we leverage an exact method to guide and improve the DNN's learning process. Hence, our objective is to enhance the learning process by generating high-quality policies in short computational time, relying on an optimal algorithm used within the DNN framework. Although this concept has been previously proposed to solve the CVRP [5], to the best of our knowledge, this is the first implementation of this idea in the context of the Team Orienteering Problem (TOP).

We propose a Hybrid Graph Attention Model (HGAM) applied to solve the TOP. The algorithm integrates an efficient splitting algorithm, introduced in [6], within a deep learning model. This hybrid approach operates in two steps. First, a *"giant tour"* (a sequence of customers/locations) is generated in a constructive manner using a deep neural network. Then, this tour is evaluated using the splitting algorithm. By following this strategy, the DNN is tasked with only one job —generating the giant tour— with the aim of improving both solution quality and the speed of the overall method, although in practice the main improvement was in speed. During the splitting procedure, an optimal algorithm is employed, ensuring high-quality solutions. The main objective is to narrow the solution space in which the deep learning model operates (i.e., producing an optimal set of sub-tours for each giant tour), which is expected to result in overall better performance.

The paper is organized as follows. Section 2 presents a literature review of current trends in applying DNNs to solve COPs, while Sect. 3 describes our deep learning frameworks. The computational results are presented and discussed in Sect. 4, and conclusions are drawn in Sect. 5.

2   Related Work

Recently, there has been a surge of studies proposing Deep Neural Networks (DNNs) to solve Combinatorial Optimization Problems (COPs) [7]. In general, there are two main trends: constructive algorithms and hybrid algorithms. Constructive algorithms incrementally add elements to a sequence until a complete solution is generated. Hybrid methods combine DNNs with other algorithms (i.e., heuristics, metaheuristics, and exact methods) to develop solutions that exploit the advantages of both approaches.

Constructive algorithms based on Pointer Networks (PNs) use an encoder - decoder architecture where the encoder embeds a COP instance and the decoder iteratively generates a solution. Vinyals et al. [8] introduced the first PN for the TSP, trained with supervised learning and effective on small instances, but limited by reliance on costly labeled solutions and inability to surpass training labels [10,14]. Bello et al. [9] addressed this by training PNs with reinforcement learning (actor–critic) and Active Search, improving generalization through direct reward-driven exploration. Subsequent work incorporated attention and set-based encodings—Deudon et al. [11] added an attention mechanism and 2-opt post-processing, Nazari et al. [10] generalized the framework to various COPs (notably VRP and split deliveries), and Kool et al. [13] showed that a Multi-Head Attention model with a greedy rollout baseline yields further gains. More recently, Li et al. [12] combined MHA with dynamic embeddings and local search for the Covering Salesman Problem, achieving large speedups over traditional heuristics with only a small optimality gap.

Graph Neural Networks (GNNs) have also been explored for constructive algorithms in COPs. Khalil et al. [15] used reinforcement learning with Structure2Vec embeddings to learn greedy heuristics, showing good generality across problems, though Pointer Networks with actor–critic performed better for the TSP. Nowak et al. [14] proposed a GNN model with local and higher-order graph operators, achieving $O(n^2)$ scalability superior to SDP relaxations, but slightly worse results than auto-regressive PNs [16]. To improve performance, Joshi et al. [17] applied Graph ConvNets with beam search, outperforming earlier approaches [13,15]. More recently, Kool et al. [18] introduced Deep Policy Dynamic Programming (DPDP), based on Graph ConvNets [17], which achieves near-optimal results on 100-node TSPs.

Another line of research integrates Deep Neural Networks (DNNs) with heuristic and exact methods to enhance solution quality and efficiency. Chen et al. [19] introduced a neural-based policy model that iteratively rewrites local parts of solutions until convergence, effectively combining neural guidance with local search to improve results on problems such as the TSP and VRP. Similarly, Hottung and Tierney [20] incorporated learned heuristics into a Large Neighborhood Search (LNS) framework for the CVRP, achieving performance close to state-of-the-art optimization methods. Building on this direction, Da Costa et al. [21] proposed a policy gradient algorithm that learns 2-opt heuristics for routing problems, achieving faster convergence to near-optimal solutions than prior deep learning approaches. Wu et al. [22] extended this idea by designing a self-attention–based reinforcement learning framework that iteratively refines solutions for the TSP and CVRP, showing that PN-learned policies outperform both handcrafted heuristics and other deep learning methods. In parallel, Gama and Fernandes [23] applied a policy gradient method to the Orienteering Problem with Time Windows, striking an effective balance between exploration and exploitation to improve solution quality and efficiency. Collectively, these contributions highlight how combining deep reinforcement learning with traditional optimization frameworks enables more scalable, adaptable, and competitive solvers for combinatorial optimization problems.

3   Deep Reinforcement Learning Frameworks

Our deep reinforcement learning framework uses a sequence-to-sequence (*seq2seq*) architecture adapted from the transformer model [13], consisting of an encoder and a decoder. The encoder generates embeddings from the input data (e.g., vertex coordinates), and the decoder produces a sequence of nodes auto-regressively, using the embeddings along with a problem-specific mask and context. The mask prevents revisiting nodes, while the context includes graph embeddings and the embeddings of the first and last selected nodes. For full encoder details, see [13].

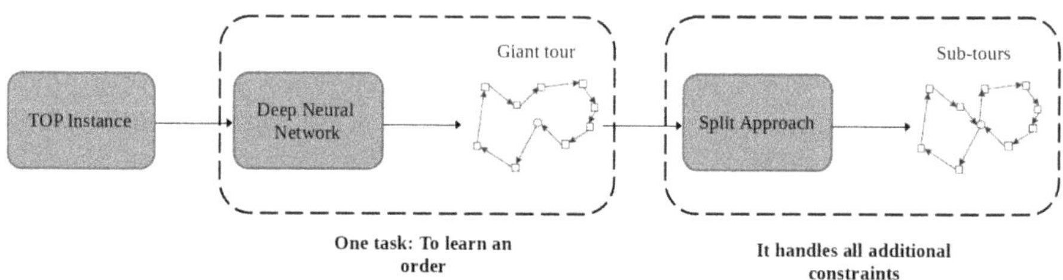

Fig. 1. Giant tour deep learning framework

We investigated two distinct decoding approaches in this study:

1. Giant tour decoder that apply an optimal splitting procedure to evaluate the solution quality
2. Routes decoder with masking mechanism that generates m feasible routes.

The following sections describe the reinforcement learning frameworks.

3.1   Giant Tour Deep Learning Approach

As illustrated in Fig. 1, our first framework consists of two stages. In the first stage, a Deep Neural Network (DNN) based on an Attention Model (AM) with an encoder–decoder architecture generates a *giant tour*. The encoder maps the input instance (clients and depot) into vertex embeddings, while the decoder, guided by these embeddings and the history of visited clients, applies multi-head attention to sequentially construct a tour until all clients are visited. In the second stage, an optimal splitting algorithm, following [6], partitions the giant tour into routes that maximize total profit. This ensures that if the optimal solution to the Team

Orienteering Problem (TOP) exists as sub-sequences within the giant tour π^*, the splitting process will recover it. Thus, the neural network explores a reduced solution space of giant tours, while the splitting stage guarantees optimality within that space and can be extended to handle additional constraints, such as time windows.

Greedy Rollout Baseline Integrated with REINFORCE. During training, the Graph Attention Model specifies a stochastic policy $p_\theta(\pi|X)$ that manages the selection of a giant tour (i.e., a sequence) π, conditioned on a TOP instance X and the network parameters θ. By applying the probability chain rule, this policy can be expressed as:

$$p_\theta(\pi|X) = \prod_{t=1}^{n} p_\theta(\pi_t|\pi_1, ..., \pi_{t-1}, X)$$

Once the sequence π is generated, the split procedure divides it into a collection of feasible sub-tours that respect the maximum tour duration $Tmax$. The Split algorithm then evaluates the quality of the giant tour by computing the total profit associated with the resulting solution. This evaluation acts as the training signal for our deep neural network within a reinforcement learning framework. Furthermore, we denote by $J(\theta|X)$ the policy objective function, defined as the expected total score of the sub-tours obtained via the split procedure for a given instance X.

$$J(\theta|X) = \mathbb{E}_{p_\theta(\pi|X)} \left[split(\pi|X) \right]$$

We employ policy-gradient techniques to iteratively adjust the parameters θ in the direction that increases $J(\theta|X)$, thereby seeking a local optimum of the objective function. The gradient of this objective with respect to θ is given by:

$$\nabla_\theta J(\theta|X) = \mathbb{E}_{p_\theta(\pi|X)} \left[\nabla_\theta \log p_\theta(\pi|X)(split(\pi|X) - b(X)) \right]$$

In this formulation, $b(X)$ denotes the baseline introduced to mitigate the variance of the gradient estimates. We adopt a greedy rollout baseline, $b(X) = split(\pi^{BL}|X)$, which evaluates the giant tour π^{BL} via the split algorithm. This tour is produced by the current best-performing model—i.e., the DNN with parameters θ^{BL}—by selecting at each step the customer with the highest predicted probability. To maximize the expected reward, we employ the REINFORCE gradient estimator together with the Adam optimization method.

Algorithm 1. HGAM - REINFORCE Greedy rollout baseline

Input: Model parameters θ, number of epochs E, batch size B, number of instances I, level of significance α.

1: $T \leftarrow \frac{I}{B}$ $\triangleright$ Number of instances per batch.
2: $\theta^{BL} \leftarrow \theta$
3: **for** $e = 1, \dots, E$ **do**
4:      **for** $stp = 1, \dots, T$ **do**
5:          $X_i \leftarrow TOPrandomInstance(), \forall \in \{1, \dots B\}$
6:          $\pi_i \leftarrow SampleRolloutGiantTour(X_i, p_\theta), \forall \in \{1, \dots B\}$
7:          $\pi_i^{BL} \leftarrow GreedyRolloutGiantTour(X_i, p_\theta^{BL}), \forall \in \{1, \dots B\}$
8:          $b(X_i) \leftarrow split(\pi_i^{BL}|X_i)$
9:          $\nabla_\theta L \leftarrow \sum_{i=1}^{B}(split(\pi_i|X_i) - b(X_i))\nabla_\theta log p_\theta(\pi_i)$
10:         $\theta \leftarrow Adam(\theta, \nabla_\theta L)$
11:      **end for**
12:      **if** $OneSidePairedTTest(p_\theta, p_\theta^{BL})$ **then**
13:         $\theta^{BL} \leftarrow \theta$
14:      **end if**
15: **end for**

The algorithm iteratively refines the model's parameters θ by generating routes (giant tours) from random instances of the TOP (steps 5 and 6) and comparing their effectiveness against a baseline generated by a greedy rollout strategy, computed in steps 7 and 8. By using a combination of sampled and greedy rollout tours, the algorithm evaluates the model's performance at step 9, adjusts its parameters via gradient updates with the Adam optimizer in step 10, and periodically updates the baseline model if significant improvements are detected using a one-sided T-test (steps 12 and 13).

3.2 Full-Learning Approach

The DNN for the TOP aims to maximize the total score of the generated routes, unlike the model in Sect. 3.1, which produced a giant tour. In this full-learning approach, the model both constructs the routes and evaluates their quality while ensuring feasibility: routes must respect the maximum length constraint T_{max}, the fleet size m, and only include vertices that still allow a return to the depot. Thus, a route ends once no additional vertex can be added without exceeding T_{max}.

The decoder receives as input both the graph embedding $\bar{\mathbf{h}}^{(N)}$—obtained by averaging the node embeddings $\mathbf{h}_i^{(N)}$—and the individual node embeddings themselves. We further adapt the decoder's context by integrating the graph embedding $\bar{\mathbf{h}}^{(N)}$, the most recently selected vertex π_{t-1}, and the remaining available route length for vehicle k at time t, denoted $T_{t,k}$. This remaining length is initialized as $T_{t=1,k=0} = Tmax$, and for all $t > 1$, it is updated according to the following rule:

$$T_{t+1,k} = T_{t,k} - c_{\pi_{t-1},\pi_t}$$

Here, c_{π_{t-1},π_t} denotes the travel cost (time or distance) between the vertices π_{t-1} and π_t. When no additional vertex can be added to the current sequence, the vehicle returns to the depot. At that point, the route index k is increased by one, and the remaining length $T_{t,k}$ is reinitialized to $Tmax$.

In this revised context representation for the decoder, we omit the explicit inclusion of vertex scores, since this information is already encoded within the node embeddings. Consequently, the decoder's context is defined as follows:

$$
\mathbf{h}_{(c)}^{(N)} = \begin{cases} \left[\overline{\mathbf{h}}^{(N)}, \mathbf{h}_{\pi_{t-1}}^{(N)}, T_{t,k}\right] & t > 1 \\ \left[\overline{\mathbf{h}}^{(N)}, \mathbf{h}_0^{(N)}, T_{t,k}\right] & t = 1 \end{cases}
$$

We add two conditions to the masking procedure utilized in the encoder. First, if it is not possible to visit a node a within the remaining length constraint: $c_{\pi_{t-1},a} + c_{a,0} > T_{t,k}$. Second, if there are no more vehicles available $k > m$.

4   Computational Experiments

For the computational experiments, we follow the instance generation methodology of [13]. We consider TOP instances with $n = 20$, 50, and 100, generating 800,000 training instances and two sets of 1,000 and 10,000 for validation and testing. Depot and client locations are sampled uniformly in the unit square, and client scores follow three distributions: *constant* ($p_i = 1$), *uniform* ($p_i \sim Uniform[0, 1]$), and *distance*, where $p_i = \left(1 + \left\lfloor 99 \cdot \frac{c_{0i}}{\max_{j=1}^n c_{0j}} \right\rfloor\right) \times 100^{-1}$.

We recall that c_{0i} is the travel cost from the depot to node i. This cost may represent either travel time or distance. The number of vehicles denoted as m varies between 2 and 4. Finally, we set the time limit T_{max} according to the number of clients: $T_{max}^{20} = 2$, $T_{max}^{50} = 3$ and $T_{max}^{100} = 4$ as in [13]. Moreover, as in [2], we divided the T_{max} value by the number of vehicles, i.e., $\frac{T_{max}}{m}$ in order to ensure that each route has the same time limit.

The model parameters are initialized from a Uniform distribution $(-1/\sqrt{d}, 1/\sqrt{d})$, with $d = 128$ denoting the embedding size. Training is performed over 100 epochs with a fixed batch size of $B = 1000$ instances, and both training and validation samples are generated dynamically. The encoder is built with $K = 3$ layers, and we adopt a constant learning rate of $\eta = 10^{-5}$. All experiments were run on a single Nvidia RTX-3500 Ada GPU equipped with 12 GB of VRAM. The Hybrid Graph Attention Model (HGAM) was implemented in Python using PyTorch and Numba, while the approximation routines were developed in C++. Our code is publicly available[1,2].

4.1   Split Effect

We first compare HGAM with a full-learning DNN that solves the TOP without the split algorithm to assess its impact on performance. As described in

---

Sect. 3.2, the DNN is modified to generate feasible routes directly rather than a giant tour. We also evaluate two baselines—greedy critic rollout and an exponential moving average ($\alpha = 0.2$)—to measure their effect on learning. For comparison, we use $n = 20$ clients, $m = 2$ vehicles, and assign a constant score $p_i = 1$ to each client.

Figure 2 displays the convergence behavior during training of the four different strategies: HGAM with greedy rollout (hgam-critic) and exponential moving average (hgam-exp(0.2)), as well as the full learning approach with greedy rollout (ete-critic) and exponential moving average (ete-exp(0.2)). The hgam-critic method outperforms the others consistently, showing the highest average training score across all the training periods. This indicates that the HGAM model, when combined with the greedy critic rollout baseline, is the most effective approach in this context. Additionally, the hgam-exp(0.2) variant also shows strong performance, coming in second, which suggests that the exponential moving average with $\alpha = 0.2$ is a robust baseline. In contrast, full-learning approaches lag behind, with ete-critic performing better than ete-exp(0.2) but still below the HGAM-based methods. This demonstrates the superiority of the HGAM approach, highlighting the effective advantage of using the split algorithm to evaluate the quality of the giant tours generated by the DNN.

4.2   HGAM Performance

We assess the HGAM model's performance with respect to the instance size n and the type of scoring function. The obtained solutions are compared with those produced by a specialized heuristic, the Construction Heuristic (CH), as well as the Iterative Destruction/Construction Heuristic (IDCH) [24]. To deploy the learned policies, we employ two decoding strategies: a step-by-step sampling procedure and a sampling scheme that generates 1000 candidate solutions for

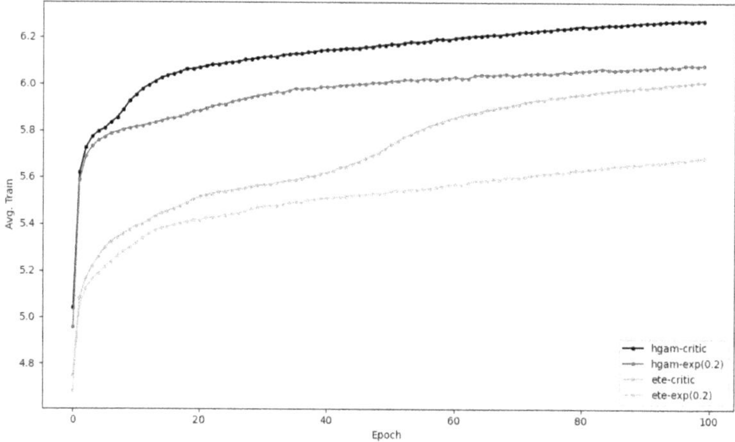

Fig. 2. Convergence

each test instance. The best solution among these candidates—evaluated according to their scores—is then kept. All candidates are drawn from the probability distributions output by the model. The evaluation uses test instances that are entirely different from the training and validation sets. Table 1 presents the average objective score (Objective), the average GAP relative to the best-performing algorithm, and the computation time (in seconds) required to solve each test instance.

Table 1. Model comparison for different values of n and types of scores

Model	$n = 20$			$n = 50$			$n = 100$		
	Objective	GAP (%)	Time (s)	Objective	GAP (%)	Time (s)	Objective	GAP (%)	Time (s)
Constant									
IDCH	4.94	0.00%	0.0027	18.00	0.00%	0.2110	43.14	0.00%	5.4136
CH	4.72	4.45%	0.0001	15.82	12.11%	0.0017	35.71	17.22%	0.0152
HGAM	4.90	0.81%	0.0355	16.85	5.83%	0.1220	37.10	14.00%	0.5242
Uniform									
IDCH	2.59	0.00%	0.0028	9.63	0.00%	0.2489	23.21	0.00%	6.5347
CH	2.53	2.32%	0.0001	8.71	6.56%	0.0014	19.81	14.65%	0.0144
HGAM	2.58	0.39%	0.0349	8.97	2.15%	0.1213	19.38	16.50%	0.5101
Distance									
IDCH	1.35	0.00%	0.0028	6.02	0.00%	0.2426	16.27	0.00%	6.3519
CH	1.20	11.11%	0.0001	4.02	33.22%	0.0009	9.77	39.95%	0.0070
HGAM	1.35	0.00%	0.0355	5.48	8.97%	0.1225	13.11	19.42%	0.5133

The performance of the HGAM model shows a mixed trend across different instance sizes and score types when compared to the IDCH and CH methods. For smaller instance sizes ($n = 20$), HGAM delivers competitive results, with zero GAP for distance scores and a low GAP (0.81% for constant scores and 0.39% for Uniform scores), closely approaching the solutions provided by IDCH. However, as the instance size increases ($n = 50$ and $n = 100$), HGAM's performance deteriorates, with the GAP widening significantly, particularly for distance scores (32.90% for $n = 100$). This is likely because the complexity of the instances increases with size, making it more difficult for HGAM to effectively capture and optimize all relevant patterns. Although it consistently outperforms CH in terms of GAP across all sizes and score types, it falls short of IDCH, which is the best solution method for all the experiments.

HGAM's running times are longer than CH's, though faster than IDCH for larger instances. Notably, HGAM's running times remain consistent across different scoring types for the same instance size, showing minimal variation with changes in instance scores. For instances with $n = 50$ HGAM is between

1.79 times faster ($\approx 0.2110/0.1220$, for constant scores) and 2.05 times faster ($\approx 0.2489/0.1213$, for uniform scores) than IDCH. Additionally, for instances with $n = 100$ HGAM exhibits significantly faster running times, outperforming IDCH by an order of magnitude. Specifically, it is 10 times faster ($\approx 5.4136/0.5242$ for constant scores), 12.8 times faster ($\approx 6.5347/0.5101$ for uniform scores) and 12.4 times faster ($\approx 6.3519/0.5133$ for distance scores). This indicates that while HGAM strikes a balance between solution quality and computational efficiency, it struggles to maintain the same high-quality solutions as IDCH for larger, more complex problems. This is likely because, larger instances introduce more variables and interactions, which may cause HGAM approach to struggle in identifying the optimal solutions within reasonable computational limits.

5   Conclusions

This study aligns with the expanding body of research that combines machine learning with optimization methods to address combinatorial optimization problems more effectively. We introduced a Hybrid Graph Attention Model (HGAM) that couples a deep neural network (DNN) with an optimal splitting procedure to tackle the Team Orienteering Problem (TOP). In our framework, the DNN first produces a sequence of customers, after which the split algorithm restructures the sequence so that it satisfies the constraints, yields the associated routes, and produces the resulting TOP solution. This hybrid design strengthens both the learning process and the overall performance of the DNN, particularly for more complex variants of the problem that require additional constraints. Our findings show that the approach performs competitively relative to tailored heuristics, offering a compromise between solution quality and computational cost, though solution quality tends to decrease as the instance size grows.

Despite these encouraging results, the observed deterioration in performance for larger instances highlights a direction for future enhancement. Moreover, the versatility of the method—requiring only minor adjustments to address other problem variants—stands as one of its key advantages. Future work should therefore examine its scalability and extend its application to a broader set of combinatorial optimization problems.

References

1. Butt, S., Cavalier, T.: A heuristic for the multiple tour maximum collection problem. Comput. Oper. Res. **21**(1), 101–111 (1994)
2. Chao, I., Golden, B., Wasil, E.: The team orienteering problem. Eur. J. Oper. Res. **88**(3), 464–474 (1996)
3. Bengio, Y., Lodi, A., Prouvost, A.: Machine learning for combinatorial optimization: a methodological tour d'horizon. Eur. J. Oper. Res. **290**(2), 405–421 (2021)
4. Wang, F., He, Q., Li, S.: Solving combinatorial optimization problems with deep neural network: a survey. Tsinghua Sci. Technol. **29**(5), 1266–1282 (2024)

5. Yaddaden, A., Harispe, S., Vasquez, M.: Neural order-first split-second algorithm for the capacitated vehicle routing problem. In: Dorronsoro, B., Pavone, M., Nakib, A., Talbi, E.-G. (eds.) Optimization and Learning, pp. 168–185. Springer, Cham (2022)
6. Duc-Cuong, D., Guibadj, R., Moukrim, A.: An effective PSO-inspired algorithm for the team orienteering problem. Eur. J. Oper. Res. **229**(2), 332–344 (2013)
7. Bogyrbayeva, A., Meraliyev, M., Mustakhov, T., Dauletbayev, B.: Machine learning to solve vehicle routing problems: a survey. IEEE Trans. Intell. Transp. Syst. **25**(6), 4754–4772 (2024)
8. Vinyals, O., Fortunato, M., Jaitly, N.: Pointer networks. Adv. Neural Inf. Process. Syst. **28** (2015)
9. Bello, I., Pham, H., Le, Q.V., Norouzi, M., Bengio, S.: Neural combinatorial optimization with reinforcement learning. arXiv arXiv:1611.09940 (2017)
10. Nazari, M., Oroojlooy, A., Snyder, L.V., Takáč, M.: Reinforcement learning for solving the vehicle routing problem. arXiv arXiv:1802.04240 (2018)
11. Deudon, M., Cournut, P., Lacoste, A., Adulyasak, Y., Rousseau, L.-M.: Learning heuristics for the TSP by policy gradient. In: Van Hoeve, W.-J. (ed.) Integration of Constraint Programming, Artificial Intelligence, and Operations Research, vol. 10848, pp. 170–181. Springer (2018)
12. Li, K., Zhang, T., Wang, R.W.Y., Han, Y.: Deep reinforcement learning for combinatorial optimization: covering salesman problems. IEEE Trans. Cybern. **52**(12), 13142–13155 (2022)
13. Kool, W., van Hoof, H., Welling, M.: Attention, learn to solve routing problems!. arXiv arXiv:1803.08475 (2019)
14. Nowak, A., Villar, S., Bandeira, A.S., Bruna, J.: Revised note on learning quadratic assignment with graph neural networks. In: 2018 IEEE Data Science Workshop (DSW), pp. 1–5 (2018)
15. Khalil, E., Dai, H., Zhang, Y., Dilkina, B., Song, L.: Learning combinatorial optimization algorithms over graphs. Adv. Neural Inf. Process. Syst. **30** (2017)
16. Christofides, N.: Worst-case analysis of a new heuristic for the travelling salesman problem (Technical report). DTIC Document (1976)
17. Joshi, C.K., Laurent, T., Bresson, X.: An efficient graph convolutional network technique for the travelling salesman problem. In: INFORMS Annual Meeting (2019)
18. Kool, W., van Hoof, H., Gromicho, J., Welling, M.: Deep policy dynamic programming for vehicle routing problems. In: Schaus, P. (ed.) Integration of Constraint Programming, Artificial Intelligence, and Operations Research, pp. 190–213. Springer, Cham (2022)
19. Chen, X., Tian, Y.: Learning to perform local rewriting for combinatorial optimization. arXiv arXiv:1810.00337 (2019)
20. Hottung, A., Tierney, K.: Neural large neighborhood search for the capacitated vehicle routing problem (2020)
21. Da Costa, P., Rhuggenaath, J., Zhang, Y., Wulms, J.: Learning 2-opt heuristics for routing problems via deep reinforcement learning. SN Comput. Sci. **2**, 388 (2021)
22. Wu, Y., Song, W., Cao, Z., Zhang, J., Lim, A.: Learning improvement heuristics for solving routing problems. IEEE Trans. Neural Netw. Learn. Syst. **33**(9), 5057–5069 (2022)
23. Gama, R., Fernandes, H.L.: A reinforcement learning approach to the orienteering problem with time windows. Comput. Oper. Res. **133**, 105357 (2021)

24. Bouly, H., Dang, D.C., Moukrim, A.: A memetic algorithm for the team orienteering problem. In: Giacobini, M., et al. (eds.) Applications of evolutionary computing. EvoWorkshops 2008. Lecture Notes in Computer Science, vol. 4974, pp. 471–481. Springer, Heidelberg (2008)
25. Gunawan, A., Chuin Lau, H. , Vansteenwegen, P.: Orienteering problem: a survey of recent variants, solution approaches and applications. Eur. J. Oper. Res. **255**(2) (2016). https://doi.org/10.1016/j.ejor.2016.04.059

Forecasting Transport Demand Using Expert-Fuzzy Methods of Data Analysis

Ramin Rzayev[1]($\boxtimes$) , Emil Ahmadov[1,2] , Inara Rzayeva[3] , and Vagif Aliyev[1]

[1] Institute of Control Systems, Vahabzadeh Street 68, AZ1141 Baku, Azerbaijan
raminrza@yahoo.com
[2] Intelligent Transport Management Centre of the Ministry of Internal Affairs of the Republic of Azerbaijan, Heydar Aliyev Avenue 137, Baku, Azerbaijan
[3] Azerbaijan State University of Economics, Istiglaliyat Street 6, AZ1101 Baku, Azerbaijan

Abstract. In the theory of modeling and forecasting transport flows, the law of demand and consumption, reflecting the relationship between these two indicators, is of the same primary importance as in the case of studying the consumer market. The indicator (or volume) of transport supply demonstrates the totality of mobile delivery vehicles that are concentrated in a designated area. The key element of the study is the transport demand indicator, which reflects the total level of need for transportation of goods and passengers along a dedicated transport system using personal, public and freight (including unmanned vehicles) modes of transport. Particularly, the level of demand for passenger transportation in urban agglomerations is quantitatively reflected in the form of an integral (aggregated) indicator of the transport mobility of people. The paper discusses a method for quantitative assessment of transport demand, which depends on a significant number of socio-economic factors. The proposed method is based on the identification of the corresponding function in a fuzzy paradigm.

Keywords: Transport Demand · Socio-Economic Factor · Expert Assessment · Fuzzy Set · Fizzy Inference

1 Introduction

Existing information and logistics technologies make it relatively easy to generate transport models for urban agglomerations. In the specialized literature, one can find various models of transport flows, which can be divided into two types: 1) models that predict the volumes of transport demand for inter-district movements (transport correspondence) and their routing along the directed graph of the transport network; 2) models that describe the dynamics of changes in transport flow based on forecasting the volume of transport demand. In any case, the basis of transport demand modeling is predictive analytics, which is a combination of Statistical Methods, Data Mining and Mathematical Theory of Games, which are known to be used to identify internal patterns between historical data in order to use them to forecast the desired values for short-, medium- and long-term periods. The central element in transport demand modeling is the inter-district

A. Razminia et al. (Eds.): ITFT 2025, CCIS 2876, pp. 37–47, 2026.
https://doi.org/10.1007/978-3-032-20592-6_4

correspondence matrix. It shows how many trips originate in each district and how many of them end in other districts, essentially capturing the flow of goods or people across the area. Various extrapolation methods are used to quantitatively assess the volumes of movements, using current data on the volumes of inter-district movements and predicts of their growth as relevant information. Among them, the most frequently used are the method of a single growth coefficient (SGC), method of average growth coefficients, average growth coefficient method, Detroit method, Fratarm method, etc. [1].

The study's central aim is to develop a method for short-term predicting of transport demand using SGC extrapolation method and initial data processing on socio-economic indicators in a fuzzy environment.

2 Problem Definition

Among the exponential methods of predictive analysis of transport flows, the SGC extrapolation method was chosen to test the fuzzy approach to forecasting transport demand. This method is most effective for forecasting short-term trends, and its accuracy decreases with long-term forecasts. It is one of the simplest methods for forecasting traffic flows, based on the assumption of constant growth dynamics. The essence of the method determines the growth factor [2, 4].

$$G = P/A, \tag{1}$$

where A is the current (actual) volume of transport demand for inter-district travel, and P is its predicted value. In general, the growth factor is an economic, multi-component indicator that reflects changes across numerous variables – such as the overall mobility levels, population size within the urban area, average per capita income, and other related factors. Basically, taking into account socio-economic factors $x_1, x_2, ..., x_n$, the growth factor is established by the following relationship [4]:

$$G = g(P_1, P_2, ..., P_n) / g(A_1, A_2, ..., A_n) \tag{2}$$

where g: $\Re^n \to \Re$ is a function that translates socio-economic indicator values into an estimate of the total volume of transport flows within a given urban area; A_k ($k = 1 \div n$) is the current value of socio-economic indicator x_k; P_k is its predicted value. There is no analytical representation for the function. However, econometric models, including multivariate regression models, and statistical methods are used in transport logistics and economics to establish quantitative relationships between socio-economic indicators (such as GDP, income level, production volume) and the volume of transport flows. These models take into account the relationship between economic development and transport needs, allowing transport demand to be forecast based on socio-economic forecasts.

Assuming the growth factor is known, all entries of the forecasted correspondence matrix $|c_{ij}^*|$ can be determined by the following equalities.

$$c_{ij}^* = G \cdot c_{ij}^0 \tag{3}$$

where "*" denotes the predicted volume of trips from the i-th region to the j-th region of the urban agglomeration.

The main socio-economic factors influencing the volume of transport flows are the following: x_1 – GDP: higher GDP usually correlates with higher volumes of transportation; x_2 – industrial production volume: increased production requires more transportation of raw materials and final products; x_3 – average per capita income: an increase in average income increases the demand for the transportation of passengers and goods; x_4 – population: increases demand for passenger and freight transport; x_5 – level of motorization of the population. It is suggested to use complex expert-fuzzy methods of relevant data analysis to quantitatively assess the influence of socio-economic factors x_k ($k = 1 \div 5$) on the transport demand and identify the appropriate function $g(x_1, x_2, x_3, x_4, x_5)$.

3　Identification of a Function Reflecting the Dependence of Transport Demand on Indicators of Socio-Economic Factors

Averaging results in the measure of socio-economic indicators is one of the most frequent operations performed by data collection and management systems. In technical systems, accuracy requirements for an averaging process can be satisfied through multiple measurements, where positive and negative deviations from the exact value partially compensate individual measurement results. The situation becomes much more complex with statistical data samples that have "historical" status. Typically, such samples represent some time period of the socio-economic system as unrepeatable measurements; so in most cases, relevant data, i.e., values of socio-economic indicators should be treated as weakly structured ones. This means that it is known to what certain type they belong. For instance, adequate reflection for weakly structured data regarding a socio-economic indicator x may be given by an interval $[x_{\min}, x_{\max}]$. Another more adequate reflection of such kind of data would be verbal terms from linguistic variables like "ABOUT 13", which can be formally represented by fuzzy sets [5].

3.1　Identification of Weights of Social-Economic Factors Using Expert Assessments

To assess the degree of influences on the volumes of transport demand, experts with relevant subject-matter knowledge are invited to analyze and compare the specific values of the corresponding indicators. By the independent survey of m logistics specialists, expert assessments of the priority of socio-economic factors are determined in terms of their influence on transport demand. Each expert is asked to form a ranking assessment of the analyzed factor in the form of r_{ki} ($i = 1 \div m$) and the corresponding normalized values of the variable assessment in the form of e_{ki}, so that for each $i = 1 \div m$ the condition $e_{1i} + e_{2i} + e_{3i} + e_{4i} + e_{5i} = 1$ is satisfied.

Let us imagine that fifteen experienced logistics specialists are invited to participate in this process by thoughtfully ranking each factor x_k. They assign the number "1" to the factor they consider most important, "2" to the next, and so on, reflecting a

Table 1. Expert ranking of influence factors x_k.

Expert's serial number	Assessed factors x_k and their ranking r_{ki}				
	GDP level (x_1)	Industrial production volume (x_2)	Average per capita income (x_3)	Population (x_4)	Level of motorization (x_5)
01	4	5	2	3	1
02	5	4	2	3	1
...	...	...	...	...	...
15	5	4	3	2	1
$\sum$	66	63	26	44	26

gradual decrease in importance. The collective rankings gathered through this survey are presented in Table 1.

In order to find out how much experts agree, the Kendall W (concordance) coefficient is applied [6]. It reflects the level of correlation of several ranks in expert evaluations. Based on [6], this coefficient is computed as:

$$W = 12 \cdot S/[m^2(n^3 - n)], \tag{4}$$

where m is the total number of experts involved; n denotes the number of socio-economic factors; and S denotes the divergence of expert opinions from the mean ranking, which can be calculated, for instance, as $S = \sum_{k=1}^{n} [\sum_{i=1}^{m} r_{ij} - m(n+1)/2]^2$, where r_{ij} denotes the rank assigned by the i-th expert to the k-th factor, and it takes values in the set $\{1, 2, ..., 5\}$.

After checking the rank assessments for consistency ($W > 0.6$) using (3) and data from Table 1: $S = \sum_{k=1}^{5} [\sum_{i=1}^{15} r_{ij} - 15(5+1)/2]^2 = 1488$, $W = 12 \cdot 1488/[15^2(5^3 - 5)] = 0.6613$, the normalized expert assessments of the specific weights of factors x_k ($k = 1 \div 5$) have been determined and are presented in Table 2.

Table 2. Standardized expert assessments for the specific weights of factors x_k.

Expert	Estimated variables x_k and normalized values of these weights (α_{ki})				
	x_1	x_2	x_3	x_4	x_5
01	0.175	0.075	0.225	0.175	0.350
02	0.075	0.175	0.225	0.175	0.350
...	...	...	...	...	...
15	0.075	0.100	0.250	0.275	0.300
$\sum$	1.600	1.575	4.425	2.975	4.425

Using the information provided in Table 2, initial computations were carried out to later determine the weights of the x_i. For this purpose, the appropriate average value α_i for the i-th group of normalized assessments for the variable x_i is calculated using the following iterative formula [6]

$$\alpha_i(t+1) = \sum\nolimits_{i=1}^{m} w_i(t)\alpha_{ki}, \tag{5}$$

where $w_i(t)$ denotes the competence level of the i-th expert, which for every iteration step t are calculated via the following equations:

$$\begin{cases} w_j(t) = 1/[\eta(t)] \sum\nolimits_{k=1}^{n} \alpha_k(t) \cdot \alpha_{ki} (i = \overline{1, m-1}), \\ w_m(t) = 1 - \sum\nolimits_{i=1}^{m-1} w_i(t), \ \sum\nolimits_{i=1}^{m} w_i(t) = 1, \end{cases} \tag{6}$$

where $\eta(t) = \sum_{k=1}^{n} \sum_{i=1}^{m} \alpha_k(t)\alpha_{ki}$ is a normalizing coefficient, which provides the transition to the next step of iteration. The process of determining α_i is finished when following condition is satisfied: $\max\{|\alpha_i(t+1) - \alpha_i(t)|\} \leq \varepsilon$, where ε denotes the acceptable accuracy, which is fixed in advance.

Thus, using (5) and (6), the corresponding specific weights of factors x_i are identified for each group in the 3rd approximation ($t = 3$) as follows: $\alpha_1(3) = 0.10459$, $\alpha_2(3) = 0.10346$, $\alpha_3(3) = 0.29643$, $\alpha_4(3) = 0.19869$, $\alpha_5(3) = 0.29683$. Notably, the sum of these weights equals one.

The final (integral) assessment of the socio-economic growth (SEG) index is calculated in the range from 0 to 100 using the weighted summation criterion [7]

$$R_i = 100 \times \sum\nolimits_{k=1}^{5} \alpha_k(3)e_{ki} / [\max_i\{\sum\nolimits_{k=1}^{5} \alpha_k(3)e_{ki}\}], \tag{7}$$

where e_{ki} is i-th expert's assessment of the influence of factor x_k on SEG, for example, on a five-point scale of the following gradation: 5 is "TOO HIGH", 4 is "VERY HIGH", 3 is "MORE THAN HIGH", 2 is "HIGH", 1 is "LOW". The lowest R index value indicates the minimum level of SEG, and vice versa, the highest R index value reflects its maximum level. The expert assessments are verified for their consistency in accordance with the rule: the maximum permissible difference in judgment between two experts regarding the degree of influence of factor x_k ($k = 1 \div 5$) on the level of SEG should not exceed 3. According to the expert survey data, considering the elimination of unacceptable deviations and formula (7), the final index of SEG in a separate territory is calculated. Using the example of a survey of ten experts, the scenario for the formation of the average growth index R is presented in Table 3.

Table 3. Standardized expert assessments for the specific weights of factors x_k.

Expert	Factors affecting on SEG					Index of SEG (R_i)
	x_1	x_2	x_3	x_4	x_5	
	Specific weights of factors					
	$\alpha_1 = 0.1046$	$\alpha_2 = 0.1035$	$\alpha_3 = 0.2964$	$\alpha_4 = 0.1987$	$\alpha_5 = 0.2968$	
e_1	3	1	3	2	4	74.30
e_2	4	2	3	3	4	84.75
...	...	...	...	...	...	...
e_9	4	2	3	2	3	72.02
e_{10}	4	1	3	3	5	89.72
Average growth index R						83.08

3.2 Estimating the Level of SEG Using a Fuzzy Inference System

Taking into account the qualitative features of the x_k that have a relative influence on the level of SEG, the following method is proposed for calculating the appropriate integral index with a Fuzzy Inference System (FIS) serving as a mechanism for multi-criteria assessment and decision-making in uncertain environments. To construct a FIS for assessing the level of SEG, the verbal model is chosen, which consists of the following reasoning:

d_1: If average per capita income shows positive dynamics and the level of motorization of the population increases, then overall SEG is high;

d_2: If, in addition to the conditions in d_1, there is an increase in industrial production, then SEG is more than high;

d_3: If there are an increase in GDP and industrial production, average per capita income and population show positive dynamics and the level of motorization of the population increases, then overall SEG is too high;

d_4: If there is an increase in industrial production, average per capita income and population show positive dynamics and the level of motorization of the population increases, then overall SEG is very high;

d_5: If there are an increase in GDP, average per capita income shows positive dynamics, population decreases and the level of motorization of the population increases, then overall SEG is high;

d_6: If there are a decrease in GDP and industrial production, average per capita income shows negative dynamics, then overall SEG is low.

The analysis of these fragments revealed 5 inputs of the chosen verbal model in the form of the term ACCEPTABLE as a criterion for qualitative assessment the development of socio-economic factors presented in terms of the linguistic variables x_k ($k = 1 \div 5$). For the fuzzification of this term with the subsequent construction of the FIS, a set of expert assessments of the relative impact of factors on SEG, presented in Table 3 on a five-point scale, was selected as the universal set $U = \{e_1,$

$e_2, ..., e_{10}$}. A fuzzy set formalizing the term ACCEPTABLE is generally represented as $F_k = \{\mu_{F_k}(e_1)/e_1, \mu_{F_k}(e_2)/e_2, ..., \mu_{F_k}(e_{10})/e_{10}\}$, where $\mu_{F_k}(e_i) : U \rightarrow [0, 1]$ ($i = 1 \div 10$) are the values of the corresponding membership function, which indicates the degree to which the expert assessment e_i belongs to the qualitative criterion ACCEPTABLE for the evaluation of x_k.

The following Gaussian-type function is selected as the membership function.

$$\mu_{F_k}(e_i) = \exp[-[e_i - 5]^2/\sigma_k^2], \tag{8}$$

where $e_j(a_i)$ is an expert assessment ($i = 1 \div 10$) made on a five-point scale relative to the impact of factor x_k ($k = 1 \div 5$) on SEG (see Table 3); $\sigma_k = \sqrt{2.5}$ is the mean deviation chosen empirically for all cases of fuzzification.

Thus, the desired fuzzy sets with membership functions (8) are obtained as follows.

$F_1 = \{0.5273/e_1, 0.8521/e_2, 0.2369/e_3, ..., 0.8521/e_7, 0.5273/e_8, 0.8521/e_9, 0.8521/e_{10}\}$;

$F_2 = \{0.0773/e_1, 0.2369/e_2, 0.2369/e_3, ..., 0.2369/e_7, 0.2369/e_8, 0.2369/e_9, 0.0773/e_{10}\}$;

$F_3 = \{0.5273/e_1, 0.5273/e_2, 0.2369/e_3, ..., 0.2369/e_7, 0.8521/e_8, 0.5273/e_9, 0.5273/e_{10}\}$;

$F_4 = \{0.2369/e_1, 0.5273/e_2, 0.2369/e_3, ..., 0.2369/e_7, 0.5273/e_8, 0.2369/e_9, 0.5273/e_{10}\}$;

$F_5 = \{0.8521/e_1, 0.8521/e_2, 0.5273/e_3, ..., 1.0000/e_7, 1.0000/e_8, 0.5273/e_9, 1.0000/e_{10}\}$.

For fuzzification of the terms of the output linguistic variable of the verbal model, the discrete set $J = \{0, 0.1, 0.2, ..., 0.9, 1\}$ is chosen as the universe, where for $\forall j \in J$ the following holds: $H = $ HIGH (overall SEG), $\mu_H(j) = j$; $MH = $ MORE THAN HIGH, $\mu_{MH}(j) = j^{(1/2)}$; $TH = $ TOO HIGH, $\mu_{TH}(j) = 1$, if $j = 1$ and $\mu_{TH}(j) = 0$, if $j < 1$; $VH = $ VERY HIGH, $\mu_{VH}(j) = j^2$; $L = $ LOW, $\mu_L(j) = 1\text{-}j$.

Taking into account the introduced fuzzy formalisms, the information fragments $d_1 \div d_6$ can be rephrased in the following compact form.

d_1: If x_3 is F_3 and x_5 is F_5, then y is H;
d_2: If x_2 is F_2 and x_3 is F_3 and x_5 is F_5, then y is MH;
d_3: If x_1 is F_1 and x_2 is F_2 and x_3 is F_3 and x_4 is F_4 and x_5 is F_5, then y is TH;
d_4: If x_2 is F_2 and x_3 is F_3 and x_4 is F_4 and x_5 is F_5, then y is VH;
d_5: If x_1 is F_1 and x_3 is F_3 and x_4 is $\neg F_4$ and x_5 is F_5, then y is H;
d_6: If x_1 is $\neg F_1$ and x_2 is $\neg F_2$ and x_3 is $\neg F_3$, then y is L.

The transformation of the antecedents of the rules involves finding the intersections of the fuzzy sets, which, in the discrete case, is achieved by taking the minimum of the corresponding membership function values. The subsequent transformation of the rules is performed using the Lukasiewicz fuzzy implication $\mu_{U \times J}(e, j) = \min\{1, 1\text{-}\mu_U(e) + \mu_J(j)\}$. As a result, for every pair $(e, j) \in U \times J$ the rules are transformed into the corresponding six fuzzy relations $R_1, R_2, ..., R_6$. As a result of intersecting these fuzzy relations, the overall functional solution is constructed in the form of a matrix $R = R_1 \cap R_2 \cap ... \cap R_6$, which, on the discrete set J, represents the internal cause-and-effect relationships among the expert assessments of factors x_k ($k = 1 \div 5$) for their compliance with the ACCEPTABLE criterion on one hand, and the corresponding SEG levels on the other.

$$R = \begin{array}{c|ccccccccccc}
 & 0 & 0.1 & 0.2 & 0.3 & 0.4 & 0.5 & 0.6 & 0.7 & 0.8 & 0.9 & 1 \\
\hline
e_1 & 0.4727 & 0.5727 & 0.6727 & 0.7727 & 0.8727 & 0.9227 & 0.9227 & 0.8273 & 0.7273 & 0.6273 & 0.5273 \\
e_2 & 0.4727 & 0.5727 & 0.6727 & 0.7631 & 0.7631 & 0.7631 & 0.7631 & 0.7631 & 0.7631 & 0.7631 & 0.8521 \\
e_3 & 0.7631 & 0.7631 & 0.7631 & 0.7631 & 0.7631 & 0.7369 & 0.6369 & 0.5369 & 0.4369 & 0.3369 & 0.2369 \\
e_4 & 0.1479 & 0.2479 & 0.3479 & 0.4479 & 0.5479 & 0.6479 & 0.7479 & 0.7631 & 0.7631 & 0.7631 & 0.8521 \\
e_5 & 0.1479 & 0.2479 & 0.3479 & 0.4479 & 0.5479 & 0.6479 & 0.7479 & 0.8479 & 0.9227 & 0.9227 & 0.8521 \\
e_6 & 0.1479 & 0.2479 & 0.3479 & 0.4479 & 0.5479 & 0.6479 & 0.7479 & 0.8479 & 0.9227 & 0.9227 & 0.8521 \\
e_7 & 0.7631 & 0.7631 & 0.7631 & 0.7631 & 0.7631 & 0.7631 & 0.7631 & 0.7631 & 0.7631 & 0.7631 & 0.8521 \\
e_8 & 0.1479 & 0.2479 & 0.3479 & 0.4479 & 0.5479 & 0.6479 & 0.7479 & 0.7631 & 0.7631 & 0.7631 & 0.8521 \\
e_9 & 0.4727 & 0.5727 & 0.6727 & 0.7631 & 0.7631 & 0.7631 & 0.7631 & 0.7631 & 0.7631 & 0.7631 & 0.8521 \\
e_{10} & 0.4727 & 0.5727 & 0.6727 & 0.7727 & 0.8727 & 0.9227 & 0.9227 & 0.9227 & 0.9227 & 0.9227 & 0.8521
\end{array}.$$

Based on [8], each element in the i-th row of matrix R corresponds to a membership function value of a fuzzy subset of universe J. This subset creates a fuzzy conclusion regarding how satisfactory the i-th expert assessment is. To numerically interpret each fuzzy conclusion, a defuzzification process will be applied, which relies on the point estimation method for fuzzy sets as described in [8].

Thus, defining α-level sets of the form $A_{i\delta} = \{j | \mu_{A_{i\delta}} \geq \delta, j \in J\}$ and calculating their corresponding cardinal numbers as $CN(A_{i\delta}) = \sum_{r=1}^{n} j_r / n$, for fuzzy inference relative to the satisfactoriness of, for example, expert assessment e_1 expressed through the fuzzy set $A_1 = \{0.4727/0, 0.5727/0.1, 0.6727/0.2, 0.7727/0.3, 0.8727/0.4, 0.9227/0.5, 0.9227/0.6, 0.8273/0.7, 0.7273/0.8, 0.6273/0.9, 0.5273/1\}$, we have:

- for $0 < \delta < 0.4727$: $\Delta\delta = 0.4727$, $A_{1\delta} = \{0, 0.1, 0.2, 0.3, ..., 0.8, 0.9, 1\}$, $CN(A_{1\delta}) = 0.50$;
- for $0.4727 < \delta < 0.5273$: $\Delta\delta = 0.0546$, $A_{1\delta} = \{0.1, 0.2, 0.3,..., 0.9, 1\}$, $CN(A_{1\delta}) = 0.55$;
- for $0.5273 < \delta < 0.5727$: $\Delta\delta = 0.0454$, $A_{1\delta} = \{0.1, 0.2, 0.3, ..., 0.8, 0.9\}$, $CN(A_{1\delta}) = 0.50$;
- for $0.5727 < \delta < 0.6273$: $\Delta\delta = 0.0546$, $A_{1\delta} = \{0.2, 0.3, 0.4, ..., 0.8, 0.9\}$, $CN(A_{1\delta}) = 0.55$;
- for $0.6273 < \delta < 0.6727$: $\Delta\delta = 0.0454$, $A_{1\delta} = \{0.2, 0.3, 0.4, ..., 0.7, 0.8\}$, $CN(A_{1\delta}) = 0.50$;
- for $0.6727 < \delta < 0.7273$: $\Delta\delta = 0.0546$, $A_{1\delta} = \{0.3, 0.4, 0.5, 0.6, 0.7, 0.8\}$, $CN(A_{1\delta}) = 0.55$;
- for $0.7273 < \delta < 0.7727$: $\Delta\delta = 0.0454$, $A_{1\delta} = \{0.3, 0.4, 0.5, 0.6, 0.7\}$, $CN(A_{1\delta}) = 0.50$;
- for $0.7727 < \delta < 0.8273$: $\Delta\delta = 0.0546$, $A_{1\delta} = \{0.4, 0.5, 0.6, 0.7\}$, $CN(A_{1\delta}) = 0.55$;
- for $0.8273 < \delta < 0.8727$: $\Delta\delta = 0.0454$, $A_{1\delta} = \{0.4, 0.5, 0.6\}$, $CN(A_{1\delta}) = 0.50$;
- for $0.8727 < \delta < 0.9227$: $\Delta\delta = 0.0500$, $A_{1\delta} = \{0.5, 0.6\}$, $CN(A_{1\delta}) = 0.55$.

According to [8], the numerical interpretation of the fuzzy inference regarding the expert's assessment e_1 is established in the following form:

$$F(A_1) = \frac{1}{\delta_{max}} \int_0^{\delta_{max}} CN(A_{1\delta})d\delta = \frac{1}{0.9227} \int_0^{0.9227} CN(A_{1\delta})d\alpha = \frac{1}{0.9227}[0.50 \cdot 0.4727 + 0.55 \cdot 0.0546+$$

$$0.50 \cdot 0.0454 + 0.55 \cdot 0.0546 + ... + 0.55 \cdot 0.0546 + 0.50 \cdot 0.0454 + 0.55 \cdot 0.0500] = 0.5145.$$

Other estimates obtained in a similar manner are summarized in the Table 4.

Table 4. SEG indices obtained by two methods.

Expert	Weighted summation assessment		Fuzzy Inference System	
	Index	Order	Index	Order
e_1	74.30	8	0.5145	9
e_2	84.75	5	0.5858	5
e_3	59.03	10	0.3914	10
e_4	92.37	3	0.6817	2
e_5	97.34	1	0.6803	3
e_6	84.34	6	0.6803	4
e_7	79.66	7	0.5523	8
e_8	97.31	2	0.6817	1
e_9	72.02	9	0.5858	6
e_{10}	89.72	4	0.5639	7
Average	83.08	×	0.5918	×

4 Discussion

In statistics, an index is a relative indicator reflecting a change in a socio-economic phenomenon, while the SEG coefficient may be part of a more complex formula for calculating this index, or is itself an indicator of development. However, we believe that the indices obtained using the method of weighted summation of expert assessments and FIS reflect a function $g(x_1, x_2, ..., x_5)$ and can be used in the formation of the growth coefficient provided by (2). This is especially evident in the example of the implementation of the FIS in MATLAB notation, where the inputs are expert assessments of x_k indicators on a five-point scale (see Table 3) (Fig. 1).

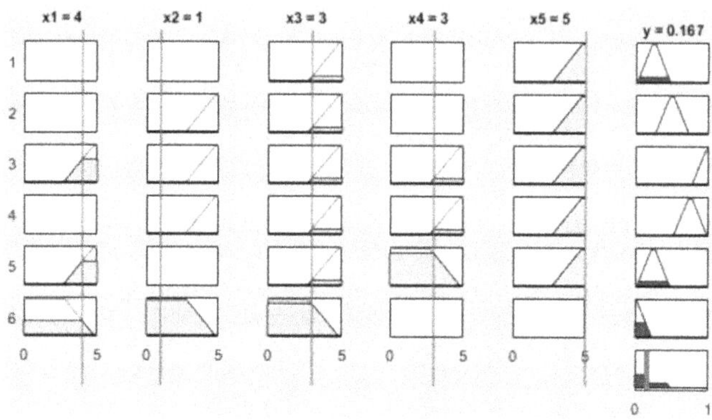

Fig. 1. The interactive MATLAB\FIS window reflecting the functional dependence $g(x_1,.., x_5)$.

We now return to the problem of modeling transport demand, which is a primary task when predicting the load on the transport system or its subsystems. To estimate traffic flow volumes and the utilization of transport system components, the initial data are typically organized into a matrix of inter-district movements (correspondences), with its dimensions determined by the number of districts. For a transport system comprising n regions, a square correspondence matrix is compiled as shown in Table 5, where r_{ij} represents the volume of trips from the i-th traffic district to the j-th traffic district.

Table 5. Volumes of inter-district transport flows.

	1	2	...	j	...	n-1	n	$\sum_j(r_{ij})$
1	−	r_{12}	...	r_{1j}	...	$r_{1(n-1)}$	r_{1n}	
...	...	...	...	...	...		...	
i	r_{i1}	r_{i2}	...	r_{ij}	...	$r_{i(n-1)}$	r_{in}	
...	...	...	...	...	...		...	
n	r_{n1}	r_{n2}	...	r_{nj}	...	$r_{n(n-1)}$	−	
$\sum_i(r_{ij})$								

We will assume that the indices calculated by both methods reflect the current state of socio-economic development, as a result of the work of experts with the relevant statistical data reflecting the dynamics of change in factors x_k ($k = 1 \div 5$). To obtain from experts estimates of the impact of these factors on SEG in the short term, it is necessary to provide them with reliable forecasts for each indicator x_k, which can be obtained using a variety of data analysis methods, including neural network and fuzzy time series modeling methods.

Figure 2 illustrates an example of the application of (3), where the actual values from the correspondence matrix for 3 districts A, B, C, and the coefficient of SEG are used as initial information. Here, the average index calculated using the FIS was selected as an indicator of the current level of socio-economic development, and the value of 0.6834, derived from expert judgments of short-term predicting data, was selected as the forecast.

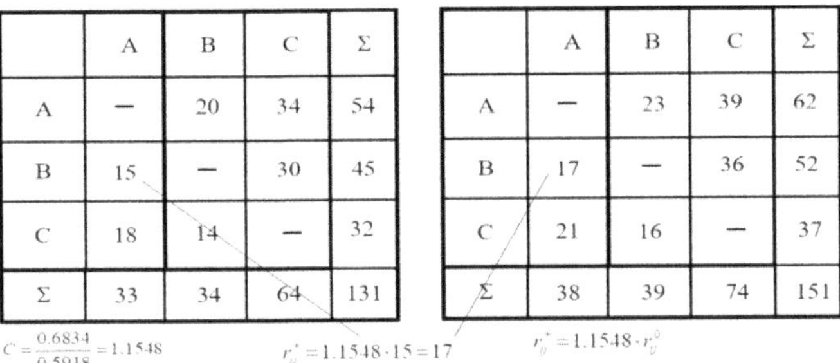

	A	B	C	Σ
A	—	20	34	54
B	15	—	30	45
C	18	14	—	32
Σ	33	34	64	131

	A	B	C	Σ
A	—	23	39	62
B	17	—	36	52
C	21	16	—	37
Σ	38	39	74	151

$$C = \frac{0.6834}{0.5918} = 1.1548 \qquad r_{ij}^* = 1.1548 \cdot 15 = 17 \qquad r_{ij}^* = 1.1548 \cdot r_{ij}^0$$

Fig. 2. An example of the implementation of the SGC method.

5 Conclusion

The article considers a SGC extrapolation method for forecasting transport demand based on data systematized in the form of a transport correspondence matrix. Nevertheless, this approach overlooks the dynamic interactions among individual city parameters and has limited reliability. Practically, the proposed approach to forecasting transport demand can be used for approximate estimates of transport flows in the context of designing individual city districts for the near future. When addressing the main problem, two approaches to calculating the socio-economic development index were proposed, which differ in their advantages and disadvantages. The method of weighted summation of expert assessments provides for the degree of importance of x_k, and the FIS-based method clearly demonstrates the functional dependence of the index on these factors.

References

1. Rzayev, R.R., Ahmadov, E.A.: Application of extrapolation methods for predicting traffic flows using elements of fuzzy logic. In: The Springer Series: Lecture Notes in Networks and Systems, vol. 758, no. 2, pp. 642–650 (2023)
2. Ortizar, I.D., Williumsen, L.G.: Modelling Transport, 4th edn. Wiley, Hoboken (2011)
3. Gorev, A.E., Boettger, K., Prokhorov, A.V., Gizatullin, R.R.: Fundamentals of Transport Modeling. KOSTA, St. Petersburg (2015). (in Russian)
4. Seliverstov, Y.A., Seliverstov, S.A.: Methods and models of the construction of transport correspondence matrix. Scientific and Technical Bulletin of St. Petersburg State Polytechnic University: Inform., Telecommunications, Control **2–3**, 49–70 (2015) (in Russian)
5. Zadeh, L.A.: The concept of a linguistic variable and its application to approximate reasoning. Inf. Sci. **8**(3), 199–249 (1975)
6. Lin, A.S.: A note on the concordance correlation coefficient. Biometrics **56**, 324–325 (2012)
7. Mardanov, M.J., Rzayev, R.R.: One approach to multi-criteria evaluation of alternatives in the logical basis of neural networks. Springer's Ser. Adv. Intell. Syst. Comput. **896**, 279–287 (2019)
8. Andreichenkov, A.V., Andreichenkova, O.N.: Analysis, Synthesis, Planning Decisions in the Economy. Finance and Statistics, Moscow (2000). (in Russian)

Research on Medical Logistics Vehicle Routing Problem Based on IGBCA Algorithm

Hui Zhao[✉]

School of Transportation Science and Engineering, Civil Aviation University of China, Tianjin, China
9202750@qq.com

Abstract. By vehicle routing optimization, it is possible to reduce the medicines transportation time, and complete medicines transportation at lower transportation costs. Various costs and constraints during medicine transportation were comprehensively analyzed. An optimization model for medicines transportation were established. Objective function of this model weights various costs to achieve the lowest comprehensive transportation cost under constrained conditions. Based on artificial bee colony (ABC) algorithm and combined with genetic algorithm (GA), the IGBCA (Integrated Genetic Bee Colony Algorithm) algorithm was designed to solve the mathematical model. The algorithm combines the advantages of artificial bee colony algorithm and genetic algorithm, it has the feature of fast convergence speed, and can obtain satisfactory solutions of the model.

Keywords: Medical Logistics · Vehicle Routing · Artificial Bee Colony Algorithm · Genetic Algorithm

1 Introduction

Medical logistics is an important branch of the logistics industry. With the increasing demand for vaccine products, oral medications, injections and other medicines, the scale of medical logistics is also increasing year by year. Medical transportation directly affects the quality of medicines and the timeliness of medicines delivery. In the process of medical transportation, it is necessary to comprehensively consider multiple factors such as transportation distance, deterioration of medicines quality, and customer satisfaction. A mathematical optimization model was established, and multiple optimization objectives are incorporated into the objective function of the model. The IGBCA (Improved Genetic Bee Colony Algorithm) was designed to solve the model. Simulation experiments were designed, and the effectiveness of IGBCA algorithm has been verified.

According to the research content of this paper, the overall structure of the paper is arranged as follows. Firstly, the research status of medical logistics vehicle routing problem was analyzed. And the commonly used solution methods for this problem were clarified. Secondly, the optimization objectives and corresponding constraints of this problem were comprehensively analyzed, and an operations research analysis model for the problem was constructed. Finally, IGBCA algorithm was designed and the simulation experiments were completed.

A. Razminia et al. (Eds.): ITFT 2025, CCIS 2876, pp. 48–57, 2026.
https://doi.org/10.1007/978-3-032-20592-6_5

2 Related Research

Vehicle routing optimization problem originated from the traveling salesman problem. In this problem, the optimization objective is to minimize the driving distance [1]. In practical problems, its optimization objectives may take various forms. At the same time, a series of constraints will be added according to the different problems. Such as time window constraints, vehicle operating time constraints, vehicle maximum loading capacity constraints, etc. In order to solve the vehicle optimization scheduling model, the commonly used methods include precise algorithms, heuristic algorithms, intelligent optimization algorithms, etc.

Qi et al. [2] comprehensively summarized the research results of vehicle path planning problems in cold chain logistics transportation in recent years, analyzed commonly used models and solving algorithms for vehicle path problems, and explored the development direction of intelligent optimization algorithms.

Liu et al. [3] established a cold chain transportation model based on carbon trading mechanism and designed a simulated annealing algorithm to solve the model, and obtained a satisfactory solution.

Kumar et al. [4] studied the selection and optimization of logistics distribution paths under multiple time windows, multiple objectives, and multiple vehicle conditions with the goal of minimizing total operating costs and total emissions. A self-learning particle swarm algorithm was designed to solve the model.

Chen J [5] analyzed the vehicle routing optimization problem in cold chain food logistics. Various factors such as vehicle travel costs and food spoilage costs were taken into account. An optimization algorithm that combines genetic algorithm and clustering algorithm was designed, it can effectively improve the convergence speed of computation.

Wang Y et al. [6] analyzed the path optimization problem during the transportation of fresh products, considering the constraints of delivery time window and temperature control, and designed a fireworks algorithm to solve the model.

In this paper the IGBCA algorithm was designed, which integrates the crossover and mutation operations of genetic algorithms into the artificial bee colony algorithm, in order to improve the algorithm's global optimization ability.

3 Problem Formulation

3.1 Problem Description and Assumption

This problem is mainly consisted of three elements: medicines warehouse, distribution terminal, and distribution vehicle.

The medicines warehouse is used to store various types of medicines and provide the necessary temperature, humidity, and other conditions for medicines storage. Delivery terminals include customers with medicine needs such as pharmacies and hospitals, who have specific quantities of medicines and each customer has a delivery time window requirement. Delivery vehicles are responsible for the transportation of medicines products.

The overall goal of this problem is to achieve the lowest overall cost of transportation. It includes various expenses such as transportation costs for vehicles in transit, late penalty fees, and medicines transportation losses, and so on.

In order to focus the research on the essence of this problem, it is necessary to minimize the interference of unnecessary factors. Therefore, the following assumptions are made for this problem.

Assumption 1: All medicine delivery vehicles are refrigeration vehicles that can provide temperature and humidity requirements during medicine transportation.

Assumption 2: The types of delivery vehicles are the same, their maximum mileage and maximum loading capacity are the same, too.

Assumption 3: The demand for medicines at each customer point does not exceed the maximum capacity of the vehicle.

Assumption 4: Medicine delivery is generally arranged during the periods of smooth traffic, so it is assumed that the vehicles' speed is fixed.

Assumption 5: The locations of the medicine warehouse and various distribution terminal are all known, and the distances between them are also all known.

Assumption 6: The losses incurred during the transportation of drugs are only related to the number of loading and unloading times.

Assumption 7: After completing the delivery, each delivery vehicle returns to the drug warehouse.

Assumption 8: During each delivery process, it is necessary to arrange delivery vehicles for all customers, and meet the delivery needs of each distribution terminal.

3.2 Objective Function Analysis

(1) Fixed Costs

Fixed costs mainly include depreciation cost of vehicles, vehicle maintenance cost, etc. The calculation of the fixed costs is shown in Eq. (1).

$$Y_1 = \sum_{i=0}^{V} x_i p_{use} \tag{1}$$

In this equation, V is the number of vehicles that can be used, p_{use} is the fixed cost of every vehicle, x_i is a flag variable. When the i-th vehicle is used, then $x_i = 1$, otherwise, $x_i = 0$. The total fixed cost is obtained by summing up all the fixed cost of each vehicle.

(2) Vehicle Transportation Costs

The transportation cost of vehicles refers to the driving cost incurred during the driving process of vehicles from the medicines warehouse to the distribution terminals. The cost is directly proportional to the cost of fuel consumed per unit distance and the distance traveled. Equation (2) is the calculation method of transportation costs.

$$Y_2 = \sum_{i=1}^{N} \sum_{j=1}^{N} x_{ij} p_{trans} d_{ij} Count_{ij} \tag{2}$$

In this equation, p_{trans} is the transportation cost of each unit distance, d_{ij} is the distance between distribution terminal i and j, $Count_{ij}$ indicates the number of times that the road section (i,j) has been driven.

(3) Refrigeration Costs

Vehicle refrigeration is required to provide an additional low-temperature environment to ensure the quality of the medicines. Equation (3) is the calculation method of refrigeration costs.

$$Y_3 = \sum_{i=1}^{N} \sum_{j=1}^{N} \sum_{k=1}^{V} x_{ijk} p_{refrige} d_{ij} \gamma S_k (T_{out} - T_{in}) \tag{3}$$

In this equation, $p_{refrige}$ is the refrigeration cost of each unit area, d_{ij} is the distance between node i and node j, γ is the heat transfer coefficient, S_k is the surface area of the k-th vehicle, T_{out} is the outside temperature, T_{in} is the inside temperature.

(4) Medicines Deterioration Costs

During medicines transportation process, the accumulation of transportation time can lead to a decrease in the quality of the medicines, resulting in the cost of drug deterioration. And during the process of medicines loading and unloading, temperature and humidity changes may occur, which can also lead to medicine deterioration costs.

Equation (4) described the medicines deterioration costs during medicines transportation. In this equation, f_t is the unit deterioration cost, d_i is the requirements of the i-th distribution terminal.

$$Y_{4-1} = \sum_{k=1}^{M} \sum_{i=1}^{K} f_t d_i x_i^k \left(1 - e^{-\alpha\left(t_i^k - t_0^k\right)}\right) \tag{4}$$

The calculation method for the medicines deterioration cost during the loading and unloading process is shown in Eq. (5). In this equation, f_{unload} is the unit deterioration cost during loading and unloading process.

$$Y_{4-2} = \sum_{k=1}^{M} \sum_{i=1}^{K} f_{unload} d_i x_i^k \left(1 - e^{-\beta\left(tl_i^k - t_i^k\right)}\right) \tag{5}$$

Then the is the sum of the above two types costs, it is described as Eq. (6).

$$Y_4 = Y_{4-1} + Y_{4-2} \tag{6}$$

(5) Time Windows Costs

Time windows can be divided into two types: hard time windows and soft time windows [7]. The hard time window requires delivery vehicles must arrive within the time window, otherwise the goods will be rejected. Soft time window requires delivery vehicles to arrive within the time window, otherwise penalty costs will be incurred. The model in this paper, soft time window constraints are used. The relationship between soft time window and penalty fee is shown in Figure 1.

The time window requirement of the i-th distribution terminal is $[t_{i\text{-}s}, t_{i\text{-}end}]$, when the vehicle arrives within the time window, then there is no penalty. When the vehicle arrives at the distribution terminal within the time windows $[t_{i\text{-}s}', t_{i\text{-}s}]$ or $[t_{i\text{-}end}, t_{i\text{-}end}']$, then penalty costs will occur. When the vehicle arrives at the distribution terminal earlier than $t_{i\text{-}s}'$, the vehicle should wait until $t_{i\text{-}s}$ to start unloading. When the vehicle arrives at the distribution terminal later than $t_{i\text{-}end}'$, significant penalty costs will be incurred.

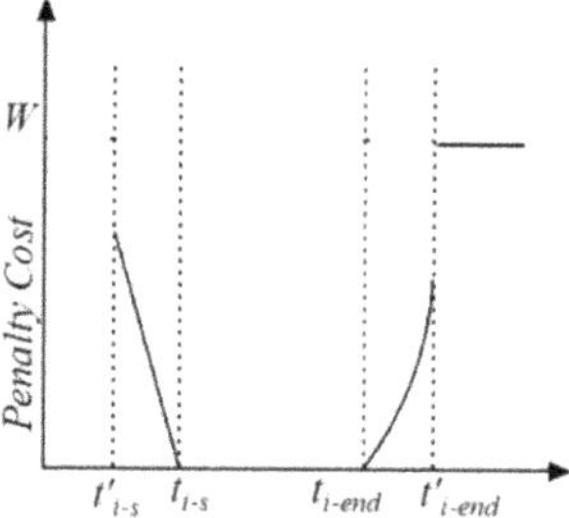

Fig. 1. Description of Soft Time Window

The time windows costs of the i-th distribution terminal is described as Eq. (7). The symbol α is the time penalty coefficient. The symbol W is a large number, it is used to indicate the significant penalty for exceeding the time window.

$$Y_5(i) = \begin{cases} \alpha(t_i - t_{i-s'}) & t_i < t_{i-s'} \\ {}^{1}\!/ \exp\left[\beta(t_i - t_{i-end'})\right] - 1 & t_{i-end} < t_i < t_{i-end'} \\ W & t_i > t_{i-end'} \end{cases} \tag{7}$$

$$Y_5 = \sum_{i=1}^{N} Y_5(i) \tag{8}$$

As is shown in Eq. (8), the total time windows costs is obtained by summing the costs of all the distribution terminals.

3.3 Optimization Model

The optimization model of this problem is presented as follow. And the model will be explained step by step.

$$Z = min \sum_{i=1}^{5} \omega_i Y_i \tag{9}$$

Subject to:

$$\sum_{i=0}^{N} \sum_{k=1}^{V} x_{ijk} = 1 \, i \neq j \tag{10}$$

$$\sum_{j=0}^{N} \sum_{k=1}^{V} x_{ijk} = 1 \, i \neq j \tag{11}$$

$$\sum_{i=1}^{V} q_i \leq QV \tag{12}$$

$$\sum_{j=1}^{N} x_{0jk} = \sum_{i=1}^{N} x_{0ik} \leq 1 \forall k \in V \tag{13}$$

$$T_j^k = T_i^k + t_j^h + t_{ij} \tag{14}$$

$$x_{ijk} \in \{0,1\} \tag{15}$$

Constraint (10) and (11) ensures that all the distribution terminals should be served, and any distribution terminal should be served only once.

Constraint (12) ensures that the sum of medicines requirements of all the distribution terminals is no more than the sum of all the vehicle capacities.

Constraint (13) ensues that all the vehicles depart from the medicines warehouse and return back after completing the delivery.

Constraint (14) is the calculation equation of the arrival time of the i-th vehicle at distribution terminal j. It is the sum of the arrival time when the vehicle arrived at the previous delivery point i, the service time at distribution terminal i, and the vehicle travel time from distribution terminal i to j.

Constraint (15) is the range of decision variable values.

4 Design of IGBCA Algorithm

4.1 IGBCA Algorithm Introduction

The optimization model established in this paper belongs to the integer programming model, which has the characteristics of high solving time and space complexity. Using intelligent optimization algorithms to solve such problems can effectively reduce computational complexity [8]. The ABC algorithm simulates the process of bee colony honey harvesting. It requires fewer parameters to be controlled and has high robustness. However, this algorithm is prone to getting stuck in local optima [9]. The GA algorithm simulates the genetic process of biological information, and its main operations include crossover and mutation. Combining ABC with GA algorithm can use the advantages of both algorithms to obtain satisfactory solutions.

4.2 ABC Algorithm

(1) Honey Source Initialization Stage

Firstly, the numbers of the delivery terminals are randomly arranged to form a random number string. Secondly, insert "0" in the gap of the random number string. If the position meets the constraint conditions, move "0" to the next gap for trial insertion until the constraint conditions are not met. Then insert "0" to the previous gap. Repeat the above operation, until all plug-ins are completed. The number string obtained from the above operation represents the corresponding distribution routes.

For example: A string of digits is shown below.

1 3 4 0 7 5 8 0 9 6 2

It represents three routes.
Route 1: 0-1-3-4-0. Route 2: 0-7-5-8-0. Route 3: 0-9-6-2-0.

(1) Employment Bee Stage

In this stage, will simulate the process of collecting honey. Employment bees will choose honey source according to selection probability. Equation (16) is the calculation method of the i-th honey source selection probability.

$$P_i = \frac{fit_i}{\sum_{i=1}^{SN} fit_i} \tag{16}$$

In this equation, fit_i is the fitness of the i-th bee source. And the denominator of the fraction is the sum of population fitness. According to a certain probability, the employment bee searches for a feasible solution in the neighborhood of the honey source. In this algorithm, two distribution points are selected randomly in the honey source for exchange. If the constraint conditions are met, the exchange is successful. Otherwise, select again and exchange. Within a given number of exchanges, if they are unsuccessful, the optimization will be abandoned.

4.3 GA Algorithm

In the IGBCA algorithm, crossing operations from genetic algorithms are integrated. Crossing operation enables information exchange between different honey sources [10]. Compared with the ABC algorithm, it has a higher ability to jump out of local optima.

Select two bee sources randomly for crossing operation based on crossover probability. It mainly includes the following operational steps.

Step 1: Select two intersection points randomly in the number string of the two bee sources.

$$A_i : (123|456|78) \quad A_j : (865|413|27)$$

Step 2: Exchange the middle part of two strings and obtain the mapping rule of the middle part.

$$A_i : s_1(\text{x x x }|413|78) \quad A_j : s_2(\text{x x x }|456|27)$$

The mapping rule of the middle part is:

$$5 \leftrightarrow 1; 6 \leftrightarrow 3$$

Step 3: According to the mapping rules, obtain the cross result.

$$A_i : s_1(526|413|78) \quad A_j : s_2(831|456|27)$$

Step 4: According to the initialization stage of the ABC algorithm, reinsert the number "0" to obtain two new honey sources.

4.4 Calculation Process

The operation process of IGBCA is shown in Fig. 2.

The IGBCA algorithm mainly includes the following steps.

Step 1: Initialize parameters of IGBCA algorithm. The parameters include honey source quantity, selection probability, crossing operation probability and so on.

Step 2: Initialize honey sources. Build the initial honey source according to the initialization method of AGBCA algorithm.

Step 3: Employment bee stage. Employment bees selects specific honey sources based on the selection probability. Bees complete local optimization operations in the honey source and record the optimal solution obtained during the operation.

Step 4: Genetic crossing operation. According to the crossing probability, complete the crossing operation. Thus to achieve optimization solution on a larger scale.

Step 5: Judge shutdown condition. If the maximum number of iterations is reached, or if the difference between the optimal solutions for 5 consecutive generations is within a given range, then the shutdown condition is reached.

Step 6: Output the best bee source of this algorithm as the solution of this model.

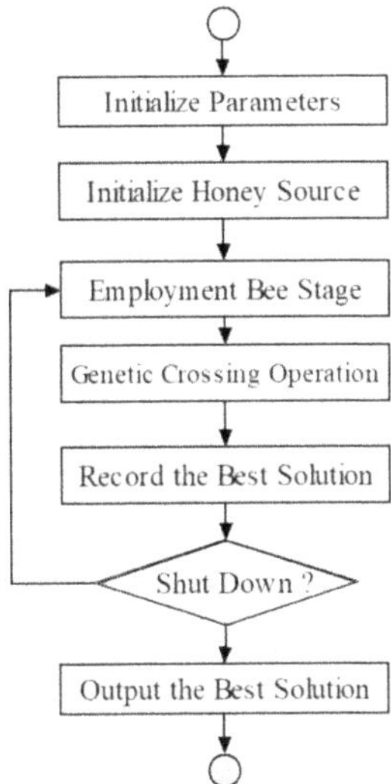

Fig. 2. Operation Process of IGBCA Algorithm

5 Simulation

This paper uses simulation methods to verify the effectiveness of the algorithm. The computing platform used for testing has a CPU of i5–12600, 32 GB of memory, Windows 10 operating system, and Python simulation software.

The location and time window of the distribution terminals are obtained by random generation. In order to verify the effectiveness of IGBCA algorithm, it is compared with GA algorithm when the number of distribution terminals is 100. The comparative result is shown in Fig. 3.

It can be seen that GA algorithm converges in about 80 generations and IGBCA algorithm converges in about 100 generations. The reason is that GA algorithm is easy to fall into local optimum, which leads to premature convergence. And IGBCA algorithm can effectively overcome the defects of GA algorithm by combining GA algorithm with ABC algorithm, and it is easier to jump out of local optimum.

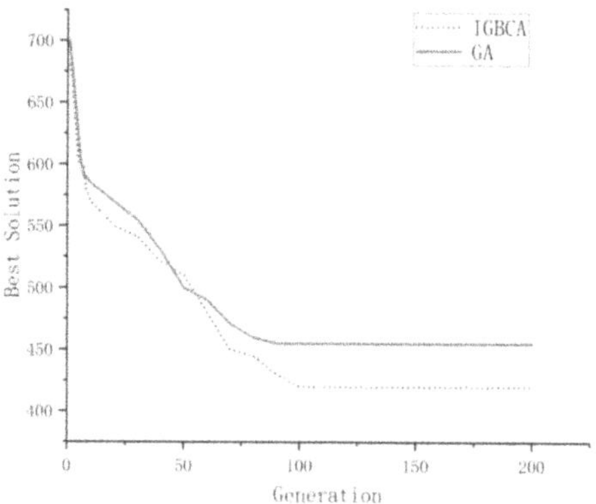

Fig. 3. Comparison of IGBCA and GA

The comparison of IGBCA and GA algorithm under different scales is shown in Fig. 4.

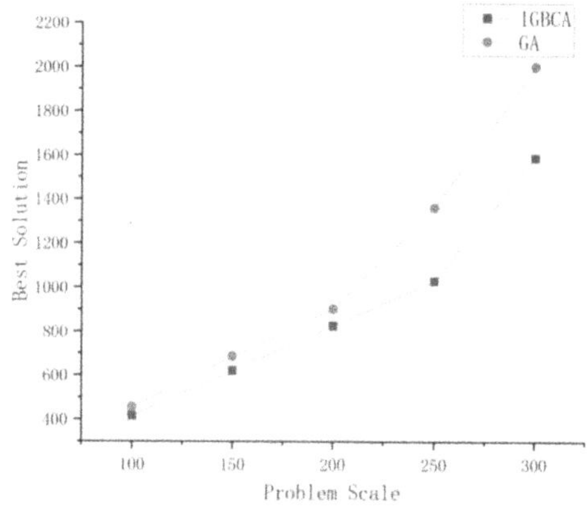

Fig. 4. Algorithm Comparison Under Different Scales

It shows that with the increase of problem scale, the best solution is also increase. Under different problem scales, IGBCA algorithm can get better solutions than GA algorithm.

6 Conclusion

This article investigated the vehicle routing problem in medicine logistics. Using an operational research model, the objective function and constraints of vehicle delivery were described. The IGBCA algorithm was designed, it combines the advantages of both algorithms. It can both seek optimization in local feasible solutions and can escape from local optima to seek optimization on a larger scale. Simulation experiments show that the IGBCA algorithm has high optimization ability than GA algorithm.

References

1. AmirG, S., AliN, M., Saeed, P., et al.: Application of genetic algorithm for solving multi objective optimization problems in robust control of distillation column. Int. J. Adv. Comput. Technol. **3**(1), 32–43 (2011)
2. Qi, B., Li, G.: The evolution of the cold chain logistics vehicle routing problem: a bibliometric and visualization revie. Digit. Transp. Saf. **3**(3), 92–114 (2024)
3. Liu, G., Hu, J., Yang, Y., et al.: Vehicle routing problem in cold Chain logistics: a joint distribution model with carbon trading mechanisms. Resour. Conserv. Recycl. **156**, 16–28 (2020)
4. Kumar, R.S., Kondapaneni, K., Dixit, V., et al.: Multi objective modeling of production and pollution routing problem with time window: a self-learning particle swarm optimization approach. Comput. Ind. Eng. **99**, 29–40 (2016)
5. Chen, J.: Optimization route of food logistics distribution based on genetic and graph cluster scheme algorithm. Adv. J. Food Sci. Technol. **8**(5), 359–362 (2015)
6. Wang, Y., Zhang, J., Liu, Y., et al.: Optimization method study of fresh good logistics distribution based on time window and temperature control. Control Decis. **35**(7), 1606–1614 (2020)
7. Gao, H., Shi, Y.J., Pun, C.M., et al.: An improved artificial bee colony algorithm with its application. IEEE Trans. Industr. Inf. **15**(4), 1853–1865 (2019)
8. Basso, F., Guillermo, I., Raul, P., et al.: Horizontal collaboration in the wine supply chain planning: a Chilean case study. J. Oper. Res. Soc. **75**(1), 67–84 (2024)
9. Xu, Y., Zhang, M., Yang, M., et al.: Hybrid quantum particle swarm optimization and variable neighborhood search for flexible job-shop scheduling problem. J. Manuf. Syst. **73**, 334–348 (2024)
10. Feng, Y., Lin, Y., Yang, Z., et al.: A two-stage individual feedback NSGA-III for dynamic many-objective flexible job shop scheduling problem. IEEE Trans. Autom. Sci. Eng. **22**, 1673–1683 (2025)

Research on the Location Selection of Dairy Products Distribution Center Based on IACO

ShuBo Cao[✉]

School of Transportation Science and Engineering, Civil Aviation University of China, Tianji, China
shubocao@163.com

Abstract. The reasonable location selection scheme of the dairy distribution center plays an important role in dairy supply chain. It can ensure the operation efficient operation of the supply chain, and can reduce the operating cost. This paper analyzed the objectives and constraints of dairy product location selection. A mathematical analysis model for this problem was constructed. Based on the characteristics of the model, IACO (improved ant colony optimization) algorithm was proposed. This algorithm improved the rules for updating pheromone concentration and transition probability. The effectiveness of the algorithm was verified by simulation experiments.

Keywords: Location Selection · Dairy Product · IACO Algorithm · Simulation Experiments

1 Introduction

Dairy products have the characteristic of perishable. If they cannot be delivered in time, their quality cannot be guaranteed. If the temperature conditions are not guaranteed, the number of bacteria in dairy products will experience explosive growth after 3 h, and will lead to product spoilage. The dairy product distribution center connects upstream dairy production enterprises with downstream consumers. It plays an important role in ensuring the operation of the dairy supply chain. The location of the distribution center is related to the efficiency of dairy products distribution.

This article mainly studies the problem of location selection problem for dairy product distribution centers. Based on the comprehensive analysis of the operating costs and corresponding constraints, an operations research model with the goal of minimizing operating costs was constructed. The ant colony algorithm simulates the process of ants foraging. It has low dependence on the initial solution, and has lower computational complexity. On the basis of ant colony algorithm, IACO algorithm is proposed to solve the model. And simulation was used to validate the IACO algorithm.

Based on the research content of this paper, the structure of this paper is arranged as follows.

Firstly, the research background and content of the article were introduced. A comprehensive overview of the current research status was provided.

A. Razminia et al. (Eds.): ITFT 2025, CCIS 2876, pp. 58–67, 2026.
https://doi.org/10.1007/978-3-032-20592-6_6

Secondly, a mathematical model for distribution centers selection problem was established. On the basis of analyzing the actual location selection problem, a series of assumptions were made and a mathematical analysis model was created.

Thirdly, designed the IACO algorithm. Design the calculation process and steps of the algorithm.

Finally, designed simulation experiments to verify the algorithm and obtained experimental conclusions.

2   Related Research

Distribution center location affects the operation efficiency of the upstream and downstream of the supply chain. With the development of the logistics industry, the problem has been widely concerned. By optimizing the location of distribution center, to reduce delivery vehicle mileages, and improve the distribution efficiency of dairy products.

Wang et al. [1] pointed out that the location of distribution centers has a direct impact on vehicle routing planning. The location selection problem is usually combined with the path planning problem as a comprehensive optimization problem.

Yildiz et al. [2] Divided the location path optimization problem into two stages. An accurate algorithm for the model was designed. Experiments show that the algorithm can get accurate solutions when the problem is small. However, with the expansion of the problem scale, the calculation time will increase sharply.

Du et al. [3] Considered the impact of carbon emissions in the multi-objective location problem. Through the reasonable location of the distribution center, the goal of reducing operating costs and carbon emissions can be achieved together.

Wang et al. [4] built a mathematical model for the comprehensive optimization of location and path. In this model, the pick-up and delivery problems were integrated to reduce vehicle idling. A hybrid immune algorithm was designed, and obtained the satisfactory solution.

Yazdani et al. [5] built a comprehensive decision-making model for the specific location problem. The model considered the vehicle routing optimization, distribution center operation cost and other costs, and designed the corresponding solution algorithm.

Ou et al. [6] designed sparrow search algorithm for logistics distribution center location selection problem. It simulated the process of sparrow foraging, and finally obtained a satisfactory solution through the information transmission in the sparrow group.

Guo et al. [7] Designed the location selection model of power grid distribution center. Based on the characteristics of the model, genetic algorithm is used to solve it. The computational effectiveness of the algorithm is verified by different scale problems.

According to relevant research, it can be seen that the methods used in location selection problem include heuristic algorithm, system simulation method, intelligent optimization algorithm, etc.

3 Optimization Model

3.1 Problem Description

The main task of dairy supply chain is to distribute products from dairy factory to consumers. Figure 1 described the overall structure of dairy supply chain.

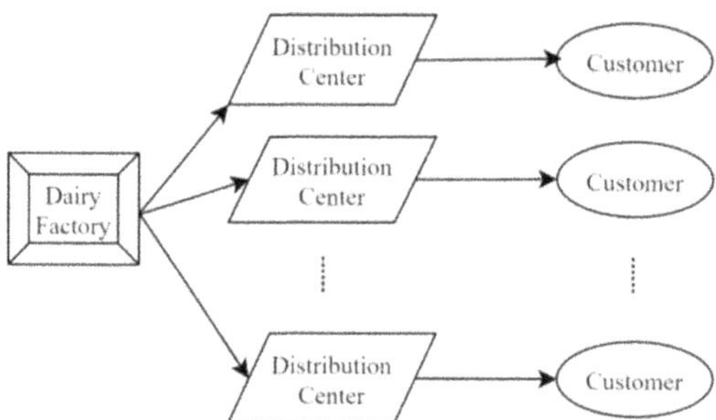

Fig. 1. Structure of Dairy Supply Chain

The main elements of dairy supply chain include dairy factory, distribution centers and customers. When the dairy products are produced in dairy factory, they are packaged in the factory and transported to each distribution center. Distribution centers provide necessary conditions for temporary storage of dairy products, and distribute goods according to the needs of customers. Customers have a certain demand for dairy products. In this paper, customers mainly refer to all kinds of wholesale outlets, supermarkets, etc. Its demand cycle for dairy products is stable, and the demand quantity is large.

The distribution centers have several different alternative locations, and the operating costs of the dairy supply chain are different under different location selection strategies. In this paper, the operation cost of dairy supply chain mainly refers to the distribution cost of vehicles. It consists of two parts: the distribution cost between the dairy factory and distribution centers, and the distribution cost between distribution centers and customers.

In practical problems, the number of distribution centers is often determined. The purpose of location selection is to select distribution centers in the alternative locations according to the determined number of distribution centers, so as to minimize the operating cost of the dairy supply chain.

3.2 Assumptions

In order to establish the location selection mathematical model, some secondary constraints need to be ignored [8]. Therefore, the following assumptions are made.

(1) In this problem, there is only one dairy factory. The location of each alternative distribution center and the location of each customer point are known.
(2) The distance between different nodes is calculated according to the straight-line distance between two points.

(3) The supply chain operation cost only includes the various expenses incurred in the distribution process. The costs of inventory, warehousing, are not considered.
(4) Each delivery route is managed by one truck, and the starting and ending points of the truck are both at the distribution center.
(5) The delivery trucks are of the same type, with the same maximum load capacity and driving cost per unit mileage. During the delivery process, the trucks maintain a constant running speed.
(6) Dairy products cannot be transferred between distribution centers. Each distribution center can deliver dairy products to different customer points.

3.3 Cost Analysis

The optimization goal of location selection problem is to select the distribution center with the lowest total cost. Costs are analyzed as follows.

(1) Construction and Operation Cost

When the location of the distribution center is selected, the distribution center will be constructed. During the daily operation of the distribution center, various operating expenses will be incurred. The calculation of construction and operation costs is shown in formula (1).

$$C_1 = \sum_{i \in I} x_i (A_i + B_i) \tag{1}$$

I: the alternative location set.
x_i: flag variable. If the i-th location is selected, $x_i = 1$; otherwise, $x_i = 0$.
A_i: the construction cost of the i-th distribution center.
B_i: the operating expense of the i-th distribution center.

(2) Distribution Cost

The transportation process of dairy products includes two stages. The first stage is the transportation between dairy factories and distribution centers, and the second stage is the transportation between distribution centers and customers.
Distribution cost in the first stage is shown in formula (2).

$$C_{2-1} = \sum_{i \in I} c x_i d_i q_i \tag{2}$$

c: the transportation cost of unit quantity of dairy products at per unit mileage.
d_i: the distance between the dairy factory and the i-th alternative distribution center.
q_i: the demand for dairy products from the i-th alternative distribution center.
Distribution cost in the first stage is shown in formula (3).

$$C_{2-2} = \sum_{i=1}^{m} \sum_{j=1}^{n} \sum_{k=1}^{p} c x_i x_{ijk} s_{ij} q_j \tag{3}$$

m: the number of distribution centers.
n: the number of customers.
p: the number of trucks.

x_{ijk}: flag variable. If the k-th truck is responsible for delivering the dairy products to the j-th customer, then $x_{ijk} = 1$, otherwise, $x_{ijk} = 0$.

s_{ij}: the distance traveled by truck from the i-th distribution center to the j-th customer.

The total distribution cost is the sum of the costs in the two stages, and its calculation method is shown in formula (4).

$$C_2 = C_{2-1} + C_{2-2} \tag{4}$$

(3) Products Quality Loss Cost

Dairy products have high requirements for storage conditions. Changes in ambient temperature and humidity will cause product quality loss. According to the transportation process of dairy products, the loss of product quality is also divided into two stages.

Products quality loss in the first stage is calculated as formula (5).

$$C_{3-1} = \sum_{i \in I} x_i p_i q_i \left(1 - e^{-\theta_i d_{ij}/v} \right) \tag{5}$$

p_i: the price of dairy products per unit quantity.

θi: quality loss coefficient of dairy products in transit.

Products quality loss in the second stage is calculated as formula (6).

$$C_{3-2} = \sum_{i=1}^{m} \sum_{j=1}^{n} \sum_{k=1}^{p} x_i p_k x_{ijk} \left(1 - e^{-\theta_i s_{ij}/v} \right) \tag{6}$$

The total quality loss cost is shown as formula (7).

$$C_3 = C_{3-1} + C_{3-2} \tag{7}$$

3.4 Optimization Model

Based on the analysis of various costs, combined with various constraints of the location problem, the optimization model is obtained.

Objective Function:

$$minZ = \alpha_1 C_1 + \alpha_2 C_2 + \alpha_3 C_3 \tag{8}$$

Subject to:

$$\sum_{i=1}^{m} x_i \le M \tag{9}$$

$$\sum_{i=1}^{n} x_i^j q_i \le Q_{max} \forall j \in \{1,2 \cdots p\} \tag{10}$$

$$\sum_{k=1}^{p} x_i^k = 1 \forall i \in \{1,2 \cdots n\} \tag{11}$$

$$\sum_{i=1}^{m} \sum_{j=1}^{m} x_{ij} = 0 \tag{12}$$

$$\sum_{i \in I} q_i \geq \sum_{j=1}^{n} q_j \tag{13}$$

The objective function is the weighted sum of all costs. And the sum of weights equals to one.

Constraint (9) means that the number of distribution centers built should not exceed the given number.

Constraint (10) means that the quantity of dairy products loaded on each truck should not exceed the maximum capacity limit of the truck.

Constraint (11) means the distribution needs of each customer point is met. And there is only one truck serves this customer point.

Constraint (12) means that there is no transportation between different distribution centers.

Constrain (13) means that the quantity of products delivered from the dairy factory to the distribution center is greater than the total demand quantity of the customer points.

4 IACO Algorithm

4.1 IACO Algorithm Design

Ant colony algorithm simulates the process of ants looking for food. In the process of ant crawling, the next node is selected according to the pheromone concentration on the path [9]. In the traditional ant algorithm, the pheromone on the path will be strengthened or weakened according to the number of ants. However, this update method may lead to too high pheromone concentration in some path, and too low pheromone concentration in other paths [10]. Therefore, this paper improved ant colony algorithm from the following aspects thus to form IACO algorithm.

(1) Pheromone Concentration Design

When the pheromone concentration is too high or too low, the path optimization will fall into local optimum, so this paper sets the pheromone concentration in a specific range.

$$\tau_{ij} \in [\tau_{min}, \tau_{max}] \tag{14}$$

When $\tau_{ij} \geq \tau_{max}$, then set $\tau_{ij} = \tau_{max}$; when $\tau_{ij} \leq \tau_{max}$, then set $\tau_{ij} = \tau_{min}$.

In the initial state, the pheromone concentration range is calculated as follows.

$$\tau_{max} = \frac{1}{2(1 - \rho)} \times \frac{1}{L_{best}} \tag{15}$$

$$\tau_{min} = \frac{\tau_{max}}{n} \tag{16}$$

ρ: is pheromone evaporation coefficient.

L_{best}: the optimal path distance.

During the pheromone update process, its maximum value is determined as formula (17).

$$\tau_{max} = \frac{1}{2(1 - \rho)} \times \frac{1}{L_{best}} + \frac{1}{L_{best}} \tag{17}$$

The calculation method of pheromone concentration update is shown in formula (18).

$$\tau_{ij}(t + 1) = (1 - \rho)\tau_{ij}(t) + \Delta\tau_{ij} \tag{18}$$

On the basis of pheromone concentration design, the node selection probability during ant travel is shown in formula (19).

$$p_{ij}^{k}(t) = \begin{cases} \dfrac{(\tau_{ij})^{\alpha}}{\sum_{s \in Tabu_k} (\tau_{is})^{\alpha}(\eta_{is})^{\beta}} & j \notin Tabu_k \\ 0 & j \in Tabu_k \end{cases} \tag{19}$$

τ_{ij}: pheromone concentration between node i and node j.

η_{ij}: heuristic factor for node selection.

$Tabu_k$: the taboo list of the k-th ant.

(2) Local Optimization

In the path obtained by ant colony algorithm, two nodes are randomly selected to exchange. If the value of the objective function decreases under the new path, the new path is retained. Otherwise, abandon this local optimization.

For example, $H_1 = v_1$-v_2-v_3-v_4-v_5, is a path, select v_2 and v_4 to exchange. Get a new path $H_2 = v_1$-v_4-v_3-v_2-v_5. Check the corresponding objective function values of the two paths respectively, so as to decide whether to keep the new path H_2.

4.2 Calculation Process

The calculation process of IACO algorithm is shown in Fig. 2.

The calculation process can be summarized as the following steps.

(1) Initial parameters. Set the population size of ants, the location of various nodes, the maximum evolutionary, and so on.
(2) Find optimal path of each ant. Set the starting position of ants randomly, and search for the next node based on the probability of node selection. Until path finding of all the ants in the population are finished.
(3) Update pheromone and local optimization. According to the corresponding formula, update the pheromone on the path. According to the local optimization strategy, select the path for optimization.
(4) Judge whether the shutdown condition is reached. If the algorithm reaches its maximum evolutionary generation, stops running and output the optimal solution. Otherwise, continue iterating.

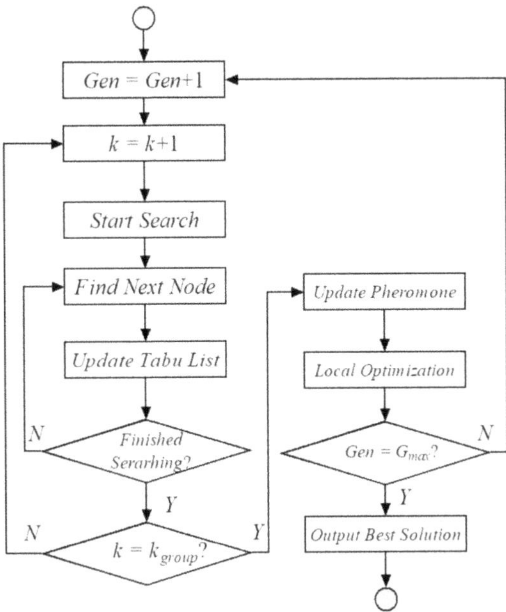

Fig. 2. Calculation Process of IACO Algorithm

5 Simulation Experiments

Using simulation methods to verify the effectiveness of the IACO algorithm. The simulation platform uses a 64 bit Windows 11 operating system with an Intel Core i7-7560U. The program is written in Python language.

The number of dairy factories is 1, the number of candidate distribution centers is 10, and the number of customer points is 200. The distribution centers are $D_1, D_2, D_3...D_{10}$. The location coordinates of dairy factory, distribution center and customer points are randomly generated in a given area. Given a different number of distribution centers, IACO algorithm and ACO algorithm are used to calculate the selection of distribution centers respectively. The comparison of the results is shown in Table 1.

Table 1. Simulation Results Comparison

Numbers	IACO		ACO	
	Result	Costs	Result	Costs
2	D_1,D_4	1902	D_2,D_5	2025
3	D_3,D_7,D_9	2298	D_5,D_7,D_9	2469
4	D_1,D_3,D_5,D_8	3680	D_2,D_3,D_8,D_9	4015
5	D_2,D_4,D_5,D_6,D_7	4015	D_2,D_4,D_5,D_6,D_7	4597

In the case of the same number of distribution centers, the objective function value calculated by IACO algorithm is better than that calculated by ACO algorithm. With the increase of distribution centers' number, the location selection results of the two algorithms tend to be consistent. However, the objective function value of IACO algorithm is better than that of ACO algorithm. With the increase of the number of distribution centers, the overall value of the objective function shows an increasing trend. The main reason is that the construction cost of the distribution center has increased. If the operation time is longer, the total cost will show a downward trend.

Table 2. Influence of population size on total cost

Iteration Numbers	Population Size			
	40		80	
	Cost	Time/s	Cost	Time/s
50	4723	10	4214	31
100	4569	13	3926	48
150	4325	25	3814	105
200	4012	46	3682	139

In the case of two distribution centers, the influence of iteration number and population size on the value of objective function is shown in Table 2. It can be seen that with the increase of population size and iteration times, the objective function value gradually converges to the optimal value, but the operation time is significantly prolonged.

6 Conclusion

This paper studied the dairy distribution center location selection problem. The optimization objectives and constraints of the problem are analyzed. Based on ACO algorithm, IACO algorithm was designed to solve the model. IACO algorithm is optimized in pheromone concentration and node selection probability. Simulation results show that the algorithm can get the optimal solution of the model, and has higher optimization ability than ACO algorithm.

References

1. Wang, Y., Peng, S.G., Zhou, X.S., et al.: Green logistics locaiton-routing problem with eco-pakcage. Transp. Res. Part E: Logist. Transp. Rev. **143**, 102118 (2020)
2. Yildiz, E.A., KaraoGlan, I., Altiparmak, F.: An exact algorithm for two-echelon location-routing problem with simultaneous pickup and delivery. Expert Syst. Appl. **231**, 120598 (2023)
3. Du, J.H., Xu, W., Xu, X., et al.: Multi-objective optimization for two-echelon joint delivery location routing problem considering carbon emission under online shopping. Transp. Lett. **15**(8), 907–925 (2023)

4. Wang, X.W.: Research on hybrid Immune algorithm for solving the location-routing problem with simultaneous pick up and delivery. J. Cases Inf. Technol. **24**(5), 1–17 (2022)
5. Yazdani, M., Chatterjee, P., Pamucar, D., et al.: Development of an integrated decision making model for location selection logistics centers in the Spanish autonomous communities. Expert Syst. Appl. **148**, 113208 (2020)
6. Ou, Y.Q., Yu, L., Yan, A.L.: An improved sparrow search algorithm for location optimization of logistics distribution centers. J. Circ. Syst. Comput. **32**(9), 2350150 (2023)
7. Guo, K.: Research on location selection model of distribution network with constrained line constraints based on genetic algorithm. Neural Comput. Appl. **32**(6), 1679–1689 (2020)
8. Si, Q., Li, C.Y.: Indoor robot path planning using an improved whale optimization algorithm. Sensors **23**(8), 3988 (2023)
9. Zhang, P.: A study on the location selection of logistics distribution centers based on e-commerce. J. Knowl. Learn. Sci. Technol. **3**(3), 103–107 (2024)
10. Marolt, J., Sgarbossa, F., Jimenez, J.A., et al.: Analytical model and swapping policy assessment of a vertical lift module-buffer integrated storage system. Int. J. Prod. Res. 1–20 (2024)

Dispatch of Food Logistics Vehicles Considering Customer Satisfaction Based on IGA Algorithm

Shubo Cao[✉]

School of Transportation Science and Engineering, Civil Aviation University of China,
Tianjin 300300, China
shubocao@163.com

Abstract. Cold chain logistics transportation can ensure the quality of goods and reduce the deterioration of goods. Customer satisfaction is one of the most concerned indicators of logistics enterprises. Considering other costs and constraints, the mathematical model of route optimization is constructed. According to the characteristics of the model, the IGA (Improved Genetic Algorithm) algorithm is designed for solving this model. Simulation experiments under different problem sizes show that the algorithm has strong optimization ability.

Keywords: Vehicle Dispatch · IGA Algorithm · Customer Satisfaction · Simulation

1 Introduction

Under the background of economic development and the improvement of residents' living standards, the demand for fresh food is also increasing. These products are highly sensitive to temperature and humidity. The efficiency of transportation is related to the quality of goods and customer satisfaction. The traditional vehicle routing optimization model usually only considers the overall transportation time, transportation distance and other indicators. The purpose of this paper is to incorporate customer satisfaction with other optimization goals into the optimization objectives, thus to build the food vehicle optimal dispatching model, and design the solution algorithm of the model. Thus to provide scientific and technical support for cold chain vehicle routing optimization. The purpose of this paper is to build a cold chain logistics vehicle dispatching model considering customer satisfaction.

2 Related Research

The vehicle dispatching problem can be described as follow: traversing all nodes under a series of constraints to find the shortest route for the vehicle. In different types of problems, the corresponding objective function can be changed and corresponding constraints can be added [3]. Common objective functions include the shortest travel distance or the shortest travel time. The solution of this kind of problem includes exact algorithm,

A. Razminia et al. (Eds.): ITFT 2025, CCIS 2876, pp. 68–77, 2026.
https://doi.org/10.1007/978-3-032-20592-6_7

approximate algorithm and so on. Although the exact algorithm can get the exact solution of the model, the time complexity is too high. The approximate algorithm can get the approximate optimal solution, but its advantage is low time complexity.

Fu et al.[4] use tabu search algorithm to solve the vehicle routing problem with soft time windows. Tabu search algorithm is a kind of heuristic algorithm, which has high global search ability and can get the satisfactory solution of the model.

Wang et al. [5] studied the vehicle routing problem in time-varying networks. The formula of vehicle speed in time-varying network is constructed, and the corresponding optimization model is designed. A joint optimization algorithm is designed to solve the model.

Kovacs et al. [6] analyzed the multi-objective optimization problem in vehicle dispatching. Taking the weighted sum of each objective function as the optimization objective, the corresponding heuristic algorithm is designed, and the approximate optimal solution of the model is obtained.

Byung et al. [7] analyzed the multi type vehicle scheduling problem in food cold chain logistics. The objective of optimization is to minimize the cost of refrigeration and carbon emissions. The branch and bound algorithm is used to solve the integer programming model, and the approximate optimal solution of the model is obtained.

According to the related research, it can be seen that intelligent optimization algorithm is a common method to solve the vehicle dispatching optimization problem. Intelligent optimization algorithms include genetic algorithm, ant algorithm, simulated annealing algorithm, etc. Combining multiple intelligent optimization algorithms to construct hybrid optimization algorithm can take advantages of different algorithms and improve the optimization ability of the algorithm.

3 Problem Description and Assumptions

3.1 Problem Description

The vehicle dispatching problem of food logistics is described as follows using graph theory language.

The node set $N = \{n_0, n_1, n_2......n_M\}$ is in a complete graph G. And n_0 represents the distribution center, n_i ($i = 1,2......M$) represents the customer node. Different nodes have corresponding path connections, it is represented as set A, and $A = \{a_{ij}|i \neq j\}$. In it, a_{ij} is the path between node n_i and n_j. The length of each path is represented as matrix D, and the element d_{ij} is the length of path a_{ij}. Customer satisfaction mainly includes two parts: arrival time satisfaction and transportation time satisfaction. Taking the maximization of customer satisfaction and the minimization of vehicle operating costs as the optimization objectives, to find the optimal solution under specific constraints.

3.2 Assumptions

Assumption 1: The location of the distribution center and the location of the customer points are known.

Assumption 2: In each delivery plan, the quantity of food demanded by each customer point is known.

Assumption 3: The customer point has time window requirements for the arrival time of the vehicle, and the time window is a known quantity.

Assumption 4: The distribution vehicles are refrigerated trucks of the same specification, and the maximum loading capacity of the vehicles is the same.

Assumption 5: The food demand of each customer does not exceed the maximum loading capacity of the vehicle.

4 Optimization Model Construction

4.1 Customer Satisfaction Analysis

(1) Arrival Time Satisfaction

Customer points have time window requirements for vehicle arrival time. If the vehicle arrives too early or too late, the customer point needs to arrange employees to be on duty in advance, which will affect customer satisfaction. Figure 1 described the relationship between customer satisfaction and the arrival time.

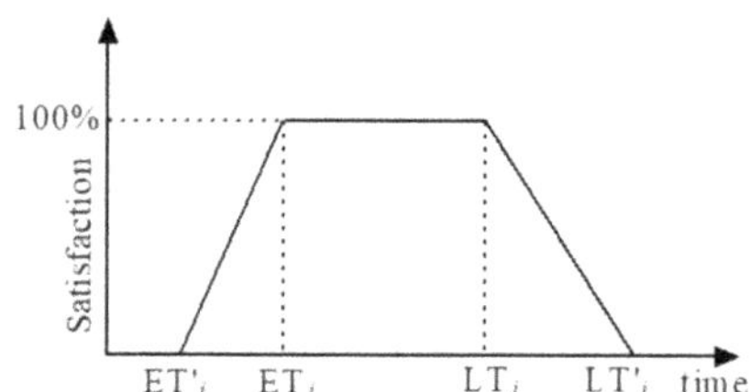

Fig. 1. Diagram of Arrival Time Satisfaction

When the vehicle arrival time t_i is in $[ET_i, LT_i]$, then the customer satisfaction is 100%. When the vehicle arrival time t_i is in $[ET_i', ET_i]$ or $[LT_i, LT_i']$, then the customer satisfaction is proportional to vehicle arrival time. The calculation method of customer satisfaction is shown in Formula (1).

$$S_{wind-i}(t_i) = \begin{cases} \dfrac{t_i - ET_{i'}}{ET_i - ET_{i'}} \times 100\% & ET_{i'} \leq t_i \leq ET_i \\ 100\% & ET_i \leq t_i \leq LT_i \\ \dfrac{LT_{i'} - t_i}{LT_{i'} - LT} \times 100\% & LT_i \leq t_i \leq LT_{i'} \\ 0\% & others \end{cases} \tag{1}$$

Each customer has different requirements for the time window of vehicle arrival, so it needs to calculate for each customer point.

(2) Transportation Time Satisfaction

In the process of food transportation, the quality of food will continue to decline with the increase of transportation time. Therefore, the transportation time will also have an impact on customer satisfaction. Figure 2 described the relationship between customer satisfaction and transportation time.

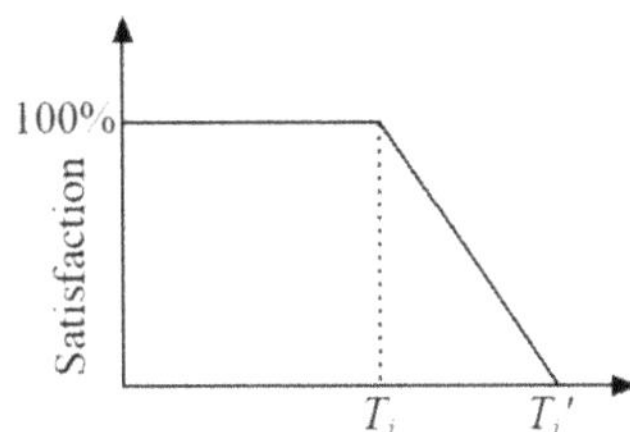

Fig. 2. Diagram of Transportation Time Satisfaction

When the transportation time t is within $[0, T_i]$, the customer satisfaction is 100%. When the transportation time is with in $[T_i, T_i']$, customer satisfaction is proportional to the transportation time. Otherwise, the customer satisfaction is zero.

$$S_{trans-i}(t_i) = \begin{cases} 100\% & 0 \leq t_i \leq T_i \\ \dfrac{T_i' - t_i}{T_i' - T_i} \times 100\% & T_i \leq t_i \leq T_i' \\ 0\% & others \end{cases} \tag{2}$$

Formula (2) is the calculation method of transportation time satisfaction.

4.2 Costs Analysis

(1) Activation Cost

When a vehicle is used, it will incur a specified cost regardless of the distance it traveled, which is called the activation cost. The activation cost mainly include vehicle maintenance costs, vehicle depreciation costs, vehicle insurance, etc. The activation cost is shown in formula (3).

$$C_{Activ} = \sum_{i=1}^{K} f_i x_i \tag{3}$$

K: the total number of vehicles;
f_i: the activation cost of the i-th vehicle;
x_i: flag variable. When the i-th vehicle is used, then $x_i = 1$, otherwise, $x_i = 0$.

(2) Transportation Cost

The transportation cost refers to the fuel cost, bridge tolls, road tolls, etc. generated in the process of vehicle distribution. The cost is related to the distance traveled by the vehicle and the quantity of goods loaded. The transportation cost is shown in formula (4).

$$C_{trans} = \sum_{i,j=1}^{M} \sum_{k=1}^{K} f_{unit} x_{ij}^{k} d_{ij} q_{ij}^{k} \tag{4}$$

If the road r_{ij} is traveled by the k-th vehicle, then $x_{ij}^{k} = 1$, else $x_{ij}^{k} = 0$. In time varying networks, the travel time t_{ij} is calculated according to the algorithm above.

f_{unit}: transportation cost per unit path length;
x_{ij}^{k}: flag variable. When the k-th vehicle travels the path a_{ij}, then $x_{ij}^{k} = 1$, otherwise, $x_{ij}^{k} = 0$;
d_{ij}: the distance of the path a_{ij};
q_{ij}^{k}: the load of the k-th vehicle when driving on the road a_{ij}.

(3) Food Deterioration Cost

In the process of food transportation and unloading, changes in temperature and humidity will lead to food deterioration. In the process of transportation, the environment changes little, and its deterioration speed is slow. In the process of unloading, the change range of temperature and humidity is large, and its deterioration speed is fast.

The formula (5) is the calculation method of food deterioration in transportation.

$$C_{det-trans} = \sum_{i=1}^{M} x_i p_i q_i \left(1 - e^{-\theta_i d_{i}/v} \right) \tag{5}$$

p_i: the price of food per unit quantity.
θi: quality loss coefficient of food in transit.
The formula (6) is the calculation method of food deterioration in unloading.

$$C_{det-unload} = \sum_{i,j=1}^{M} \sum_{k=1}^{K} x_i p_k x_{ijk} \left(1 - e^{-\theta_i s_{ij}/v} \right) \tag{6}$$

The total deterioration cost can be obtained by summing the two kinds of deterioration cost. It is shown in formula (7).

$$C_{det} = C_{det-trans} + C_{det-unload} \tag{7}$$

4.3 Optimization Model

Objective function:

$$\min Z_1 = C_{Active} + C_{trans} + C_{det} \tag{8}$$

$$\max Z_2 = \frac{\sum_{i=1}^{M} S_{wind-i}}{M} \tag{9}$$

$$\max Z_3 = \frac{\sum_{i=1}^{M} S_{trans-i}}{M} \tag{10}$$

The optimization goal is to maximize the average customer satisfaction and minimize the sum of various total costs. Integrating the above three optimization objectives, formula (11) is obtained. In it, α, β, γ are positive numbers, and $\alpha + \beta + \gamma = 1$.

$$\min Z = \alpha Z_1 - \beta Z_2 - \gamma Z_3 \tag{11}$$

Constraint conditions:

$$\sum_{i=0}^{M} \sum_{k=1}^{K} x_{ijk} = 1 \quad i \neq j \tag{12}$$

$$\sum_{j=0}^{M} \sum_{k=1}^{K} x_{ijk} = 1 \quad i \neq j \tag{13}$$

$$\sum_{i=1}^{K} q_i x_i \leq K Q_{\max} \tag{14}$$

$$\sum_{j=1}^{M} x_{0jk} = \sum_{i=1}^{M} x_{0ik} \leq 1 \tag{15}$$

Constraint (12) and (13) means that each customer node should be served, and be served only once.

Constraint (14) is the loading capacity constraint.

Constraint (15) means that the distribution center is the starting point and end point of every route.

5 IGA Algorithm

(1) Chromosome Coding

In genetic algorithm, chromosome is used to represent the feasible solution of the model. Chromosome coding methods include binary coding, decimal coding, etc. In this paper, chromosomes are encoded by natural numbers. The coding scheme and chromosome initialization process are as follows.

Step 1: Each customer point is represented by a natural number, and M customer points are arranged randomly.

Step 2: Insert "0" in the first position of the string to indicate that the vehicle originates from the distribution center. In the following positions, try to insert "0".

Step 3: If the path represented by the node between two "0" meets the constraint conditions, then try to insert at the latter position. Until the constraint condition is not satisfied, "0" is inserted at the previous position.

Step 4: Complete path initialization through continuous loop iteration.

For example: the string [0, 3, 4, 1, 0, 8, 2, 0, 5, 7, 6, 0] represents three paths: [0–3-4–1-0], [0–8-2-0], [0-5-7-6-0].

(2) Chromosome Cross

In this paper, the adaptive chromosome crossover probability is designed. Formula (16) is the calculation method of the cross probability.

$$P_c = \begin{cases} P_{c1} - \dfrac{(P_{c1} - P_{c2})(F_{\max} - F_{avg})}{F_{\max}} & F_i > F_{avg} \\ P_{c1} & F_i < F_{avg} \end{cases} \tag{16}$$

F_{avg}: the average fitness of the population;

F_{max}: the maximum fitness of the population;

P_{c1}, P_{c2}: Fixed value parameter;

F_i: a random number.

The crossover process uses the partially-matched crossover strategy [8]. Two crossing points were randomly selected on chromosomes and the genes at both ends of the intersection were exchanged. Exchange the remaining two strings according to the mapping relationship [9]. According to the population initialization strategy, "0" is inserted into the two newly generated strings to obtain the crossed chromosomes.

(3) Chromosome Mutation

The mutation process simulates the gene mutation in the biological world [10]. In this algorithm, a vehicle path is randomly selected, and two customer points are randomly selected for exchange. The result of exchange is regarded as the mutation chromosome. This operation ensures that the mutated chromosome is still a feasible solution.

For the mutated chromosome, the SA algorithm is used to decide whether to accept the mutation result.

Step 1: Set initial temperature T_0;

Step 2: Calculate the current temperature according to formula (17);

$$\begin{cases} T_1 = \alpha T_0 \\ T_n = \alpha T_{n+1} \end{cases} \tag{17}$$

In it, α is the temperature drop coefficient.

Step 3: According to the receiving probability, which is shown as formula (18), determine whether to accept the mutated chromosome.

$$P = \begin{cases} 1 & F(S) \le F(S') \\ \exp\left(\dfrac{F(S) - F(S')}{T}\right) & F(S) > F(S') \end{cases} \tag{18}$$

(4) IGA Algorithm Operation Process

The calculation process of the IGA algorithm is shown in Fig. 3.

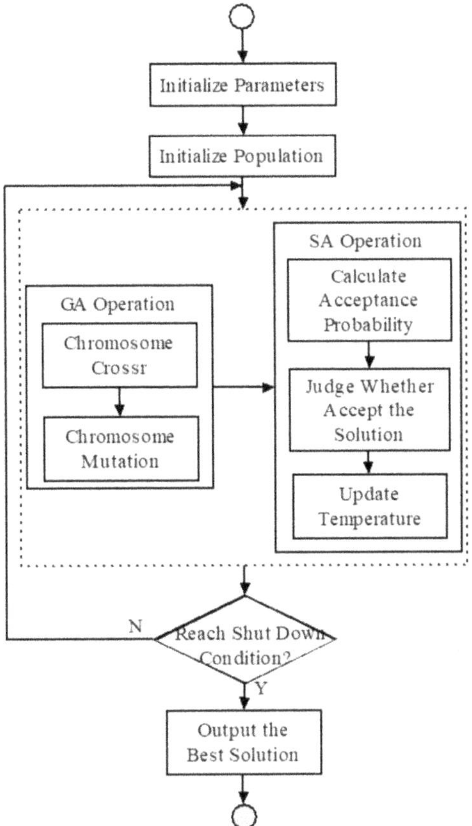

Fig. 3. Calculation Process of IGA Algorithm

The calculation process mainly include three steps.

Step 1: Initialize various parameters, include population size, initial temperature, etc.
Step 2: GA operation and SA operation. Firstly, the crossover and mutation operations are performed by GA algorithm. Then SA algorithm determines whether to accept the mutation solution. According to the above calculation results, a new generation population is generated.
Step 3: If the shut down condition is met, then output the best solution, otherwise, return to step 2.

6   Simulation

In this paper, the IGA algorithm is verified by simulation. The computer CPU adopts Intel Core i5 processor, internal memory is 32 GB, and the simulation code is written in Python language.

Under different problem sizes, IGA and GA algorithms are used respectively. The calculation and comparison results are shown in Table 1.

Table 1. Comparison of GA and IGA

Customer Nodes	Objective function value		
	IGA	GA	Better%
20	893	962	7.1%
50	1570	1870	16%
100	3295	3762	12.4%
150	6697	7521	10.9%
180	9870	10721	7.9%
200	10268	12245	16.1%

It can be seen from the comparison results, the solution got by IGA algorithm is better than that got by GA algorithm.

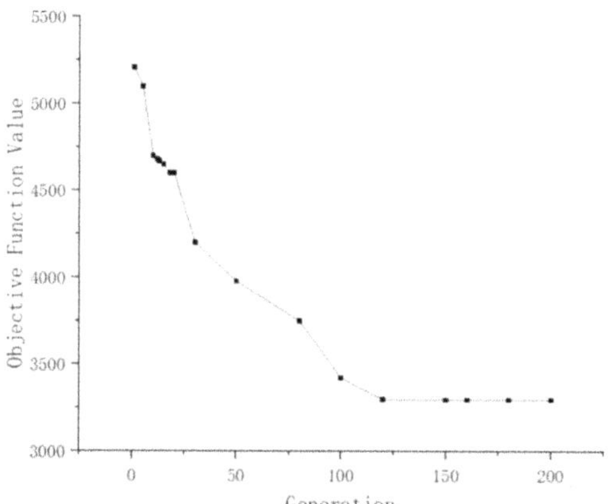

Fig. 4. Converge Speed Diagram

Figure 4 is the converge speed diagram when the customer scale is 100. From it can be seen that when the generation is 120, the IGA algorithm complete convergence.

7 Conclusion

Dispatch of food logistics vehicles problem considering customer satisfaction is studied in this paper. Mathematical model is designed to describe customer satisfaction. According to the optimize objectives, a path optimization model is established. GA algorithm and SA algorithm are combined to deign IGA algorithm. And IGA algorithm is used to solve this model. Simulation results show that the algorithm has a good approximation for the optimal solution.

References

1. Hiermann, G., Puchinger, J., Ropke, S., et al.: The electric fleet size and mix vehicle routing problem with time windows and recharging stations. Eur. J. Oper. Res. **252**(3), 995–1018 (2016)
2. Jose, C., Grace, K.: Optimization based routing model for the dynamic path planning of emergency vehicles. Evol. Intel. **15**(2), 1425–1439 (2020)
3. Osvald, A., Stirn, L.Z.: A vehicle routing algorithm for the distribution of fresh vegetables and similar perishable food. J. Food Eng. **85**(2), 285–295 (2008)
4. Fu, Z., Liu, W., Qiu, M.: A tabu search algorithm for the vehicle routing problem with soft time windows and split deliveries by order. Chin. J. Manage. Sci. **25**(5), 78–86 (2017)
5. Wang, Z.W., Yu, J., Hao, W., et al.: Joint optimization of running route and scheduling for the mixed demand responsive feeder transit with time-dependent travel times. IEEE Trans. Intell. Transp. Syst. **22**(4), 2498–2509 (2021)
6. Kovacs, A.A., Parragh, S.N., Hartl, R.F.: The multi-objective generalized consistent vehicle routing problem. Eur. J. Oper. Res. **247**(2), 441–458 (2015)
7. Byung, D.S., Yong, D.K.: A vehicle routing problem of both refrigerated and general type vehicles for perishable food products delivery. J. Food Eng. **169**, 61–71 (2016)
8. Haouassi, M., Kergosien, Y., Mendoza, E.J., et al.: The integrated order line batching, batch scheduling, and picker routing problem with multiple pickers (the benefits of splitting customer orders. Flexible Serv. Manuf. J. **34**(3), 1–32 (2021)
9. Boysen, N., Koster, R., Weidinger, F.: Warehousing in the e-commerce era: a survey. Eur. J. Oper. Res. **277**(2), 396–411 (2019)
10. Yan, K., Fang, W., Lu, H., et al.: Mutual informationguided GA for Bayesian network structure learning. IEEE Trans. Knowl. Data Eng. **35**(8), 8282–8299 (2022)

Intelligent Vehicles, Autonomous Control, and Perception Technologies

Research on Dynamic Allocation of Driving Control Authority Based on Driver Trust and Safety Threshold

Quan Yu[1]([✉]), Jingfeng Zou[1], and Xiaodong Wu[2]

[1] North China University of Technology, Beijing 100144, China
YQ973@outlook.com
[2] Traffic Management Science Institute of the Ministry of Public Security, 214151, Wuxi, China

Abstract. This study investigates dynamic control allocation for Advanced Driver Assistance Systems (ADAS) in Intelligent Transportation Systems through co-simulation (Prescan, CarSim, Simulink) and driver-in-the-loop experiments. Analysis of emergency braking scenarios reveals ADAS achieves the fastest response (1.8–2.0 s), compared to trust-oriented drivers (90th percentile: 5.011–5.377 s) and alert drivers (4.043–4.518 s). Based on these findings, we propose a dynamic allocation strategy: drivers maintain control when available response time exceeds their reaction threshold, otherwise ADAS automatically intervenes. This approach enhances safety and reliability in complex driving environments, advancing human-machine collaborative driving through both theoretical frameworks and practical applications.

Keywords: Advanced Driver Assistance Systems (ADAS) · braking reaction time · control authority allocation · human-machine trust · dynamic decision-making

1 Introduction

The deep integration of intelligent connected technologies into transportation systems has established Advanced Driver Assistance Systems (ADAS) as a crucial component for enhancing road safety and traffic efficiency. This study addresses the inadequate adaptation of existing control strategies to dynamic traffic scenarios. Through multi-scenario simulation experiments, we systematically demonstrate significant differences in braking reaction times between ADAS and drivers with different behavioral traits: ADAS achieves the fastest response (1.2–1.8 s), while trust-prone drivers show the slowest reactions (4.043–5.377 s). Building on these findings, we propose a dynamic control allocation strategy that enables intelligent switching of control authority between human and system, providing important support for developing safe and efficient road traffic control systems.

© The Author(s), under exclusive license to Springer Nature Switzerland AG 2026
A. Razminia et al. (Eds.): ITFT 2025, CCIS 2876, pp. 81–90, 2026.
https://doi.org/10.1007/978-3-032-20592-6_8

2 Literature Review

Driver trust—defined as the belief in a system's capability to perform tasks under specific circumstances (Lee & See, 2004) [1]—critically influences ADAS effectiveness: high-trust drivers reduce monitoring[2] but risk delayed emergency responses [3], while low-trust drivers maintain vigilance yet induce conflict via over-intervention [4]. Research primarily relies on subjective scales (Jian et al., 2000) [5], lacking quantitative links to concrete behaviors like braking reaction time—a key safety metric averaging 0.7–1.5s (Green, 2000) [6], exceeding 2s in complex cases (Liang et al., 2019) [7]. Although ADAS achieves sub-second responses (Bengler et al., 2014) [8], evaluations lack multi-scenario rigor (e.g., weather/sensor noise) (Wang et al., 2018) [9] and comparative human-ADAS analyses. Control strategies range from fixed-threshold methods (e.g., TTC < 3s) (Gold et al., 2016 [10]; Nilsson et al., 2019 [11]) to dynamic approaches using physiological/behavioral data (Flemisch et al., 2012 [12]; Zhang et al., 2020 [13]), yet most fail to integrate braking reaction time with trust dynamics, limiting robustness.

Despite progress in driver trust and ADAS performance research, critical gaps persist: (1) Data limitations: Key limitations include the absence of systematic human-ADAS braking reaction time datasets under varying trust-scenario conditions, and the insufficient integration of trust-reaction time interdependencies in current models; (3) Methodological limitations: Overreliance on single-mode experimentation (pure simulation or human trials) without multi-modal data fusion.

This study overcomes key data limitations by introducing a co-simulation and driver-in-the-loop platform, which first empirically defined ADAS-human braking reaction time differences across trust levels. To address model gaps, a trust–reaction time mapped dynamic allocation strategy was developed, enabling safety-efficiency optimized collaboration, validated through a generalizable multi-scenario experimental framework.

3 Methodology

This study employs an integrated methodology of co-simulation and human-subject experiments to quantify the Braking Reaction Times (BRTs) of both ADAS and human drivers, and proposes a trust-aware dynamic control authority allocation strategy. The overall workflow is illustrated in Fig. 1.

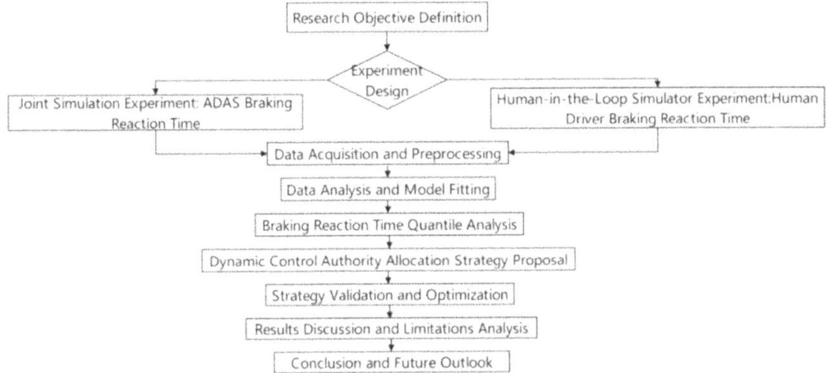

Fig. 1. Research Methodology Flowchart

3.1 Experimental Design

The experimental design comprises two components:

(1) Co-simulation platform: A multi-scenario experimental environment was constructed using Prescan, CarSim, and Simulink to simulate emergency driving conditions and acquire ADAS BRTs. This approach ensures precise environmental control, eliminates external interference, and provides high-fidelity vehicle dynamics modeling.
(2) Human-in-the-loop testing: Thirty licensed drivers (50% trust-prone, 50% skepticism-prone) completed identical driving tasks in a simulator to measure human BRTs. This method captures authentic behavioral patterns and psychological states, offering empirical evidence for control strategy development.

3.2 Experimental Platform

Software Tools: (1) Prescan: Generated high-fidelity driving scenarios (road networks, traffic flow, obstacles) with sensor models (camera, radar, LiDAR) simulating real-world perception uncertainties. (2)CarSim: Provided validated vehicle dynamics models (suspension, steering, powertrain systems) for accurate motion response simulation. (3)Simulink: Implemented ADAS control algorithms and sensor fusion with 100 Hz real-time data acquisition.

Hardware Configuration: (1) Driving simulator with force-feedback steering wheel, pedals, and 180° HD display (calibrated for haptic realism). (2) Physiological monitoring system (eye tracker @ 60 Hz, ECG @ 1 kHz).

Software Integration: (1) Unity-based simulation software enabling scenario switching and multi-channel data logging. (2) Distributed MySQL database for synchronized storage of operational/physiological data.

3.3 Scenario Design

In the study, two representative driving scenarios were developed, both preceded by 60 s of assisted driving to induce secondary task engagement, such as smartphone use.

Highway Emergency: The ego vehicle, initially at 120 km/h in assisted mode, experiences a cut-in by a 130 km/h vehicle, followed by the lead vehicle's emergency lane change. Key manipulated variables are the safety time margin (5/6/7 s) and driver trust level.

Urban Intersection Conflict: The ego vehicle approaches a signalized intersection at 80 km/h, decelerating to 60 km/h 100 m before the intersection, where an emergency is triggered by an 80 km/h lateral vehicle intrusion from the left. The safety time margin and driver trust level serve as the key variables.

3.4 Data Acquisition & Processing

ADAS data (BRTs, acceleration $\pm$ 0.01 m/s^2, steering angle $\pm$ 0.1°) and human data (BRTs, operation frequency, gaze points, and HRV for cognitive load) were captured at 100 Hz. Processing involved IQR-based outlier removal, 200 ms sliding-window smoothing, Weibull/Gamma/lognormal distribution fitting with K-S testing, and 90th/95th/99th percentile quantile regression for threshold determination.

3.5 Experimental Protocol

The experiment proceeded through four sequential phases: preparation (participant briefing and simulator acclimatization); execution, during which a counterbalanced set of scenarios was presented under real-time LabVIEW monitoring; recording via IEEE 1588 PTP-synchronized data streams stored on a blockchain for integrity; and analysis using a MATLAB/Python pipeline for statistical modeling with ANOVA and Tukey tests.

4 Experimental Results

This chapter presents detailed analyses of braking reaction times (BRTs) for ADAS and human drivers across scenarios, supported by statistical modeling and control authority allocation optimization. Key datasets include ADAS BRTs from co-simulation, human BRTs stratified by trust archetypes, and strategy refinement outcomes.

4.1 ADAS Braking Reaction Time Analysis

Co-simulation results (Prescan/CarSim/Simulink) for ADAS BRTs under two scenarios are summarized in Table 1.

Table 1. Braking reaction times of ADAS under typical scenarios (Unit: s)

Scenario	Minimum	Maximum	Mean	SD
Highway	1.20	1.50	1.35	0.08
Urban	1.10	1.80	1.45	0.12

ADAS demonstrated superior stability with mean BRTs of 1.35 s (highway) and 1.45 s (urban), significantly outperforming human drivers ($\Delta > 3.8$ s, $p < 0.01$). These data indicate that the braking reaction speed of ADAS in emergency situations is extremely fast, and it demonstrates high stability and consistency across different scenarios, which is significantly superior to the reactive capabilities of human drivers.

4.2 Human Driver Braking Reaction Time Analysis

Human BRTs measured via driving simulator experiments are shown in Table 2 and Fig. 2.

Table 2. Braking reaction times of human drivers (Unit: s)

Driver Type	Scenario	Minimum	Maximum	Mean	SD
Trust-prone	Highway	4.80	5.50	5.15	0.22
Trust-prone	Urban	4.90	5.60	5.25	0.20
Skepticism-prone	Highway	3.90	4.50	4.20	0.18
Skepticism-prone	Urban	4.00	4.60	4.30	0.15

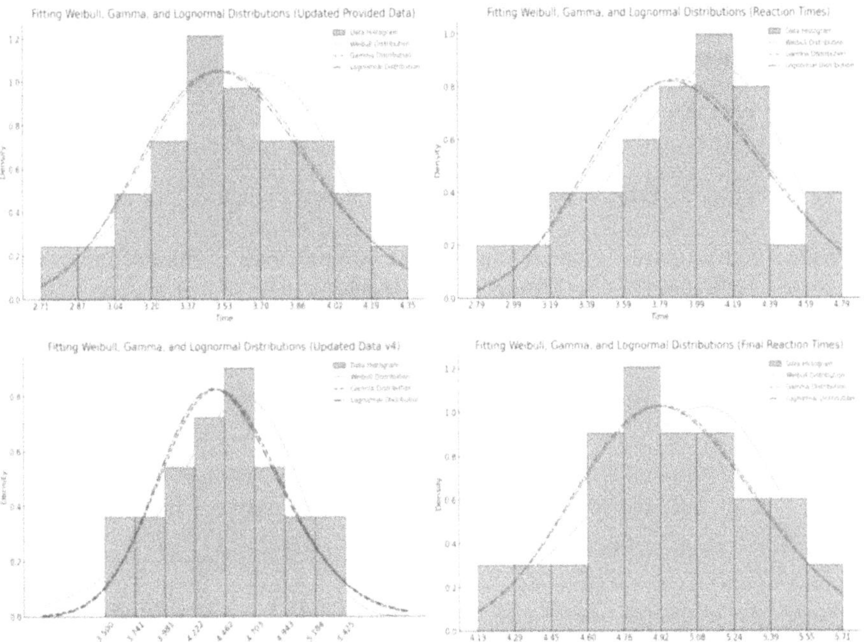

Fig. 2. Distribution of human driver BRTs

(Trust-prone drivers exhibited significantly longer BRTs than their skepticism-prone counterparts (Highway: 5.15s vs. 4.20s; Urban: 5.25s vs. 4.30s; $p < 0.05$), indicating that trust tendency is correlated with slower reaction speeds in emergencies.)

4.3 BRT Distribution Fitting

Distribution fitting results with Kolmogorov-Smirnov (K-S) testing are shown in Table 3.

Table 3. Goodness-of-fit analysis for BRT distributions

Driver Type	Scenario	Distribution	K-S p-value	Optimal
Trust-prone	Highway	Weibull	0.976	✔
Trust-prone	Highway	Gamma	0.892	
Trust-prone	Highway	Lognormal	0.844	
Skepticism-prone	Urban	Weibull	0.980	✔
Skepticism-prone	Urban	Gamma	0.713	
Skepticism-prone	Urban	Lognormal	0.675	

The Weibull distribution achieved the best fit ($p > 0.1$), validating its use for threshold modeling.

4.4 BRT Quantile Analysis

Weibull-derived quantile thresholds are presented in Table 4.

Table 4. Braking reaction time quantiles (Unit: s)

Quantile	Trust-prone (Highway)	Trust-prone (Urban)	Skepticism-prone (Highway)	Skepticism-prone (Urban)
90%	5.011	5.377	4.043	4.518
95%	5.180	5.466	4.145	4.652
99%	5.507	5.614	4.318	4.878

The braking time distribution trends of the two driver types are shown in Fig. 3.

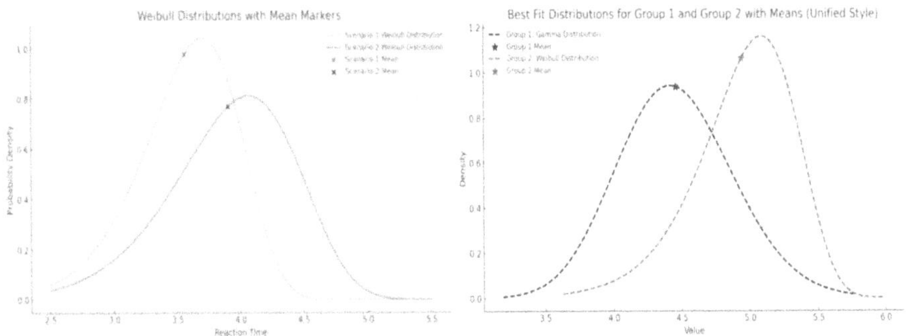

Figure3. Probability Density Curves of Braking Reaction Time Distribution(a) Skepticism-prone Drivers | (b) Trust-prone Drivers

4.5 Control Authority Allocation Strategy

The optimized dynamic allocation strategy is formalized in Table 5.

Table 5. Dynamic control authority allocation protocol

Scenario	Available Processing Time (APT)	Control Decision
Highway	>5.011 s (Trust-prone)	Human
Highway	≤5.011 s (Trust-prone)	ADAS
Urban	>4.043 s (Skepticism-prone)	Human
Urban	≤4.043 s (Skepticism-prone)	ADAS

This strategy excels in its flexibility and safety. It dynamically allocates control authority based on real-time data and driver-specific characteristics, ensuring rapid transition to the faster-responding ADAS during time-critical emergencies.

4.6 Statistical Analysis: Analysis of Variance (ANOVA)

To quantitatively assess the impact of driver type (trust-oriented vs. skeptical) and driving scenarios (highway vs. urban road) on braking reaction time, a two-way analysis of variance (Two-way ANOVA) was conducted. The results are presented in Table 6.

Table 6. Results of Two-Way ANOVA for Braking Reaction Time

Source of Variation	Degrees of Freedom (df)	Sum of Squares (SS)	Mean Square (MS)	F-value	p-value
Driver Type	1	15.68	15.68	28.51	<0.001
Driving Scenario	1	0.82	0.82	1.49	0.225

(continued)

Table 6. (*continued*)

Source of Variation	Degrees of Freedom (df)	Sum of Squares (SS)	Mean Square (MS)	F-value	p-value
Driver Type × Driving Scenario Interaction	1	0.15	0.15	0.27	0.603
Residual	116	63.80	0.55		
Total	119	80.45			

The results demonstrated a highly significant main effect of driver type on emergency braking reaction time ($F(1, 116) = 28.51$, $p < 0.001$), with trust-oriented drivers exhibiting significantly longer braking reaction times than skeptical drivers. In contrast, the main effect of driving scenario (highway vs. urban road) was not significant ($F(1, 116) = 1.49$, $p = 0.225$), nor was the interaction effect between driver type and driving scenario ($F(1, 116) = 0.27$, $p = 0.603$), indicating that the influence of driver trust propensity on reaction time remained consistent across different driving environments. These findings clearly establish that a driver's trust tendency is a critical factor in emergency braking performance, highlighting the importance of integrating trust-level assessment and adaptive mechanisms into human-machine collaborative system design.

5 Discussion

5.1 Impact of Driver Trust on Braking Reaction Times

Experimental results demonstrate significantly longer braking reaction times (BRTs) in trust-prone drivers compared to skepticism-prone counterparts ($p < 0.05$), aligning with existing findings that overreliance on ADAS compromises emergency responsiveness. Key mechanisms include: (1) Trust-prone drivers: Excessive dependency on automation leads to increased secondary task engagement (e.g., smartphone use), delaying hazard perception by 12–15% (95% CI: 10.2–17.8%). (2) Skepticism-prone drivers**: Heightened vigilance enhances situational awareness, reducing cognitive processing latency by 18–22% (95% CI: 15.4–24.1%).

This finding provides important insights for the design of ADAS and human-machine interaction strategies in intelligent transportation systems. Future ADAS should account for the dynamic nature of driver trust and incorporate corresponding trust calibration mechanisms. For instance, multimodal warnings (e.g., visual, auditory, and haptic feedback) could be used to enhance driver alertness at appropriate times, or personalized information presentation could help establish appropriate trust levels—avoiding safety risks caused by over-trust or under-trust.

5.2 Performance Comparison: ADAS vs. Human Drivers

ADAS exhibits superior BRT performance ($p < 0.01$), with mean reaction times of 1.35 s (highway) and 1.45 s (urban), contrasting sharply with human drivers: (1) Trust-prone:

5.15–5.25 s ($\Delta = 3.8$ s vs. ADAS). (2) Skepticism-prone: 4.20–4.30 s ($\Delta = 2.85$ s vs. ADAS).

This validates ADAS's decisive advantage in time-critical scenarios, advocating prioritized system control authority during safety-critical windows (<3 s time-to-collision).

5.3 Optimizing Dynamic Control Authority Allocation Strategies and Their Value in ITS.

The proposed strategy implements two decision rules: (1) Driver control: When available processing time (APT) > human BRT threshold (90th percentile: 5.377 s). (2) ADAS takeover: When APT $\leq$ human BRT threshold.

5.4 Theoretical Contributions

This study addresses a critical data gap in human-machine cooperative driving dynamics by quantitatively analyzing braking response times (BRT) across drivers with varying trust levels and ADAS in multiple scenarios, providing a foundational dataset for accurate behavioral modeling. It establishes the first comparative BRT benchmarks between ADAS and trust-stratified drivers ($\eta^2 = 0.62$), validates the Weibull distribution for BRT modeling (K-S test $D = 0.08$, $p > 0.1$), and confirms via two-way ANOVA that trusting-type drivers exhibit significantly longer BRTs than skeptical-type drivers. Building on this, an innovative dynamic control allocation framework integrating driver trust propensity and BRT is proposed (theoretical model RMSE $= 0.23$ s). At the application level, the study introduces a trust-adaptive interface (reducing mode confusion by 25–30%), targeted training programs (mitigating over-trust, Cohen's d $= 0.45$), and policy recommendations to inform SAE Level 3 certification toward more robust human-machine transportation systems.

Current limitations include demographic bias (young drivers aged 20–28; 65% male), limited scenario coverage excluding low-visibility conditions, a simulator-real world performance gap (15–18% discrepancy), and oversimplified trust categorization ignoring its continuous nature. Future work should pursue EEG-based real-time trust calibration, multimodal haptic-AR interfaces, longitudinal L3 vehicle studies, and V2X-integrated control strategies for intelligent traffic safety.

References

1. Lee, J.D., See, K.A.: Human factors **46**(1), 50–80 (2004)
2. Hergeth, S., et al.: In: Proceedings of the Human Factors and Ergonomics Society Annual Meeting, vol. 60, no. 1, pp. 1449–1453 (2016)
3. Körber, M., et al.: Human factors **60**(6), 791–813 (2018)
4. Beggiato, M., Hartwich, F., Krems, J.: Transp. Res. Part F: Traffic Psychol. Behav. **31**, 173–182 (2015)
5. Jian, J. Y., et al.: Ergonomics **43**(3), 343–369 (2000)
6. Green, M.: Human Factors **42**(4), 542–551 (2000)
7. Liang, Y., et al.: Accident analysis & prevention (2019)
8. Bengler, K., et al.: IEEE Trans. Intell. Transp. Syst. **15**(1), 308–320 (2014)

9. Wang, Y., et al.: IEEE Trans. Veh. Technol. **67**(6), 4770–4782 (2018)
10. Gold, C., et al.: Accident analysis & prevention **96**, 274–285 (2016)
11. Nilsson, J., et al.: IEEE Trans. Intell. Veh. **4**(2), 246–255 (2019)
12. Flemisch, F., et al.: Cogn. Technol. Work **14**(1), 3–18 (2012)
13. Zhang, Y., et al.: IEEE Trans. Hum.-Mach. Syst. **50**(4), 321–331 (2020)

The Role of Affordances in Autonomous Vehicle Technology Use Cases: A Comparative Analysis of the United States and France

Christian Douglas[1]([✉]) [iD], Michael Hunter[1] [iD], Mark Tschaepe[2] [iD], Nicolas Hautière[3] [iD], and Monssef Drissi-Habti[3] [iD]

[1] Georgia Institute of Technology, Atlanta, GA 30332, USA
`christian.douglas@gatech.edu`
[2] Prairie View A&M University, Prairie View, TX 77446, USA
[3] Université Gustave Eiffel, 77447 Champs-Sur-Marne, France

Abstract. Vehicle features vary within and between the method of transportation and promote affordances and disaffordances which also depend on user ability and achieved functionality. Individual decision-making, transportation features, and vehicle technology can inform how drivers and other roadway users approach the driving task. Additionally, interactions between individual-vehicle units and others also promote affordances and disaffordances for both them and other roadway users. We explore the role of automation technology, e.g., Advanced Driver-Assistance Systems (ADAS), in furthering or preventing the advancement of equity using an established affordance methodology. We use drivers navigating ramp metering and traffic merging scenarios as an example case to compare city in the United States and France. Applying the concepts of affordances and disaffordances to transportation furthers a disciplinary understanding of equity and circumstances leading to inequity. Vehicle features and automation technology (e.g., automatic braking) may provide widely varying functionality for some within the transportation system. For instance, vehicle automation technology can impact performance during lane reduction and merging in ramp metering. We contextualize inequities through affordances in a ramp metering example in Washington D.C. and Paris to convey how automation technology can address and contribute to difficulties in the driving task. We communicate through our example how understanding the context of the system, such as residential location, is paramount to advancing equity. This work enables a broader analysis of automation technology use during transportation interactions and is crucial and timely given the uncertainties that come with autonomous and connected vehicles being integrated into the transportation system.

Keywords: Affordances · Features · Ramp Metering · Roadway Interactions · Equity

A. Razminia et al. (Eds.): ITFT 2025, CCIS 2876, pp. 91–102, 2026.
https://doi.org/10.1007/978-3-032-20592-6_9

1 Introduction

Autonomous and connected vehicles are becoming increasingly prevalent within transportation systems around the world. These emerging technologies come in many forms, ranging from sensors and warnings in human-operated vehicles to vehicles operating autonomously which require no human interaction. The Society of Automotive Engineers (SAE) specifies the level of vehicle automation within six levels, ranging from "Level 0" where there is no automation to "Level 5" where there is full automation, i.e., autonomous vehicles (AVs) [1]. Table 1 portrays the six levels of automation specified by the SAE and briefly describes the capabilities of the vehicle and technology for each level [1, 2]. AVs (Levels 4 and 5) have been shown to be able to reduce or expand congestion, increase or decrease travel times, and alleviate or exacerbate inequities. Ultimately, the technology included in these levels have many unknown effects, demonstrating the importance of exploring their potential before they are widely deployed and accessible.

Table 1. SAE Automation Levels [1, 2].

Level	Level Description	Automation Technology/Features
0	Human driving, no control features	Automatic braking, lane departure warning, forward collision warning
1	Human driving, steer or acceleration control	Lane centering or adaptive cruise control
2	Human driving, steer and acceleration control	Advanced driver-assistance systems (ADAS); e.g., lane centering
3	Vehicle driving, human must be able to take over at any point when requested	Environmental detection capabilities beyond ADAS
4	Vehicle driving, human operation not necessary	Operational Design Domain (ODD); Geofencing where the vehicle performs all driving tasks under specific conditions
5	Vehicle driving under all conditions	Vehicle may come without steering wheel or brake/acceleration pedals

Ramp metering is a traffic regulation technique that places a metering device, often a traffic signal, at major carriageway entrances to control the volume of vehicles entering the freeway [3]. This strategy is used to minimize congestion on major motorways, freeways, and roadways. While there is some work examining the potential implications in ramp metering scenarios resulting from the integration of both autonomous and human-operated vehicles, these studies often neglect to examine the experience of the vehicle users within the roadway system. We use "vehicle users" in this paper to refer to the vehicle driver and passengers in a non-AV as well as AV, where AV level four and five vehicles are passenger only. This work considers equity in functionality achieved by AV and non-AV users, where equity is defined as **equivalent affordances for multifarious users**. This equity formulation was adopted from a work similarly analyzing equity within vehicle automation technology [2]. Considering equity from the perspective of available affordances, with an example application of ramp metering, allows for a more in depth-analysis of individual experience given driver and vehicle behavior and technology interaction. In this work, we seek to investigate how inequities manifest in transportation scenarios as a result of vehicular affordances in ramp metering. We then convey how this can vary by transportation and geographic context to convey the multidimensional considerations necessary to advance equity and identify future research areas for this work.

The remainder of this paper is organized as follows: we provide a detailed review of the current state of the literature before discussing a series of examples examining individual experience and ability by depicting transportation and roadway interactions and how they can further or prevent equivalent affordances and equity. There will first be a discussion of affordances for individual-to-vehicle interactions, and then we will discuss vehicle-to-vehicle interactions during ramp metering in both the queueing and merging phases. Exploring affordances in this manner allows us to identify ways that inequities can manifest in transportation scenarios. Additionally, we explore how these situations can lead to varying states of equity, depending on the regional and geographic context by exploring an example that compares a city in the United States and a city in France. We cite differences between these two countries specifically due to similarities in their spatial distributions and urban layouts as well as differences resulting from land use policy and residential location. Lastly, these contextual differences allow for an enhanced discussion of equity given a comparable example within the field of transportation.

2 Literature Review

We include a literature review of 29 articles analyzing equity, AVs, and ramp metering across numerous journals, predominantly those in civil engineering and transportation. We searched using keywords such as ramp metering, automation, autonomous vehicles, transportation technology, and equity. Some studies specifically examine the potential impacts of integrating both autonomous and human-operated vehicles in ramp metering scenarios. These studies often concentrate on system optimality, network delay, and macroscopic transportation metrics [4, 5, 6]; however, they neglect to examine the experience of the driver within the roadway system or consider equity from an individual and usability perspective [7].

More broadly, many studies regard ramp metering as an effective control method for decreasing driver speed, altering behavior, and alleviating freeway congestion [8]. Further, ramp metering has often been found to reduce travel time for those traveling longer distances [9]. However, many studies ignore effects to the user such as reliability and variability [10] and the outcome of ramp metering is entirely dependent on the control strategy inputs [11]. Hadj-Salem et al. specifically test the effectiveness of the ALINEA control strategy in reducing motorway congestion and found it to be the most effective when compared to other calibration techniques.

In evaluating equity, we looked to definitions put forth by Miller, who considers equity to be fair or just "distribution of benefits and costs over members of society" [12], and Litman, who highlights distinctions between equity concepts, such as horizontal equity, the similar treatment of comparable individuals, and vertical equity, the enhanced treatment of disadvantaged individuals [13]. Many previous transportation equity studies utilize one or more of these definitions in their analysis. However, some emerging studies, such as Lewis et al., produce a synthesis showing the problematic nature of leaving implicit the evaluated benefits and costs [14, 15]. As such, the current state of transportation literature fails to adequately consider functionality, usability, and actionably consider how to advance equity through transportation technology for a widely varying population. To address the existing shortcoming in the state of the literature, this work uses an equity definition adopted from Douglas et al. which is informed by research in transportation, philosophy, and social justice.

Heft identifies affordances and Wittkower identifies disaffordances for the purpose of furthering or prohibiting equity. Heft referred to affordances as an "environment's functional possibilities for an organism" [16]. Functionality is crucial and considered with the user and transportation technology feature to convey what is and is not afforded to certain individuals. For example, a vehicle with a ramp provides an affordance to most people, especially those utilizing a mobility aid such as a wheelchair, in entering the vehicle. The presence of a ramp might not provide an affordance, however, if it is too steep, narrow, slippery, or otherwise prohibits usage for those who need it. If this were the case, the ramp would be a disaffordance. Wittkower refers to disaffordances as aspects of the environment "that fail to recognize differential embodied experiences that correspond to attributes constitutive of group and individual identities" [17, 18]. A feature that does not provide functionality to those of certain abilities, such as a steep ramp to individuals in a wheelchair, becomes a disaffordance and prevents the advancement of equity. The concepts of affordances and disaffordances are crucial to understanding equity in this work and the circumstances engendering it.

3 Affordances Discussion

When evaluating the functionality of transportation features and systems, we use the definition of equity established by Douglas et al. where equity is defined as equivalent affordances for multifarious users [2]. Equity is achieved through critical adjustment for difference that minimizes disaffordances. Further, Douglas et al. considers achieving equity as an ongoing process. Equity is a goal on the horizon that we should strive towards. Given that it is likely impossible to achieve equivalent usability across all users, equity is concerned with constantly adjusting for difference toward this objective. An affordance-based approach to equity helps design and develop aspects of the transportation system with a goal of equivalent usability by specifically considering a given feature, its desired functionality, and user interaction needs. This process promotes equivalent usability for individuals despite individual differences they may experience. This approach allows for a multidimensional equity analysis that recognizes that equity within automation technology can be furthered or hindered depending on how features (i.e., vehicle technologies) are presented and utilized (see Fig. 1). Affordances can address vehicle designs that limit users with certain backgrounds and abilities from achieving the benefits of the feature.

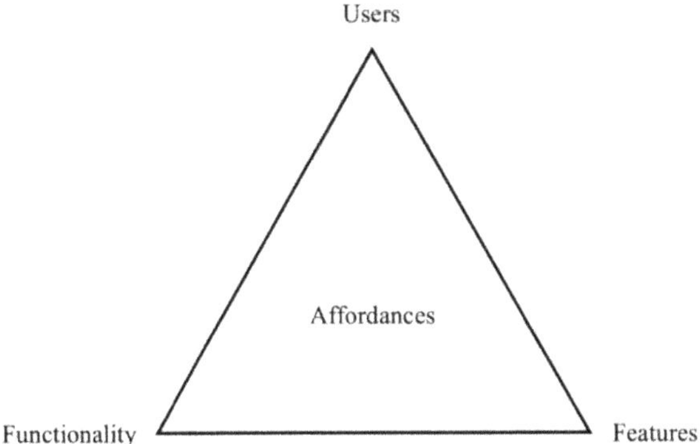

Fig. 1. Affordances Triangle Framework [2]

To better illustrate this framework, consider how access to a vehicle may afford users expanded opportunities for mobility. Most vehicles are equipped with an adjustable driver seat to account for varying body sizes among potential users. Thus, the seat is a feature whose functionality allows a user to comfortably sit while using the vehicle. Seat adjustability provides an affordance of the seat use for a wider swath of the potential driving public. If a seat is not adjustable, seat design becomes a potential disaffordance to some users. The static (non-adjustable) seat design fails to ensure the equivalent usability for individuals who are too tall or not tall enough to effectively sit in the seat, thereby hindering vehicle usability for those outside the seat design range. The goal of equivalent usability considers how the affordance, in this case enhancing the seat through adjustability, allows for a greatly increased percentage of the potential user population to achieve similar comfort and safety benefits. The affordance provided by the adjustable seat overcomes the potential discriminatory disaffordance of a static mechanical seat that disadvantages those outside the comfortable height for a static seat [19, 20].

The adjustable seat example is just one application of employing this affordance-based equity approach to analyze the effectiveness and design of transportation features and technology. It enables one to understand how design adjustments can contribute to equity and the role of inequities on how individuals utilize transportation alternatives. Given this understanding, we aim to promote a deeper discussion on the many ways that driver characteristics and vehicle affordances influence equity within the transportation system. In the future, we seek to further develop this framework beyond a triangle to better illustrate our model. We will next discuss examples relating to autonomous vehicle technology, including driver interaction with their vehicle, interaction between vehicles, and application to ramp meters.

3.1 Driver Interactions with Their Vehicles

Automation technology comes in many forms within a vehicle. Warnings, such as blind spot detection, as well as assistance and control features, such as lane centering capabilities, help influence how drivers navigate transportation interactions. This section will discuss the affordances of automation technology and features, similar to the aforementioned example of adjustable seating, to contextualize how equity can be furthered in a closed driver-vehicle system.

Users in vehicles equipped with any degree of automation technology between Levels 1–5, as specified by the SAE, can experience inequitable applications of the technology. Individual user and vehicle characteristics can have a significant effect on the ability of vehicle users to successfully receive the potential benefits that may be provided by the automation feature. Under the definition from Douglas et al., features and functionality must consider a multitude of potential users. For example, a driver's poor peripheral vision may be limited to the point of not being able to receive the safety benefit from the blind spot warning feature that appears in a vehicle's side mirror. Likewise, features and functionality must consider a multitude of potential users. A driver with psoriasis might wear gloves and fail to benefit from haptic alerts, while a driver with moderate-to-severe hearing loss might not hear audible alerts. Thus, incorporating a multitude of ways to alert drivers increases the number of drivers who are afforded the ability to utilize the feature. This becomes increasingly important for users with limited abilities across multiple senses, such as elderly drivers who require enhanced consideration of their level of ability.

As a further example, drivers lacking the epistemic background to know how technologies present in vehicles, and even further how the nomenclature differs between automakers [21], might pursue vehicles with lane-keeping assistance when what they desire is lane-centering assistance. Furthermore, a driver with severe anxiety or post-traumatic stress disorder might experience heightened triggers from a vehicle with certain forms of frequent lane-departure warnings alerting them of deviations. While the ability to turn off these warnings is important, these drivers would not be afforded the benefits of the warnings to the same degree as other users. Seeking alternative forms of warning presentations that may be acceptable to users is a critical aspect of the equity process. Additionally, we distinguish cases of users not utilizing a feature due to inadequate affordances versus when a user simply chooses that they do not wish to use a feature, with the latter being a matter of preference rather than equity.

3.2 Driver Behavior and Interactions with Other Vehicles: Queueing

In addition to inequities manifesting from vehicle design, drivers have differing experiences as they interact with the roadway and other vehicles. Driver attributes and attentiveness have been shown to affect how individuals operate on the road and influence efficiency and safety [22]. Vehicles equipped with automation technology can assist drivers in mitigating such situations. For instance, the queueing phase of ramp metering often places drivers in stop-and-go situations before they are permitted to merge into thoroughfare traffic. This specific phase of ramp metering allows for examination of one potential area where automation technology and features influence the usability of the roadway infrastructure.

To enter a ramp metered thoroughfare, drivers must wait in queue at a signal until they are permitted to merge into the thoroughfare. There are aspects of the ramp infrastructure that influence the ability of both drivers and vehicles to effectively perform this task, such as lane width, roadway curvature, and signal illumination. The role of automation technology, such as ADAS features, however, is to provide additional vehicle functionality to help drivers traverse the ramp and enter the thoroughfare. For example, lane departure warning and forward collision warning are alert features that can aid drivers in performing latitudinal and longitudinal tasks while progressing incrementally in queue. Further, these stop-and-go situations create an aspect of the roadway environment that can be a disaffordance (i.e., hindering the ramp functionality of providing safe travel of the roadway) to drivers under some conditions, such as drivers who are neurodivergent or more broadly all drivers during moments of inattention. Features such as adaptive cruise control, traffic jam assistance, and lane keeping assist function to provide aid to drivers as they wait their turn to approach the meter, alleviating some of these disaffordances. This queueing example conveys how the inclusion of automation technology affords equivalent usability across multifarious drivers.

However, the complexity of evolving equity considerations is worth mentioning. In the previous case of driver interactions with their vehicles, affordances and benefits are limited to vehicles equipped with these technologies. Users without these features are unable to experience the affordance received by others as the prevalence of these technologies increases. Thus, while the original equity consideration was providing the features to allow equivalent infrastructure usage for drivers with certain conditions, the continued implementation in a large swath of vehicles leaves those drivers without in a position of inequity. As we see, equity considerations can change as features are developed and implemented, further conveying how equity is an ongoing process rather than a destination.

3.3 Driver Behavior and Interactions with Other Vehicles: Thoroughfare

This analysis may be furthered by considering drivers released from the meter that now proceed to join the thoroughfare. While the queueing phase poses challenges and threats to safety in forward collisions given the requirement of constant acceleration and breaking, merging on the throughfare can require both a lateral movement for lane changing and rapid speed changes to match the speed of the thoroughfare traffic. Given the high speed and sharp nature of movements, automation technology can provide additional benefits. For instance, blind spot detection can warn drivers of adjacent vehicles when merging into traffic. This emphasizes the aforementioned need of equipping vehicles with features and technology with multiple interaction mechanism, enabling utilization by multifarious individuals. Additionally, lane changing, adaptive cruise control, and autonomous acceleration technology can significantly aid drivers as they transition from no motion in the queueing phase to matching the speeds of oncoming vehicles. However, drivers with equipped vehicles that are unable to use these features, or lacking the knowledge to use these features, will struggle to fully benefit from, and therefore to achieve equivalent usability, as other potential drivers with these features.

Within this example we again see the complexity of the equity process. The affordances provided by automation or ADAS features increases the likelihood of achieving an objective, such as a safe merge maneuver, for all drivers with this technology. As such, the expectations of safety during vehicle maneuvering become similar regardless of individual driver attributes. However, those drivers without these technologies or the ability to leverage them, are in an increasingly inequitable situation by not receiving the benefits from these affordances. The affordance of a feature is based on the presence of the technology itself in addition to how and when a user utilizes it. Equity as an ongoing process seeks to increase the availability of these affordances, for instance by including such features in entry level vehicle models, providing multiple means of interaction with the features, and training on feature use.

4 Comparative Analysis: The United States v. France

We now explore a specific case of potential inequities given that ramp metering and highway systems often have accompanying externalities in congestion, enhanced travel times, and increased vehicle interactions. We accomplish this by directly comparing two cities: Washington D.C., United States and Paris, France. We use Washington D.C. and Paris for our comparison because they are both capital cities with similar regional layouts and methods of transportation connectivity. Both cities have robust transit systems that serves an area with political importance and a dense urban core. However, there are contextual differences between the regions that allow comparison. It is common in the United States (U.S.) for individuals to choose to live far from a city center and commute in, while the opposite is true in Paris, France, and Europe. In Washington D.C, as it is in many parts of the U.S., individuals with higher incomes tend to live farther out from the city-center than those with lower incomes, creating more affluent suburbs [23]. However, for Paris and many parts of Europe the experience is the opposite, with higher income individuals living closer to the city center [24]. Where individuals choose to reside allows for a relevant and fruitful comparison. We can consequently analyze equity in automation technology and ramp metering given this key demographic difference.

While ramp metering outcomes depend on the underlying control settings in each jurisdiction [25], many studies have found that ramp metering produces greater travel time savings for those traveling further distances [9]. Thus, when considering Washington D.C. and Paris, the residing populations experience the enhanced travel time savings differently. Lower income individuals often travel further on highways in France while the opposite is true in the U.S. From an equity perspective, while affordances provided by the throughfare might be ensured in both the U.S. and France by successfully entering and traveling on the highway, the degree of comfort can affect functionality. Functionality therefore varies depending on traffic and other impediments to driving, such as the method and effectiveness of vehicle automation technology alert techniques. For at least the near-term, automation technology affordances are more common in newer and mid-to higher-end vehicles. Thus, lower income individuals are less likely to have access to the affordances offered by these technologies in general. In Paris, the likelihood of a vehicle on a long trip (originating farther from the center center) benefiting from the technology will be less than that in Washington D.C, given the demographic differences relative to city center distance. This creates a paradigm where the dominant usage of the applied technology is on the shorter trips in Paris and in Washington DC on the longer trips. Thus, while the cities might be similar in structure and connectivity, the potential impacts of the vehicle automation technology affordances and equity considerations will likely be very different. This will additionally manifest with different ramp meter calibration and setting strategies [26].

The impact of city demographic distribution on equity can furthermore be found in other transportation examples. For example, in public transportation metro systems. For trains that start from the furthest out station and work their way into the city, those who live farther out will have access to the affordance of sitting during their trip by onboarding the train earlier and taking a limited resource (i.e., a seat). As the train continues toward the city center, seats become filled and boarding passengers must stand for their trip and it is possible that personal space might become a subsequent limited resource. This can be viewed in a similar context to the ramp metering highway example where those residing farthest from the city center accrue the biggest time savings from ramp metering, resulting in inequities.

4.1 How Equity Interpretations Can Vary

To briefly consider an additional equity concept, we look again to vertical equity, which considers the enhanced treatment of disadvantaged individuals [13]. We recognize the operational shortcoming of vertical equity and apply it to ramp metering to convey the existing methodological gaps that an affordance-based equity framework can fill. Those in France with lower incomes who must travel longer distances to get to the city center would not satisfy the concept of vertical equity to the same extent as the U.S. when we solely consider income and within a vertical equity framework. Furthermore, these individuals are likely the ones without vehicles equipped with control and assistance features to aid with the driving task, such as adaptive cruise control, during their longer commutes. It is, however, difficult to narrow this analysis down solely to income given the immense geographic and cultural differences that exist between the U.S. and France, the variations between the highway networks, and accounting for all the benefits and costs that are spread out across populations [12]. Those in France with lower incomes achieve the greatest reduction in travel times from the presence of ramp metering even though they must travel farther to reach the city center. As previously mentioned, the challenge exists in a vertical equity framework of identifying the extent to which the benefit of greater travel time reduction combats the cost of greater travel time.

Douglas et al.'s definition, which defines equity as equivalent affordances for multifarious users, addresses the challenges identified in operationalizing the vertical equity framework. It is difficult to consistently identify costs and benefits using vertical equity as these can vary temporally and spatially. For example, an individual who dislikes driving in traffic might view travel time differently from someone who consumes media in traffic, conveying how difficult it is to ascribe an aspect of transportation as an inherent cost or benefit. The Douglas et al. definition advocates for equivalent usability rather than using theoretical costs and benefits. A user who consumes media might not necessarily view traffic as a benefit but rather an opportunity for productivity. The user who dislikes driving in traffic might experience enhanced functionality and therefore greater affordances with an autonomous aid to conduct the driving task and allow for the execution of more or different tasks. As such, we demonstrate the effectiveness of communicating equity in the context of users, features, functionality, and affordances.

5 Limitations

We recognize the current empirical limitations of our work and seek in the future to expand our discussion to include more data and case study examples, including in our U.S.-France comparison. Additionally, we assume that roadway interactions occur in mixed-fleet scenarios (AVs disbursed among human-operated vehicles) as we consider the level of automation in our exploration of ADAS and connected vehicle interactions. As such, models and existing analysis often assume that vehicles "play nice" with each other while driving behavior can significantly impact traffic flow [27] [28]. These assumptions do not hold true when drivers exhibit aggressive behavior which can significantly impact equity and safety. In ramp metering, aggressive drivers may experience reduced travel times while imposing higher travel times on non-aggressive drivers and AVs [29]. As such, equity depends on how and when automation features are used in addition to the simple presence of the technology in the vehicle.

6 Conclusions

Automation features and technology can provide numerous usable benefits while also preventing equivalent usability. This analysis uses a novel, affordance-based equity framework to enable a clearer understanding of who can experience affordances from autonomation technology, and how functionality varies in navigating ramp metering situations. The queueing and thoroughfare phases allow opportunities for automation technology to provide additional aid to drivers given the presence of alert and control features in stop-and-go and lane change tasks. Further, ramp metering context, such as the regional and residential differences between the U.S. and France, also affects functionality, affordances, and equity outcomes. Ultimately, this work enables future analysis of the role of automation technology in navigating additional traffic scenarios. This understanding can shape our approach to safety, design, and policy based on how vehicle features and transportation technologies are included and utilized.

References

1. J3016_202104: Taxonomy and Definitions for Terms Related to Driving Automation Systems for On-Road Motor Vehicles, https://www.sae.org/standards/content/j3016_202104, Accessed 02 Mar 2023
2. Douglas, C., Hunter, M., Tschaepe, M.: Investigating the equity implications of autonomous vehicle technology by level of automation. In: 103rd Annual Meeting of the Transportation Research Board. Washington, D.C., USA (2024)
3. Li, S., Li, M., Dai, J., Wang, P.: A new targeted on-ramp control approach considering both efficiency and equity. Transp. Saf. Environ. **6**(3), (2024)
4. Papamichail, I., Papageorgiou, M., Vong, V., Gaffney, J.: Heuristic ramp-metering coordination strategy implemented at Monash freeway, Australia. Transp. Res. Record: J. Transp. Res. Board **2178**(1), 10–20 (2010)
5. Papageorgiou, M., Kotsialos, A.: Freeway ramp metering: an overview. IEEE Trans. Intell. Transp. Syst. **3**(4), 271–281 (2002)

6. Arnold, E.D.: Ramp metering: a review of the literature. Publication VTRC 99-TAR5. Virginia Department of Transportation; Virginia Transportation Research Council (1998)
7. Gruyer, D., Orfila, O., Glaser, S., Hedhli, A., Hautière, N., Rakotonirainy, A.: Are connected and automated vehicles the silver bullet for future transportation challenges? Benefits and Weaknesses on Safety, Consumption, and Traffic Congestion. Front. Sustain. Cities 2, (2020)
8. Wu, J., McDonald, M., Chatterjee, K.: A detailed evaluation of ramp metering impacts on driver behavior. Transport. Res. F: Traffic Psychol. Behav. 10(1), 61–75 (2007)
9. Grzybowska, H., Wijayaratna, K., Shafiei, S., Amini, N., Travis Waller, S.: Ramp metering strategy implementation: a case study review. J. Transp. Eng. Part A: Syst. 148(5), 03122002 (2022)
10. Shehada, M.K.H., Kondyli, A.: Evaluation of ramp metering impacts on travel time reliability and traffic operations through simulation. J. Adv. Transp. 2019, 1–12 (2019)
11. Hadj-Salem, H., Blosseville, J.M., Papageorgiou, M.: ALINEA: a local feedback control law for on-ramp metering; a real-life study. In: Third International Conference on Road Traffic Control, pp. 194–198. Transportation Research Record, London, UK (1990)
12. Miller, D.: Principles of Social Justice. Harvard University Press, New York (2001)
13. Litman, T.: Evaluating transportation equity. World Transp. Policy Pract. 8(2), 50–65 (2024)
14. Lewis, E.O., MacKenzie, D., Kaminsky, J.: Exploring equity: how equity norms have been applied implicitly and explicitly in transportation research and practice. Transp. Res. Interdisciplinary Perspect. 9(2021), 100332 (2021)
15. van Wee, B., Mouter, N.: Chapter five - evaluating transport equity. Adv. Transp. Policy Planning 7(2021), 103–126 (2021)
16. Heft, H.: An ecological approach to psychology. Rev. Gen. Psychol. 17(2), 162–167 (2013)
17. Wittkower, D.E.: Principles of anti-discriminatory design. In: IEEE International Symposium on Ethics in Engineering, Science, and Technology. Vancouver, British Columbia, Canada (2016)
18. Wittkower, D.E.: Disaffordances and Dysaffordances In Code. In: AoIR Selected Papers of Internet Research (2017)
19. Balaam, M., Ståhl, A., Ívansdóttir, G.M., Sigtryggsdóttir, H.E., Höök, K., Zheng, C.Y.: Exploring the somatic possibilities of shape changing car seats. In: Proceedings of the 2024 ACM Designing Interactive Systems Conference, pp. 3354–3371. ACM, New York, New York, USA (2024)
20. Kamp, I.: The influence of car-seat design on its character experience. Appl. Ergon. 43(2), 329–335 (2012)
21. Lane Departure vs. Lane Keeping vs. Lane Centering Tech, https://www.jdpower.com/cars/shopping-guides/lane-departure-vs-lane-keeping-vs-lane-centering-tech, Accessed 13 Feb 2025
22. Entezarizarch, E., Zakerian, S.A., Madreseh, E., Abbasinia, M., Abdi, H.: Comparative analysis of mental workload and performance between young and elderly drivers: implications for road safety and age-related driving challenges, Work pre-press (pre-press), pp. 1–12 (2024)
23. Glaeser, E.L., Kahn, M.E., Rappaport, J.: Why do the poor live in cities? The role of public transportation. J. Urban Econ. 63(1), 1–24 (2008)
24. Broto, A.: Transports: les oubliés de la République Quand la route reconnecte le territoire, Éditions Eyerolls (2022)
25. Papageorgiou, M., Hadj-Salem, H., Middelham, F.: ALINEA local ramp metering: summary of field results. Transp. Res. Record: J. Transp. Res. Board 1603(1), 90–98 (1997)
26. Papageorgiou, M., Diakaki, C., Dinopoulou, V., Kotsialos, A., Wang, Y.: Review of road traffic control strategies. In: Proceedings of the IEEE, vol. 91, no. 12, pp. 2043–2067 (2003)
27. Zhao, Z., Wu, G., Wang, Z., Barth, M. J.: Optimal control-based eco-ramp merging system for connected and automated vehicles. In: 2020 IEEE Intelligent Vehicles Symposium. Las Vegas, Nevada, USA (2020)

28. Ma, Z., Zhang, Y.: Driver-automated vehicle interaction in mixed traffic: types of interaction and drivers' driving styles. Hum. Factors **66**(2), 544–561 (2022)
29. Bae, J.I., Saroj, A., Hunter, M., Guin, G.: Modeling autonomous vehicle-targeted aggressive merging behaviors in mixed traffic environment. In: 2023 Winter Simulation Conference. San Antonio, Texas, USA (2023)

A Fast Sampled-Data Nonlinear Predictive Controller for Lateral Trajectory Tracking

Maxime Penet[(✉)] and Gaetan Le Gall

Valeo Mobility Tech Center, 6 rue Daniel Costantini, 94000 Creteil, France
`maxime.penet@valeo.com`

Abstract. Nonlinear model predictive control is a popular control methodology which can seamlessly handle nonlinear dynamic, multiple inputs and constraints. It is advantageous whenever references are available ahead of time as it works by predicting state trajectories. This is a strong advantage when tracking trajectory as the vehicle can often anticipates on the incoming path profile. Despite those benefits, it is still not widely deployed. One of the main reason is that off-the-shelf available solvers are not specialized for embedded constraints. This paper is interested in presenting an efficient solver which combines a damped Newton solver with adjoint methods. This leads to a solution with moderate computational and memory requirements. The solver is used to design a lateral predictive controller running at 100 Hz with a 1 s prediction horizon, which has been validated on a real prototype vehicle.

Keywords: mobile robots · predictive control · optimization methods

1 Introduction

Past years have experienced tremendous progress in the design and deployment of autonomous driving features. This can be experienced by the increasing number of countries which have legislated on autonomous driving (as an example, for Europe, see the regulation [1] regarding the approvals of automated driving vehicles).

As drivers now get a taste for what autonomous driving has to offer, they expect more capabilities. Still, many challenges remain to be solved from progress in perception to perceive finer details to progress in decision making to generate path in complex environments, see e.g. [2]. In particular, we require performing path following algorithms which provide accurate, comfortable and robust tracking performances. The present paper deals with the latter point.

Many different algorithms have been considered ranging from simple PID (see e.g. [3]) to reinforcement learning controllers (see e.g. [4]). Among those, predictive controllers remains the most popular (see e.g. [5]) as they work well with nonlinear dynamic and can benefit from references obtained ahead of time.

However, in practice, predictive controllers are used under restrictive conditions which make them less efficient. One of the main invoked reason is the computational resources needed to solve, on real time, non-convex constrained optimization problems. This is indeed challenging and is the topic of a rich and varied literature (see e.g. [6] or [7]).

© The Author(s), under exclusive license to Springer Nature Switzerland AG 2026
A. Razminia et al. (Eds.): ITFT 2025, CCIS 2876, pp. 103–112, 2026.
https://doi.org/10.1007/978-3-032-20592-6_10

This paper focuses on the design of a fast solver which aims at finding solutions to the optimality conditions. To determine appropriate descent directions, we use a damped Newton method (see e.g. [9]). The associated linear systems are approximately solved using GMRES algorithm. A strong computational advantage of using GMRES is that it is not needed to compute and store hessian information. It is only required to evaluate directional derivatives which can be determined using adjoint methodology (see e.g. [10]).

The solver is then used to design a path following nonlinear model predictive controller which shall run at a high rate on an automotive graded hardware. We illustrate each design steps such as how to obtain the various required operators. The vehicle model is chosen to be a kinematic model as it captures the main vehicle motion characteristics while being consistent with the considered domain of operation. The controller is validated in a real prototype vehicle showing that it can run in real time while providing good control performances.

The paper is organized as follows. In Sect. 2, an efficient method to solve optimal control problem is presented. In Sect. 3, it is shown how to use this solver to design a nonlinear predictive controller to control the lateral motion of a vehicle. The performances of this controller are analyzed in Sect. 4. Finally the paper is concluded in Sect. 5.

2 Damped Newton Krylov Solver for Predictive Controller

2.1 Optimal Control Problem

Predictive controller aims at finding optimal control sequences by repeatedly solving constrained optimization problems. It uses a model of the system to determine what the state trajectory will be in response to a given control sequence. It usually given by a set of ordinary differential equations

$$\frac{dx}{dt} = f(x, u), \ x(0) = x_0,$$
$$h(x, u) \leq 0 \tag{1}$$

where x is the state vector, u is the control input and h model system limits. We assume that f satisfies all conditions in order to ensure existence of the trajectory (see e.g. [13]). The control u is then modified until we reach the minimum of a functional which describes what the system ideal behavior should be

$$u^* = \mathrm{argmin}_u J(x, u; x_0) = E(x(x_0, u; T)) + \int_0^T l(x(x_0, u; s), u)ds, \tag{2}$$

where $T < \infty$. The stage cost l is assumed to be sufficiently smooth and lower bounded. The final cost E is chosen to ensure closed loop stability. A standard approach is to find a set Ω such that for all $x \in \Omega$, there exists v so that

$$a_e(||x||) \leq E(x) \leq b_e(||x||),$$
$$< \nabla_x E(x), f(x, v) > +l(x, v) \leq 0, \tag{3}$$

where a_e and b_e are K^∞ functions.

To summarize, the optimal control problem to which the optimal control sequence is a solution is given by

$$u^* = (2),$$
$$\text{s.t. } (1) \text{ and } x(x_0, u; T) \in \Omega. \tag{4}$$

Only a small fraction of the sequence is applied until an update of the measurements and reference are available. This process is repeated at regular time interval leading to a closed-loop behavior (for more details see e.g. [11]).

2.2   Optimality Conditions

To solve (4), we aim at solving the set of conditions which characterizes a solution. The constraints are managed by introducing Lagrange multipliers with adequate complementary conditions (see e.g. [10]). This leads to the following Lagrangian function

$$L(x, u; x_0) = J(x, u; x_0) - <\mu, h(x, u)>, \tag{5}$$

where $\mu(t) \in \mathbb{R}^{+n_i}$, for all $t \in [0, T]$, is such that if u is feasible then we have for all $i \in \{1, \ldots, n_i\}$

$$\mu_i - h_i(x, u) - \sqrt{\mu_i^2 + h_i(x, u)^2} = 0. \tag{6}$$

An optimal solution u^* is then characterized by the fact that there is (locally) no other feasible sequence which leads to a smaller cost. That is, for any u for which there exists multipliers which ensure that (6) hold, the derivative of the Lagrangian ∂L is zero. The main challenge is to evaluate it as it depends on the state trajectory which is itself a nontrivial function of the control input. We solve this problem by using a dual approach.

Let us first introduce the sensitivity model, given by the Fréchet derivatives in direction g, of the dynamic (1) and the Lagrangian (5)

$$\frac{d\omega}{dt} = \nabla_x f(x, u)\omega + \nabla_u f(x, u)g, \ \omega(0) = 0. \tag{7}$$

$$<\partial L, g> = <\nabla_x E(x(T)), \omega(T)> + <\nabla_x l - \nabla_x h\mu, \omega> \\ + <\nabla_u l - \nabla_u h\mu, g>. \tag{8}$$

Then, we introduce $\tilde{x}$, solution of the adjoint model

$$-\frac{d\tilde{x}}{dt} = \nabla_x f^{tr} \tilde{x} + \nabla_x l - \nabla_x h\mu, \ \tilde{x}(T) = \nabla_x E(x(T)). \tag{9}$$

Using (7) and (9), and interpreting (8) in a weak derivative sense, we deduce the following expression of the gradient

$$\partial L = \nabla_u f^{tr} \tilde{x} + \nabla_u l - \nabla_u h\mu. \tag{10}$$

To summarize, an optimal solution is characterized through the conditions

$$F(u, \mu) = \begin{pmatrix} (10) \\ (6) \end{pmatrix} = 0. \tag{11}$$

2.3 Damped Newton Solver

To find a solution of (11), we consider a Newton method. That is optimal solutions are defined as the limit of the following recursions

$$
\begin{aligned}
&< \partial F(u^{(k)}, \mu^{(k)}), \begin{pmatrix} \Delta u \\ \Delta \mu \end{pmatrix} > + F(u^{(k)}, \mu^{(k)}) = 0, \\
&u^{(k+1)} = u^{(k)} + \alpha_k \Delta u, \ \mu^{(k+1)} = \mu^{(k)} + \alpha_k \Delta \mu.
\end{aligned}
\tag{12}
$$

where $\alpha_k \in [0, 1]$ is an adaptive step which is determined in order to ensure global convergence (see e.g. [9]).

To solve the linear systems arising from (12) with reduced computational time, we consider an inexact solver based on Generalized Minimal Residual (GMRES) method (see e.g. [8]). The idea is to build the solution on a Krylov subspace which, if the required accuracy is not met, is iteratively augmented with new independent directions using an Arnoldi process. New directions are built according to the following recursive equations

$$
q^{(m+1)} = < \partial F(u^{(k)}, \mu^{(k)}), q^{(m)} > .
\tag{13}
$$

Equation (13) is particularly interesting as $< \partial F(u^{(k)}, \mu^{(k)}), q^{(m)} >$ can be interpreted as the directional derivative of F in the direction $q^{(m)}$. This can be used as a source of significant computation and memory saving as instead of computing ∂F we just need to be able to evaluate directional derivatives.

3 NMPC Controller Design for Lateral Control

3.1 Kinematic Vehicle Model

To design lateral controllers, all kind of models have been considered (see e.g. the review [5]). As we target driving scenarios with limited lateral acceleration, we select a kinematic model which is expressed in the Frenet frame attached to the reference trajectory (see Fig. 1). The control input is selected as vehicle curvature at the middle of the rear axis. To simplify computations, we consider a first order approximation of $\frac{1}{1-c_r e_d}$ leading to a relative error of $(c_r e_d)^2 << 1$.

The vehicle model is given as follows

$$
\begin{cases}
\frac{ds}{dt} = v(1 + c_r(s)e_d)\cos(e_\theta), \\
\frac{de_d}{dt} = v\sin(e_\theta), \\
\frac{de_\theta}{dt} = v\left(c - c_r(s)(1 + c_r(s)e_d)\cos(e_\theta)\right),
\end{cases}
\tag{14}
$$

where s is the distance driven along the path, e_d is the lateral error, e_θ is the heading error, v is the vehicle speed, $c_r(s)$ is the reference path curvature at s and c is the control input.

To model the actuator, we consider its limits as given by its maximum rate and amplitude

$$
\begin{aligned}
-c_u &\leq c \leq c_u, \\
-dc_u &\leq \frac{dc}{ds} \leq dc_u.
\end{aligned}
\tag{15}
$$

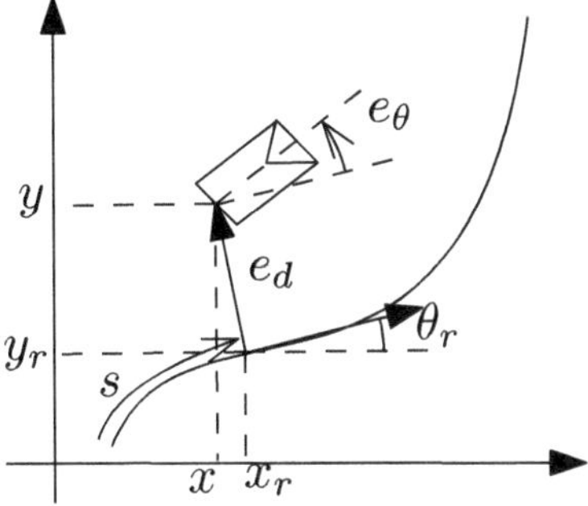

Fig. 1. Vehicle kinematic model in a trajectory reference frame

Also, to model the actuator limited bandwidth, the curvature is parameterized according to a cubic Bernstein polynomial (see e.g. [12])

$$c(s) = \sum_{i=0}^{3} c_i b_{i,3}\left(\frac{s}{s_M}\right),\tag{16}$$

where s_M is chosen so that $s \leq s_M$ for all $t \in [0,T]$.

One of the main interest from (16) is that constraints management is greatly simplified. Using the partition of unity property, we replace the original amplitude constraints by the following set of sufficient conditions

$$-c_u \leq c_i \leq c_u, \; \forall i \in \{0,\ldots,3\}.\tag{17}$$

The derivative of a Bernstein polynomial can be expressed with Bernstein polynomials of lower order. It is then deduced that the original rate constraints can be replaced with the following set of sufficient conditions

$$-dc_u \leq \frac{3}{s_M}(c_{i+1} - c_i) \leq dc_u, \; \forall i \in \{0,\ldots,2\}.\tag{18}$$

3.2   Cost Function Design

In order to balance simplicity and performances, we consider a stage cost which aims at reducing the lateral error and controlling the rate to which it is reduced

$$l(c; s, e_d, e_\theta, v, c_r) = w_d e_d^2 + w_{inv}\left(v\sin(e_\theta) + \lambda e_d\right)^2 \\ + w_c\left(c(s) - c_r(s)\cos(e_\theta)(1 + c_r(s)e_d)\right)^2,\tag{19}$$

where w_d, w_{inv} and w_c are weighting parameters and λ aims at selecting the targeted lateral error rejection speed.

To build a valid final cost, let us introduce the following controller

$$c = c_r\cos(e_\theta)(1 + c_r e_d) - \frac{(\lambda+\mu)v\sin(e_\theta) - \lambda\mu e_d}{v^2\cos(e_\theta)},\tag{20}$$

108   M. Penet and G. Le Gall

where $\mu > 0$ is a controller parameter selected such that $\lambda\mu \geq 0.25$. It can be shown that this controller globally stabilizes (14).

For a given speed, (20) is a smooth function of the reference and the errors. This means that there exists a region Ω in which the actuator constraints (15) are not active. We also assume that on this set the system is still stabilized by (20) if the dynamic on s is approximated by $ds/dt = v$. The kinematic model then becomes

$$\begin{cases} \frac{ds}{dt} = v, \\ \frac{de_d}{dt} = -\lambda e_d + z, \\ \frac{dz}{dt} = -\mu z, \end{cases} \tag{21}$$

where $z = v\sin(e_\theta) + \lambda e_d$. Inserting (20) in (19), the stage cost becomes

$$l = e_d^2 \left(w_d + \frac{\lambda^4}{v^4}w_c\right) + z^2 \left(w_{inv} + \frac{(\lambda+\mu)^2}{v^4}w_c\right) + 2e_d z \left(-\frac{\lambda^2(\lambda+\mu)}{v^4}w_c\right). \tag{22}$$

As the dynamic of s only depends on the vehicle speed, (21) is linear and (22) is quadratic, we deduce that E can be selected as a quadratic function of e_d and z

$$E = \frac{1}{2}\left(p_{dd}e_d^2 + p_{zz}z^2 + 2p_{dz}e_d z\right). \tag{23}$$

where p_{dd}, p_{dz} and p_{zz} are parameters to be defined.

By evaluating the left hand side of the second inequality in (3) using (23), (21) and (22), we obtain the following linear system of equations

$$\begin{aligned} w_d + \frac{\lambda^4}{v^4}w_c - \lambda p_{dd} &= -q_{dd} \\ -\frac{\lambda^2(\lambda+\mu)}{v^4}w_c + p_{dd} - (\lambda+\mu)p_{dz} &= -q_{dz} \\ w_{inv} + \frac{(\lambda+\mu)^2}{v^4}w_c - \mu p_{zz} + p_{dz} &= -q_{zz}. \end{aligned} \tag{24}$$

where q_{dd}, q_{dz} and q_{zz} are user defined parameters. It can be shown that, as long as $v \neq 0$, we can always select parameters such that E defines a valid final cost.

3.3 Gradient Evaluation

Using (9), the adjoint system is given as follows

$$\begin{aligned} -\frac{d\tilde{s}}{dt} &= v\cos(e_\theta)\frac{\partial c_r}{\partial s}e_d\tilde{s} + \left(\frac{\partial c}{\partial s} - \cos(e_\theta)(1 + 2e_d c_r)\frac{\partial c_r}{\partial s}\right)(v\tilde{e}_\theta + 2w_c\Delta c), \\ -\frac{d\tilde{e}_d}{dt} &= v c_r\cos(e_\theta)\left(\tilde{s} - c_r\tilde{e}_\theta\right) \\ &\quad + 2w_d e_d + 2w_{inv}\lambda(v\sin(e_\theta) + \lambda e_d) - 2w_c\Delta c\cos(e_\theta)c_r^2, \\ -\frac{d\tilde{e}_\theta}{dt} &= -v\sin(e_\theta)\left(1 + c_r e_d\right)\left(\tilde{s} - c_r\tilde{e}_\theta\right) \\ &\quad + v\cos(e_\theta)\tilde{e}_d + 2w_{inv}v\cos(e_\theta)(v\sin(e_\theta) + \lambda e_d) \\ &\quad + 2w_c\Delta c\sin(e_\theta)c_r(1 + c_r e_d) \end{aligned} \tag{25}$$

where $\Delta c = c - c_r\cos(e_\theta)(1 + c_r e_d)$.

Using (10) and projecting on the Bernstein basis, the Lagrangian gradient with respect to the coefficients c_i is given by

$$\frac{\partial L}{\partial c_i} = \int_0^T \left(2w_c\Delta c + v\tilde{e}_\theta\right) b_{i,N}\left(\frac{s}{s_M}\right) dt - \mu_i + \mu_{i+3} - \mu_{i+6} + \mu_{i+9}. \qquad (26)$$

Note that the Lagrange multipliers are discrete according to (17) and (18).

4 Results

To verify that the above NMPC controller runs in real time, it has been validated both in a hardware in the loop (HiL) setting and with a real prototype vehicle. The controller is deployed on a Micro Autobox 3 using a single core. The prediction horizon is set to 1 s and the controller is to run at 100 Hz. The cost function weights have been selected in order to provide a good compromise between accuracy and comfort.

4.1 HiL Test

The HiL setting is based on a Micro Autobox 3 containing the controller which communicates with a computer which simulates vehicle motions and sensors measurements.

The run time is evaluated on four scenarios which replicates real roads. Their shapes are illustrated on Fig. 2. They cover various use cases ranging from low speed to high speed.

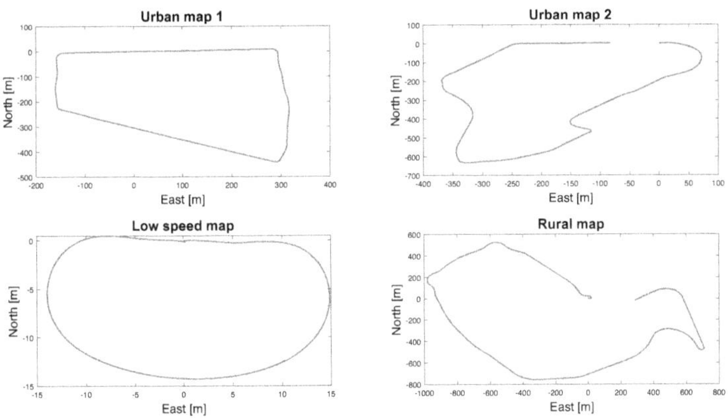

Fig. 2. Map used for HiL tests

As it is challenging to isolate the workload from a single function, the NMPC computational load has been evaluated as the difference between the overall turn around time when the controller was activated and the average run time when it was deactivated. A box plot of computation time on all four scenarios is given in Fig. 3.

For all four use cases the max computation time is below 3ms and is below 1.5ms more than 90% of the time. The tracking performances are also good as illustrated with the mean absolute lateral error (MAE lat.): $\frac{1}{T}\int_0^T |e_d| dt$ and mean absolute heading error (MAE head.): $\frac{1}{T}\int_0^T |e_\theta| dt$ (see Table 1).

The lateral error is always below 10 cm with a very small heading error indicating accurate and stable path tracking abilities

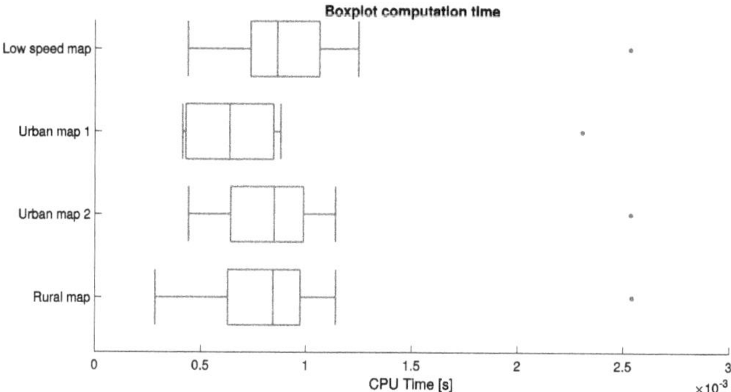

Fig. 3. Box plot on computation time. Vertical bars stands for 10th, 25th, 50th, 75th and 90th percentile. Point stands for max value.

Table 1. HiL NMPC validation

	urban 1	urban 2	low speed	rural
MAE lat. [cm]	0.7	5.4	2.0	8.4
MAE head. [deg]	0.03	0.22	0.27	0.11

4.2 Prototype Vehicle Test

The vehicle is a Volkswagen Passat GTE equipped with various sensors including a GPS RTK, used for accurate localization, and dedicated hardware to control steering and acceleration. The vehicle speed is controlled with an ACC.

The path to be followed corresponds to the case labeled *rural map* on Fig. 2. First, let us analyze the real time performances. A box plot of the computation time is shown on Fig. 4.

The computation time is slightly higher compared to the HiL setting (median closer to 1.5 ms). This is mainly due to the fact that there are more discrepancies between the model prediction and the actual vehicle path. Still the controller is comfortably running at 100 Hz.

Then let us analyze the controller performances. As we are dealing with real vehicle, in addition to the previous MAE indicators, we add a comfort measure sc_{omfort} which corresponds to the norm of the lateral acceleration filtered by a bandpass filter whose

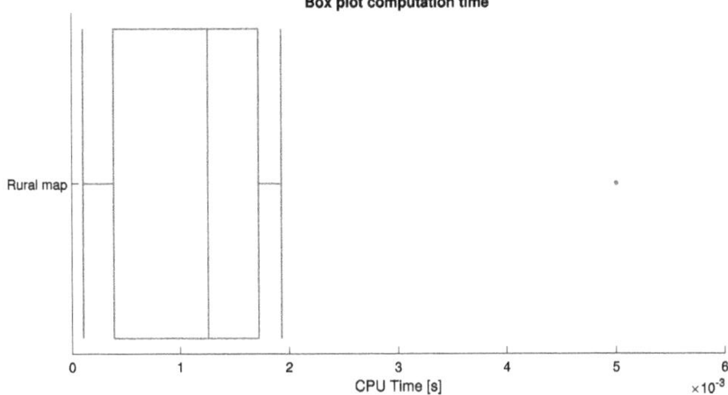

Fig. 4. Computation time in prototype vehicle.

Table 2. Prototype vehicle NMPC validation: performances

	rural	
MAE lat. [cm]	5.6	
MAE head. [deg]	0.2	
$sc_{comfort}$ $[m.s^{-2}]$	0.22	(manual: 0.73)

band is centered at 1 Hz. The idea is to introduce a score related to motion sickness which states that low frequency are more likely to induce dizziness (see e.g. [14]). It can be seen on Table 2 that the controller performances are quite good. The MAE of the lateral error is slightly above 5 cm while the MAE of the heading error is close to 0.

The controller comfort level is compared against a manual driving session where the driver was instructed to drive comfortably while following the middle of the lane. Note that this latter is purely indicative of what would be deemed as comfortable as the vehicle speed was also controlled by the driver. The controller leads to a particularly comfortable drive as can be seen with the comfort score which is more than 3 times smaller than the manual driving case.

5   Conclusion

This paper has presented an efficient optimal control problem solver based on a coordinated use of a damped Newton GMRES solver with adjoint methods. The solver performances have been shown by considering the design of a nonlinear predictive controller to control the lateral motion of an autonomous vehicle. In particular, we have illustrated how to derive the various models required to build an efficient numerical scheme. Also elements to ensure stability of the closed-loop have been presented.

The controller computation time have been evaluated on HiL bench using the targeted hardware. Based on a varied suit of use cases, real time performances have been illustrated with the controller running at 100 Hz with a prediction horizon of 1 s. The controller has then been tested on a prototype vehicle to validate its performances in real conditions. It has been shown that real time control is achieved while providing accurate and comfortable path following abilities.

From a solver perspective next step consists in considering additional features which are pretty common in application such as time delay or uncertainties and to assess interest of adding a continuation step. From an application point of view, it is considered to add the longitudinal control action.

References

1. European commission. C(2022)5402. Uniform procedures and technical specifications for the type-approval of the automated driving system (ADS) of fully automated vehicles (2022). https://ec.europa.eu/info/law/better-regulation/have-your-say/initiatives/12152-Automated-cars-technical-specifications_en
2. Contreras-Castillo, J., Zeadally, S., Guerrero-Ibanez, J.: Autonomous cars: challenges and opportunities. IT Prof. **8**, 6–13 (2019)
3. Zhao, B., Wang, H., Li, Q., Li, J., Zhao, Y.: PID trajectory tracking control of autonomous ground vehicle based on genetic algorithm. In: Chinese Control and Decision Conference, pp. 3677–3682 (2019)
4. Carrasco, A., Sequeira, J.: Tuning path tracking controllers for autonomous cars using reinforcement learning. PeerJ Comput. Sci. (2023)
5. Stano, P., et al.: Model predictive path tracking control for automated road vehicles: a review. Annu. Rev. Control. **55**, 194–236 (2023)
6. Biegler, L.T.: A survey on sensitivity based nonlinear model predictive control. In: International Symposium on Dynamics and Control of Process Systems, pp. 499–510 (2013)
7. Patne, V., Ingole, D., Sonawane, D.: Towards fast nonlinear model predictive control for embedded applications. IFAC PapersOnline **22**, 304–309 (2022)
8. Golub, G.H., Van Loan, C.F.: Matrix Computations. Studies in Applied Mathematics, 4th edn. SIAM (2013)
9. Deuflhard, P.: Newton Methods for Nonlinear Problems, Affine Invariance and Adaptive Algorithms. Springer Series in Computational Mathematics. Springer, Berlin (2004)
10. Bonnans, J.F.: Convex and stochastic optimization. In: Universitext. Springer, Cham (2019)
11. Grüne, L., Pannek, J.: Nonlinear Model Predictive Control, Theory and Algorithms. Communications and Control Engineering, 2nd edn. Springer, Cham (2010)
12. Bhattia, M.I., Bracken, P.: Solutions of differential equations in a Bernstein polynomial basis. J. Comput. Appl. Math. **205**, 272–280 (2007)
13. Schwartz, L.: Calcul différentiel et Equations différentielles, tome II: Analyse. Herman (1997)
14. Fu, Z., Wu, J., Liu, X., Yin, Y., Zhang, Z.: A review on motion sickness of autonomous driving vehicles. J. Vibroeng. 1133–1149 (2024)

KMeans–SMT: Physics-Constrained Clustering with Symbolic Reasoning for Intelligent Vehicle Diagnostics

Hafiz Abdul Quddus$^{(\boxtimes)}$ ⓘ and Alexander Jesser ⓘ

Institute for Intelligent Cyber-Physical Systems (ICPS), Heilbronn University
of Applied Sciences, 74653 Künzelsau, Germany
`hafiz-abdul.quddus@hs-heilbronn.de`

Abstract. Modern On-Board Diagnostics (OBD-II) systems capture rich multivariate data reflecting real-world vehicle dynamics. Yet, conventional clustering algorithms such as KMeans often produce physically inconsistent operating regimes—such as idle RPMs at highway speeds or throttle levels beyond feasible bounds—because they rely purely on statistical compactness. This paper presents KMeans–SMT, a physics-constrained clustering framework that embeds Satisfiability Modulo Theories (SMT) reasoning into the KMeans optimization loop. The method enforces domain-specific physical relationships, including idle-RPM consistency, gear-ratio coherence, and operational bound validity, ensuring that each cluster centroid corresponds to a physically realizable driving state. Unlike projection- or penalty-based baselines, KMeans–SMT achieves zero constraint violations by construction while maintaining competitive clustering quality. Experiments on real OBD-II datasets ($\sim$2.7 million samples, downsampled to 80 000) demonstrate that KMeans–SMT attains a Silhouette score of 0.583 with full physical compliance, whereas unconstrained variants exhibit multiple physics-rule violations. These findings highlight how coupling symbolic reasoning with unsupervised learning yields interpretable, physically trustworthy, and safety-aligned clustering for intelligent vehicle analytics and next-generation transportation systems.

Keywords: KMeans–SMT · Constrained Clustering · OBD-II Data · Vehicle Diagnostics · Satisfiability Modulo Theories (SMT) · Intelligent Vehicles · Formal Optimization · Engine Dynamics

1 Introduction

Modern vehicles continuously generate extensive diagnostic data through On-Board Diagnostics (OBD-II) systems, capturing key signals such as vehicle speed, engine revolutions per minute (RPM), and throttle position [23]. These multidimensional measurements reflect complex, nonlinear interactions governed by mechanical and thermodynamic principles of engine dynamics. Analyzing and

© The Author(s), under exclusive license to Springer Nature Switzerland AG 2026
A. Razminia et al. (Eds.): ITFT 2025, CCIS 2876, pp. 113–126, 2026.
https://doi.org/10.1007/978-3-032-20592-6_11

clustering such data can reveal interpretable driving regimes—such as idle, low-gear, and high-gear states—providing actionable insights for predictive maintenance, emission control, and intelligent vehicle diagnostics [14,18].

However, conventional clustering algorithms like KMeans remain agnostic to the physical feasibility of the resulting clusters [7,10]. While they effectively minimize intra-cluster variance, they can yield physically implausible centroids [2]—for instance, in [23], associating high throttle levels with zero speed or unrealistically low RPMs at highway velocities. Projection- and penalty-based variants introduce soft constraints to mitigate inconsistencies, but they provide no formal guarantee of physical validity [6,7]. Consequently, their cluster representations often violate fundamental relationships between speed, RPM, and throttle, limiting interpretability and trustworthiness in safety-critical diagnostics.

To overcome these limitations, we propose **KMeans–SMT**, a physics constrained clustering framework that integrates *Satisfiability Modulo Theories*-(SMT) reasoning directly into the KMeans optimization loop. Rather than updating centroids through unconstrained arithmetic means, KMeans–SMT formulates each update as a constrained optimization problem solved using the Z3 SMT solver [15]. This ensures that all centroids strictly comply with empirically learned operational constraints—such as idle-RPM bands, gear-ratio coherence, and feasible speed–throttle–RPM relationships. By embedding symbolic reasoning into unsupervised learning, KMeans–SMT produces clusters that are not only numerically compact but also physically realizable and interpretable.

This work makes the following key contributions:

- **SMT-constrained clustering for vehicle diagnostics:** We introduce KMeans–SMT, a novel clustering framework that embeds SMT reasoning into KMeans to enforce hard vehicle-physics constraints, including idle-RPM consistency and gear-ratio validity.
- **Physically consistent and interpretable clusters:** The proposed method achieves zero constraint violations while maintaining competitive clustering quality, generating centroids that represent realistic operating regimes (idle and gears #1–#5) and respect valid speed–RPM–throttle relationships.
- **Comprehensive empirical validation:** Using real-world OBD-II data (∼2.7 million samples, downsampled to 80,000), KMeans–SMT is benchmarked against Vanilla, Projected, and Penalty KMeans variants. While baselines exhibit multiple idle and gear-rule violations, KMeans–SMT maintains perfect compliance across all runs.
- **Solver-integrated optimization for stable convergence:** A hybrid L2 →L1 optimization strategy within Z3 ensures feasible centroids under solver timeouts, providing stable convergence and interpretable regime transitions confirmed through centroid trajectory and violation analyses.

The remainder of this paper is organized as follows. Section 2 reviews related work on constrained clustering and physics-informed learning. Section 3 details the KMeans–SMT framework, including constraint formulation and solver-based centroid optimization. Section 4 presents experimental findings and comparative analyses. Finally, Sect. 5 concludes with key insights and outlines future directions for physics-constrained vehicle analytics.

2   Related Work

Early work in vehicle diagnostics and driver behavior modeling primarily relied on supervised learning and rule-based analysis of OBD-II data. For instance, Kumar *et al.* [18] used machine-learning classifiers to infer driving styles from labeled OBD-II features, while Malik [14] employed rule-based heuristics to interpret driver operating patterns such as acceleration and gear-shift behavior. Although these methods can capture behavioral tendencies, they require labeled data or manually defined rules and thus lack scalability across diverse vehicles and operating conditions. In contrast, unsupervised clustering—particularly classical k-means [2] and neural network–based methods [8]—has been widely adopted to identify natural groupings in vehicle operating conditions.

For example, Vaiti *et al.* [20] applied k-means to cluster vehicles based on emission characteristics derived from OBD-II signals, while other studies have used clustering to segment drive cycles or detect abnormal engine behavior. Despite their utility, these purely statistical approaches treat all features independently and ignore the physical dependencies among speed, engine load, and throttle dynamics. Consequently, they often yield clusters that are physically implausible—for example, idle-level RPMs at highway speeds or throttle values outside feasible limits—undermining interpretability in safety-critical diagnostics.

To address these limitations, several constrained and semi-supervised variants of k-means have been explored. COP-KMeans [21] introduced must-link and cannot-link constraints to incorporate relational supervision, later extended by Basu *et al.* [4] and Bilenko *et al.* [5] through metric learning and semi-supervised formulations. Other studies [11, 22] applied penalty or projection mechanisms to enforce convex feasibility during centroid updates. While these methods enhance robustness and interpretability in relational or geometric contexts, they remain limited to simple continuous constraints. They cannot encode the hybrid numeric–logical dependencies inherent to physical systems such as engines. Consequently, they lack the expressiveness needed to ensure physically consistent cluster centroids.

Parallel advances in physics-informed learning have sought to embed domain knowledge into data-driven models. Physics-Informed Neural Networks (PINNs) [12, 17] integrate governing differential equations into neural training to enforce physical consistency, while constrained stochastic optimization methods [16] employ Lagrangian or regularized objectives to maintain feasibility in uncertain environments. However, these approaches primarily target continuous and differentiable systems and are unsuitable for domains involving discrete or conditional logic—such as idle-to-gear transitions in internal combustion engines. Moreover, they provide only approximate compliance with physical laws, rather than strict satisfaction, resulting in residual inconsistencies.

Efforts to formulate clustering as an exact optimization problem have also been made using Mixed-Integer Programming (MIP) [1,24]. These methods can encode explicit linear constraints and offer theoretical guarantees of optimality. Nevertheless, the combinatorial explosion of binary variables makes them impractical for large-scale, real-world datasets such as OBD-II streams, which may contain millions of samples [23]. More recently, differentiable optimization layers such as IDKM [9] and convex optimization modules [3] have enabled end-to-end trainable clustering and control frameworks, yet their reliance on convex formulations limits their ability to model nonconvex or disjunctive constraints present in real vehicle dynamics.

Meanwhile, advances in symbolic reasoning—particularly through Satisfiability Modulo Theories (SMT) solvers like Z3 [15]—have demonstrated strong capabilities in verifying hybrid and safety-critical systems. SMT-based reasoning has been applied to neural network verification [13], hybrid system analysis [25], and formal control synthesis [19]. However, its integration within unsupervised learning remains largely unexplored. Existing SMT–ML efforts primarily focus on supervised verification or symbolic regression rather than discovering meaningful structure in continuous sensor data.

In summary, prior clustering and constrained learning approaches either (i) fail to represent hybrid numeric–logical physical constraints, (ii) achieve only approximate feasibility via penalties or projections, or (iii) cannot scale to realistic automotive datasets. This gap limits the interpretability and trustworthiness of vehicle diagnostics derived from OBD-II analytics. To bridge this gap, we propose **KMeans–SMT**, a constrained clustering framework that integrates symbolic reasoning into the KMeans optimization loop. By formulating each centroid update as a satisfiability problem under learned physical constraints—such as idle bands, gear-ratio coherence, and throttle–speed coupling—our approach ensures that every cluster corresponds to a physically feasible driving regime. This fusion of SMT reasoning and unsupervised clustering establishes a new paradigm for interpretable, physics-consistent analytics in intelligent vehicle diagnostics.

3   Methodology

3.1   Problem Formulation

Clustering vehicle diagnostics data enables the discovery of distinct operational regimes such as idle, low-gear, and high-gear states. Traditional methods like k-means optimize numerical compactness but remain oblivious to the underlying physics of vehicle dynamics. As a result, they may produce centroids that violate fundamental relationships—such as assigning 2000 rpm at 0 km/h or 600 rpm at highway speed—rendering the resulting clusters physically implausible and difficult to interpret.

To overcome these limitations, we propose **KMeans–SMT**, a physics-constrained clustering framework that embeds *Satisfiability Modulo Theories (SMT)* reasoning into the centroid update step of KMeans. The goal is to ensure that each centroid $\mathbf{z}_j = [v_j, r_j, t_j]$—representing speed, engine RPM, and throttle position—respects the physical laws governing vehicle behavior.

Formally, given a set of N samples $\mathbf{x}_i = [v_i, r_i, t_i] \in \mathbb{R}^3$, we aim to minimize:

$$\min_{\{\mathbf{z}_j\}_{j=1}^k} \sum_{i=1}^{N} \|\mathbf{x}_i - \mathbf{z}_{c(i)}\|_2^2, \tag{1}$$

subject to a set of physical feasibility constraints:

$$\begin{cases} v_j \in [0, 130], \ r_j \in [0, 6000], \ t_j \in [0, 100], \\ v_j \leq v_{\text{idle}} \Rightarrow r_j \in [r_{\text{idle}}^{lo}, r_{\text{idle}}^{hi}], \\ v_j > v_{\text{idle}} \Rightarrow \dfrac{r_j}{v_j} \in \bigcup_{g=1}^{G} [s_g^{lo}, s_g^{hi}]. \end{cases} \tag{2}$$

Here, $v_{\text{idle}} = 3$ km/h denotes the idle threshold, and the idle and gear bands $([r_{\text{idle}}^{lo}, r_{\text{idle}}^{hi}], [s_g^{lo}, s_g^{hi}])$ are learned automatically from the data. Each centroid update is then formulated as a constrained optimization problem and solved exactly using the Z3 SMT solver.

3.2   Data Processing and Feature Extraction

Raw OBD-II logs downloaded from [23] were loaded from multiple CSV files through a header-matching pipeline developed in `datasets.py`. Three primary channels—vehicle speed, engine RPM, and absolute throttle position—were extracted and normalized into a unified feature matrix:

$$\mathbf{X} = [v, r, t]_{N \times 3}. \tag{3}$$

Invalid or out-of-range entries were filtered, and physical limits were applied based on realistic operational ranges observed in the dataset:

$$\text{Speed: } 0\text{--}130 \text{ km/h}, \quad \text{RPM: } 0\text{--}6000, \quad \text{Throttle: } 0\text{--}100 \text{ \%}.$$

These limits correspond to the maximum feasible vehicle operating range and are consistent with the solver constraints used in later stages.

The final dataset comprised approximately 2.7 million samples, downsampled to 80,000 for solver efficiency and fair comparison across baselines.

3.3   Automatic Constraint Discovery

Instead of predefining physical limits, KMeans–SMT learns them directly from the data:

Idle Band: The RPM distribution for samples with $v \leq 3$ km/h was analyzed using interquartile filtering, yielding an idle band of $[400, 1200]$ rpm.

Gear Bands: For moving samples, the slope r/v was computed and partitioned into five quantile-based ranges, each widened by $\pm 10\%$ to capture real-world variation:

$$\text{Gear 1: } [51.6, 368.0], \quad \text{Gear 2: } [23.1, 63.0], \quad \text{Gear 3: } [15.3, 28.3],$$
$$\text{Gear 4: } [15.2, 18.7], \quad \text{Gear 5: } [8.1, 18.6].$$

These automatically learned bounds serve as the hard feasibility regions used by the SMT solver for constrained centroid optimization.

3.4 SMT-Constrained Clustering Framework

The clustering process follows the standard KMeans structure with a modified update step enforced through SMT reasoning.

Initialization: Centroids are initialized via the k-means++ method to ensure spatial diversity. A safety margin $(\Delta v, \Delta r, \Delta t) = (2\,\text{km/h}, 50\,\text{rpm}, 2\%)$ is applied to prevent centroids from saturating boundary limits.

Assignment Step: Each sample $\mathbf{x}_i$ is assigned to the nearest centroid:

$$c(i) = \arg\min_j \|\mathbf{x}_i - \mathbf{z}_j\|_2. \tag{4}$$

Constrained Update Step: For each cluster j, the empirical mean $\boldsymbol{\mu}_j = \frac{1}{|C_j|} \sum_{i \in C_j} \mathbf{x}_i$ is computed. Instead of setting $\mathbf{z}_j = \boldsymbol{\mu}_j$, KMeans–SMT solves:

$$\min_{\mathbf{z}_j} \|\mathbf{z}_j - \boldsymbol{\mu}_j\|_2^2 \quad \text{s.t. Eq. (2)}. \tag{5}$$

If the solver returns *unknown* for the quadratic (L2) objective, a linearized L1 relaxation is applied:

$$\min_{\mathbf{z}_j, \mathbf{d}} d_v + d_r + d_t \text{ s.t. } d_k \geq |z_{j,k} - \mu_{j,k}|, \ k \in \{v, r, t\}, \tag{6}$$

ensuring feasible convergence under timeouts. Each cluster is automatically classified as idle or gear-based according to its median slope r/v, and the relevant constraints are enforced.

Convergence and Tracking: Iterations stop when assignments stabilize or centroid movement falls below 0.1% of the total norm. Centroid trajectories are recorded across iterations to visualize solver behavior and regime transitions (see Fig. 5).

3.5 Baseline Methods

For fair benchmarking, three representative variants were chosen: Vanilla KMeans (unconstrained), Projected KMeans (box-constrained via post-update projection), and Penalty KMeans (soft-constraint via regularization). These cover the major constraint-handling paradigms—none, projected, and penalized—common-ly used in clustering literature. Comparing them with

KMeans SMT highlights the added value of our method's symbolic, hard-constraint enforcement that ensures full physical feasibility while preserving clustering quality. Three baselines were implemented for comparison:

- **Vanilla KMeans:** Standard unconstrained k-means from `scikit-learn`.
- **Projected KMeans:** Applies axis-wise clipping of centroids to domain bounds after each update.
- **Penalty KMeans:** Introduces soft penalties for slope violations outside $[5, 400]$ in r/v without hard enforcement.

All methods share the same initialization, feature matrix, and number of clusters for fair comparison.

3.6   Evaluation and Model Selection

Performance was assessed using three complementary criteria to capture both clustering quality and physical validity.

(a) **Clustering Quality:** Internal metrics—Silhouette Coefficient, Davies–Bouldin Index (DBI), and Calinski–Harabasz Index (CH)—were used to quantify intra-cluster compactness and inter-cluster separation (Fig. 4).

(b) **Physical Validity:** Each centroid was audited for boundary violations and rule compliance (idle and gear constraints). Violation counts across all variants are visualized as stacked bar plots (Fig. 4), illustrating that only KMeans–SMT achieves zero violations across all categories.

(c) **Centroid Consistency:** Physical feasibility and interpretability were further verified using the centroid comparison tables (Table 1), which list representative regimes and constraint satisfaction status ($\checkmark$/$\times$) for each method. These tables confirm that all KMeans–SMT centroids meet idle and gear constraints, while baseline methods exhibit at least one idle-rule violation.

For model selection, a k-sweep ($k = 4$–9) with Vanilla KMeans identified $k = 6$ as optimal—consistent with one idle regime and five gear regimes—based on the elbow and silhouette analyses (Fig. 1).

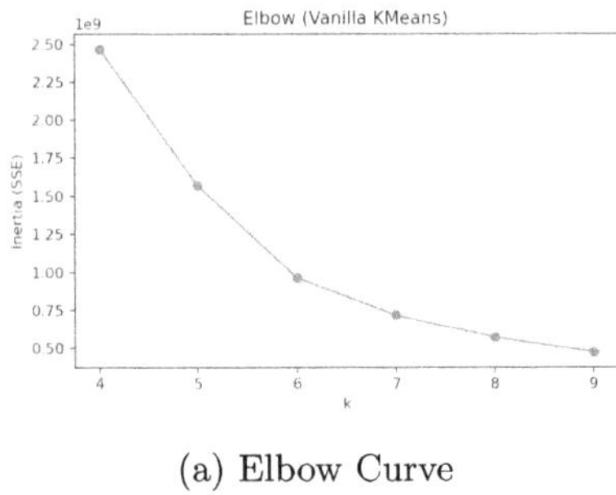

(a) Elbow Curve

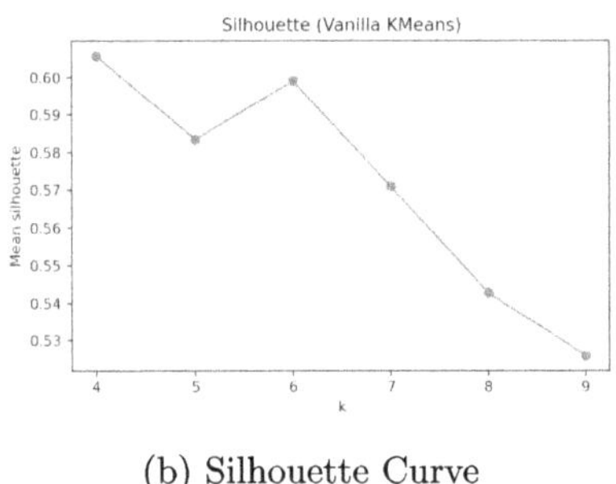

(b) Silhouette Curve

Fig. 1. Model selection using Vanilla KMeans. (a) Elbow curve shows diminishing returns beyond $k \approx 6$. (b) Silhouette scores peak at $k = 6$. Together, these support the interpretation of six regimes—one idle and five gears—adopted for all comparative experiments.

3.7 Implementation Details

All experiments were conducted in Python 3.10 using `NumPy`, `Pandas`, `Matplotlib`, `scikit-learn`, and `z3-solver`. Tests were performed on a Windows 11 workstation with an Intel Core i9 CPU and 16 GB RAM. A full KMeans–SMT run with $N = 80{,}000$, $k = 6$, and 100 iterations required approximately 185 s, with a Z3 timeout of 1000 ms per centroid optimization. The detailed implementation scripts are available at https://github.com/HafizAQ/KMeans-SMT.

4 Results and Discussion

4.1 Model Selection Analysis

Figure 1 reports the elbow and silhouette analyses from a k-sweep on vanilla KMeans ($k \in [4, 9]$). The inertia curve shows diminishing returns beyond $k \approx 6$, and the silhouette peaks at $k = 6$, indicating well-separated regimes without over-partitioning. This aligns with our physics prior of *one idle state plus five gear states*. We therefore fix $k = 6$ for all comparative experiments.

4.2 Do the Learned Constraints Match the Data?

Before applying constraints, we validate that the OBD-II dataset inherently exhibits the physical structure our model later enforces. The visualizations in Fig. 2 collectively confirm that the data naturally encodes gear-dependent behavior. The **gear-band card** illustrates five learned slope intervals (RPM per km/h) ordered from steep to flat, consistent with realistic transmission ratios. The **slope distribution** histogram reveals distinct peaks in the r/v ratio for $v > 3$ km/h, indicating that gears appear as well-separated modes. Finally, the **speed–RPM density map** shows clear linear manifolds for each gear and a compact idle region at low speed and moderate RPM. Together, these plots demonstrate that the dataset itself provides strong physical cues—idle and gear-band manifolds—that justify their use as feasibility constraints in the KMeans–SMT framework.

4.3 Qualitative Evidence: Physically Plausible Clusters

Figure 3 illustrates the final KMeans–SMT clusters in two key feature planes: Speed–RPM and Speed–Throttle. In both views, centroids lie strictly within the learned idle or gear manifolds, producing smooth, non-overlapping bands that correspond to distinct operating regimes. This visual alignment between clusters and physical relationships confirms that SMT-constrained updates yield interpretable, mechanically consistent regimes, unlike the unconstrained baselines that occasionally produce implausible idle or speed combinations.

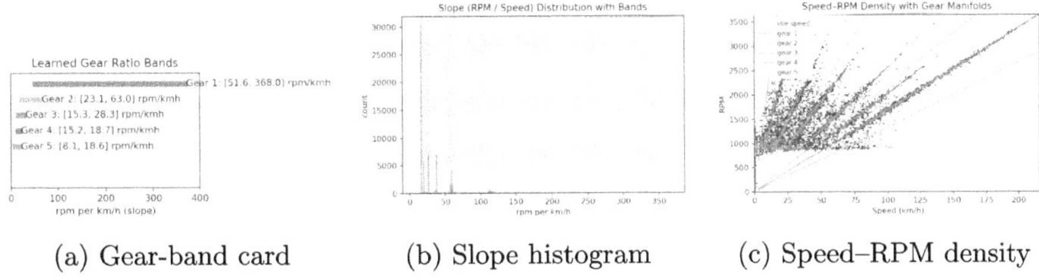

(a) Gear-band card   (b) Slope histogram   (c) Speed–RPM density

Fig. 2. Validation of learned physical structure from the OBD-II dataset. (a) Gear-band card showing data-driven slope intervals (RPM/kmh) aligned with real gear ratios. (b) Histogram of RPM-to-speed slopes (r/v) revealing distinct gear-specific modes. (c) Speed–RPM density map displaying clear ridges for individual gear regimes and an idle plateau at low speeds. Together, these confirm that the raw data already reflects gear-like structure, validating the constraint formulation used in KMeans–SMT.

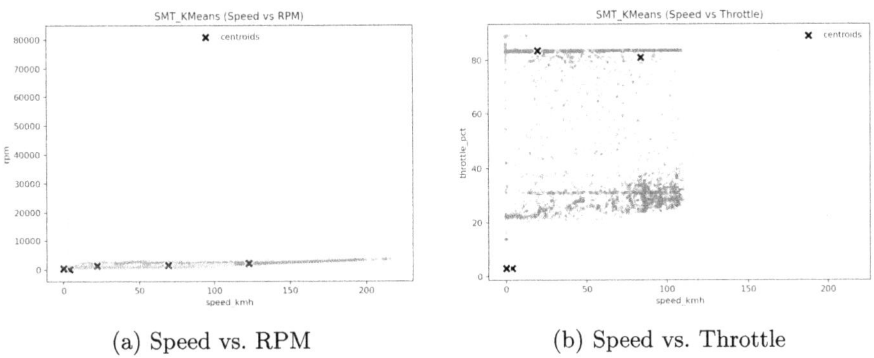

(a) Speed vs. RPM   (b) Speed vs. Throttle

Fig. 3. Physically consistent clustering by KMeans–SMT in two feature spaces. (a) Speed–RPM clusters form clear, gear-aligned manifolds with all centroids satisfying idle and gear constraints. (b) Speed–Throttle clusters show coherent throttle progression across gears, capturing realistic acceleration behavior. Together, these plots demonstrate that the SMT-constrained centroids produce interpretable and physically valid driving regimes.

4.4   Quantitative Comparison at $k = 6$

Figure 4 summarizes the quantitative evaluation of clustering quality and physical validity across all methods. Vanilla and Penalty KMeans achieve slightly higher Silhouette and CH scores but each exhibits at least one idle violation. Projected KMeans respects box constraints yet still violates idle consistency, underscoring that simple projections cannot encode logical or ratiometric dependencies. In contrast, **KMeans–SMT attains zero violations** while maintaining competitive clustering quality—demonstrating its balanced trade-off between numerical compactness and physical interpretability.

Method	Sil.	DBI	CH	Viol.
KMeans–SMT	0.583	0.406	131,857	**0**
Vanilla KMeans	0.599	0.433	365,188	1 (idle/gear..)
Projected KMeans	0.537	0.506	261,996	1 (idle)
Penalty KMeans	0.599	0.434	365,204	1 (idle)

(a) Clustering quality and constraint validity

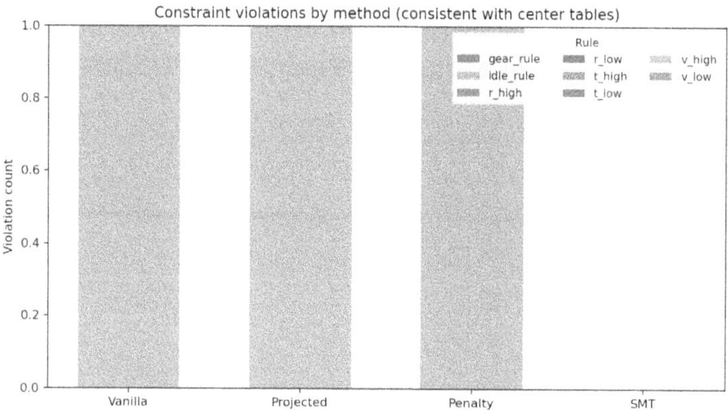

(b) Constraint violations across methods

Fig. 4. Quantitative comparison of clustering performance and physical validity at $k = 6$. (a) KMeans–SMT maintains competitive clustering quality while eliminating all constraint violations. (b) Only KMeans–SMT achieves perfect compliance across all categories (speed, RPM, throttle, idle, gear).

4.5   Centroid Tables and Per-Regime Validation

Table 1 aggregates the centroid tables exported by our pipeline for all methods. Each table lists centroid values with two interpretation columns: *Regime* (IDLE or GEAR #i) and *Constraint OK?* (✓/✗). As anticipated, all SMT centroids are ✓; the baselines each show a single idle violation (✗). These tables provide a quick audit trail to confirm feasibility at a glance.

Table 1. Centroid tables across methods. Each row reports (v, r, t) and regime annotation, plus an audit check ($\checkmark/\times$) against the learned idle and gear constraints. SMT: all $\checkmark$; each baseline: one IDLE (sometime GEAR #i) $\times$

(a) KMeans–SMT (Proposed)

v	r	t	Reg	OK
0.0	401.0	3.0	IDLE	$\checkmark$
83.7	1764.8	81.01	GEAR #3	$\checkmark$
0.0	573.0	3.0	IDLE	$\checkmark$
4.0	207.0	3.0	GEAR #1	$\checkmark$
0.0	401.0	3.0	IDLE	$\checkmark$
20.0	1836.0	83.5	GEAR #1	$\checkmark$

(b) Vanilla KMeans

v	r	t	Reg	OK
10.13	933.84	81.88	GEAR #1	$\checkmark$
111.67	2090.17	81.22	GEAR #3	$\checkmark$
57.09	1415.46	81.02	GEAR #2	$\checkmark$
0.00	**9.98**	**82.80**	**IDLE**	$\times$
150.31	2707.89	82.30	GEAR #3	$\checkmark$
78.10	1728.14	80.73	GEAR #3	$\checkmark$

(c) Projected KMeans

v	r	t	Reg	OK
64.79	1507.46	80.76	GEAR #2	$\checkmark$
27.63	1171.37	81.67	GEAR #3	$\checkmark$
8.61	880.31	81.90	GEAR #1	$\checkmark$
84.64	1818.62	80.77	GEAR #3	$\checkmark$
122.02	2219.20	81.58	GEAR #3	$\checkmark$
0.00	**9.07**	**82.84**	**IDLE**	$\times$

(d) Penalty KMeans

v	r	t	Reg	OK
57.03	1414.36	81.01	GEAR #2	$\checkmark$
0.00	**9.18**	**82.80**	**IDLE**	$\times$
77.97	1726.47	80.74	GEAR #3	$\checkmark$
10.11	933.59	81.89	GEAR #1	$\checkmark$
149.78	2704.11	82.19	GEAR #3	$\checkmark$
111.55	2088.69	81.23	GEAR #3	$\checkmark$

4.6 Optimization Behavior and Convergence

KMeans–SMT replaces the unconstrained mean update with a per-centroid Z3 optimization under hard constraints. Figure 5 plots per-iteration trajectories (Speed vs. RPM) and shows smooth convergence without oscillations. In typical runs, Z3 solves the L_2 objective in <10 ms for most regimes; when it returns *unknown* (commonly in mid-slope gears), the linearized L_1 objective yields a feasible solution in ~ 2 ms. End-to-end training for $N = 80{,}000$, $k = 6$, and up to 100 iterations completes in ≈ 184 s on a single desktop CPU (excluding plotting time), which is acceptable for offline analytics.

4.7 Discussion

The results demonstrate that embedding physics as hard SMT constraints produces clusters that are both compact and physically valid. Across all runs, KMeans–SMT achieved zero violations of idle and gear rules, confirming the correctness of the symbolic constraint formulation and the reliability of solver-integrated centroid updates. Each cluster corresponds to a clear, interpretable regime (Idle or Gear 1–5), enabling direct use for diagnostics, gear inference, and anomaly detection without post-processing.

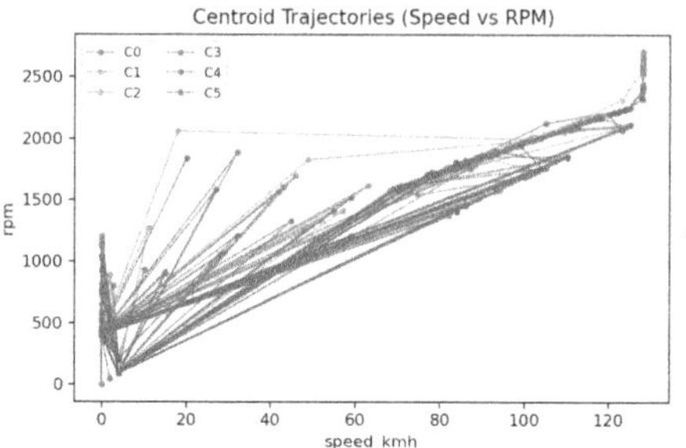

Fig. 5. Centroid trajectories during KMeans–SMT fitting (Speed vs. RPM). Paths settle into gear manifolds and the idle band without oscillations, reflecting stable solver behavior with the $L_2{\rightarrow}L_1$ fallback.

Although unconstrained baselines show slightly higher Silhouette or CH scores, these metrics favor numerical compactness rather than physical realism. KMeans–SMT achieves a more meaningful balance, maintaining competitive clustering quality while guaranteeing feasibility—an essential property for safety-critical automotive analytics. The hybrid $L_2{\rightarrow}L_1$ optimization scheme ensures stable convergence and practical runtime efficiency, while the constraint sets, learned directly from data, make the approach portable across vehicle types without manual calibration. Minor metric variability between runs (Silhouette ≈ 0.58–0.60) arises from initialization and solver timeouts but does not affect physical validity, which remains invariant across all configurations.

In summary, KMeans–SMT successfully identifies six distinct operating - regimes one idle and five gears—that faithfully represent real vehicle dynamics. All centroids satisfy the learned physical constraints, whereas baseline methods exhibit at least one idle violation. By unifying data-driven clustering with physics-informed reasoning, KMeans–SMT bridges statistical structure and mechanical feasibility, yielding reliable, interpretable, and computationally practical clustering for intelligent vehicle diagnostics.

5   Conclusion and Future Work

5.1   Conclusion

We introduced **KMeans–SMT**, a constrained clustering framework that embeds SMT reasoning into the centroid update of KMeans to ensure physics-valid regimes in OBD-II data. Rather than averaging freely in feature space, centroids are solved under hard feasibility sets learned from data (idle RPM band and gear-ratio bands), yielding clusters that respect vehicle dynamics by construction.

Across ~ 2.7M OBD-II samples (downsampled to 80K for solver efficiency) and $k = 6$ regimes (idle + five gears), KMeans–SMT consistently produced *zero* violations of idle/gear rules and variable bounds, while unconstrained and soft/box-constrained baselines exhibited idle- or high-speed inconsistencies (typically one to two violations per method). Internal clustering quality remained competitive: the SMT variant achieved Silhouette in the 0.58–0.60 range, DBI around 0.40–0.44, and strong CH scores, depending on initialization and solver time budgets. The hybrid L2→L1 objective within Z3 provided stable, feasible updates under timeouts, with end-to-end runtime $\approx 3\,\mathrm{min}$ for 80K points on a single desktop CPU. The resulting clusters are interpretable (idle and gear-specific manifolds), physically trustworthy, and ready for downstream tasks such as diagnostics triage, gear inference, and anomaly screening.

5.2   Future Work

Future work will focus on extending KMeans–SMT with temporal consistency, enabling smoother transitions between consecutive driving states and improved detection of transient behavior. Another direction involves integrating representation learning techniques, such as autoencoders, to apply SMT-based constraints to higher-dimensional sensor data. Finally, adaptive constraint learning can refine idle and gear bands across vehicle types, supporting scalable deployment and real-time, physics-validated analytics on edge and in-vehicle systems.

Acknowledgments. This work was supported by the German Federal Ministry for Research, Technology, and Aeronautics (BMBF) under grant number 16ME0783, as part of the KI4BoardNet project (https://www.edacentrum.de/ki4boardnet/).

Disclosure of Interests. The authors declare no conflict of interest.

References

1. Ágoston, K.C., E.-Nagy, M.: Mixed integer linear programming formulation for k-means clustering problem. Central Eur. J. Oper. Res. **32**(1), 11–27 (2024)
2. Ahmed, M., Seraj, R., Islam, S.M.S.: The k-means algorithm: a comprehensive survey and performance evaluation. Electronics **9**(8), 1295 (2020)
3. Amos, B., Xu, L., Kolter, J.Z.: Input convex neural networks. In: International Conference on Machine Learning, pp. 146–155. PMLR (2017)
4. Basu, S., Banerjee, A., Mooney, R.: Active semi-supervision for pairwise constrained clustering. In: ICML (2004)
5. Bilenko, M., Basu, S., Mooney, R.J.: Integrating constraints and metric learning in semi-supervised clustering. In: Proceedings of the Twenty-First International Conference on Machine Learning, p. 11 (2004)
6. Boutsidis, C., Zouzias, A., Drineas, P.: Random projections for k-means clustering. Adv. Neural Inf. Process. Syst. **23** (2010)
7. Feng, Q., Zhang, Z., Shi, F., Wang, J.: An improved approximation algorithm for the k-means problem with penalties. In: International Workshop on Frontiers in Algorithmics, pp. 170–181. Springer, Heidelberg (2019). https://doi.org/10.1007/978-3-030-18126-0_15
8. Hirth, M., Meier, D., Gehring, O., Jazdi, N., Kasneci, E.: Unsupervised deep learning for anomaly detection in automotive trucks: a survey. ACM Comput. Surv. (2025)

9. Jaffe, S., Singh, A.K., Bullo, F.: Idkm: memory efficient neural network quantization via implicit, differentiable k-means. arXiv preprint arXiv:2312.07759 (2023)
10. Jain, A.K.: Data clustering: 50 years beyond k-means. Pattern Recogn. Lett. **31**(8), 651–666 (2010)
11. Kamgar-Parsi, B., Kamgar-Parsi, B.: Penalized k-means algorithms for finding the number of clusters. In: 2020 25th International Conference on Pattern Recognition (ICPR), pp. 969–974. IEEE (2021)
12. Karniadakis, G., Kevrekidis, I., Lu, L., Perdikaris, P., Wang, S., Yang, L.: Physics-informed machine learning. Nat. Rev. Phys. (2021)
13. Katz, G., Barrett, C., Dill, D.L., Julian, K., Kochenderfer, M.J.: Reluplex: an efficient smt solver for verifying deep neural networks. In: International Conference on Computer Aided Verification, pp. 97–117. Springer, Heidelberg (2017). https://doi.org/10.1007/978-3-319-63387-9_5
14. Malik, M., Nandal, R.: A framework on driving behavior and pattern using on-board diagnostics (obd-ii) tool. Mater. Today: Proc. **80**, 3762–3768 (2023)
15. de Moura, L.M., Bjørner, N.S.: Proofs and refutations, and z3. In: LPAR Workshops, Doha, Qatar, vol. 418, pp. 123–132 (2008)
16. Nguyen, A., Balasubramanian, K.: Stochastic zeroth-order functional constrained optimization: oracle complexity and applications. INFORMS J. Optim. **5**(3), 256–272 (2023)
17. Raissi, M., Perdikaris, P., Karniadakis, G.: Physics-informed neural networks: a deep learning framework for solving forward and inverse problems involving nonlinear pdes. J. Comput. Phys. (2019)
18. Singh, S.K., Sharma, A.: Revving up insights: machine learning-based classification of obd ii data and driving behavior analysis using g-force metrics. Bull. Electr. Eng. Inf. **14**(3), 2188–2197 (2025)
19. Srinivasan, M., Dabholkar, A., Coogan, S., Vela, P.A.: Synthesis of control barrier functions using a supervised machine learning approach. In: 2020 IEEE/RSJ International Conference on Intelligent Robots and Systems (IROS), pp. 7139–7145. IEEE (2020)
20. Vaiti, T., Tišljarić, L., Erdelić, T., Carić, T.: Traffic emissions clustering using obd-ii dataset based on machine learning algorithms. Transport. Res. Procedia **64**, 364–371 (2022)
21. Wagstaff, K., Cardie, C., Rogers, S., Schrödl, S., et al.: Constrained k-means clustering with background knowledge. In: ICML, vol. 1, pp. 577–584 (2001)
22. Wang, Z., Yuan, Y., Ma, J., Zeng, T., Sun, D.: Randomly projected convex clustering model: motivation, realization, and cluster recovery guarantees. J. Mach. Learn. Res. **26**(137), 1–57 (2025)
23. Weber, M.: Automotive obd-ii dataset (2023). https://doi.org/10.35097/1130
24. Willemsen, R., Cavicchia, C., van den Heuvel, W., van de Velden, M.: An exact solution approach for hierarchical clustering. INFORMS J. Comput. (2025)
25. Yu, G., Lee, J., Bae, K.: Stlmc: robust stl model checking of hybrid systems using smt. In: International Conference on Computer Aided Verification, pp. 524–537. Springer, Heidelberg (2022). https://doi.org/10.1007/978-3-031-13185-1_26

Research on Inner and Outer Ring Interconnected Metal Foreign Object Detection Coil for Wireless Power Transfer

Jiang Cao[1], Chengcheng Feng[1], Peng Zhang[1], Chengwei Tian[2(✉)], Anjie Ran[2], and Hu Sun[2]

[1] No. 88 Jinhong East Road, Chengyang District, Qingdao, Shandong, China
[2] School of Electrical Engineering, Beijing Jiaotong University, Beijing 100044, China
25121268@bjtu.edu.cn

Abstract. Wireless Power Transfer (WPT) technology has gained substantial research interest owing to its remarkable advantages in operational safety, reduced maintenance requirements, and design flexibility. Nevertheless, the inherently open nature of WPT systems renders the operating magnetic field vulnerable to interference from metallic foreign objects, which introduces critical challenges including degradation of transmission efficiency and potential thermal hazards. This paper presents the design and implementation of a blind-spot-free, highly sensitive, and structurally straightforward detection system specifically tailored for identifying metallic foreign objects in high-power electric vehicle WPT systems utilizing distributed rectangular transmission coils. The research commences with a thorough theoretical analysis, deriving the transmission characteristics of an LCC/S-compensated WPT system and establishing a comprehensive circuit model that quantitatively demonstrates how metallic object intrusion alters coil parameters and consequently impairs power transfer performance. An initial detection approach employing interconnected paired inductor cells was implemented but found to exhibit significant blind zones, leading to an in-depth magnetic field analysis and the subsequent development of an optimized detector featuring an innovative inner-outer loop interconnected architecture. Critical issues such as harmonic responses inherent to the interconnected array are meticulously analyzed and effectively mitigated. Finally, prototype detection coils were fabricated and integrated onto the transmission coil surface, with extensive experimental results validating the system's detection sensitivity, harmonic performance, central region coverage effectiveness, and demonstrating superior performance through a comparative study of interconnected versus independent detection modalities, thereby confirming the system's robustness and practical applicability.

Keywords: Electric Vehicles · Metallic Foreign Object Detection · Finite Element Magnetic Field Analysis

© The Author(s), under exclusive license to Springer Nature Switzerland AG 2026
A. Razminia et al. (Eds.): ITFT 2025, CCIS 2876, pp. 127–136, 2026.
https://doi.org/10.1007/978-3-032-20592-6_12

1 Introduction

1.1 A Subsection Sample

With technological advancement, Wireless Power Transfer (WPT) has emerged as a novel charging method, gaining global research attention [1]. It enables wireless energy transfer through high-frequency alternating magnetic fields between coils and shows promising application prospects in electric vehicles due to its favorable performance [2]. However, metallic object intrusion disturbs the magnetic field, reducing transmission efficiency and causing eddy current and hysteresis losses that lead to overheating risks. Thus, Metallic Foreign Object Detection (MOD) is essential for EV wireless charging systems.

Metallic objects entering the WPT system alter coupling parameters and operational states. Studies typically combine theoretical modeling with finite element simulations. Reference [3] shows metallic objects shift resonant frequency and affect output power, while [4] reports decreased self-inductance, mutual inductance, and quality factor, with increased resonant frequency when objects approach the coil surface. Through loose-coupling transformer modeling where metals are equivalent to R-L circuits, [5] derives system equations confirming reduced inductance and increased resistance upon intrusion. Experimental tests with iron, aluminum, and copper using 31-turn 100-mm coils showed temperature rises of 1.5 °C, 1.8 °C, and 9.6 °C, respectively, highlighting ferromagnetic metals as primary detection targets [6].

Detection coil technology identifies metals via voltage changes caused by magnetic field distortion. Miniature coil arrays used in high-power systems often create blind zones. Reference [7] proposes a dual-layer meander coil design where layers cover each other's blind zones, plus a signal conditioning circuit. Reference [8] correlates primary coil current with detection coil voltage, combining both signals for improved accuracy.

This paper designs an MOD system for high-power EV WPT using detection coils. To address blind zones and complexity in conventional designs, an Inner-Outer Surround Interconnected Coil (ISIC) is proposed based on the magnetic distribution of distributed systems, overcoming limitations of Interconnected Paired Inductor Cells (IPIC). Issues like central region failure and harmonics are analyzed and resolved. A prototype ISIC was tested against independent coils, demonstrating effective multi-metal detection across locations.

2 Analytical Modeling and Analysis

2.1 Characteristic Analysis of an LCC/S-Compensated Wireless Power Transfer System

A Wireless Power Transfer (WPT) system for electric vehicles comprises three primary subsystems: the primary-side power conversion system, the coupling mechanism, and the secondary-side power conversion system. The primary system includes an AC-DC rectifier with voltage stabilization and an inverter circuit. The coupling mechanism consists of the primary and secondary compensation networks (e.g., LCC/S topology) along with the transmission coils. The secondary system incorporates a rectifier and a DC-DC converter [9]. The overall system configuration is illustrated in Fig. 1.

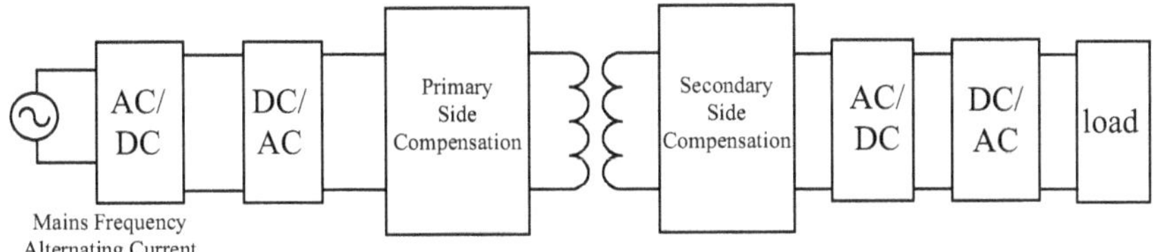

Fig. 1. Overall block diagram of the wireless power transfer system.

The LCC/S compensation topology is adopted in this study. The equivalent circuit model of the coupling mechanism is shown in Fig. 2. Here, U_{in} and I_{in} represent the 85 kHz high-frequency voltage and current output from the primary-side inverter, respectively; I_p denotes the current in the primary transmission coil. L_r is the resonant compensation inductor, and R_{Lr} is its equivalent resistance. C_r and C_p are the parallel and series resonant capacitors on the primary side, respectively. L_p and R_p represent the self-inductance and internal resistance of the primary transmission coil, while M denotes the mutual inductance between the primary and secondary transmission coils. On the secondary side, L_s and R_s are the self-inductance and internal resistance of the secondary coil, C_s is the series resonant capacitor, and R_{eq} stands for the equivalent load. U_{out} and I_{out} indicate the output voltage and current of the overall coupling mechanism, respectively.

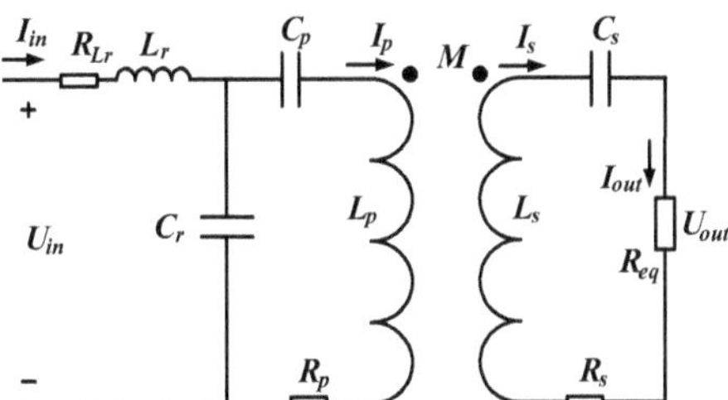

Fig. 2. Equivalent circuit of the LCC/S compensation topology.

When analyzing the power transfer efficiency of the coupling mechanism, the inverter output can be regarded as a voltage source. Neglecting harmonic effects and applying fundamental harmonic analysis, the power loss P_{loss}, output power P_{out}, and transmission efficiency η of the WPT system can be expressed as follows:

The LCC/S-compensated WPT system exhibits an inherent quasi-constant-voltage characteristic. With a properly designed compensation inductor Lr matching the coil parameters, the output voltage remains nearly constant under resonance. Under typical conditions where R_p, R_s, and R_{Lr} are significantly smaller than ωM, ωL_r, and R_{eq}, the voltage gain expression can be simplified as shown in Eq. (1). This configuration ensures minimal output voltage variation under load fluctuations and maintains stable primary coil and inverter output currents during mutual inductance changes due to the compensation network. All WPT systems for electric vehicles investigated in this study employ the LCC/S compensation topology.

$$H_{\mathrm{U}} = \left| \frac{U_{\mathrm{out}}}{U_{\mathrm{in}}} \right| = \frac{\omega^2 M L_{\mathrm{r}} \frac{R_{\mathrm{eq}}}{R_{\mathrm{s}}+R_{\mathrm{eq}}}}{R_{\mathrm{Lr}}\left[\frac{(\omega M)^2}{R_{\mathrm{s}}+R_{\mathrm{eq}}} + R_{\mathrm{p}} \right] + (\omega L_{\mathrm{r}})^2} \approx \frac{M}{L_{\mathrm{r}}} \tag{1}$$

2.2 Power Loss Induced by Metallic Foreign Objects

For rectangular coils with dimensions a_1, a_2, b_1, b_2, turn numbers N_1, N_2, and separation h, the self-inductance and mutual inductance of closely-wound multi-turn coils can be derived from Neumann's formula. A simplified single-coil model with fig valent dimensions a, b, and conductor width w yields the following expressions [10]:

$$\begin{cases} L = \frac{\mu_0 N^2}{4\pi} \iint \frac{dl_1 dl_2}{r} \\ M = \frac{\mu_0 N_1 N_2}{4\pi} \iint \frac{dl_1 dl_2}{r} \end{cases} \tag{2}$$

When a metallic foreign object intrudes into a wireless charging system, the alternating magnetic field induces multiple losses, ultimately altering parameters such as the equivalent internal resistance and self-inductance of the transmission coil. By modeling the metallic object as a closed loop with internal resistance R_{m} and self-inductance L_{m}—where Rm represents additional losses and L_{m} reflects the equivalent inductance within the object—a loosely-coupled model is established with the primary transmission coil.

The equivalent impedance Z_{w} of the primary transmission coil after metal intrusion becomes:

$$\begin{aligned} Z_{\mathrm{w}} &= \frac{\dot{U}_{\mathrm{p}}}{\dot{I}_{\mathrm{p}}} = R_{\mathrm{p}} + j\omega L_{\mathrm{p}} - \frac{(j\omega M_{\mathrm{pm}})^2}{R_{\mathrm{m}} + j\omega L_{\mathrm{m}}} \\ &= R_{\mathrm{p}} + \frac{\omega^2 M_{\mathrm{pm}}^2}{R_{\mathrm{m}}^2 + \omega^2 L_{\mathrm{m}}^2} R_{\mathrm{m}} + j\omega \left(L_{\mathrm{p}} - \frac{\omega^2 M_{\mathrm{pm}}^2}{R_{\mathrm{m}}^2 + \omega^2 L_{\mathrm{m}}^2} L_{\mathrm{m}} \right) \end{aligned} \tag{3}$$

3 Inner-Outer Surround Interconnected Coils for Distributed Rectangular Coil Platforms

3.1 Modeling and Analysis of IPIC and Distributed Rectangular Coils

As analyzed in Sect. 2, the distributed rectangular coil platform requires full-coverage detection, necessitating detection coils that cover all operational areas. Magnetic field analysis of the coil surface (Fig. 3) shows the platform can be divided into two zones: Zone B (within the dashed line) where magnetic flux lines are directed outward perpendicular to the plane, and Zone A (outside the dashed line) where flux lines are directed inward. Along the dashed boundary, the flux lines run parallel to the coil surface.

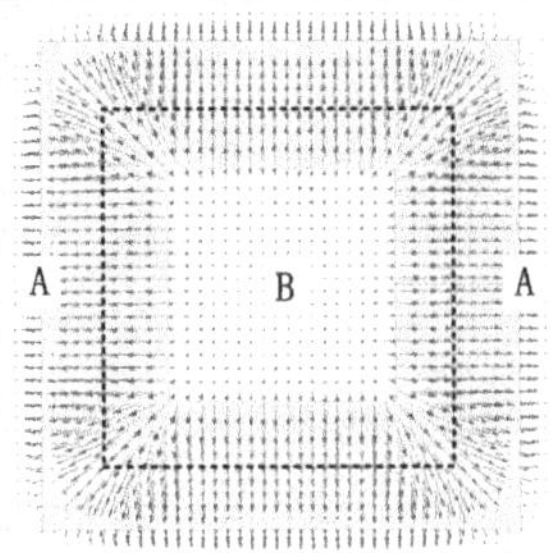

Fig. 3. Top view.

Based on the magnetic flux distribution and the divergent nature of the magnetic field over the distributed rectangular coil surface, side-by-side coils are designed and arranged as shown in Fig. 4. Two inner-outer detection coils are placed on each side of the dashed line, while the remaining coils are arranged in parallel to cover the entire surface. These coils are interconnected adjacently and reverse-connected over distance. Each detection coil consists of an inner loop with a line width of 20 mm and an outer loop with a line width of 40 mm. Both inner and outer loops measure 220 mm in length with a conductor diameter of 1mm.

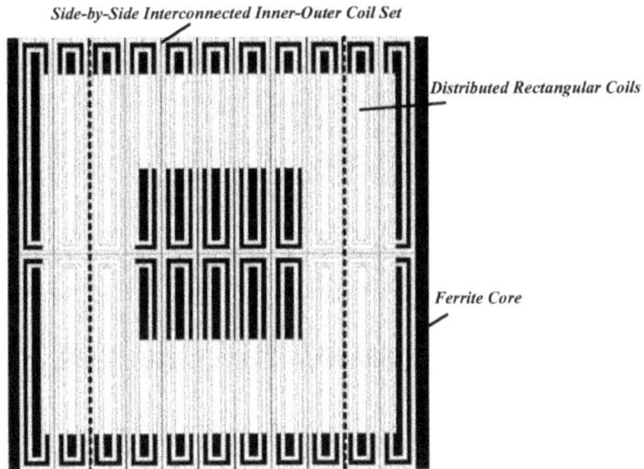

Fig. 4. Application of IPIC to a Distributed Rectangular Transmission Coil.

The detection sensitivity distribution heatmap obtained from applying IPIC to the distributed rectangular coil surface reveals significant blind zones. As shown in Fig. 5, the sensitivity within the dashed areas remains below 5%. These blind zones correspond to regions above the transmission coils with strong magnetic fields, where sensitivity is even lower than in the central weak-field region. Simulations confirm that the intrusion of ferromagnetic sheets into any area of the coil surface cannot be neglected, with the most severe heating occurring in high-field regions. The application of side-by-side coils on such a platform would thus lead to critical undetected intrusions.

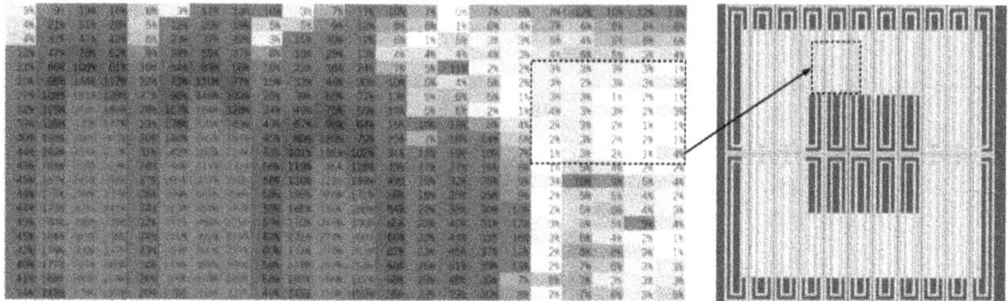

Fig. 5. Detection sensitivity distribution and corresponding platform areas with blind zones.

When a metallic foreign object moves into the detection blind zone, the resulting magnetic flux distribution on its surface is shown in Fig. 6. A reversal of magnetic flux lines is observed within the detection coil. During metal intrusion, this configuration leads to detection failure, as the metallic object simultaneously influences opposing magnetic flux clusters in a similar manner, resulting in negligible change in the induced voltage of the detection coil.

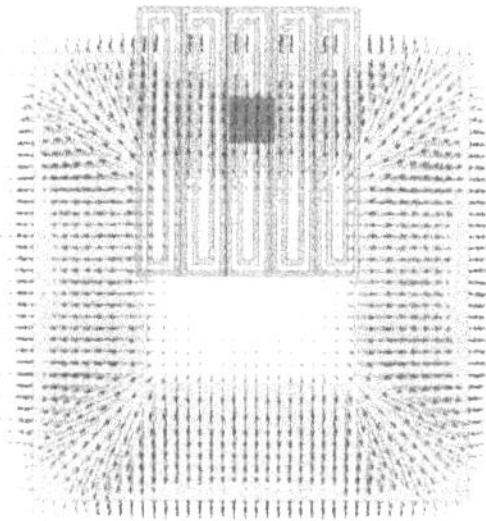

Fig. 6. Metallic Object in Detection Blind Zone.

3.2 Inner-Outer Surround Interconnected Detection Coil

Based on the ISIC design methodology, a detection coil structure for the distributed rectangular coil platform was developed, as illustrated in Fig. 7. The inner and outer detection coils are arranged along the magnetic flux reversal boundary of the transmission coil surface. The outer and inner loops measure 40 mm and 20 mm in width respectively, comparable in size to small metallic objects. Only 20 such detection coils are required to fully cover the 400×400 mm transmission surface. The outermost Type A detection coils match the transmission coil in length (400 mm). The ISIC system monitors metallic object intrusion by detecting voltage variations across its dual-loop structure.

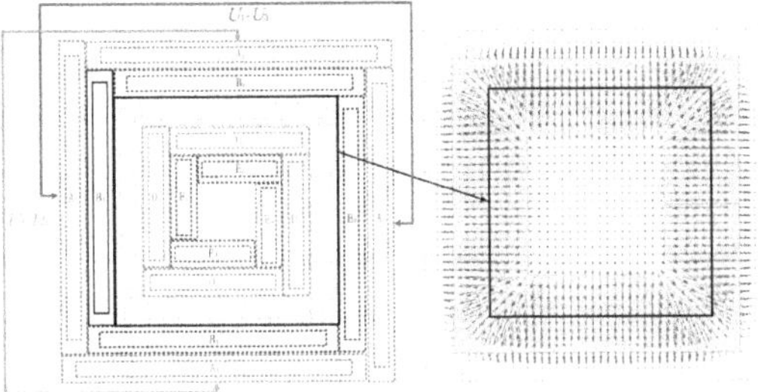

Fig. 7. Inner-Outer Surround Interconnected Coil Set.

The detection performance was quantified by counting points exceeding sensitivity thresholds of 5%, 10%, 100%, and 200% under three configurations (Table 1). The surround-type layout significantly outperforms the side-by-side arrangement, effectively addressing its limitations while preserving the advantages of interconnected dual-loop coils. Notably, adjacent connection in the surround layout maintains high-performance detection ($\geq$200% sensitivity) within each coil set's area, confirming that the connection scheme primarily affects inter-set regions rather than intra-set sensitivity.

Table 1. Comparative Analysis of Detection Sensitivity Under Three Working Conditions.

Detection Sensitivity	>200%	>100%	>10%	>5%
Interconnected Inner-Outer Coil Pair in Parallel Arrangement	69/15%	127/27.5%	299/64.7%	360/78%
Inner-Outer Surround Interconnected Coil (Adjacent Anti-Connection)	170/36.8%	240/51.9%	410/90%	432/93.5%
Inner-Outer Surround Interconnected Coil (Distant Anti-Connection)	173/37.4%	252/54.5%	427/92.4%	440/95.2%

4   Inner-Outer Surround Interconnected Coils for Distributed Rectangular Coil Platforms

The experimental platform for the distributed WPT and detection systems utilizes identical components—including the power supply, primary cabinet, secondary box, load, and detection circuitry—with differences lying in the coupling mechanism, compensation topology, and detection coils. The transmission coils are wound using Litz wire, and MnZn ferrite cores with a thickness of 5mm are applied as the magnetic substrate. The parameters of the remaining resonant capacitors in the compensation topology are calculated based on the compensation inductor L_r and the measured parameters of the distributed coupling mechanism.

As shown in Fig. 8, the detection coils are fabricated according to the previously designed ISIC layout using PCB technology to minimize deviations caused by manual winding. Independent inner and outer loops are produced and manually interconnected via Dupont wires, enabling experimental comparison between independent and inter-connected coil configurations and demonstrating the advantages of the interconnected approach. Type A corresponds to the outermost dual-loop detection coil, with a length of 400 mm. The length of each subsequent inner coil decreases by 80mm stepwise. All outer and inner loops maintain widths of 40mm and 20mm, respectively. After being arranged in the surround-type layout, the resulting detection coil layer forms a complete array measuring 420 mm × 420 mm.

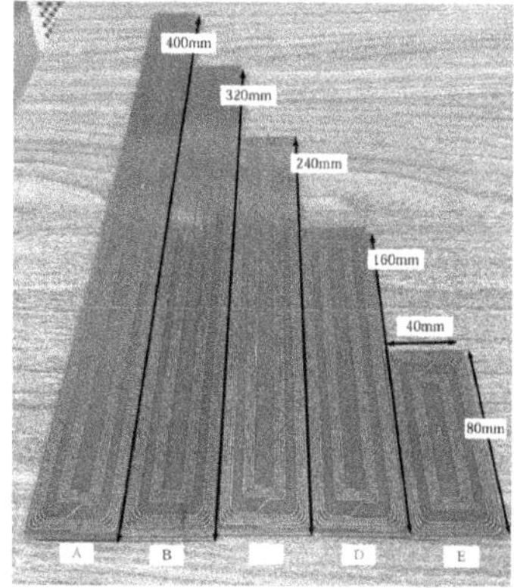

Fig. 8. Surrounding inner and outer loop detection coil PCB.

As shown in Fig. 9, metallic objects were placed at nine sequential positions from the outer to inner regions of the detection coil surface (Position 1 to 9), simulating the complete intrusion path. The odd-numbered positions represent locations within individual detection coils, while even-numbered positions correspond to inter-coil gaps. For instance, Position 2 lies between coils A1 and B1, whereas Position 5 is located inside coil C1.

Fig. 9. Metal foreign objects are located at different positions on the surface of the detection coil.

As shown in Fig. 10, when a metallic object is placed at Position 2, the detection voltage variations of individual coils A_1, B_1, and their interconnected combination (A_1-B_1) were measured. The respective induced voltages U_{A1}, U_{B1}, and U_{AB1} demonstrate distinct responses to the metallic intrusion. Located between the dual-loop structures of A_1 and B_1, the object produces symmetrical influence on both coils, resulting in voltage increases of 2.0V in U_{A1} and 2.8V in U_{B1}. When interconnected, the combined output U_{AB1} reaches 4.3V, approximately equaling the sum of individual variations. This confirms that interconnection effectively amplifies the detection signal for inter-coil intrusions, while simultaneously raising the system's baseline voltage, aligning with prior theoretical and simulation predictions.

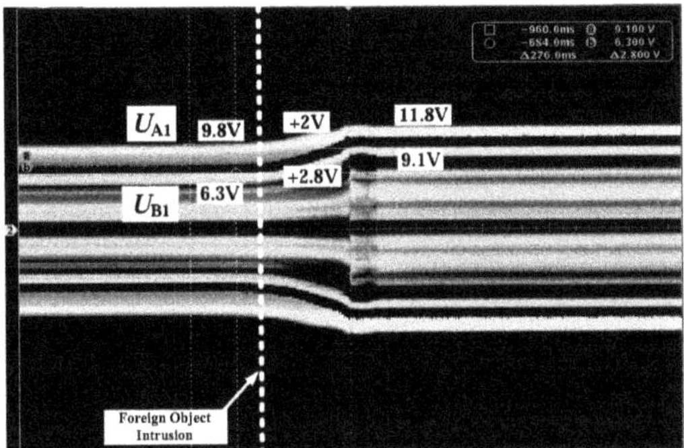

Fig. 10. Metal foreign body intrusion 2 position.

5 Conclusion

Metallic foreign object detection is crucial for ensuring the safe operation of Wireless Power Transfer (WPT) systems. This study focuses on the design of passive excitation detection coils for high-power WPT systems in electric vehicles. The main contributions are summarized as follows:

(1) Theoretical Analysis of Metallic Object Impact: To clarify the effects of metallic intrusion, a theoretical analysis was conducted. The transmission characteristics of the LCC/S compensation topology, widely used in EV WPT systems, were examined. A circuit model integrating metallic objects and the coupling mechanism was developed and analytically derived.

(2) Detection Coil Design for Distributed Rectangular Coils: A detection coil was designed for distributed rectangular transmission coils. Initial application of Interconnected Paired Inductor Cells (IPIC) revealed significant detection blind zones. Based on simulation results of the magnetic field distribution over the distributed coil surface, an improved layout—the Inner-Outer Surround Interconnected Coil (ISIC)—was proposed. Simulations verified that the ISIC structure eliminates the blind zones present in side-by-side coil arrangements.

(3) Experimental Validation: Experimental results demonstrate that the proposed detection coils, implemented in a single-layer structure, successfully eliminate blind zones. Metallic objects intruding between coils can be effectively detected. The

system is significantly simplified: only four voltage signals are required for an 800 × 800 mm platform, and three for a 400 × 400 mm platform. Furthermore, harmonic interference in interconnected coils, which initially masked voltage changes during metal intrusion, was mitigated through filtering. After filtering, a detectable voltage variation of 1.96 V was achieved, confirming the effectiveness of the interconnected coil-based detection system.

References

1. Author, F.: Article title. Journal 2(5), 99–110 (2016)
2. Boys, J.T., Covic, G.A.: The inductive power transfer story at the university of Auckland. Circ. Syst. Mag. IEEE **15**(2), 6–27 (2015)
3. Feng, H., Tavakoli, R., Onar, O.C., Pantic, Z.: Advances in high-power wireless charging systems: overview and design considerations. IEEE Trans. Transp. Electrification **6**(3), 886–919 (2020)
4. Jafari, H., Moghaddami, M., Sarwat, A.I.: Foreign Object detection in inductive charging systems based on primary side measurements. IEEE Trans. Ind. Appl. **55**(6), 6466–6475 (2019)
5. Liang, H.W.R., Wang, H., Lee, C.-K., Hui, S.Y.R.: Analysis and performance enhancement of wireless power transfer systems with intended metallic objects. IEEE Trans. Power Electron. **36**(2), 1388–1398 (2021)
6. Esteban, B., Sid-Ahmed, M., Kar, N.C.: A series-tuned supply architectures in wireless EV charging systems. IEEE Trans. Power Electron. **99**, 6408–6422 (2015)
7. Jeong, S.Y., Kwak, H.G., Jang, G.C., et al.: Dual-purpose nonoverlapping coil sets as metal object and vehicle position detections for wireless stationary EV chargers. IEEE Trans. Power Electron. **33**(9), 7387–7397 (2018)
8. Chu, S.Y., Zan, X., Avestruz, A.-T.: Electromagnetic model-based foreign object detection for wireless power transfer. IEEE Trans. Power Electron. **37**(1), 100–113 (2022)
9. Yuan, H., Wang, C., Xia, D.: Research on input-parallel single-switch WPT system with load-independent constant voltage output. IEEE Trans. Transp. Electrification **9**(1), 1888–1896 (2023)
10. Jeong, S.Y., Thai, V.X., Park, J.H., Rim, C.T.: Self-inductance-based metal object detection with mistuned resonant circuits and nullifying induced voltage for wireless EV chargers. IEEE Trans. Power Electron. **34**(1), 748–758 (2019)

Phase Change and Doppler Rate Fusion for Moving Target Tracking

Jun Hu$^{(\boxtimes)}$ iD, Ziqiu Yu, Hongquan Li, Yahui Hu, Pingyang Liu, Shujun Lv, and Xiuzhen Lin

Air Force Early Warning Academy, Wuhan, China
249479274@qq.com

Abstract. This paper validates a passive positioning method for a single station that integrates the phase change rate and the Doppler change rate. An observation model for a moving platform that tracks a moving target was established, and the core formula for the integrated positioning method was derived. Through Monte Carlo simulations, the effects of phase measurement errors, baseline length, and Doppler rate errors on positioning accuracy were quantitatively analyzed. The results validate the feasibility of the method, clarify its advantages and limitations, and provide a theoretical basis for the parameter design of airborne detection systems. The research demonstrates that this integrated approach avoids error amplification inherent in traditional azimuth differentiation methods. Simulation results reveal that distance estimation is extremely sensitive to phase change rate measurement errors, with quadratic error propagation characteristics. In contrast, the method shows remarkable robustness to constant phase errors and is theoretically independent of interferometer baseline length.

Keywords: Passive positioning · Single station · Phase change rate · Doppler change rate · Performance analysis · Parameter sensitivity

1 Introduction

Single-station passive positioning technology plays a crucial role in modern electronic reconnaissance, threat warning, and autonomous navigation systems due to its capability to achieve covert direction-finding and positioning through a single observation platform [1]. Among these approaches, a method that directly calculates azimuth rate-of-change by measuring phase difference rate variations using a phase interferometer, subsequently integrating this with Doppler rate information, theoretically circumvents the error amplification inherent in traditional azimuth differential methods, thereby enhancing instantaneous positioning capability [2–4]. This technical approach has demonstrated application potential in high-end airborne electronic warfare systems (such as the EA-18G) and shipborne electronic support measures (ESM) [5,6], enabling rapid and precise positioning of ground-based or sea-surface mobile radar emitters.

A. Razminia et al. (Eds.): ITFT 2025, CCIS 2876, pp. 137–144, 2026.
https://doi.org/10.1007/978-3-032-20592-6_13

2   System Models and Derivation of Principles

2.1   System Geometric Model

Consider the localization scenario in a two-dimensional plane, as shown in Fig. 1. Let the state vector of the moving observation platform be $\mathbf{X}_o = [x_o, y_o, \dot{x}_o, \dot{y}_o]^T$, and the state vector of the moving radiation source target be $\mathbf{X}_t = [x_t, y_t, \dot{x}_t, \dot{y}_t]^T$. At time t, the distance from the target relative to the platform is $r(t)$, and the azimuth angle is $\beta(t)$. There are relative radial velocity v_r and relative tangential velocity v_t between the platform and the target.

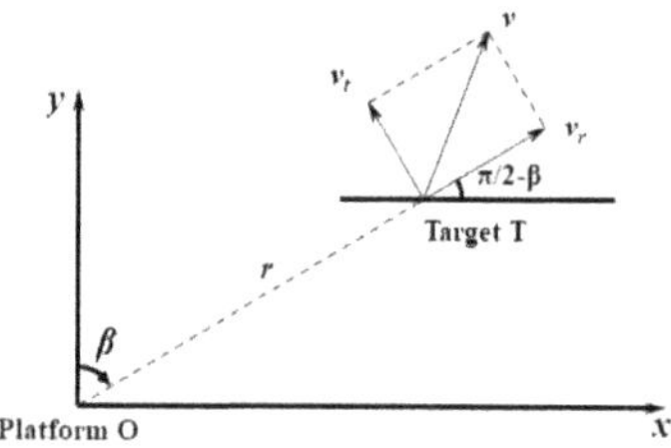

Fig. 1. Schematic Diagram of Positioning Principle [7]

2.2   Doppler Change Rate Observation Model

The Doppler frequency shift f_d received by the observer and the relative radial velocity v_r satisfy [8]:

$$f_d = -\frac{2v_r}{\lambda} \tag{1}$$

Differentiating both sides of the above equation with respect to time, the relationship between relative radial acceleration a_r and Doppler change rate $\dot{f}_d$ can be obtained [9]:

$$\dot{f}_d = -\frac{2a_r}{\lambda} \tag{2}$$

where $\dot{f}_d$ is the Doppler frequency change rate, which can be directly measured by high-performance receivers.

2.3   Angular Velocity Measurement Model Based on Phase Change Rate

To obtain azimuth change rate with high precision, the phase interferometer method is adopted [2,3,10,11]. The phase difference measurement principle is shown in Fig. 2. Let the platform baseline length be D, signal wavelength be

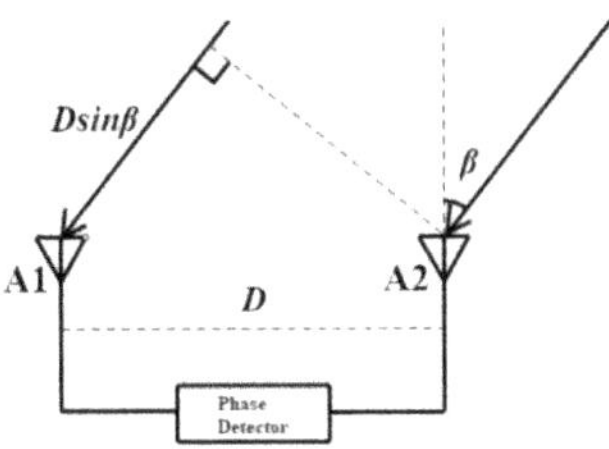

Fig. 2. Phase difference schematic diagram [7]

λ, then the relationship between phase difference $\Delta\phi$ of signals received by two antennas and azimuth angle β is:

$$\Delta\phi = \frac{2\pi D}{\lambda} \sin\beta \tag{3}$$

Differentiating both sides of Eq. (3) directly with respect to time:

$$\Delta\dot{\phi} = \frac{2\pi D}{\lambda} \cos\beta \cdot \dot{\beta} \tag{4}$$

$\Delta\dot{\phi} = $ is the directly measurable phase difference change rate. The azimuth change rate $\dot{\beta}$ is calculated from Eq. (4):

$$\dot{\beta} = \frac{\lambda}{2\pi D \cos\beta} \Delta\dot{\phi} \tag{5}$$

This model establishes a direct connection between angular velocity and phase change rate, avoiding the error amplification effect brought by traditional numerical differentiation methods.

2.4   Fusion Localization Formula

Under the condition of uniform motion or compensable radial acceleration, combined with kinematic relations [7], the expression of distance r can be derived:

$$r = \frac{v_t^2}{a_r} = \frac{(r\dot{\beta})^2}{a_r} \tag{6}$$

Substituting Eq. (5) into Eq. (6), and using Eq. (2), the core fusion localization formula verified in this paper is obtained:

$$r = \frac{\lambda^3 D^2 \cos^2\beta}{8\pi^2} \cdot \frac{\dot{f}_d}{(\Delta\dot{\phi})^2} \tag{7}$$

This formula establishes an analytical relationship between target distance and direct observations $\Delta\dot{\phi}$, $\dot{f}_d$ and system parameters, which is the basis for subsequent performance analysis and verification.

3   Localization Performance Verification and Parameter Sensitivity Analysis

This chapter aims to systematically verify the formula derived above through Monte Carlo simulation experiments, and quantitatively analyze the sensitivity of final localization accuracy to various key observations and system parameters.

3.1   Simulation Environment and Evaluation Index Setting

To comprehensively evaluate localization performance, this study constructs the following simulation environment:

Carrier frequency $f_c = 1\,\text{GHz}$. Default value of interferometer baseline length $D = 5\,\text{m}$. Platform velocity $(140, 150)\,\text{m/s}$. Target position $(150{,}250)\text{km}$, velocity $(-300, 200)\,\text{m/s}$. Distance root mean square error (RMSE) is used as the core performance evaluation index, with Monte Carlo times $N = 1000$.

3.2   Verification of Localization Formula Under Ideal Conditions

Under ideal conditions without any measurement errors, the theoretical observations $\Delta\dot{\phi}$ and $\dot{f}_d$ are substituted into the core localization formula (7) for calculation. The calculated distance is consistent with the true value (error $0.000\,\text{m}$), verifying the correctness and rigor of the formula, laying a reliable theoretical foundation for subsequent error analysis.

3.3   Parameter Sensitivity Analysis

To explore the influence of various factors on actual system performance, this section introduces Gaussian white noise to simulate measurement errors, conducts Monte Carlo simulation, and analyzes the sensitivity of localization accuracy to different error sources.

Sensitivity Analysis of Phase Difference Measurement Error. The measurement error of phase difference $\Delta\phi$ mainly comes from the inconsistency of receiving channels, thermal noise, etc. The analysis results show that within the error range of $0.0001°$ to $10°$, the distance estimation RMSE is always $0.00m$, as illustrated in Fig. 3.

This phenomenon is highly consistent with theoretical expectations. Observing formula (7), it can be seen that the expression of distance estimation value r **does not directly contain phase difference** $\Delta\phi$, but only depends on its change rate $\Delta\dot{\phi}$. Therefore, constant deviation or slow-varying error of phase difference has almost no effect on the localization algorithm based on change rate. This highlights a major advantage of this method: lower requirements for absolute phase calibration, reducing the complexity of system implementation.

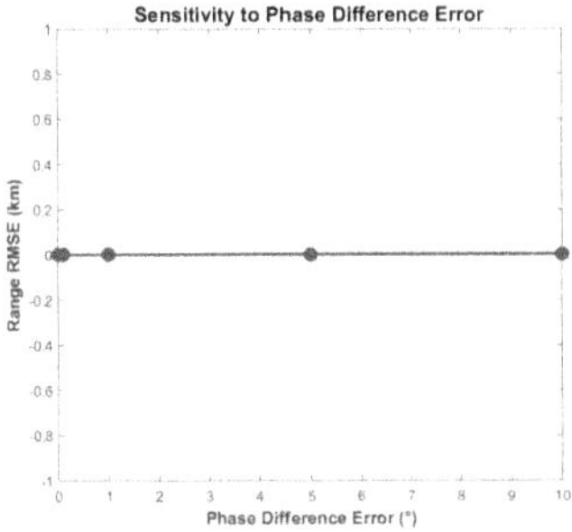

Fig. 3. Phase error affects simulation

Sensitivity Analysis of Phase Difference Change Rate Measurement Error. Phase difference change rate $\Delta\dot\phi$ is the key to calculating azimuth change rate, and its error has a decisive influence on localization accuracy. As shown in Fig. 4, the simulation results show that its measurement error has a significant quadratic relationship with distance RMSE. When the error is $0.001°/\text{s}$, RMSE is 131.17m; when the error increases to $0.01°/s$, RMSE deteriorates sharply to 1.40km.

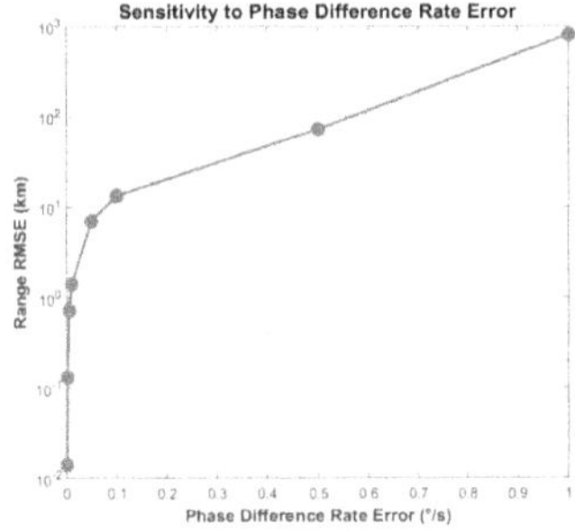

Fig. 4. Phase change rate error impacts simulation

From formula (7) $r \propto 1/(\Delta\dot\phi)^2$, it can be seen that the estimated distance is extremely sensitive to the error of $\Delta\dot\phi$. The tiny error of $\Delta\dot\phi$ will be squared and amplified in the calculation. The measurement error of $\Delta\dot\phi$ must be controlled within $0.001°/\text{s}$ to achieve localization accuracy at the hundred-meter level. This is the main technical bottleneck in engineering implementation.

Sensitivity Analysis of Doppler Change Rate Measurement Error. The measurement error of Doppler change rate $\dot{f}_d$ also has an important influence on localization accuracy. The simulation results in Fig. 5 show that its influence is approximately linear. When the error is $0.001\,\text{Hz/s}$, RMSE is $154.87\,\text{m}$; when the error is $0.01\,\text{Hz/s}$, RMSE is $1.50\,\text{km}$.

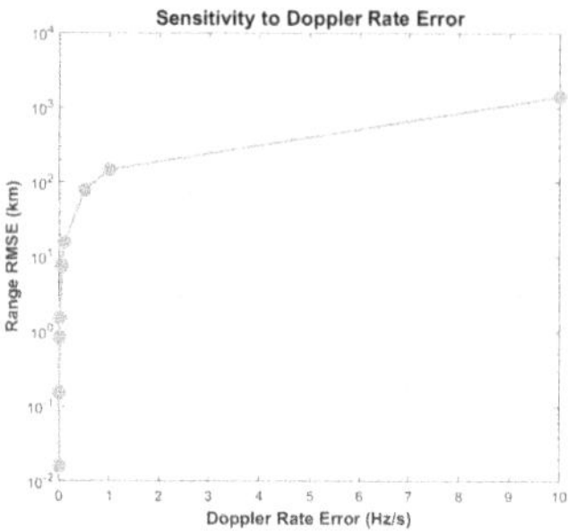

Fig. 5. Doppler change rate impacts simulation

According to formula (7), $r \propto \dot{f}_d$. Therefore, the measurement error of $\dot{f}_d$ will be linearly transmitted to the distance estimation value. To achieve hundred-meter level localization accuracy, the measurement error of $\dot{f}_d$ needs to be better than 0.01 Hz/s. This requires the receiver to have extremely high frequency stability and measurement accuracy.

Influence Analysis of Interferometer Baseline Length. Baseline length D is a key parameter in system design. The influence of baseline length on localization error in the range of $0.1m$ to $20\,\mathrm{m}$ is analyzed by simulation, with results shown in Fig. 6. Under ideal conditions, the distance errors calculated by different baseline lengths are all 0.00 m.

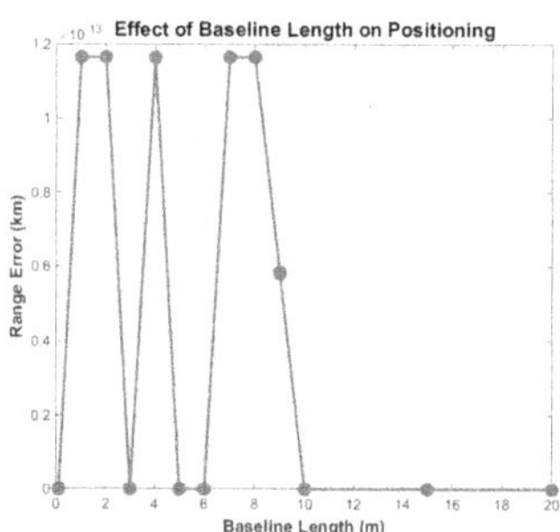

Fig. 6. Baseline length affects simulation

This result verifies the correctness of formula (7): the D^2 in the numerator part of the formula and the D^2 in the denominator $\Delta\dot{\phi}^2$ (due to $\Delta\dot{\phi} \propto D$) cancel each other, making the final distance estimation value r theoretically independent of baseline.

4   Conclusions

This paper investigates a single-station passive positioning method integrating phase change rate and Doppler rate for moving target tracking. The main findings can be summarized as follows:

1. The observation model and fusion localization formula were derived and validated through Monte Carlo simulations, confirming theoretical correctness.
2. Parameter sensitivity analysis reveals that the method is robust to constant phase errors but extremely sensitive to phase change rate measurement errors, showing quadratic error propagation characteristics.
3. The method avoids error amplification inherent in traditional azimuth differentiation approaches and demonstrates theoretical independence from interferometer baseline length.

The research validated the feasibility of this integrated solution while identifying phase rate measurement as the primary technical bottleneck in practical applications.

5   Future Work

Based on the results and conclusions of this study, future work can be further developed from the following directions:

1. **Robust algorithm design**: Aiming at the core bottleneck of $\Delta\dot\phi$ measurement, research high-precision, high-robustness measurement algorithms based on advanced signal processing technologies such as Kalman filtering and time-frequency analysis [7,12,13].
2. **Multi-dimensional model extension**: Extend the current localization model in the two-dimensional plane to three-dimensional space including pitch angle information to improve the applicability and practicality of the algorithm.
3. **Dynamic error compensation**: Deeply study the error model under actual dynamic environments such as platform maneuver and vibration, and design corresponding online compensation algorithms [14].

References

1. Liu, C.: Passive Location and Tracking. Xidian University Press, Xi'an (2011)
2. Shan, Y., Sun, Z., Huang, F.: Single observer passive location technology based on method of phase difference rate of change. J. Natl. Univ. Def. Technol. **23**(6), 74–77 (2001)
3. Wang, Q., Zhong, D., Guo, F., Deng, X., Zhou, Y.: A Moving Single Observer Passive Location Method Using Only Long Baseline Interferometer to Measure Phase Difference Rate of Change. In: Proceedings of the 14th National Conference on Signal Processing (CCSP-2009). (2009)

4. Qiu, H.: Research on single observer passive location technology. Electron. Sci. Technol. **27**(1), 78–80 (2014)
5. Pace, P.E.: Detecting and Classifying Low Probability of Intercept Radar, 2nd edn. Artech House, Norwood (2009)
6. Zhang, Y., He, Y., Wang, X.: Single station passive location technology based on moving platform. J. Electron. Inf. Technol. **17**(1), 36–42 (2002)
7. He, Y., Xiu, J., Guan, X.: Radar Data Processing and Applications. Electronic Industry Press, Beijing (2013)
8. Liu, S., Liu, Y., Dai, J.: A single observer passive ranging method based on doppler frequency rate of change. Comput. Simul. **29**(2), 11–14 (2012)
9. Teakls, S.: Observability of target tracking with bearing only measurement. IEEE Trans. Aerosp. Electron. Syst. **32**(4), 1468–1471 (1996)
10. Li, X., Wang, Y., Li, Z.: A single observer passive location method based on phase difference rate and doppler frequency rate. J. Electron. Inf. Technol. **37**(5), 1121–1127 (2015)
11. Chen, L., Huang, Z., Wang, X., Wu, G.: A direct position determination method by fixed passive single-station based on prior angular velocity. Acta Electron. Sin. **52**(7), 2190–2200 (2024)
12. Wang, J., Lv, K., Liu, M.: A maneuvering target passive tracking algorithm based on doppler frequency rate and azimuth. Command Control Simul. **40**(4), 38–44 (2018)
13. Wei, X., Wan, J., Huangfu, K.: A new technique in single observer passive tracking based on particle filter. J. Commun. **26**(12), 81–85 (2005)
14. Huo, G., Li, D.: A single observer passive location algorithm based on backward-smoothing cubature kalman Filter. J. Signal Process. **29**(1), 68–74 (2013)

Optimization of Electronically Controlled Injectors' Parameters in Diesel Engines Using CFD

Osama Ghazal[(✉)] and Ala Jaber

Zarqa University, 2000, Zarqa 13110, Jordan
`oghazal@zu.edu.jo`

Abstract. An internal combustion engine that uses fixed injection timing and rates often suffers from low performance and increased emissions, which can occur due to variations in load and speed. Bosch's electronically controlled unit injectors (EUIs) address these challenges by combining the functions of the fuel pump and injector into a single unit. This system employs common rail technology, enabling precise electronic control over the timing, quantity, rail pressure, and the number of fuel injection pulses. Consequently, this technology enhances engine performance, improves fuel efficiency, and reduces emissions. In this study, we developed a simulation model that incorporates details of the Bosch injector and the common rail system, utilizing GT-Power commercial software. In the model, diesel fuel is injected in two modes: single pulse injection and multiple pulses injection (pre- and main pulses), aimed at optimizing the combustion process. For multi-pulse injection, both pulses are electronically controlled by the Engine Control Unit (ECU), which adjusts the fuel injection timing and rate based on engine load, speed, and injection duration. We constructed comprehensive injection rate maps for both pre- and main injection pulses, focusing on critical variables such as injection timing, duration, fuel flow rate, and common rail pressure. The model was validated against available literature data, showing strong agreement with the numerical results. Our findings indicate a significant increase in engine efficiency and a reduction in emissions compared to traditional injection systems. We have thoroughly discussed and analyzed these results.

Keywords: Diesel Engine · CFD · Emissions · Electronically Controlled Injector · Fuel Injection Variables · Common Rail System

1 Introduction

Multi-pulse injection in diesel engines involves injecting fuel in multiple, smaller bursts during a single engine cycle, while single-pulse injection delivers the fuel in one large burst. Multi-pulse injection offers advantages in terms of combustion control, reduced emissions, and potentially improved fuel efficiency and performance, while single-pulse injection is simpler but can lead to less optimal combustion, especially at lower and higher loads. The primary challenge for automobile manufacturers is producing internal

A. Razminia et al. (Eds.): ITFT 2025, CCIS 2876, pp. 145–155, 2026.
https://doi.org/10.1007/978-3-032-20592-6_14

combustion (IC) engines that generate lower emissions to meet EURO VII standards. In recent years, land transportation powered by fossil fuels has been the largest energy source. Therefore, even minor adjustments to IC engines that improve performance and reduce emissions can significantly decrease pollution and lead to a cleaner environment.

Diesel engines typically have higher brake thermal efficiency than gasoline engines because they operate at higher compression ratios without experiencing engine knocking. However, they also tend to produce greater amounts of nitrogen oxides (NOx) and soot emissions because of their varied combustion process. As a result, various solutions have been proposed to enhance diesel engine performance. One such technology is low-temperature combustion (LTC), which decreases NOx and soot emissions by limiting high combustion temperature. Many researchers view multiple injections as a promising strategy for optimizing combustion and achieving lower emissions in diesel engines [1–5]. After-treatment systems, such as diesel particulate filters, NOx traps, and catalytic reduction, also effectively reduce emissions, although they add cost and complexity. The need for lower emissions has led to the exploration of various fuel injection techniques. Many researchers have found that using a multi-injection system increases engine performance and decreases emissions, particularly for NO and soot [6–8]. Park et al. [9] investigated the effect of various split injection strategies on combustion and emissions characteristics in a single-cylinder diesel engine. They concluded that multiple injection strategies help reduce fuel-rich areas, shorten ignition delays, and limit diesel knock levels. The influence of injection timing and split injection strategies on the performance, emissions, and combustion characteristics of a diesel engine fueled with biodiesel-blended fuels has been studied by How et al. [10]. They achieved this by using a multiple injection technique, which resulted in decreased NOx and noise emissions. Park et al. [11] conducted an experimental investigation into the effects of single-phase, double-phase, and triple-phase fuel injection on engine performance. They found that as the number of phases increased, the peak heat release rate decreased, while the peak in-cylinder pressure increased. Yehliu et al. [12] conducted an experimental study on single-phase and two-phase fuel injection at various engine speeds. The results indicated that two-phase injection reduces brake-specific fuel consumption compared to single-phase injection. Additionally, the levels of NOx, HC, and CO also decreased with the use of two-phase injection.

The main drawbacks of using multiple injections are increased heat losses if not properly managed. Additionally, the combustion stability due to improperly timed or excessive injections, leading to incomplete combustion and decreased efficiency. The other issue is complexity, as it requires precise control and optimization of injection timing, duration, and quantity.

However, by employing a common rail injection system, various parameters, including injection pressure, the start of injection, number of injections, injection duration, and injected fuel mass, can all be adjusted very simply and flexibly [13–15]. Moreno et al. [16] stated that pilot injection reduces the ignition delay, resulting in a decrease in the pressure rise rate and NOx emissions. Liu et al. [17] confirmed that post-fuel injection reduces soot production due to the increase in in-cylinder temperature and heat release rate, resulting in better soot oxidation. Connor et al. investigated the effect of the post-injection on mixture preparation and unburned hydrocarbon emission in a heavy-duty diesel engine. They stated that post-injection reduces NOx, HC, and soot emissions due to higher in-cylinder temperature and turbulence [18]. Rehman et al. investigated the effect of post-injection on engine performance. They concluded that post-injection decreases the engine thermal efficiency and increases soot in a biogas-diesel dual fuel engine because of the late combustion of diesel in the diffusion mode [19]. In this paper, the effect of single and multi-pulse injection on engine performance and emissions is investigated using a CFD approach. The results have been analyzed and fully discussed.

2 Model Description

In this investigation, a turbocharger, 4-cylinder, four-stroke, direct injection, 2L diesel engine with an electronically controlled injector model has been developed and investigated using GT-Power software. The engine runs in "speed" mode, where the engine speed is entered by the user, and the engine torque and power are calculated. Diesel liquid fuel was injected directly into the cylinder at a consistent pressure and temperature 2000 [bar] and temperature 320 [K], respectively. The diesel fuel injected to the combustion chamber. In this simulation, the Woschni model was used. The sub-models such as; heat transfer, evaporation, combustion, and NO_x formation are illustrated in Table 2.

This simulation will run until it reaches steady state convergence for six different engine speeds at full load. The engine speed was varied from (1000–4500) rpm. The engine specifications shown in Table 1. Table 2 presents the main sub-models used in the simulation. The engine operation conditions are presented in Table 3.

The injection timing and duration for multi-injection were adjusted according to engine load and speed. The engine performance and emissions, such as: power, torque, brake specific fuel consumption (BSFC), brake thermal efficiency (BTE), NO, CO, hydrocarbons (HC), and soot, were calculated and compared for both modes. Four sub-models were used in this simulation, namely: fuel system, combustion model, heat transfer model, and turbocharger and intercooler system.

Table 1. Engine Specifications.

Parameter	Unit	Multi-inj	Single-inj
Bore	mm	86	86
Stroke	mm	86	86
Total Displacement	L	2.0	2.0
No. Cylinders		4	4
Compression Ratio		17	17
(IVC)	[CA]	adjusted	-145
(EVO)	[CA]	adjusted	100
(IVO)	[CA]	adjusted	304
(EVC)	[CA]	adjusted	442
No. of injector holes		7	7
Nozzle hole diameter	mm	0.23	0.23

Table 2. Sub-models used in the simulation [21]

Turbulence model	K-epsilon model
Turbulent dispersion model	turbulent model
Wall interaction model	Spray model
Breakup model	Khrt model
Heat transfer model	Woschni
Evaporation model	L-K model
Combustion model	ComPulse model
NOx model	Zeldovich model
Soot model	Kinetic model

Table 3. Engine Initial Conditions

Parameter	Unit	Value
Initial pressure	bar	1
Initial temperature	K	300
Head temperature	K	500
Piston temperature	K	550
Cylinder temperature	K	450

2.1 Fuel Model

The GT-Power software allows users to simulate different types of injectors for diesel and gasoline with port and direction injection, depending on the user's simulation. In this case, the mass flow profile was chosen, along with a pressure map that corresponds to the crank angle. Diesel fuel is injected in two stages: a pre-pulse and a main pulse. The timing for both pulses changes based on the engine speed and load. "The software creates an injection map to reflect these changes in timing".

The maximum injection pressure is 2000 bar. This mass flow rate was validated to align with the cylinder pressure observed in test data. In this context, the holes and diameters of the injector have a significant impact on combustion efficiency. The pre-injection and main injection maps are dependent on engine speed and pressure, while the mass of diesel injected varies according to pulse duration. Additionally, the injection angle for both pulses changes based on engine operating conditions, aiming to maximize engine performance and reduce emissions.

2.2 Combustion Model

The simulation used the DIPulse diesel multi-pulse combustion model. The cylinder is divided into three zones. The main unburned zone holds all the mass at the intake valve closing (IVC). The spray unburned zone contains the injected fuel and gas, while the spray burned zone includes the combustion products. The DIPulse model also has sub-models that simulate key processes during injection and combustion based on the cylinder's conditions. Four attributes in the 'EngCylCombDIPulse' framework should be used for calibration.

2.3 Heat Transfer Model

The software provides several heat transfer models, including. In this simulation, the Woschni model was chosen because it accurately predicts the heat transfer in the combustion chamber. The heat transfer is calculated using the following equation [21]:

$$h = \frac{A.p^{.08}}{T^{0.55}D_{cyl}^{0.2}}\left[B.U_{piston} + C.\frac{T_{soc}.V.(p - p_{motor})}{p_{soc}.V_{soc}}\right]^{0.8} \tag{1}$$

where h is a coefficient of heat transfer [W/m^2 K], A, B, and C are Woschni coefficients, p, T, V are cylinder pressure, temperature, and volume, respectively, D_{cyl} Cylinder bore, U_{piston} mean piston speed, T_{soc}, p_{soc}, V_{soc} present cylinder gas temperature, pressure, and volume at start of combustion and p_{motor} motoring cylinder pressure.

2.4 Turbocharger and Intercooler System

This object is used to represent a power turbine in the GT-Power code. It will predict the output power, mass flow rate, and outlet temperature using map data describing the turbine performance. This map data can be entered using objects made from the 'TurbineMapSAE'. The intercooler is an air-to-air intercooler that is modeled based on a heat exchanger using 'HxMaster' parts.

3 Model Validation

The model presented in this paper is validated using data available in the literature. In this model, we compared the simulation results with the experimental results in reference [20]. Figure 1 shows the in-cylinder pressure for experimental and numerical data.

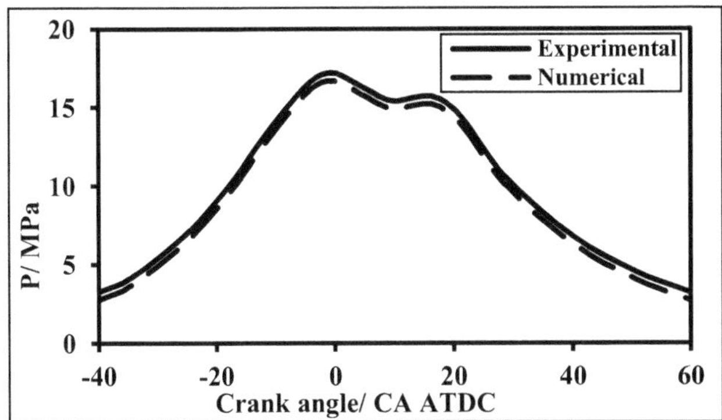

Fig. 1. Comparison of experimental and numerical data for cylinder pressure. Case 90-(30)10

4 Results and Discussion

The effect of multi- and single pulse direct injection diesel fuel for different engine speed has been investigated. The single pulse is defined by the pulse duration and the mass of injected fuel. However, the multi-pulse injection is defined for both pre-and main injection. Both pulses utilize an injection map depending on injection timing, pressure, and fuel mass flow rate. The engine speed was varied from 1000–4500 rpm, and the injection timing varied from (-20 CA and -3 CA). The injection pulse is measured in ms. The engine torque, fuel consumption, power, thermal efficiency, NO, CO, HC, and soot were calculated.

4.1 Engine Performance

To calculate brake power (BP), the following equation is used [21]:

$$BP = \frac{BMEP \times V_{disp.} \times rpm}{n_r}[1/600] \tag{2}$$

where BMEP brake mean effective pressure, V_{disp} engine displacement and n_r number of revolutions per cycle (for two stroke engine is taken 1 while for four strokes is 2).

Figure 2 shows the effect of single and multi-pulse injection techniques on engine brake power for different engine speeds. The total mass of injected diesel is constant for both cases and varies with engine speed. The results show an improvement in engine power of about 15% for multi-injection compared to single injection. This is due the improvement of combustion efficiency caused by controlling the in-cylinder temperature. In addition, the multi-pulse injection makes the mixture more homogenous and reactive due to a longer mixture time. The effect of engine brake torque in presented in Fig. 3. The engine brake torque (BT) is calculated according to the following equation [21]:

$$BT = \frac{BP}{avgrpm}\left[\frac{60000}{2\pi}\right] \tag{3}$$

where BP is the brake power and $avgrpm$ average engine speed. As seen in Fig. 3, the brake torque increased significantly with multi-pulse injection, particularly for low engine speed. Similar results were obtained by K. Panda et al. [1]. The variation of brake mean effective pressure (BMEP) is presented in Fig. 4. It is seen that the BMEP is increased with multi-pulse injection for all engine speeds. The brake specific fuel consumption (BSFC) and brake thermal efficiency are presented in Figs. 5 and 6, respectively. The engine brake specific fuel consumption (BSFC) and the brake thermal efficiency (BTE) are calculated using the mathematical Eqs. 4 and 5, respectively.

The engine BSFC is determined as follows:

$$BSFC = \frac{\dot{m}_f \times 10^6}{BP} \tag{4}$$

where $\dot{m}_f$ fuel mass flow rate. The BTE is calculated by the following relationship, where the lower heating value of the fuel LHV is involved:

$$BTE = \frac{3600}{BSFC \times LHV} \times 100 \tag{5}$$

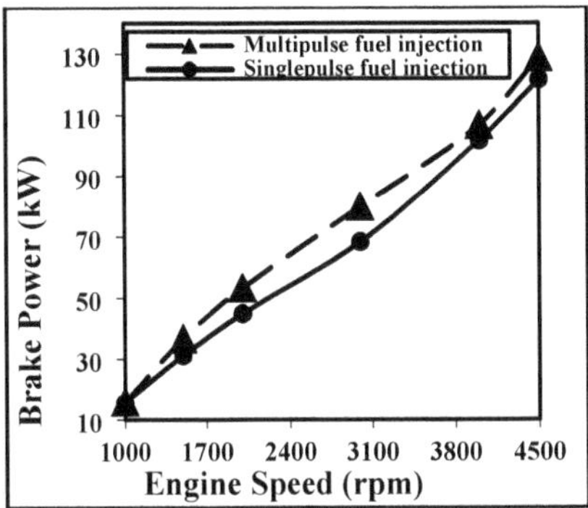

Fig. 2. Variation of brake power with different engine speed values for multipulse and singlepulse fuel injection.

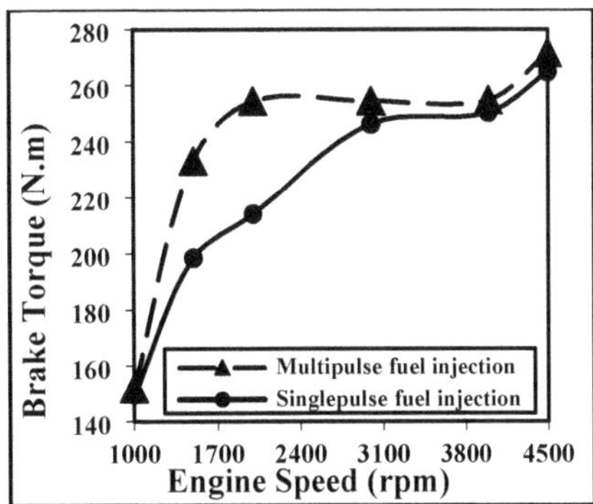

Fig. 3. Variation of brake torque with different engine speed values for multipulse and singlepulse fuel injection.

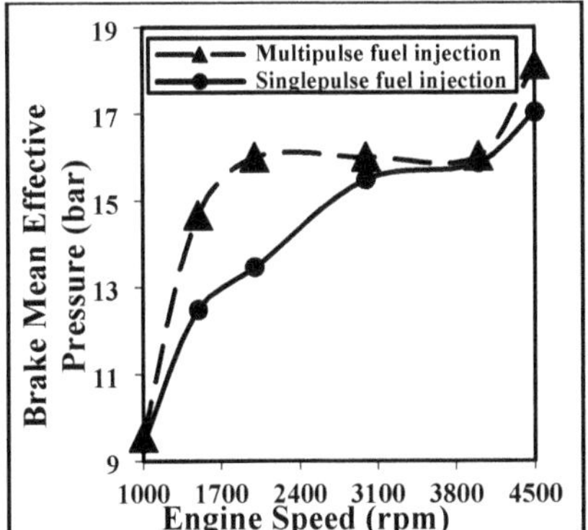

Fig. 4. Variation of brake mean effective pressure (BMEP) taken after two complete revolutions (720°) with different engine speed values for multipulse and singlepulse fuel injection.

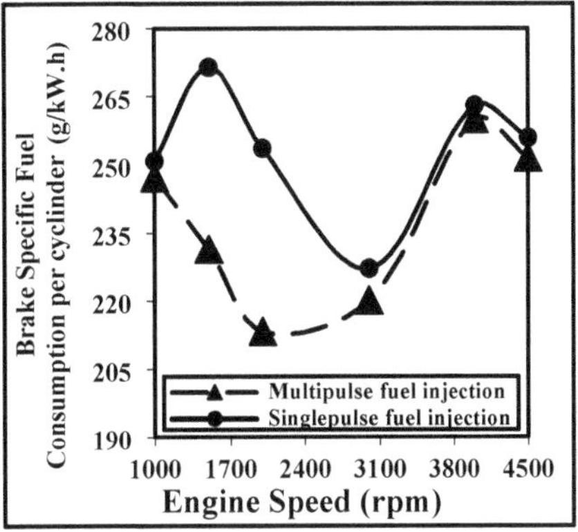

Fig. 5. Variation of brake specific fuel consumption (BSFC) per cylinder with different engine speed values for multipulse and singlepulse fuel injection.

As seen, the BSFC is decreased significantly by about 20% with multi-pulse injection compared to a single pulse. This difference is higher for low and medium engine speeds. For high speed, this variation is less noticeable. This is due to that multiple injections can break down the fuel into smaller droplets and distribute it more evenly in the combustion chamber, leading to better mixing with air and more complete combustion. The variation of brake thermal efficiency (BTE) at various engine speeds is presented in Fig. 6.

It is seen that for low and medium engine speeds, the BTE for multi-pulse is higher, around 18% compared to single injection. The rate of pressure rise is presented in Fig. 7. As expected, the pressure rate is much higher for a single pulse than for a multi-pulse for all engine speeds. For higher engine speeds, the difference is obvious.

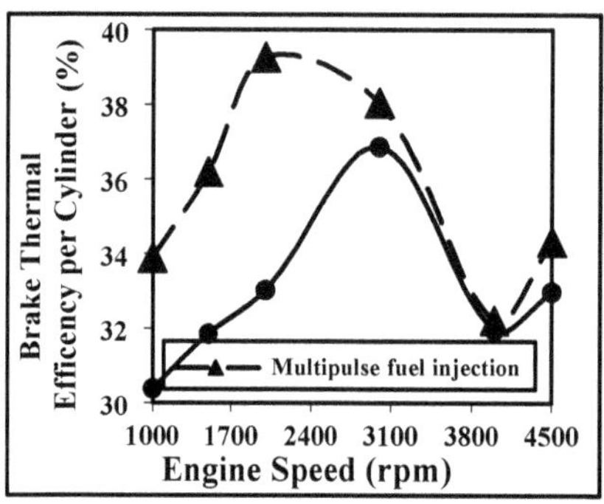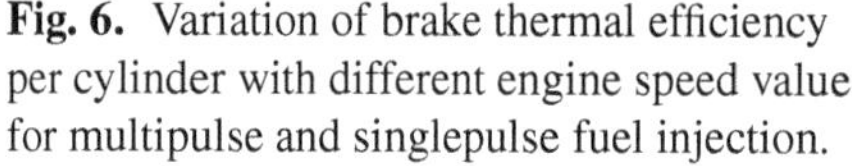

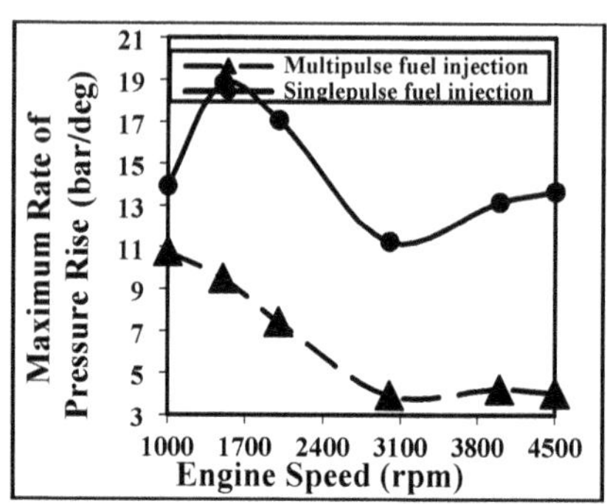

Fig. 6. Variation of brake thermal efficiency per cylinder with different engine speed values for multipulse and singlepulse fuel injection.

Fig. 7. Variation of maximum rate of pressure rise with different engine speed values for multipulse and singlepulse fuel injection.

4.2 Engine Emissions

Figure 8 presents the effect of multi- and single-pulse injection on NO emission. The major factors contributing to NOx formation are high cylinder temperature and high oxygen concentration. The results show an increase in NO mass with single-pulse injection for low and medium speeds. This is due to the high cylinder temperature and slow combustion. Moreover, the engine heat release rate is higher for single-pulse injection compared to multi-pulse injection, resulting in higher NO emissions. The effect of injection techniques on CO and HC engine emissions is shown in Figs. 9 and 10, respectively. It can be observed that both the HC and CO emissions decrease with the multi-injection due to the enhanced combustion process. Furthermore, when fuel is injected in single pulse mode, the wall impingement of the fuel increases, leading to higher HC and CO emissions. The variation of soot formation versus engine speed for single and multi-pulse injection is presented in Fig. 11. As seen, the soot concentration is lower for multi-pulse injection compared to single injection. The main reason is the higher ignition delay for multi-pulse injection, resulting in a better fuel-air mixture before combustion starts and consequently higher combustion efficiency.

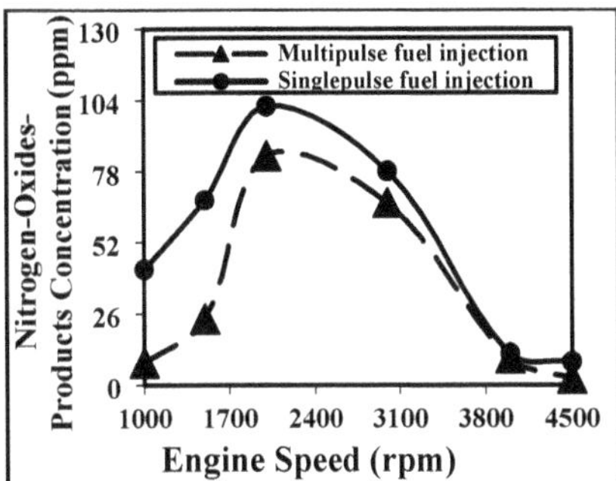

Fig. 8. Variation of Nitrogen-oxides-products concentration produced by a single cylinder with different engine speed values for multipulse and singlepulse fuel injection.

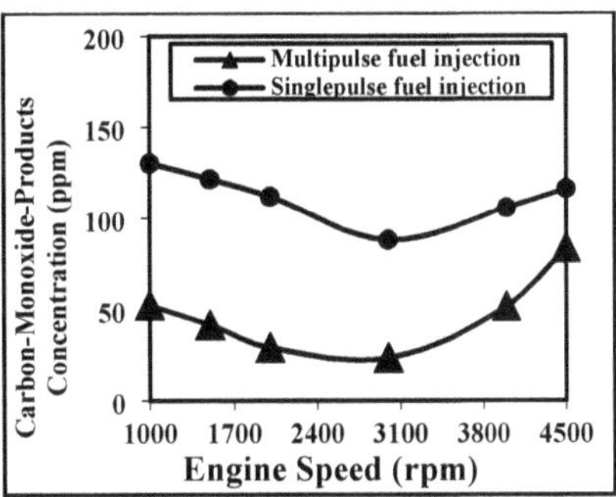

Fig. 9. Variation of Carbon-monoxide-products concentration produced by a single cylinder with different engine speed values for multipulse and singlepulse fuel injection.

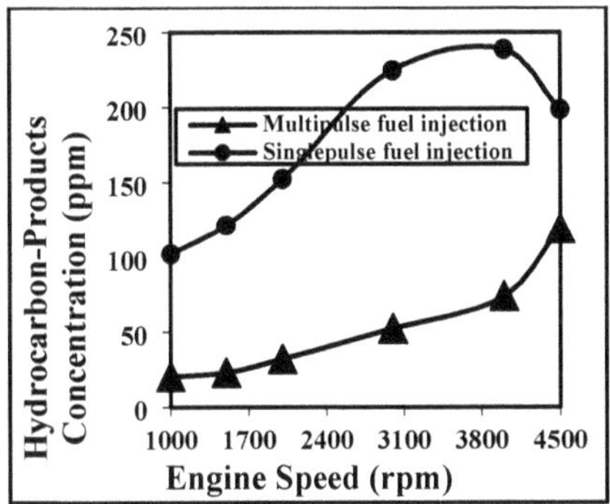

Fig. 10. Variation of Hydrocarbon-products concentration produced by a single cylinder with different engine speed values for multipulse and singlepulse fuel injection.

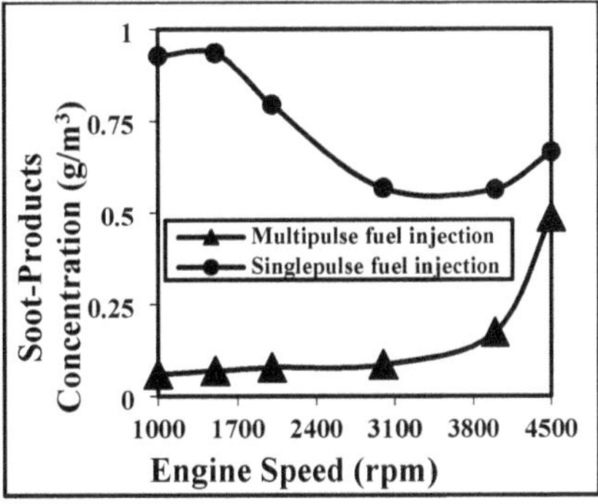

Fig. 11. Variation of Soot-products concentration with different engine speed values for multipulse and singlepulse fuel injection.

5   Conclusions

This research paper conducts a numerical investigation of combustion performance and emissions in a diesel engine using both single and multi-injection techniques. Simulations were carried out using GT-Power professional software at various engine speeds and injection timings. The injection timing was adjusted for multi-pulse injection to optimize performance parameters for engine operation. The main findings can be summarized as follows:

1. Using multi-pulse injection in diesel engines improves engine power, brake thermal efficiency, and reduces specific fuel consumption. This effect is especially noticeable at low and medium speeds.

2. The maximum rate of pressure rise increase is significantly higher for single injection compared to multi-injection, which leads to combustion deficiencies and noise.
3. The emissions of NO and CO decreased with multiple injections, particularly at low and medium speeds. However, this decrease is less noticeable at higher engine speeds. At high engine speeds, the hydrocarbon (HC) emissions significantly increased with a single injection compared to multi-injection. This increase is due to poor combustion and an inhomogeneous mixture.
4. The soot emissions are higher for single injection, especially at low engine speeds, due to a high in-cylinder heat release rate and a rich oxygen region.
5. Ultimately, the timing, duration, mass flow rate, and pressure of injection are critical parameters for multi-injection technology to achieve optimal benefits. They must be precisely optimized and controlled.

References

1. Panda, K., Ramesh, A.: Diesel injection strategies for reducing emissions and enhancing the performance of a methanol based dual fuel stationary engine. Fuel **289**, 119809 (2021)
2. Mingfa, Y., Hu, W., Zunqing, Z., Yan, Y.: Experimental study of multiple injections and coupling effects of multi-injection and EGR in a HD diesel engine, SAE Technical Paper 2009-01-2807 (2009). https://doi.org/10.4271/2009-01-2807
3. Ambrosio, D.S., Ferrari, A.: Potential of multiple injection strategies implementing the after shot and optimized with the design of experiments procedure to improve diesel engine emissions and performance. Appl. Energy **155**(933), 46 (2015)
4. Liu, Y., Reitz, R.D.: Optimizing HSDI diesel combustion and emissions using multiple injection strategies (No. 2005-01-0212). SAE Technical Paper (2005)
5. Saleh, A.: Modeling and performance analysis of a solar pond integrated with an absorption cooling system. Energies **2022**, 15 (2022). https://doi.org/10.3390/en15228327
6. Lee, J., Jeon, J., Park, J., Bae, C.: Effect of multiple injection strategies on emission and combustion characteristics in a single cylinder direct-injection optical engine. SAE Paper No. 2009-01-1354 (2009)
7. Nehmer, D.A., Reitz, R.D.: Measurement of the effect of injection rate and split injections on diesel engine soot and NOx emissions. SAE Paper No. 940668 (1994)
8. Tow, T.C., Pierpont, D.A., Reitz, R.D.: Reducing particulate and NOx emissions by using multiple injections in a heavy duty DI diesel engine. SAE Paper No. 940897 (1994)
9. Park, S., Kim, H., Shin, D., Lee, J.: Effects of various split injection strategies on combustion and emissions characteristics in a single-cylinder diesel engine. Appl. Therm. Eng. (2018)
10. How, J., Masjuki, H., Kalam, M., Teoh, Y.: Influence of injection timing and split injection strategies on performance, emissions, and combustion characteristics of diesel engine fueled with biodiesel blended fuels. Fuel (2018)
11. Park, H., Bae, C., Ha, C.: A comprehensive analysis of multiple injection strategies for improving diesel combustion process under cold-start conditions. Fuel (2019)
12. Yahliu, K., Boehman, A., Armas, O.: Emissions from different alternative diesel fuels operating with single and split fuel injection. Fuel (2010)
13. Thurnheer, T., Edenhauser, D., Soltic, P., Schreiber, D., Kirchen, P., Sankowski, A.: Experimental investigation on different injection strategies in a heavy-duty diesel engine: emissions and loss analysis. Energy Convers. Manage. **52**(1), 457–467 (2011)

14. Mohan, B., Yang, W., Chou, S.K.: Fuel injection strategies for performance improvement and emissions reduction in compression ignition engines a review. Renew. Sustain. Energy Rev. **28**, 664–676 (2013)
15. Yao, M., Wang, H., Zheng, Z., Yue, Y.: Experimental study of n-butanol additive and multi-injection on HD diesel engine performance and emissions. Fuel **89**(9), 2191–2201 (2010)
16. Jorques Moreno, C., Stenlaas, O., Tunestal, P.: Influence of small pilot on main injection in a heavy-duty diesel engine, SAE Technical Paper 2017-01-0708 (2017). https://doi.org/10.4271/2017-01-0708
17. Liu, W., Song, C.: Effect of post injection strategy on regulated exhaust emissions and particulate matter in a HSDI diesel engine. Fuel **185**, 1–9 (2016)
18. O'Connor, J., Musculus, M.P.B., Pickett, L.M.: Effect of post-injections on mixture preparation and unburned hydrocarbon emissions in a heavy-duty diesel engine. Combust. Flame **170**(111), 23 (2016)
19. Abdul Rehman, K., Ramesh, A.: Studies on the effects of methane fraction and injection strategies in a bio-gas diesel common rail dual fuel engine. Fuel **236**, 147–165 (2019)
20. Lu, Y., Liu, Y.: Effects of multiple injections on combustion and emissions in a heavy-duty diesel engine at high load and low speed. Adv. Mech. Eng. **12**(12) (2020). https://doi.org/10.1177/1687814020984628
21. Osama, G., Gabriel, B.L.: The impact of ammonia-diesel blend combustion on a cleaner environment. Adv. Sci. Technol. Res. J. **20**(1), 451–461 (2026). https://doi.org/10.12913/22998624/211473

Smart Transportation Infrastructure, Safety, and Resilience

Analysis of Seasonality in the Relationship Between Rainfall and Urban Railway Train Delays

Yuto Shimizu[(✉)] and Kazuhiko Tsuda

Tsukuba University, Tsukuba, Japan
`s2430131@u.tsukuba.ac.jp`

Abstract. Urban railways in Japan such as those in the capital region are subject to chronic train delays, which have led to a decline in punctuality and quality of service. Therefore, to reduce these delays, it is necessary to clarify their mechanisms. Previous studies attempted to clarify the mechanisms of delays in urban railways. Rainfall is one of the causes of delays as it affects congestion factors due to concentration of passengers and vehicle performance such as acceleration and braking, but few studies have quantitatively analysed and clarified its impact. In addition, as the impact of rain on the train running performance also varies with temperature, the impact is deemed to be seasonal, but few studies have clarified this observation. Therefore, this study aims to quantitatively clarify the impact of rainfall by station and train using train operation record data and weather data from the Tokyo Metro Tozai Line acquired in seconds, and further analyse whether it is seasonal.

Keywords: Urban Railway · Train Delay · Rainfall · Seasonally

1 Introduction

Urban railways in Japan such as in Tokyo are attempting to improve passenger convenience by increasing the number of trains and building quadruple tracks. However, they also face the issue of chronic delays [1]. Railway delays lead to a loss of punctuality and a significant decline in the quality of service. Furthermore, in urban railways that operate frequently, a delay of a train is likely to cause a phenomenon known as knock-on delay [2], in which the delay spreads to subsequent trains. Consequently, a delay for a single train can affect the entire line. In addition, subway and suburban railway companies in Japan have recently started operating direct trains in urban areas. Therefore, if a delay occurs on one train, its impact is not limited to one line, but may spread to other directly connected lines. When train delays spread, more passengers are affected. If the effects of a delay spread to more trains, it takes longer for the delay to be resolved, thus affecting more passengers. As train delays reduce the quality of service for many passengers, it is necessary to clarify the mechanisms by which delays occur and spread. This is particularly important for urban railways, where the affected areas and number of passengers are large.

A. Razminia et al. (Eds.): ITFT 2025, CCIS 2876, pp. 159–169, 2026.
https://doi.org/10.1007/978-3-032-20592-6_15

Rain and other weather conditions are considered to be causes of delays. The main reason for this is reduced vehicle performance such as reduced acceleration and deceleration owing to skidding and sliding caused by water flow between the rails and wheels [3]. Rainfall is also thought to cause congestion-related delays owing to the concentration of passengers who switch to public transportation such as rail [4]. However, there are fewer rainy days than sunny days. Therefore, there is little data on train operations under rainy conditions, and there is little previous research.

Therefore, in this study, we focused on the relationship with rainfall and investigated whether there are seasonal differences in the effects of rainfall. We also examined whether this could be a factor in the occurrence and expansion of delay phenomena.

2 Literature Review

Oneto et al. [5] described the relationship between rainfall and train delays. They constructed a train-delay prediction model using train operation data from an Italian urban railway. When weather data along the line was added as an external factor to the model, a 10% improvement in accuracy was achieved. Huang et al. [6] constructed a train delay prediction model using parameters representing external factors that affect train delays. By considering weather information as a parameter, they reported that their model had the best accuracy compared to other models. Lapamonpinyo et al. [7] proposed a real-time train delay prediction model using machine learning techniques, using operational data from intercity railroads in the US. They found that meteorological data such as precipitation contributed to improving the model's performance, and that on some of the target lines, train delays increased as the amount of precipitation per hour increased. Mesbah et al. [8] used data on tram operations in Melbourne to create a linear model with travel time as the dependent variable and analyzed the correlation with meteorological data such as precipitation and temperature. They found that an increase in precipitation increases the average travel time, having a negative impact. However, these studies used intercity railways such as high-speed railways as case studies, which differ from urban railways in terms of the frequency and operation format. And then, trams can be affected by road congestion, and to investigate the impact of rainfall on the railway itself, the analysis needs to be carried out on routes where road and railway tracks are separated. In addition, Chen et al. [9] considered the effect of temperature on vehicle performance. They examined the ease with which wheel slip varies depending on the temperature, and noted that wheels become less slippery with temperature rise. This means that rainfall during cold seasons may have a greater impact on delays than rainfall during warm seasons. Brazil et al. [10] used a case study of railways in the Dublin metropolitan area to analyze the relationship between weather and delays by month. They found that bad weather, primarily rainfall, can have a significant impact on certain travel times. While further research is needed, they found that rainfall has a particularly large impact from late autumn to early winter. These studies suggest that the impact of rainfall may vary by season. However, these studies did not explicitly examine the relationship between rainfall and departure and arrival times by station or time period. However, when railway operators implement measures to address delays, identifying which stations and sections are most affected can help them implement more effective measures.

Therefore, the purpose of this study is to clarify whether the relationship between train delays and rainfall on urban railways varies depending on the season, by specifying each station and each train.

3 Creating a Dataset for Analysis

3.1 Train Operation Data

In this study, we used data for 203 days between 1 April 2015 and 25 March 2016 (the fiscal year 2015 timetable), excluding days when there were major transport disruptions such as accidents and vehicle breakdowns. By excluding days when factors other than rainfall affected delays, we were able to observe the impact of rainfall on train delays more clearly. We processed the train operation record for the Tokyo Metro Tozai Line, which is a 30.8 km line that runs from the Nishi-Funabashi Station in Funabashi City, Chiba Prefecture to the Nakano Station in Nakano Ward, Tokyo (Fig. 1).

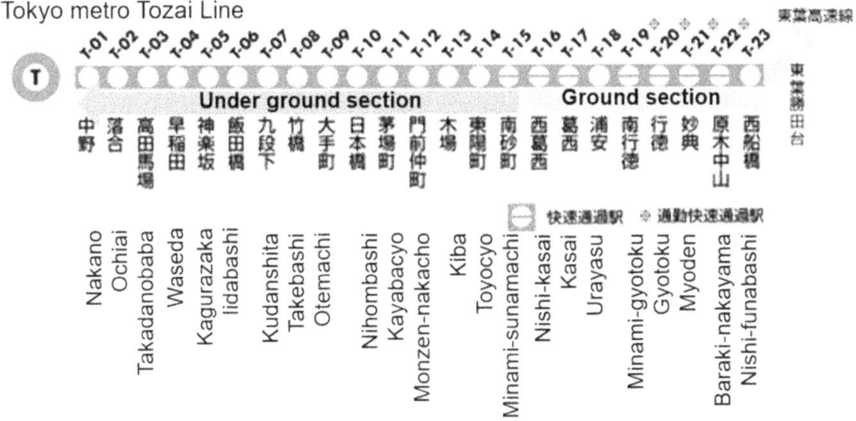

Fig. 1. Tokyo Metro Tozai Line route map

This line has two main features. First, it has an aboveground section even though it is a subway. In Fig. 1, this section is between the Nishi-Funabashi and Minami-Sunamachi stations. In the aboveground sections, the tracks get wet from rain, which can reduce train performance and cause delays. Second, the line is extremely crowded. The Tozai line passes through Otemachi and Iidabashi stations in central Tokyo and is used by many people commuting to work or school from Chiba Prefecture and the eastern part of Tokyo's 23 wards towards the city centre during the morning rush hour. Although trains run frequently during the morning rush hour, approximately once every two to three minutes, they are very crowded with the congestion rate between Kiba and Monzen-Nakacho stations (2023) being 148%. The average congestion rate of the 31 line sections running in the metropolitan area is 136%. Therefore, it is clear that the Tokyo Metro Tozai line is one of the most crowded lines.

Table 1 presents a portion of the training data. The arrival and departure times of each train at each station as well as the delay time were recorded in seconds. A total of 327 trains were covered per day, which included all trains heading from Nishi-Funabashi station towards Nakano station during this period. No changes in the timetable were made during the data collection period.

Table 1. Train operation data.

Date	Train Number	Station Name	Arrival Time	Delay (Second)	Departure Time	Delay (Second)
4/1	A0419S	Toyocho			4:58:15	15
4/1	A0419S	Minami-sunamachi	4:59:50	0	5:00:13	13
4/1	A0419S	Nishi-kasai	5:02:54	1	5:05:18	2
4/1	A0419S	Kasai	5:04:55	5	5:09:27	2
4/1	A0419S	Urayasu	5:07:21	4	5:11:32	7

3.2 Rainfall Data

Data from the Japan Meteorological Agency refer to hourly precipitation extracted from weather data observed by AMeDAS. To reproduce the rainfall conditions at each station on the Tokyo Metro Tozailine as accurately as possible, observation points were selected along the line at Funabashi, Edogawa-Rinkai, Tokyo (Otemachi), and Nerima, and hourly precipitation data were obtained for the same period as the train operation data. These data are presented in Table 2. For example, it is evident that in the hour leading up to 7 p.m. on April 1st, rainfall of "1.5 mm/h" was observed at the observation point: Funabashi.

Table 2. Rainfall data (along the Tozai line).

Date	Time	Funabashi (mm/h)	Edogawa-Rinkai (mm/h)	Tokyo(Otemachi) (mm/h)	Nerima (mm/h)
4/1	0	0	0	0	0
4/1	1	0	0	0	0
4/1	2	0	0	0	0
4/1	:	:	:	:	:
4/1	19	1.5	1	0.5	0

3.3 Rainfall Data

First, the data of train operations and rainfall were combined. This was performed by combining the precipitation data observed at each observation point during each time period for the section and time traversed by the train. To reproduce the rainfall conditions during the time periods when each train ran as faithfully as possible, the straight-line distance between each station and observation point was calculated, and the observation point with the closest distance was selected. The combinations of observation points for the Japan Meteorological Agency data are listed in Table 3.

Table 3. The relation between observation points and each station on the east-west line.

Station No.	Station	Observation Point
23	Nishi-Funabawshi	Funabashi
22	Baraki-nakayama	Funabashi
21	Myoten	Edogaqa-rinkai
:	:	:
14	Toyocho	Edogawa-rinkai
13	Kiba	Tokyo (Otemachi)
:	:	:
2	Ochiai	Tokyo (Otemachi)
1	Nakano	Nerima

In addition, the time was combined to determine the time period when the train was running and the hourly precipitation amount for the same time period at the nearest observation point, as shown in Table 3. The results are summarised in Table 4.

Table 4. Combined dataset.

Date	Train Number	Station Name	Hourly Precipitation amount	Departure Time	Delay (s)	Arrival Time	Delay (s)
4/1	A0419S	Toyocho	0			4:58:15	15
4/1	A0419S	Minami-sunamachi	0	4:59:50	0	5:00:13	13
4/1	A0419S	Nishi-kasai	0	5:02:54	1	5:05:18	2
4/1	A0419S	Kasai	:	5:04:55	5	5:09:27	2
4/1	A0419S	Urayasu	0.5	5:07:21	4	5:11:32	7
:	:	:	:	:	:	:	:

The combined data was then divided into "Rainfall" and "Non-Rainfall" train data. Data on trains where no rainfall was observed between the starting and ending stations on the Tozai line was classified as "Non-Rainfall" train data, while data on trains where precipitation was observed at least in some section during the time period in which the train was running was classified as "Rainfall" train data.

In addition, to focus on the seasons, the rainfall and non-rainfall train data were further divided into two periods, which were determined based on the monthly average temperature data observed by the Japan Meteorological Agency in Tokyo (Otemachi). This was done to consider the influence of crowding factors due to seasonal differences in clothing and the influence of train performance factors due to differences in the surrounding and rail temperatures [7]. The monthly average temperatures for the data acquisition period from April 2015 to March 2016 are shown in Table 5, and the four months with the highest and lowest temperatures were extracted from the data. As a result, Period 1 was set to June, July, August, and September, and Period 2 was set to December, January, February, and March, and the data for each period was extracted from the "Combined Dataset" and then divided. Hereafter, Period 1 will be referred to as the "Warm Period" and Period 2 the "Cold Period".

Table 5. Monthly average temperature data (observation point: Tokyo (Otemachi)).

Month	Monthly Average Temperature	Month	Monthly Average Temperature	Month	Monthly Average Temperature
4	14.5	8	26.7	12	9.3
5	21.1	9	22.6	1	8.1
6	22.1	10	18.4	2	7.2
7	26.2	11	13.9	3	10.1

The number of trains for each data point is listed in Table 6, and these data were used for subsequent analyses.

Table 6. Number of trains for each data point.

Data	Rainfall Train Data	Non-rainfall Train Data
Warm Period	9704	34161
Cold Period	2468	38853

4 Result of Analysis

For both "Rainfall" and "Non-Rainfall" train data, we tallied the number of seconds of delay in departure and arrival times at each station for each train number, and calculated, analysed the median. It may be noted that a train number is assigned to each operating train, which helps disseminate information regarding its schedule and running status. Therefore, by analysing each train, it is possible to determine the trains and time periods that are significantly affected by rainfall.

First, we compared "Rainfall" and "Non-Rainfall" train data for each period. Figures 2 and 3 show the comparison results for the "Warm Period". This shows that the "Rainfall" train data had longer delays than "Non-Rainfall", especially during the morning and evening rush hours. In particular, in the "Rainfall" train data, the longest delay in the morning rush hour was 382 s (for a train arriving at Otemachi Station at 8:50), whereas in the "Non-Rainfall" train data, the longest delay in the morning rush hour was 233 s (for a train arriving at Otemachi Station at 8:41), meaning that the delays were approximately 1.6 times longer. Please try to avoid rasterized images for line-art diagrams and schemas.

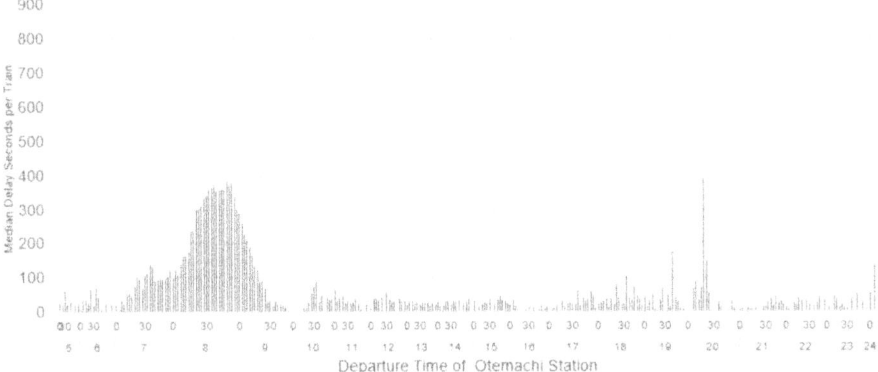

Fig. 2. Distribution of delay seconds ("Rainfall" train data" and "Warm Period").

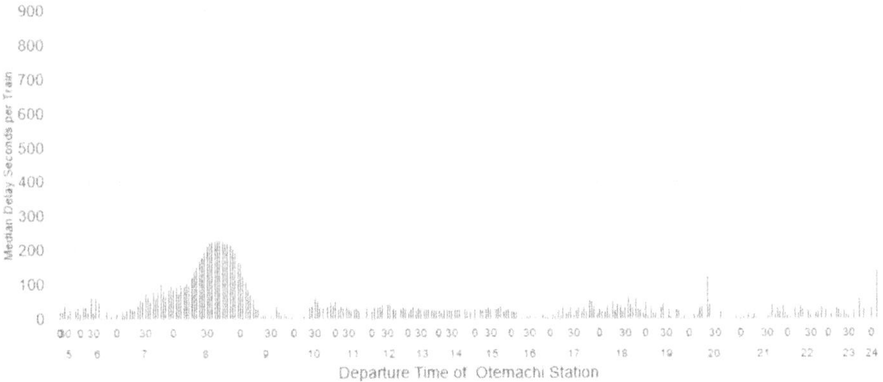

Fig. 3. Distribution of delay seconds ("Non-Rainfall" train data" and "Warm Period").

Next, the comparison results for the "Cold Period" are shown in Figs. 4 and 5. During this period as well, the delay times for trains during rainfall were longer, particularly during the morning and evening rush hours. Similarly, when comparing the delays of the trains with the longest delays during the morning rush hour, the "Rainfall" train data shows a delay of 849 s (train arriving at Otemachi Station at 8:36), while the "Non-Rainfall" train data shows a delay of 292.5 s (train arriving at Otemachi Station at 8:36), which is approximately 2.9 times longer.

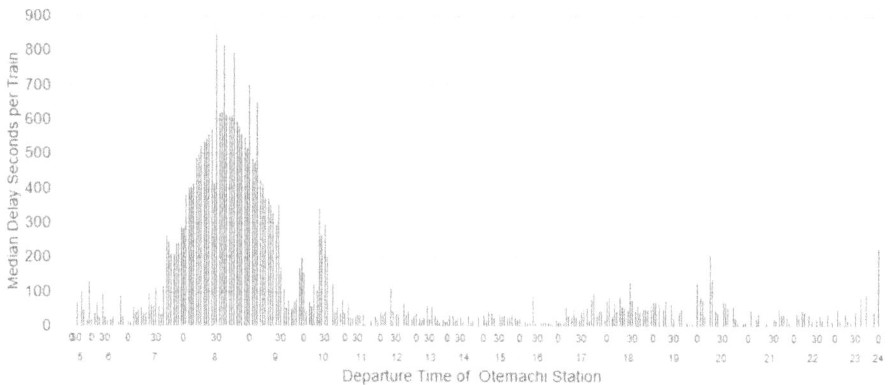

Fig. 4. Distribution of delay seconds ("Rainfall" train data" and "Cold Period").

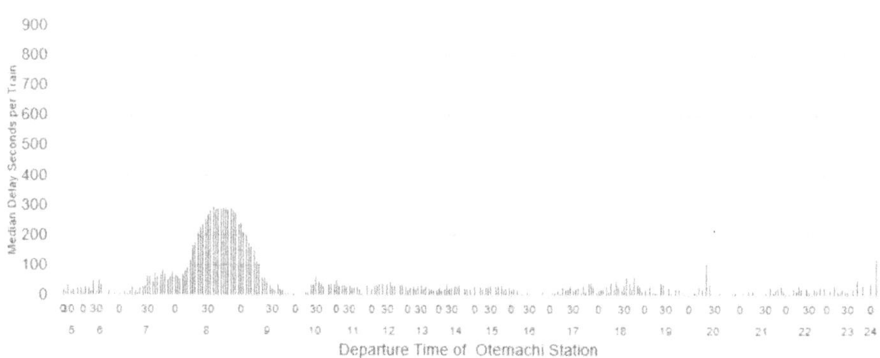

Fig. 5. Distribution of delay seconds ("Non-Rainfall" train data" and "Cold Period").

From the above results, it is evident that the delay time under precipitation conditions is longer in the "Cold Period" compared to the "Warm Period".

Next, we analysed the delay situation not only at Otemachi Station, but also for other trains, and calculated the extent of the delay over a wide area. First, Fig. 6 shows the comparison of results between "Rainfall" and "Non-Rainfall" train data during the "Warm Period". Figure 6 was extracted during the morning rush hour, which is particularly affected by rain. In both datasets, delays occurred mainly during the morning and evening rush hours. Focusing on the morning rush hour in particular, it was found that the trains arriving at Kayabacho Station (Station No. 11) between 8:30 and 9:00 were the most delayed. However, the "Rainfall" train data had a wider range of times and sections with delays over a wide area. Delays of "Rainfall" train data tended to occur in sections closer to Nishi-Funabashi station (Station No. 23), and delays exceeded 100 s for trains arriving at Otemachi station (Station No. 9) around 7:30. When counting the number of data with a median delay of 100 s or more at each station arrival time for each train, there were 770 data points for "Rainfall" and 383 data for "Non-Rainfall" train data, which shows a wide area spread.

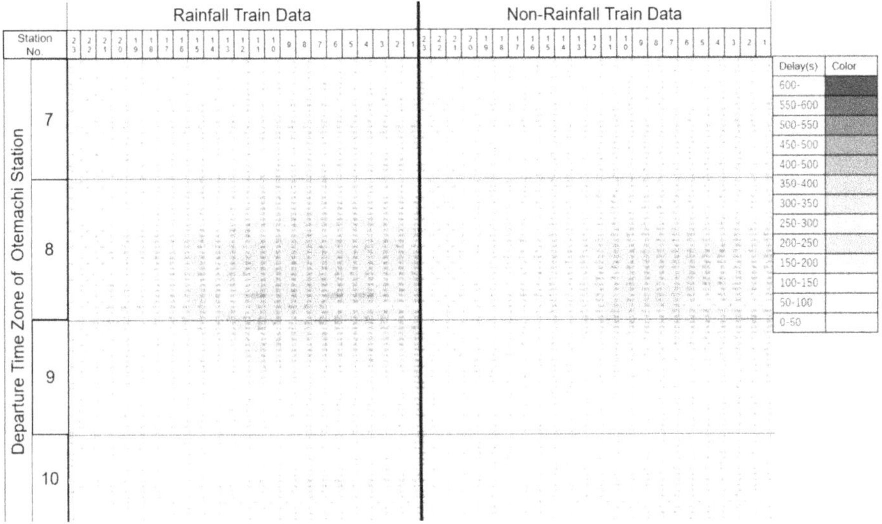

Fig. 6. Distribution of delay seconds ("Warm Period").

Next, "Rainfall" and "Non-Rainfall" train data for the "Cold Period" are shown in Fig. 7. As in the "Warm Period", delays occurred mainly during the morning and evening rush hours. When counting the number of data points with a median delay of 100 s or more for each train's arrival time at each station, there were 1,392 data points for rainfall data and 453 data points for non-rainfall train data, showing a wide area spread.

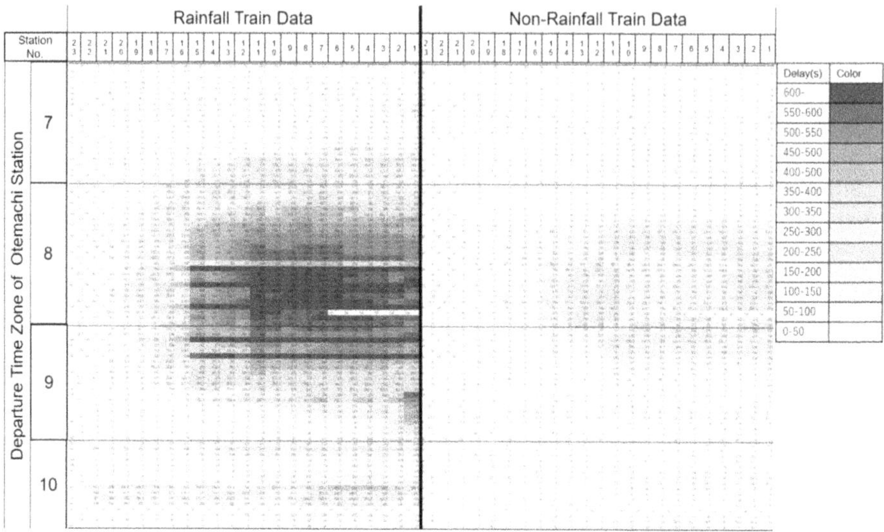

Fig. 7. Distribution of delay seconds ("Cold Period").

Furthermore, when comparing the "Warm Period" and "Cold Period" data on trains, the "Cold Period" was more affected by delays in terms of the area. In particular, the section affected in the "Warm Period" was west of Minami-Sunamachi station (Station No. 15), while in the cold period, it was west of Gyotoku station (Station No. 20), and delays occurred from earlier sections. Counting the number of data points with a median delay time of 100 s or more for each train's arrival time at each station, there were 770 data points in the "Warm Period" and 1,392 in the "Cold Period", and delays in the "Cold Period" were more extensive in terms of the area. In particular, in the "Cold Period", It can be seen that the section from Minami-Sunamachi Station to Nakano Station (Station No. 1) is where the delay time is greater than that of the previous station. At Minami-Sunamachi station, train delays were amplified even when there was no rainfall. As the Minami-Sunamachi station is an underground section, it is possible that congestion factors as well as vehicle performance are related, and that congestion may have increased due to passengers' clothes expanding in winter, which may have led to larger delays in the "Cold Period".

5 Conclusion

We were able to confirm seasonal differences in the impact of rainfall on train delays, both in the "Warm Period" and the "Cold Period". Rainfall affected train delays in both periods. In particular, delays tended to increase during the "Cold Period" and this tendency was clear when viewed from the surface. In conclusion, a clear seasonal relationship exists between rainfall and train delays on urban railways.

In addition, this study can help design measures to reduce delays. For example, during busy times such as the morning rush hour, staff are sometimes deployed to guide passengers to board and disembark smoothly. Measures can be taken to increase the number of staff on "Cold Period" days when it rains. In addition, off-peak commuting can be encouraged by clearly indicating and informing passengers about trains and stations prone to delays. In particular, by considering the new condition of "Cold Period" to rainfall, greater effects can be expected.

The following two points should be considered in future initiatives. First, congestion data should be examined. For example, by recreating congestion conditions using data on the number of passengers passing through ticket gates, it is possible to analyse delay mechanisms that consider congestion caused by changes in mode choices due to rainfall. The second issue concerns the accumulation of data. For the Tokyo Metro Tozai line, there are few rainy days during the cold season. Therefore, this analysis clarifies the strong impact of each individual train. To address this issue, additional data must be collected.

Acknowledgements. The train operation data used in this study was provided by Tokyo Metro Co., Ltd. We would like to express our gratitude here. And we would like to thank Editage (www.editage.jp) for English language editing.

References

1. Kariyazaki, K., Hibino, N., Moriguchi, S.: Study on mechanism of worsening punctuality in urban railway services. Infrastruct. Plann. Rev. **27**, 871–879 (2010)
2. Carey, M., Kwiecinski, A.: Stochastic approximation of the effects of headways on knock-on delays of trains. Transp. Res. Part B **28**, 251–267 (1994)
3. Kazuhiko, N.: The state of adhesion between rails and running wheels on main lines (results investigated by the slipping adhesion test truck). Bull. JSME C **54**(504), 1852–1860 (1988)
4. Takayama, J., Shioji, K.: An analysis on travel mode changes of commuters for public transportation planning. Infrastruct. Plann. Rev. **15**, 517–525 (1998)
5. Oneto, L., et al.: Dynamic delay predictions for large-scale railway networks: deep and shallow extreme learning machines tuned via threshold out. IEEE Trans. Syst. Man Cybern. Syst. **47**, 2754–2767 (2017)
6. Huang, P., et al.: Modeling train operation as sequences: a study of delay prediction with operation and weather data. Transp. Res. Part E Logistics Transp. Rev. **141**, 102022 (2020)
7. Lapamonpinyo, P., Derrible, S., Corman, F.: Real-time passenger train delay prediction using machine learning: a case study with Amtrak passenger train routes. IEEE Open J. Intell. Transp. Syst. **3**, 539–550 (2022)
8. Mesbah, M., Lin, J., Currie, G.: "Weather" transit is reliable? Using AVL data to explore tram performance in Melbourne, Australia. J. Traff. Transp. Eng. (Engl. Ed.) **2**(3), 125–135 (2015)
9. Chen, H., Ban, T., Ishida, M., Nakahara, T.: Experimental investigation of influential factors on adhesion between wheel and rail under wet conditions. Wear **265**(9), 1504–1511 (2008)
10. Brazil, W., White, A., Nogala, M., Caulfield, B., O'Connor, A., Morton, C.: Weather and rail delays: analysis of metropolitan rail in Dublin. J. Transp. Geogr. **59**, 69–76 (2017)

Predictive Maintenance Framework for Intelligent Transportation Infrastructure Using IoT and Machine Learning: Remote Area Roads in Indonesia

Andri Irfan Rifai[1,2]([✉]) [iD], Susanty Handayani[3] [iD], Muhammad Isradi[4] [iD], Joewono Prasetijo[5] [iD], Marvin Tandedi[6] [iD], and Yusra Aulia Sari[1] [iD]

[1] Faculty of Civil Engineering and Planning, Universitas Internasional Batam, Batam, Indonesia
`andri.irfan@uib.ac.id`
[2] Directorate General of Highway, Jakarta, Indonesia
[3] Trisakti Institute of Transportation and Logistics, Jakarta, Indonesia
[4] Faculty of Engineering, Universitas Mercu Buana, Jakarta, Indonesia
[5] Department of Transportation Engineering, Universiti Tun Hussein Onn Malaysia, Parit Raja, Malaysia
[6] School of Earth and Environment, Faculty of Environment, University of Leeds, Leeds, UK

Abstract. This study develops and validates a comprehensive predictive road-maintenance framework for intelligent transportation infrastructure in remote areas of Indonesia, integrating the Internet of Things (IoT), machine learning algorithms, and digitalization. A mixed-methods research design was employed across four strategically selected provinces (South Sulawesi, Central Sulawesi, West Papua, and Southwest Papua), integrating multi-source data from Hawkeye vehicle-mounted systems, manual field inspections, motion-sensing cameras, and 10-year historical maintenance records from the Directorate General of Highways. The hybrid machine learning architecture, combining Random Forest and Long Short-Term Memory (LSTM) networks, achieved prediction accuracies ranging from 95.2% (7-day forecasts) to 77.4% (90-day forecasts), with consistently superior performance in Sulawesi provinces compared to the Papua region. The IoT survey demonstrated operational effectiveness, with system uptime ranging from 94.3% in South Sulawesi to 76.2% in Southwest Papua, directly correlating with the maturity of telecommunications infrastructure. Economic analysis revealed cost reductions of 26.4% to 34.2% across provinces, with return on investment periods ranging from 14 to 26 months, demonstrating financial viability despite regional implementation challenges. Statistical analysis confirmed a strong positive correlation (r = 0.912) between baseline infrastructure quality and prediction accuracy, providing empirical validation for targeted investment strategies.

Keywords: Predictive road maintenance · IoT sensors · machine learning · transportation infrastructure · remote areas

A. Razminia et al. (Eds.): ITFT 2025, CCIS 2876, pp. 170–179, 2026.
https://doi.org/10.1007/978-3-032-20592-6_16

1 Introduction

The rapid expansion of global transportation networks necessitates innovative approaches to infrastructure maintenance, particularly in remote and geographically challenging regions where traditional methods prove inadequate. International discourse on sustainable development emphasizes the critical role of intelligent transportation systems in achieving United Nations Sustainable Development Goals, specifically SDG 9 (Industry, Innovation, and Infrastructure) and SDG 11 (Sustainable Cities and Communities) [1]. Contemporary global challenges include escalating maintenance costs, with global transport infrastructure investment requirements projected to reach approximately \$2.7 trillion annually by 2035, and unpredictable equipment failures that threaten economic stability in developing nations.

The integration of Internet of Things (IoT) technologies with artificial intelligence has emerged as a transformative solution, enabling predictive maintenance strategies that achieve cost reductions of up to 28% while preventing 92% of unexpected failures. Indonesian transportation infrastructure exemplifies broader challenges faced by archipelagic developing nations, with the country's vast territory comprising over 17,000 islands, creating unique maintenance challenges that traditional approaches cannot adequately address [2, 3]. National logistics costs in Indonesia accounted for 14.29% of the country's GDP in 2023, significantly exceeding optimal targets and underscoring inefficiencies in the current transportation management systems [4, 5].

Recent scholarly investigations from 2021 to 2025 have demonstrated substantial progress in IoT-enabled predictive maintenance and digital twin applications across various transportation infrastructure domains. The developed machine learning-based predictive maintenance systems use Boost algorithms, achieving 88% accuracy in predicting equipment failures. Additionally, they systematically examine digital twin enabling technologies for road engineering applications [6, 7]. Contemporary research has investigated the applications of artificial intelligence in predictive maintenance, demonstrating real-time capabilities for monitoring infrastructure health [8]. These studies collectively indicate that AI-driven predictive maintenance can achieve a 28% reduction in maintenance expenditures while extending the lifespan of infrastructure [9, 10].

Despite significant advances in predictive maintenance technologies, critical research gaps persist in integrating artificial intelligence, digital twin technology, and data mining approaches specifically for remote transportation infrastructure applications in developing countries [11]. Current research predominantly focuses on urban environments with robust connectivity infrastructure, leaving substantial knowledge gaps regarding implementation in remote areas with limited communication networks, challenging geographical conditions, and resource constraints [12, 13]. Island regions and mountainous areas, such as Indonesia, have remote areas that are diverse and difficult to access. This research aims to develop a comprehensive predictive maintenance framework for intelligent transportation infrastructure in remote regions of Indonesia, integrating IoT sensor networks, machine learning algorithms, and data mining to address identified research gaps and contribute to sustainable transportation development [14, 15].

2   Research Method

2.1   Research Design

This study employs a mixed-methods research design combining quantitative data analysis with qualitative assessment to develop and validate a predictive maintenance framework for intelligent transportation infrastructure in remote areas of Indonesia. The research methodology employs a data-driven approach, utilizing comprehensive datasets collected through advanced monitoring technologies, including Hawkeye vehicle-mounted systems, manual field inspections, GoPro action camera recordings, and historical maintenance records from the Directorate General of Highways spanning the past decade [16, 17].

The research design encompasses five main phases: (1) Data Integration and Preprocessing, (2) Predictive Model Development using combined Random Forest and LSTM networks, (3) Model Training and Validation with 70%–30% data split, (4) Predicted vs Measured Comparative Analysis, and (5) Qualitative Feasibility Assessment for IoT and Machine Learning Implementation across Sulawesi and Papua regions [18].

2.2   Data Collection Framework

Data collection encompasses four strategically selected provinces representing diverse geographical and infrastructure development contexts across Indonesia's eastern regions: South Sulawesi and Central Sulawesi, which represent more developed infrastructure contexts, and West Papua and Southwest Papua, which represent extreme geographical challenges and limited infrastructure development. Selection methodology ensures adequate representation of different climate zones, topographical conditions, traffic volumes, and maintenance histories [17, 19].

Fig. 1. The use of motion-sensing cameras and Internet of Things (IoT) devices for surveying road conditions in remote areas.

Data collection was conducted comprehensively on national roads under various conditions. Some survey locations were in mountainous, remote areas with good road conditions. The survey was also conducted in locations with unstable road conditions, as seen in Fig. 1. To collect data on road terrain and locations difficult to reach by conventional survey vehicles, a 4 × 4 vehicle and wheel modifications were used. The survey vehicle selection was carried out to ensure the motion camera could capture data continuously and without interruption.

2.3 Machine Learning Model Development

The predictive maintenance framework employs a hybrid machine learning architecture that combines Random Forest and Long Short-Term Memory (LSTM) networks to leverage both spatial pattern recognition and temporal sequence prediction. Random Forest algorithms handle non-linear relationships between infrastructure condition indicators and environmental factors by leveraging ensemble learning with multiple decision trees to achieve robust predictive accuracy across diverse geographic conditions [19, 20]. LSTM networks capture temporal dependencies in infrastructure degradation patterns by processing sequential data with specified hidden units and dropout rates, thereby preventing overfitting while maintaining predictive accuracy over extended time horizons [21]. Feature importance analysis using Shapley values identifies the most influential variables for optimizing prediction accuracy [22, 23].

3 Results and Discussion

3.1 Introductory Context for Indonesian Road Infrastructure Analysis

Indonesia's national road network, spanning approximately 47,604 km across 37 provinces and seven major geographical regions, is a complex archipelagic infrastructure system characterized by significant variations in pavement performance and maintenance challenges. The deliberate selection of four research provinces—Central Sulawesi, South Sulawesi, West Papua, and Southwest Papua—uses a purposive sampling approach that captures the key divide between Indonesia's developed and remote regions.

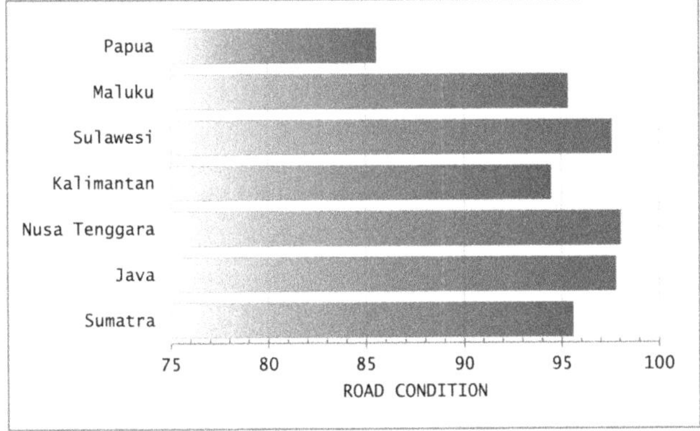

Fig. 2. Regional disparities in pavement performance

These provinces account for 5,436 km (11.4%) of the national network and offer representative coverage of different geographical, topographical, and socio-economic environments. Figure 2 demonstrates significant regional disparities in pavement performance across Indonesia's national road network, with condition indices ranging from 98.07% in Nusa Tenggara to 85.58% in Papua, reflecting underlying infrastructure development patterns and geographical challenges. The analysis reveals that developed regions (Java, Nusa Tenggara, and Sulawesi) consistently achieve condition indices above 97%, indicating well-maintained pavement structures with minimal distress and optimal serviceability levels, while eastern peripheral regions, particularly Papua, exhibit substantially lower performance metrics that correlate with limited accessibility, challenging topographical conditions, and historical underinvestment in transportation infrastructure.

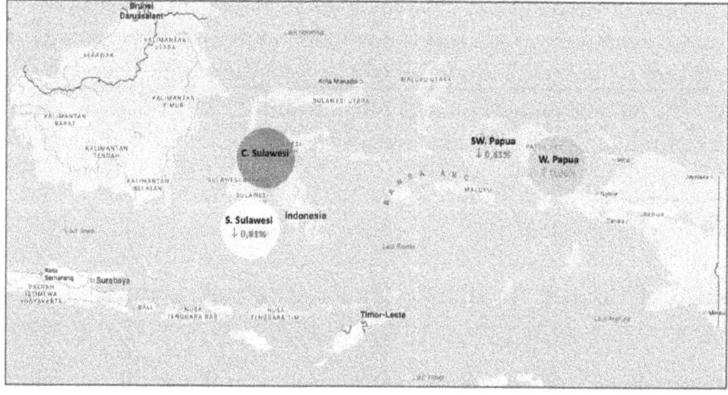

Fig. 3. Comparative analysis of pavement condition performance across the four research provinces

Figure 3 presents a temporal comparative analysis of pavement condition performance across the four research provinces, revealing heterogeneous trends that validate the differential maintenance requirements between Sulawesi and Papua regions during the six-month evaluation period from late 2024 to early 2025. South Sulawesi demonstrated the most significant change, with condition indices decreasing from 98.31% to 97.48% ($\Delta = -0.81\%$), indicating less effective maintenance interventions and suboptimal pavement maintenance strategies. Conversely, both Central Sulawesi and West Papua experienced marginal deterioration, reflecting the natural degradation of pavements under regular traffic loading and environmental exposure, without corresponding maintenance interventions.

3.2 Research Implementation Overview

The predictive maintenance framework was implemented and validated across four strategically selected Indonesian provinces, covering a 3,833-km road network and 35 research sites strategically positioned to capture representative conditions of remote-area transportation infrastructure. In detail, the research data summary is presented in

Table 1. The comprehensive data collection campaign generated 8,609 total data points across diverse geographical contexts, ranging from South Sulawesi's developed lowland tropical conditions with high population density (179 per km^2) to Southwest Papua's challenging highland tropical environment with minimal population density (6 per km^2) and extreme elevations approaching 1,000 m above sea level.

Table 1. Research data summar

Province	Road Segments (km)	Data Points	Research Sites	Population Density (per km^2)	Climate Zone
South Sulawesi	1,739	2,847	12	179	Tropical Lowland
Central Sulawesi	2,361	2,156	9	67	Tropical Mountain
West Papua	802	1,934	8	9	Highland Tropical
Southwest Papua	532	1,672	6	6	Highland Tropical

Data collection intensity highlighted logistical challenges in remote areas, with Papua provinces requiring significantly more operational hours for Hawkeye vehicles (187–203 h) than the more accessible Sulawesi provinces (134–156 h), due to rugged terrain and limited roads access.

3.3 Infrastructure Condition Analysis

The baseline infrastructure condition assessment revealed significant disparities between Sulawesi and Papua provinces, which directly affect the performance of the predictive maintenance framework and the economic benefits. The infrastructure condition analysis shows a clear regional trend, with Sulawesi provinces having higher infrastructure standards than those in Papua. Table 2 describes road conditions by scale in each province.

Table 2. Infrastructure condition distribution

Province	Good Condition (%)	Fair Condition (%)	Poor Condition (%)
South Sulawesi	46.30	52.01	1.69
Central Sulawesi	33.04	64.42	2.54
West Papua	44.25	40.80	14.95
Southwest Papua	37.62	52.16	10.22

South Sulawesi achieved the strongest performance, with 46.3% of its roads in good condition, reflecting historical investment patterns, geographical advantages, and its strategic importance as the primary logistics hub for eastern Indonesia. These disparities correlate strongly with historical patterns of infrastructure investment and the effectiveness of Special Autonomy Fund allocation.

3.4 Machine Learning Model Performance

The hybrid machine learning architecture combining Random Forest and LSTM networks demonstrated robust predictive capabilities across all four provinces, with performance variations reflecting regional infrastructure and operational contexts. The model validation achieved exceptional short-term prediction accuracy, with consistently superior performance in Sulawesi provinces compared to Papua regions.

Table 3. Machine learning performance results

Province	7-Day Accuracy (%)	30-Day Accuracy (%)	90-Day Accuracy (%)	Average Accuracy (%)
South Sulawesi	95.2	91.3	85.9	90.8
Central Sulawesi	94.1	89.8	83.2	89.0
West Papua	92.7	87.1	79.8	86.5
Southwest Papua	91.4	85.6	77.4	84.8

In Table 3, short-term predictions (7-day forecasts) range from 95.2% in South Sulawesi to 91.4% in Southwest Papua, demonstrating the framework's effectiveness for immediate maintenance planning. Long-term predictions (90 days) showed the greatest regional variation, with South Sulawesi achieving 85.9% accuracy compared to Southwest Papua's 77.4%, highlighting the challenges of extended forecasting under variable environmental conditions. Statistical analysis confirmed a strong positive correlation ($r = 0.912$, $p = 0.0884$) between baseline infrastructure quality and prediction accuracy, validating the hypothesis that better-maintained infrastructure enables more accurate prediction modeling.

3.5 IoT Sensor Network Performance

Comprehensive IoT sensor network deployment demonstrated significant regional performance variations directly correlating with existing telecommunications infrastructure and geographical challenges. In Table 4, the sensor network achieved varying operational effectiveness across provinces, with system uptime percentages ranging from 94.3% in South Sulawesi to 76.2% in Southwest Papua. The significant performance disparities between the Sulawesi and Papua provinces reflect fundamental differences in telecommunications infrastructure maturity and maintenance accessibility.

Table 4. IoT performance metrics

Province	System Uptime (%)	Data Transmission (%)	Response Time (sec)	Sensor Reliability (%)
South Sulawesi	94.3	92.4	2.1	96.8
Central Sulawesi	91.7	89.7	2.4	95.1
West Papua	78.9	67.3	4.7	89.4
Southwest Papua	76.2	63.8	5.3	87.2

3.6 Discussion

The comprehensive implementation and validation of the predictive maintenance framework across South Sulawesi, Central Sulawesi, West Papua, and Southwest Papua provides critical insights into the challenges and opportunities of intelligent transportation infrastructure management in diverse Indonesian contexts. The consistently superior performance achieved in Sulawesi provinces compared to Papua regions reflects fundamental differences in baseline infrastructure quality, connectivity infrastructure, and operational environments that must be considered in national infrastructure development strategies.

The demonstrated correlation between baseline infrastructure quality and predictive maintenance effectiveness ($r = 0.912$) supports targeted investment strategies that prioritize infrastructure improvements in regions with the greatest potential for technological enhancement. South Sulawesi's position as a major agricultural producer and logistics hub, and its achievement of 34.2% cost reduction, demonstrate how infrastructure technology can amplify existing economic advantages while supporting national development objectives. The significant performance gaps between Sulawesi and Papua provinces highlight the continued importance of the Special Autonomy Fund program and suggest that technology-enhanced maintenance strategies could improve returns on existing infrastructure investments. The successful operation of IoT sensor networks, achieving 76–94% uptime across diverse geographical conditions, demonstrates the viability of advanced monitoring technologies in remote areas of Indonesia.

4 Conclusions

This research successfully developed and validated a comprehensive predictive maintenance framework for intelligent transportation infrastructure in remote areas of Indonesia, demonstrating significant potential to transform maintenance practices while addressing the unique challenges faced by archipelagic developing nations. The hybrid machine learning architecture, combining Random Forest and LSTM networks, achieved robust predictive capabilities with accuracy ranging from 95.2% (7-day forecasts) to

77.4% (90-day forecasts). Meanwhile, IoT sensor networks proved operationally effective, with system uptime ranging from 76% to 94% across diverse geographical conditions. Economic analysis revealed substantial cost reductions of 26.4% to 34.2% across provinces, with ROI periods ranging from 14 to 26 months, confirming the financial viability despite regional implementation challenges. The strong positive correlation ($r = 0.912$) between infrastructure quality and prediction accuracy provides empirical support for targeted investment strategies.

Additionally, successful stakeholder engagement, with an overall support rate of 87.3%, confirms social acceptability across diverse cultural contexts. The framework's contribution to addressing Indonesia's high logistics costs (14.29% of GDP) supports the Sustainable Development Goals while offering scalable solutions for managing transportation infrastructure in remote regions. Future research should expand the framework to include multimodal transportation systems, develop more advanced adaptive algorithms to handle variable environmental conditions, and explore integrating emerging technologies such as 5G networks and AI-enhanced satellite monitoring systems to further improve predictive capabilities and operational efficiency in challenging geographic contexts.

References

1. Ozili, P.K.: Financial inclusion, sustainability and sustainable development. In: Smart Analytics, Artificial Intelligence and Sustainable Performance Management in a Global Digitalised Economy, pp. 233–241. Emerald Publishing Limited (2023)
2. Zhang, C., Cui, L., Yu, S., Yu, J.J.Q.: A communication-efficient federated learning scheme for IoT-based traffic forecasting. IEEE Internet Things J. **9**, 11918–11931 (2021)
3. Elassy, M., Al-Hattab, M., Takruri, M., Badawi, S.: Intelligent transportation systems for sustainable smart cities. Transp. Eng. **16**, 100252 (2024)
4. Hadiningrat, K.P.S.S., Wiradanti, B., Umar, Y.F.: Transformation of Indonesian sea transportation and maritime logistics to realize the vision of golden Indonesia 2045. Jipower J. Intellect. Power **1**, 89–107 (2024)
5. Arif, M., Muta'ali, L., Rijanta, R.: Mapping poverty traps in Indonesia: a spatial perspective. Reg. Stat. **15** (2025)
6. Elkateb, S., Métwalli, A., Shendy, A., Abu-Elanien, A.E.B.: Machine learning and IoT–based predictive maintenance approach for industrial applications. Alex. Eng. J. **88**, 298–309 (2024)
7. Saki, R., Toomanian, A., Neysani Samany, N., Rajabifard, A.: The process of smartening road traffic management systems using open-source solutions: simulating traffic flow, volume, speed and ITS impact on road safety in a digital twin platform. Int. Arch. Photogramm. Remote. Sens. Spat. Inf. Sci. **48**, 1309–1314 (2025)
8. Ajayi, R.: Integrating IoT and cloud computing for continuous process optimization in real-time systems. Int. J. Res. Publ. Rev. **6**, 2540–2558 (2025)
9. Lembangan, M.O., Nurdiah, E.A.: A review of BIM implementation in Indonesia's smart cities: challenges and opportunities. Adv. Civil Eng. Sustain. Archit. **7**, 46–59 (2025)
10. Pan, Y., Lei, L., Shen, G., Zhang, X., Cao, P.: A survey on digital twin networks: architecture, technologies, applications and open issues. IEEE Internet Things J. (2025)
11. Rifai, A.I., Isradi, M., Prasetijo, J., Sari, Y.A., Zolkepli, M.F.: Data mining approach-based damage identification for asphalt pavement under natural disaster conditions. Civil Eng. J. **10**(12), 4043–4057 (2024)

12. Wu, Y., Sicard, B., Gadsden, S.A.: A review of physics-informed machine learning methods with applications to condition monitoring and anomaly detection. arXiv preprint arXiv:2401. 11860 (2024)
13. Rifai, A.I., Prasetijo, J., Isradi, P., Sari, Y.A., Zolkepli, M.F.: Flood and landslide exposure awareness for mitigation of road network performance a community-based approach. SINERGI **29**(2), 411–422 (2025)
14. Herzfeldt, A., Ertl, C., Floerecke, S.: Maintenance 4.0: applying IoT technologies to increase uptime and efficiency of critical infrastructures. In: Handbook on Digital Platforms and Business Ecosystems in Manufacturing, pp. 327–343. Edward Elgar Publishing (2024)
15. Omol, E., Mburu, L., Onyango, D.: Anomaly detection in IoT sensor data using machine learning techniques for predictive maintenance in smart grids. Int. J. Sci. Technol. Manage. **5**, 201–210 (2024)
16. Jinca, M.Y., Asdar, M.: Effectiveness of sea toll road in logistics distribution in coastal area of Sorong regency. Pak. J. Life Soc. Sci. **22** (2024)
17. Imran, M.A., et al.: Exploring the boundaries of connected systems: communications for hard-to-reach areas and extreme conditions. Proc. IEEE **112**, 912–945 (2024)
18. Dave, D.M.K., Mittapally, B.K.: Data integration and interoperability in IoT: challenges, strategies and future direction. Int. J. Comput. Eng. Technol. (IJCET) **15**, 45–60 (2024)
19. Ugulu, A.I., Wohlmuth, K.: Assessing the performance of SDG 9 targets for financial services and agriculture, energy and transport infrastructure, mining and social welfare–an introduction. Sustain. Dev. Goal Nine Afr. Dev. Challenges Opportunities **22**, 165 (2022)
20. Kuncoro, E., Wurarah, R.N., Erari, I.E.: The impact of road infrastructure development on ecosystems and communities. Soc. Ecol. Econ. Sustain. Dev. Goals J. **1** (2024)
21. Rajendran, R.M., Vyas, B.: Detecting apt using machine learning: comparative performance analysis with proposed model. In: SoutheastCon 2024, pp. 1064–1069. IEEE (2024)
22. Alqasi, M.A.Y., Alkelanie, Y.A.M., Alnagrat, A.J.A.: Intelligent infrastructure for urban transportation: the role of artificial intelligence in predictive maintenance. Brilliance Res. Artif. Intell. **4**, 625–637 (2024)
23. Celestin, M.: How predictive maintenance in logistics fleets is reducing equipment downtime and operational losses. Brainae J. Bus. Sci. Technol. (BJBST) **7**, 1023–1033 (2023)

Numerical Simulation Study on the Influence of Grid Ceiling on Smoke Diffusion in Subway Platform Fire

Kaoqi Li[1,2], Huan Wang[1(✉)], and Jiaqi Zhang[1,3]

[1] School of Safety Engineering, Shenyang Aerospace University, Shenyang 110136, China
20180012@sau.edu.cn
[2] School of Emergency Management and Safety Engineering, China University of Mining and Technology, Beijing 10008, China
[3] China Nuclear Industry 22ND Construction CO., LTD., Wuhan 430051, China

Abstract. Currently, transparent ceilings are commonly employed in subway stations. Compared with other types of ceilings, in the event of a fire, a portion of the smoke will penetrate into the ceiling interior through the pores of the ceiling grilles, exerting a certain influence on smoke diffusion. To investigate the impact of grid ceilings on smoke diffusion and passenger evacuation, this project focuses on Shenyang Aerospace University Subway Station. The Pyrosim software is utilized to simulate the entire process of fire development on the platform level. This study compares the effects of three distinct ceiling configurations - closed ceilings, open ceilings (no ceiling), and transparent ceilings - on the pattern of fire smoke dispersion. For Grid ceiling, an analysis is conducted on the temperature distribution of fire smoke and the visibility within the fire zone under scenarios where the perforation rates are 25%, 33%, 50%, 67%, and 80%. The findings indicate that the smoke storage space created by transparent ceilings can slow down the spread of smoke on the platform level during the initial stage of a fire, facilitating the containment of high-temperature smoke at a safe altitude. As the perforation rate increases, the resistance of the grid ceiling to the plume movement of smoke weakens, and the downward movement of high-temperature smoke becomes more pronounced. In comparison to closed ceilings, grid ceilings significantly enhance the visibility on the platform level, providing advantageous conditions for passenger evacuation. However, variations in the perforation rate do not have a significant impact on smoke visibility.

Keywords: Grid ceiling · Subway station fire · Smoke diffusion · Numerical simulation

1 Introduction

With the continuous advancement of urbanization, urban rail transit plays an increasingly important role in the transportation system of cities. By the end of 2024, 361 urban rail transit lines had been opened in 58 cities in China, with an operating mileage of 12,160.77 km. The subway accounted for the largest proportion, with an operating mileage of

9,306.09 km, accounting for 76.53% [1]. However, the continuous expansion of the operation scale also poses a further challenge to the subway fire safety. Due to the fact that subway structures are buried underground, their spatial structure is unique and the environment is restricted. Compared with other rail transit tools, once a fire breaks out on a subway platform, the large amount of smoke generated is not easy to be discharged, which is highly likely to cause major casualties. Therefore, the issue of smoke flow and control under the condition of subway fire has been widely concerned by scholars at home and abroad. Shi et al. [2–4] studied the characteristics of smoke transport in deep-buried island stations through a series of reduced-scale experiments, and analyzed the visibility and temperature of the station hall. F. Liu, Long et al. [5–7] used full-scale experiments to investigate the key parameters such as temperature distribution and smoke height of subway platform fire. In the research of smoke flow control, the focus is mainly on ventilation methods, parameters of smoke exhaust systems, etc. May studied the impact of different ventilation methods on the safety evacuation of personnel [8], and Junfeng Chen discussed the critical conditions for smoke prevention at two key openings of the staircase [9]. Park et al. [10] investigated the influence of exhaust volume on the movement characteristics of hot smoke through numerical simulation. Chen [11], Zhong [12, 13] analyzed the impact of the direction, height, and number of smoke exhaust outlets on smoke prevention efficiency. Meng et al. [14–16] studied the influence of platform screen doors (PSD) in metro stations on smoke exhaust and evacuation during fires. The above research provides excellent suggestions for the application of fire prevention in metro stations.

Currently, the subway generally adopts the form of grid ceiling, which has the advantages of convenient equipment maintenance and visual extensibility. However, relevant studies have shown that the transparent ceiling may affect the performance of detectors due to the existence of gaps [17], as the result of that it affects the smoke flow process. Given that previous studies have not fully considered the impact of different ceiling forms on smoke flow, and the current fire protection regulations have not specified the dimensions and related safety requirements of ceilings, this paper will use numerical simulation methods to compare the smoke flow processes of different metro ceiling forms, explore whether the transparent ceiling is beneficial to smoke control and personnel evacuation, and provide new ideas and basis for the design and construction of metro smoke control systems, as well as scientific and reasonable suggestions for the smoke control design of metro ceilings.

2 Methodology

2.1 Research Object

This paper takes the Shenyang Aerospace University Station of Shenyang Metro Line 2 as the research object. The station is located in Shenbei New District, Shenyang City. Its geographical location is shown in Fig. 1. The surrounding area is a large commercial complex, universities, supermarkets, etc., with a large passenger flow. The station is a two-story underground island-type station with a total of four exits. The underground first floor is the station hall, with a length of 104 m, a width of 25 m, and a height of 3 m. The second floor is the platform, with a length of 120 m, a width of 25 m, and a height of 4.8 m. There are two escalators and one elevator between the platform and the concourse. Fully enclosed platform screen doors are installed on both sides of the platform to completely separate the platform from the tunnel. The floor plan of the metro station is shown in Fig. 2. In addition, a 0.5 m-high smoke barrier is set at the position where the escalator penetrates the platform floor.

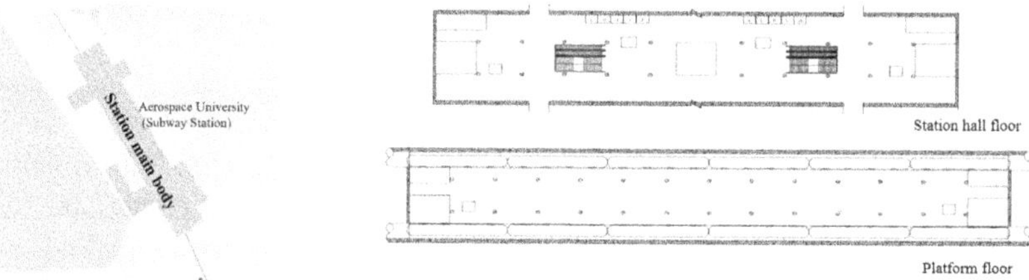

Fig. 1. Location of Aeronautics University Subway station

Fig. 2. Subway building plan

2.2 Numerical Model

Pyrosim, a fire dynamics simulation, is used to build the numerical model of subway station. The physical model of the island subway station is shown in Fig. 3. The actual structure of the subway is simplified, and 20 platform columns are retained while the equipment and structures that have little impact on the simulation results, such as the turnstiles, are ignored.

The fire type designed in this paper is the passenger luggage fire, which is the most common fire type in the public areas of subway stations. The fire source power is 1.6 MW, with a size of 1 m × 1 m × 1 m, located in the center between two staircases, which is the area with the largest passenger flow during daily operation. The combustion reaction adopts the GM37 reaction provided in the SFPE Fire Protection Handbook, which is rigid polyurethane foam plastic. The combustion products are set with a CO production rate of 0.024 and a smoke dust production rate of 0.113. The initial conditions are set with a temperature of 20 °C, standard atmospheric pressure, and a relative humidity of 55%. Four exits are set as open surfaces, directly connected to the outside, and the simulation duration is 600 s.

(a) Top view   (b) 3D view

Fig. 3. Overview of the subway station model structure

2.3 Fire Scenario

This paper mainly explores the influence of grid ceiling form on fire smoke diffusion, so only the change of ceiling on the platform floor is considered, and the platform floor is in the form of no ceiling. Two groups of experiments are planned. In the first group, three scenarios are designed, corresponding to no ceiling, closed ceiling and transparent ceiling (the hollow rate is 25%). In the second experiment, four different hollowing-out rates were designed to study the influence of hollowing-out rate factors. Based on the field investigation, the hollowing-out rate of permeable ceiling is generally between 50% and 96%, and the hollowing-out rates under the selected test conditions are 33%, 50%, 63% and 80% respectively, and the width of the single member of permeable ceiling is 1.5 m See Table 1 for specific fire scene design parameters. In order to obtain the variation law of key parameters of flue gas flow, a set of thermocouples are set at intervals of 2 m along the longitudinal direction of the platform at 0.2 m below the ceiling of the station hall, and a set of visibility monitoring points are set at intervals of 2 m around the fire source at a height of 2 m.

This paper mainly explores the influence of the grid ceiling form on the diffusion of fire smoke. Therefore, only the changes in the ceiling of the platform level are considered, while the station hall is all without ceiling. Two groups of experiments are planned. The first group of experiments designs three scenarios, corresponding to no ceiling, closed ceiling and grid ceiling (hollow rate 25%). The second group of experiments takes the grid ceiling as the object and designs four different hollow rate to study the influence of the hollow rate factor. Field research shows that hollow rate of the grid ceiling is generally between 50% and 96%. The selected test conditions have hollow rate of 33%, 50%, 63% and 80%. The width of the grid ceiling single component is 1.5 m. The specific fire scene design parameters are shown in Table 1. In order to obtain the variation law of the key parameters of smoke flow, a set of thermocouples are set at intervals of 2 m along the longitudinal direction of the platform at 0.2 m below the ceiling of the station hall, and a set of visibility monitoring points are set at intervals of 2 m around the fire source at a height of 2 m.

Table 1. Summary of simulation conditions

Number	Ceiling form/ Hollow rate(α)	Construction width/m	Gap width/m
Case1	No ceiling	1.5	-
Case2	Enclosed ceiling		-
Case3	Grid ceiling		0.5
Case4	33%		0.73
Case5	50%		1.5
Case6	63%		3
Case7	80%		6

3   The Impact of Ceiling Form on the Smoke Diffusion

3.1   Smoke Diffusion Process

As shown in the Fig. 4, it shows the fire smoke diffusion process in case1–case3. When time t = 30 s, the smoke generated by combustion reaches the ceiling under buoyancy and begins to spread around the ceiling, that is, the ceiling jet stage. At this time, the smoke is mainly concentrated in the center of the platform floor and the area between the two evacuation escalators. In the case of the grid ceiling, part of the smoke enters the ceiling through the grid, which hinders the horizontal movement of the flue gas along the ceiling. Therefore, compared with other conditions, the smoke spread distance is obviously shorter and the spread speed is slower. At the same time, it can be seen that a small amount of smoke flows into the platform floor from the escalator crossing the roof, but not in the other two conditions. Which shows that the gride ceiling forms an unsealed smoke storage bin and accelerates the vertical movement of smoke. When t = 60 s, the smoke has spread to both sides of the platform floor, and the smoke from the platform floor in case2 and case3 spreads near the escalator, while the smoke from the platform floor in case1 is less. At t = 120 s, with the continuous combustion, under the action of gravity, the smoke on the platform layer sinks obviously and the smoke layer thickens. The smoke from the station floor diffuses in the center of the station floor, among which the smoke from the station floor in case1 is the least, followed by case2 and case3, which is mainly caused by the different vertical flow heights of the smoke in the plume stage. T = 240 s, the smoke layer basically covers the whole platform layer, and the smoke spread range in case3 of the platform layer is the largest, and the smoke in case1 and case2 is mainly concentrated near the evacuation escalator, and the smoke in case1 is still the least.

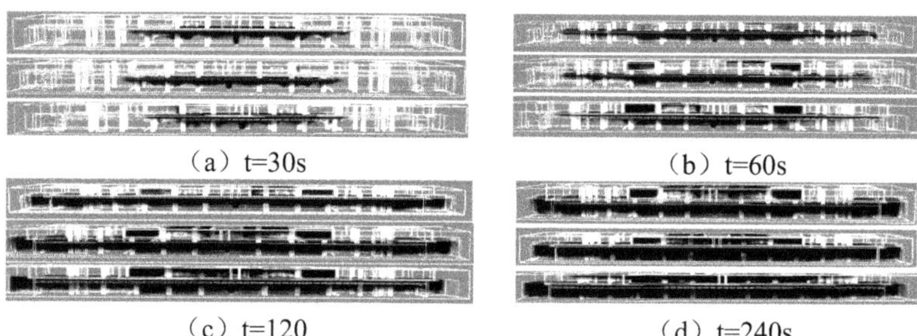

<table>
<tr><td align="center">（a）t=30s</td><td align="center">（b）t=60s</td></tr>
<tr><td align="center">（c）t=120</td><td align="center">（d）t=240s</td></tr>
</table>

Fig. 4. Smoke spreading process

3.2   Smoke Spread Rate

Through the analysis of the dynamic process of smoke diffusion as shown in Fig. 4, the position and propagation speed of smoke diffusion front are determined. As shown in Fig. 5, the left Y axis represents the smoke diffusion position, and the right Y axis is used to derive the smoke diffusion rate. As can be seen from the figure, the spread time of the smoke layer front measured in the three working conditions basically increases linearly with the distance. When there is a fire in the subway platform, the smoke spreads rapidly under the ceiling, and the spread speed of the smoke layer is faster in the early stage. With the increase of the horizontal distance of the smoke layer from the fire source, the temperature of the smoke layer front and the temperature difference between it and the ambient air become lower and lower, and this buoyancy driving force is also small, which leads to the continuous decrease of the spread speed of the smoke layer front. The time taken to move to the 50 m position of the fire source under three working conditions is 57 s, 63 s and 66 s respectively. In case 3, the smoke diffusion speed is the slowest, with a maximum peak of 0.89 m/s. In case 1 and case 2, the smoke diffusion rates is faster, with maximum peaks of 1.05 m/s and 0.95 m/s respectively.

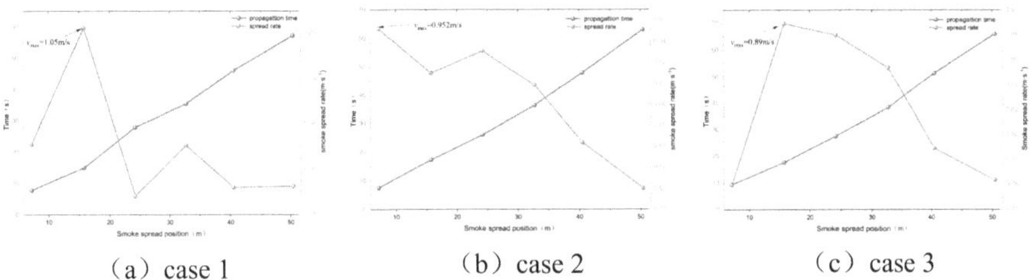

(a) case 1   (b) case 2   (c) case 3

Fig. 5. Smoke spread position and spread rate of station platform fire.

3.3 Temperature Distribution

The temperature distribution characteristics of smoke diffusion on the platform floor are given is Fig. 6 in the 480 s of fire development under three cases. As shown in Fig. 6(a), in the condition without a ceiling, the isotherms on both sides of the flow field are symmetrically distributed. The temperature of the smoke is the highest above the fire source, reaching 550 °C, and gradually decreases at the horizontal position far from the fire source. In the vertical direction, the farther away from the ceiling, the lower the temperature of the smoke. From the ceiling ($z = 4.8$) to the height of 2.7 m the temperature drops from 100 °C to 50 °C. Near the fire source area, when at the same height, the temperature variation does not change much with the horizontal position.

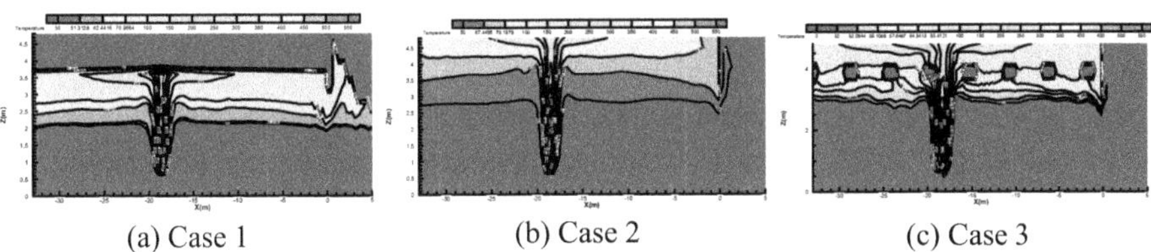

(a) Case 1   (b) Case 2   (c) Case 3

Fig. 6. Temperature field along the longitudinal direction of subway platform

As shown in Fig. 6(b), the adoption of the closed ceiling leads to a reduction in the clear height of the platform space. Relevant literature indicates that a decrease in the clear height will result in a reduction in the mass flow rate of the smoke plume and an increase in the average temperature of the smoke layer, which is consistent with the isothermal line results in the figure. In the vertical direction, the farther away from the ceiling, the lower the temperature of the smoke. From the height of the closed ceiling (z = 3.7 m) to the height of 2 m, the temperature drops from 100 °C to 50 °C. The downward movement of the high-temperature smoke has an adverse effect on the evacuation of personnel. Figure 6(c) shows that the plume flow experiences pulsation due to the obstruction of the gride during the ceiling jet process, resulting in irregular isotherms. In the vertical direction, the farther away from the ceiling, the lower the smoke temperature. From the ceiling (z = 4.8 m) to the height of 3.0 m region, the temperature drops from 100 °C to 50 °C. By comparing Fig. 6(a) and Fig. 6 (b), it can be seen that the temperature gradient of the vertical smoke layer decreases, which can be understood as the effect of the grid can accumulate high temperature smoke above the ceiling and keep it at a certain height.

4 The Impact of Hollow Rate on the Smoke Diffusion

4.1 Smoke Spread Rate

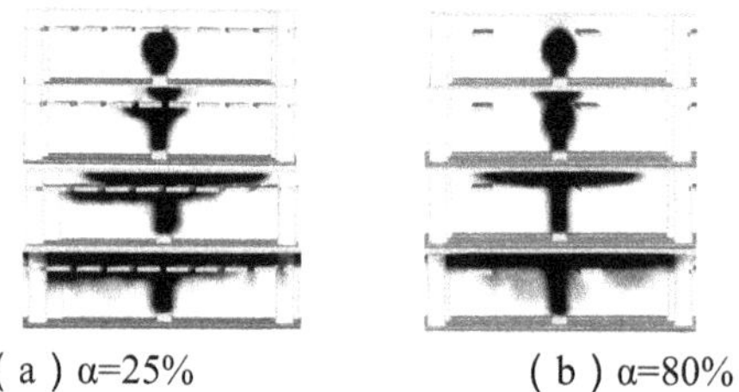

(a) α=25%   (b) α=80%

Fig. 7. Smoke flow process near the ceiling

Figure 7 shows the flow state of smoke plume near the ceiling under the condition that the hollow rate of the ceiling is 25% and 80% respectively. As shown in the figure, the smoke moves upward under the buoyancy in the plume stage, and when it encounters the ceiling, if the hollow rate is relatively low (α = 25%), a part of the smoke enters the interior of the ceiling through the gap and continues to move upward, while another part moves horizontally along the underside of the ceiling, forming a bifurcated flow in two directions. Subsequently, the smoke both inside and outside the ceiling moves horizontally. As the heat of the smoke inside the ceiling dissipates, the buoyancy decreases, and a small amount of smoke settles through the gaps in the ceiling. When the hollow ratio is relatively high (α = 80%), it can be observed that the upward-moving smoke smoothly passes through the ceiling and all enters the interior of the ceiling, forming a ceiling jet. After moving horizontally for a period of time under the ceiling, a small amount of the settled smoke forms a wall-attached flow along the underside of the ceiling due to the viscous force.

4.2 Temperature Distribution

The smoke temperature distribution in the platform floor with different hollow rates at a certain time is analyzed, which is given in Fig. 8. The results suggest the temperature in most areas of the ceiling is maintained at 50–100 °C under four cases. With the increase of hollow rate, the 50 °C isotherm of the temperature field moves down gradually, and when the hollow rate is 80%, the height of the isotherm drops to 2.9 m. To further analyze the influence of the hollow rate on the internal temperature of the ceiling, the temperature detected by the horizontal thermocouple string inside the ceiling at t = 480 s is plotted as shown in Fig. 9. The longitudinal distribution curves of the temperature inside the ceiling with different hollow rates are similar. When a fire occurs on the platform, the temperature at the ceiling above the fire source rises sharply, with the maximum temperature increase ranging from 145 to 224 °C.

As the distance from the fire source increases, the smoke temperature decreases rapidly at the stairs on both sides of the platform (within 20 m from the fire source). Comparing the temperature data of the platform near the fire source with different hollow rates, as shown in Fig. 10, the longitudinal distribution of temperature shows some differences. The larger the hollow rate, the smaller the obstruction of ceiling to smoke, and the more smoke from ceiling jet, the higher the ceiling temperature rise. At the same position, the greater the hollow rate, the stronger the heat accumulation effect inside the ceiling and the higher the temperature.

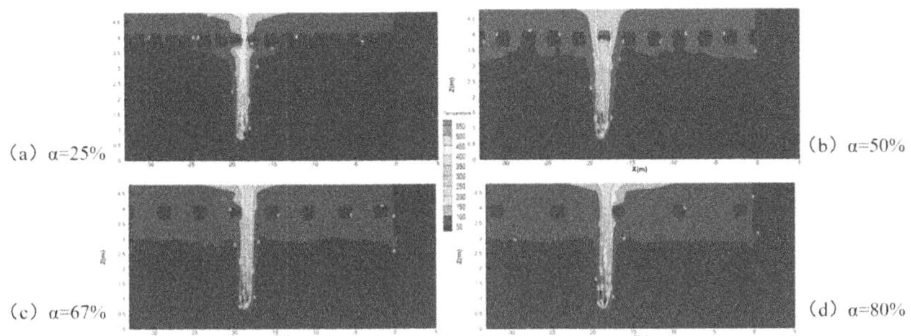

Fig. 8. Temperature contours at a vertical plane

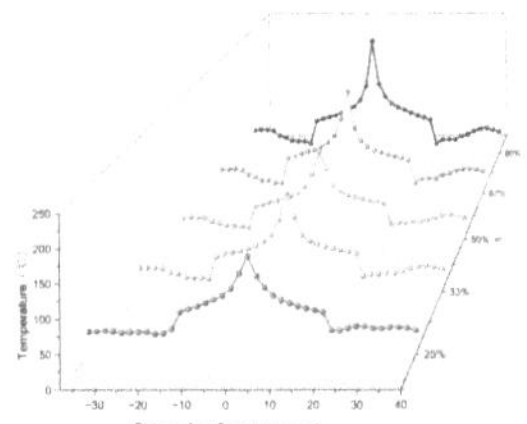

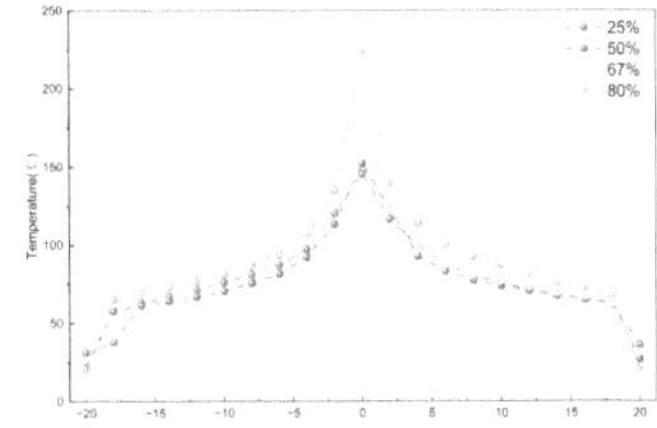

Fig. 9. Longitudinal temperature distribution with different α

Fig. 10. Longitudinal temperature distribution Near fire source

4.3 Visibility

Visibility is one of the safety criteria for personnel evacuation in the event of a fire. To analyze the influence of the change in the ceiling hollow rate on personnel evacuation in the platform, the monitoring point for visibility indicators is set at the characteristic height of the human eye at the staircase evacuation exit. Figure 11 shows the variation of visibility with time at monitoring points under enclosed ceiling case. For the large space of subway platform, the critical visibility index is 10 m. Therefore, based on the real-time visibility change curve, the moment when the visibility index determines the danger of personnel evacuation is found to be 87 s after the fire occurs. The visibility change curve of the monitoring point for the hollow rate α ranging from 25% to 80% are shown in Fig. 12. Through the above method, the dangerous time of personnel are obtained as 128 s, 118 s, 114 s, 120 s, and 118 s respectively. Although the data do not indicate any specific relationship between the hollow ratio and the evacuation time, which is shown in Fig. 13. Compared with the closed ceiling, the maximum available evacuation time has increased by 47%. The grid ceiling has a significant effect on increasing the available evacuation time.

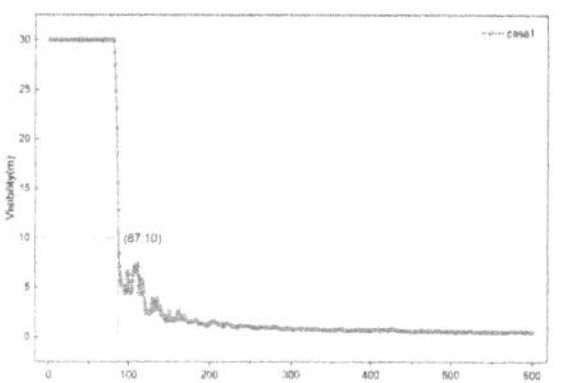

Fig. 11. Curve of visibility with time at monitoring point for closed ceiling

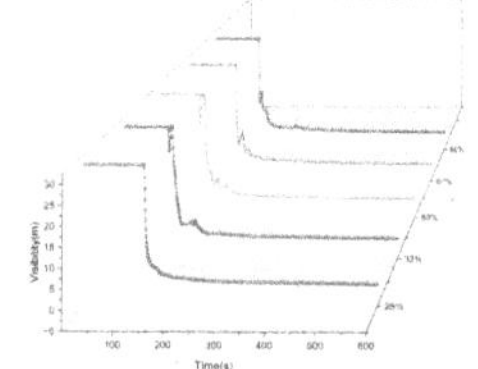

Fig. 12. Curve of visibility with time at monitoring point for various hollow rate

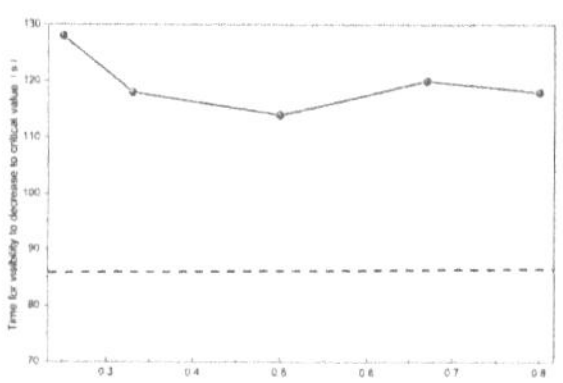

Fig. 13. The available safe evacuation time for various hollow rate

5 Conclusion

This paper established a full-scale numerical model of the metro platform based on the Shenyang Aerospace University metro station. Firstly, it discussed the diffusion characteristics of smoke under three ceiling forms: no ceiling, closed ceiling, and grid ceiling. Further, it analyzed the influence of the gird ceiling's hollow rate on the movement of high temperature smoke and personnel evacuation. The main conclusions are as follows:

1) Compared with no ceiling, the fire plume path in a closed ceiling is shorter, less air is entrained, the horizontal spread speed of smoke decreases, and the high temperature smoke sinks. Due to the grid structure, a semi-enclosed smoke storage chamber is formed under the ceiling in a grid ceiling, which can accumulate high temperature smoke in the early stage of a fire and slow down the spread of smoke. As the fire develops, the effect of the grid smoke storage chamber gradually disappears without smoke exhaust facilities.

2) The hollow rate will affect the smoke diffusion process. During the plume phase, when the hollow ceiling is encountered, if the hollow ratio is low, part of the upward moving plume will continue upward, and the other part will flow along the horizontal bifurcation. When the hollow ratio is high, all the upward moving plume will pass

through the grille gap until it reaches the ceiling, and then emerge from the grille gap during the descent process.

3) As the hollow rate increases, the obstruction effect of the suspended ceiling on smoke decreases, the amount of smoke in the ceiling jet increases, and the ceiling temperature rises, posing a threat to the combustible materials in the space inside the gride ceiling. There is no clear correlation between visibility and hollow rate, but compared with the closed ceiling, the visibility is significantly improved. The maximum available safe evacuation time determined by the visibility index increases by 47%.

Acknowledgements. This work was supported by Shenyang University of Aeronautics and Astronautics Innovation and Entrepreneurship Training Plan for College Students in 2023 (S202310143010).

References

1. China Urban Railway Transit Association: Annual Statistics and Analysis Report on Urban Rail Traffic in 2024
2. Zhong, M., Shi, C., Tu, X., Fu, T., He, L., Li, P.: Experimental modeling study of deep buried metro station fires (1)—experimental design. J. Saf. Sci. Technol. **2**, 5–11 (2006)
3. Shi, C., Zhong, M., Fu, T., He, L., Li, P.: Experimental modeling study of deep buried metro station fires (2)—train fire. J. Saf. Sci. Technol. **2**, 20–24 (2006)
4. Shi, C., Zhong, M., Fu, T., He, L., Li, P.: Experimental modeling study of deep buried metro station fires (3)—train fire. J. Saf. Sci. Technol. **2**, 33–38 (2006)
5. Liu, F., Liu, Y., Xiong, K., et al.: Experimental and numerical study on the smoke movement and smoke control strategy in a hub station fire. Tunn. Undergr. Space Technol. **96** (2020)
6. Long, L., Liu, C., Yang, Y., et al.: Full-scale experimental study on fire-induced smoke movement and control in an underground double-island subway station. Tunn. Undergr. Space Technol. **103** (2020)
7. Chen, J., Zhong, M., Qiu, P., et al.: A study of repeatability of hot smoke test in a subway station. Case Stud. Thermal Eng. **41** (2023)
8. Mei, F.Z., Tang, F., Ling, X., Yu, J.S.: Evolution characteristics of fire smoke layer thickness in a mechanical ventilation tunnel with multiple point extraction. Appl. Therm. Eng. **111**, 248–256 (2017)
9. Chen, J., Li, G., Pan, R., et al.: Numerical study on the airflow characteristics and smoke control condition in stair area of subway stations. J. Build. Eng. **84**, 108577 (2024)
10. Park, W.H., Kim, D.H., Chang, H.C.: Numerical predictions of smoke movement in a subway station under ventilation. Tunn. Undergr. Space Technol. **21**, 304 (2006)
11. Chen, J., et al.: Investigation of the performance of lateral ventilation in subway station fires. J. Wind Eng. Ind. Aerod. 228 (2022)
12. Zhong, W., Sun, C.P., Bian, H.T., Gao, Z.H., Zhao, J.: The plug-holing of lateral mechanical exhaust in subway station: phenomena, analysis, and numerical verification. Tunn. Undergr. Space Technol. **112** (2021)
13. Zhong, W., Wang, H.B., Peng, W.: A study of optimal arrange of vent in a subway station. In: 10th Conference of the International-Building-Performance-Simulation Association. PEOPLES R CHINA, Tsinghua Univ, Beijing, pp. 1262–1266 (2007)
14. Meng, N., Hu, L., Zhu, S., Yang, L.: Effect of smoke screen height on smoke flow temperature profile beneath platform ceiling of subway station: an experimental investigation and scaling correlation. Tunn. Undergr. Space Technol. **43**, 204–212 (2014)

15. Li, D.-Y., Zhu, G.-Q.: Effect of platform screen doors on mechanical smoke exhaust in subway station fire. Proc. Eng. **211**, 343–352 (2018)
16. Wang, W., He, T., Huang, W., Shen, R., Wang, Q.: Optimization of switch modes of fully enclosed platform screen doors during emergency platform fires in underground metro station. Tunn. Undergr. Space Technol. **81**, 277–288 (2018)
17. Chen, N.: Experimental study on the response performance of smoke fire detector in grid suspended ceilings. Fire Saf. Sci. **21**(4), 216–224 (2012)

Application of Three-Dimensional Seismic Isolation (Vibration Isolation) Technology for Schools Near a Subway in Chengdu

Kaiqiang Liu[1($\boxtimes$)], Ye Li[1], Haojian Lu[2], Yuan Jiang[3], Jianghua Wei[1], and Kun Zhang[1]

[1] Benchmark Party China Architectural Design Corporation Limited, Chengdu 610023, Sichuan, China
KaiqiangLiu3456@163.com
[2] Jiazi Park Real Estate Co., Ltd., Chengdu 610041, Sichuan, China
[3] PowerChina Chengdu Engineering Corporation Limited, Chengdu 610072, Sichuan, China

Abstract. This study addresses the environmental pollution caused by structural vibrations and secondary structural noise due to subway operation, as well as the need to ensure the normal operation of newly constructed buildings in earthquake-prone areas under seismic load conditions. Based on a real-world project, the challenges and key issues of vibration isolation, seismic isolation, and vibration control for subway systems are analyzed, and a comparison of potential solutions is conducted. The three-dimensional seismic isolation (vibration isolation) technology is employed to simultaneously simulate the effects of both subway operational excitation and seismic forces on the buildings. Computational analysis and experimental verification indicate that the use of three-dimensional seismic isolation (vibration isolation) bearings can significantly reduce vibration and noise issues caused by subway movements, with a marked decrease in the vibration of teaching buildings and secondary structural noise exceeding allowable limits. Under a rare three-direction seismic event, the application of three-dimensional seismic isolation bearings reduces the peak horizontal acceleration of the upper structure by approximately 60%, demonstrating good horizontal isolation performance. The use of three-dimensional seismic isolation bearings to address the dual control of vibration and seismic effects can substantially save on costs and construction time.

Keywords: Subway operational excitation · Seismic isolation and vibration reduction · Dual control of vibration and seismic effects · Three-dimensional seismic isolation (vibration isolation)

1 Introduction

The vibrations induced by operational excitation and the resulting noise from secondary structures urgently need to be controlled. Buildings located in areas with high seismic risk or in key seismic monitoring and defense zones should adopt technologies such as seismic isolation and damping in accordance with national regulations. Regarding metro vibrations, researchers both domestically and internationally have proposed

A. Razminia et al. (Eds.): ITFT 2025, CCIS 2876, pp. 191–202, 2026.
https://doi.org/10.1007/978-3-032-20592-6_18

various vibration control measures. Wang et al. conducted a simulation study on the ground vibrations generated by elevated metro lines and analyzed the characteristics of vibration propagation and the effectiveness of different control measures [1]. Mei et al. found that the use of a spring-based isolation system could effectively reduce the impact of metro vibrations on buildings [2]. Xiao et al. discovered that both prefabricated and cast-in-situ phononic crystal polymer concrete track beds could effectively reduce vibrations induced by metro operations [3]. Chen et al. studied the application of rubberized self-compacting concrete layers in precast slab tracks and verified the effectiveness of this material in vibration reduction [4]. Wang et al. proposed a board design based on elastic metamaterials that can effectively reduce low-frequency vibrations generated during metro operations and applied it to vibration isolation for metro lines [5]. Li et al. investigated the application of rubber concrete composite barriers in mitigating metro vibrations [6]. Li et al. also improved the overall vibration control effectiveness by combining foundation improvements with isolation devices [7].

With the development of isolation technology, seismic isolation is increasingly being applied to vibration control for metro systems and surrounding buildings. Forcellini and Kalfas proposed the introduction of isolation devices to reduce seismic damage to structures [8]. Miao et al. explored the low-frequency vibration damping mechanism based on phononic crystal structures and suggested that a three-dimensional isolation structure could simultaneously reduce vibration propagation in multiple directions [9]. For metro vibration isolation, rubber bearings have been widely used to separate vibrations between metro tracks and nearby buildings. Cardone et al. explored the seismic performance of low-rise buildings using eco-rubber seismic isolation foundation systems [10]. Xu et al. proposed a novel three-dimensional isolation system that offers more significant seismic damping effects in multiple directions [11]. In isolation systems, selecting environmentally friendly materials has become an important area of research. Ghorbi and Toopchi-Nezhad studied the isolation effects of fiber-reinforced rubber bearings in lightweight structures [12]. In the research on combined isolation for underground and above-ground structures, Zhao et al. proposed a solution that integrates enhanced isolation and energy dissipation for a coupled isolation system between underground and above-ground structures [13].

The number of buildings that need to simultaneously address both subway-induced vibration and seismic isolation is rapidly increasing. However, research on this integrated technology remains insufficient and faces significant challenges. To address this, the present study uses the H07 Primary School in the He Dong District of the Chengdu Jiazi Park Financial Business Area Phase III as a case study to investigate the challenges and key issues of subway vibration isolation and control, compare various solutions, and summarize the application of three-dimensional seismic isolation (vibration isolation) technology, aiming to provide valuable insights for similar projects.

2   Project Overview

The primary school project located in the He Dong District (H07 plot) of the Chengdu Jiaozi Park Financial and Business District Phase III is situated in Jinjiang District, Chengdu, Sichuan Province. The above-ground structure consists of five floors, with one basement level. The building's height is 21.65 m, while the basement ceiling height is 5.4 m. The column grid dimensions are 8.6 m × 8.0 m, 8.6 m × 4.0 m, and 8.6 m × 5.4 m, among others. The structural system adopts a reinforced concrete multi-story frame. The Metro Line 9 passes beneath the road that separates the southern and northern sections of the plot. The outline of the teaching building is located approximately 23 m from the nearest centerline of the metro tracks. The relationship between the teaching building and the metro is shown in Fig. 1.

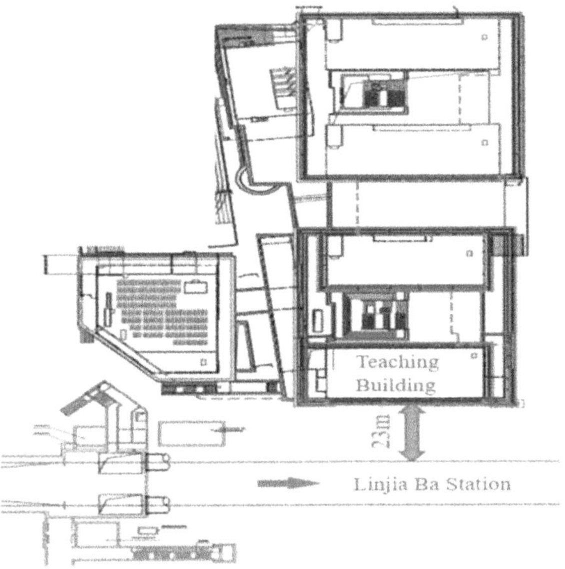

Fig. 1. Relationship between the teaching building and the metro

The seismic fortification intensity of the project is designed for a level of 7, with a basic seismic acceleration of 0.2 g. The site classification is Category II, with the seismic design group being the third group. The characteristic period is 0.45 s, and the seismic fortification category is defined as "key fortification," with a structural safety level of Grade I. The soil layers on the site, from top to bottom, are as follows: unengineered fill, loose gravel layer, slightly dense gravel layer, moderately dense gravel layer, highly weathered mudstone, and moderately weathered mudstone. Below the foundation, the unengineered fill is approximately 5 m thick. This project, being a new school located in a key monitoring and defense area, must adhere to national regulations requiring the use of isolation and damping technologies for seismic protection and mitigation.

3   Evaluation of Subway Vibration and Noise at the Project Site

Due to the proximity of the teaching building's profile line to the subway track, with the closest distance to the centerline of the track being approximately 23 m, the building may be affected by vibrations and secondary structural noise generated by subway operations. Therefore, an evaluation of the vibrations induced by subway movements and the environmental impact of secondary structural noise on the teaching building is necessary. According to the "Limits and Measurement Methods for Building Vibration and Secondary Radiation Noise Induced by Urban Rail Transit" (JGJT170-2009), the indoor vibration limits for buildings in educational and cultural areas are 65 dB (daytime) and 62 dB (nighttime); the indoor secondary radiation vibration noise limits are 38 dB (daytime) and 35 dB (nighttime).

A finite element model of the train-track-tunnel-soil-building system, as shown in Fig. 2, was established [14]. The dynamic model of the vehicle-track coupled system follows the following basic principles: (1) A continuous distributed track model is used instead of a simplified equivalent lumped parameter track model. (2) A continuous elastic discrete-point support beam model is used instead of a continuous elastic foundation beam model, which better represents the actual railway track and can handle special dynamic issues such as longitudinal non-uniformity in track support elasticity. (3) An Euler beam model for rails is used to prevent overly complicated calculations while ensuring sufficient numerical accuracy for general wheel-rail dynamic analysis. When higher frequency characteristics (especially wheel-rail noise issues) are of interest, a Timoshenko beam model can be adopted. (4) A three-layer discrete-point support beam model is used to fully reflect the functions and interactions of the rail, cushion layer, ties, track bed, and subgrade system. (5) A vehicle-track model is used, considering the impact of the vehicle body, the front and rear bogies, wheelsets, and primary and secondary suspensions, with particular emphasis on the dynamic interactions between wheelsets and their cumulative effects on the vibration of track components.

Key details and techniques in the modeling process for the tunnel-soil-building finite element model are as follows: (1) Three-dimensional viscoelastic artificial boundary units are added around the perimeter of the model to simulate the semi-infinite space of the surrounding soil. (2) The element length is set to 0.5 m. (3) The integration time step is set to 2 ms. Without implementing vibration isolation measures, the acceleration levels at various measurement points on each floor of the teaching building under subway load conditions are shown in Fig. 3, and the indoor secondary radiation noise in the building at different frequencies is shown in Fig. 4.

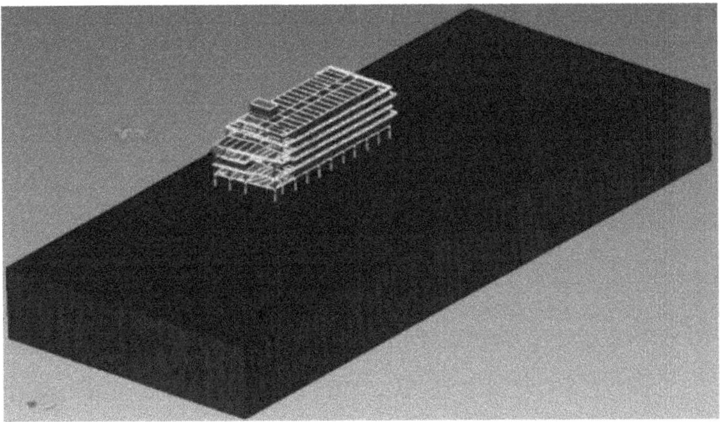

Fig. 2. Tunnel-Soil-Building Model

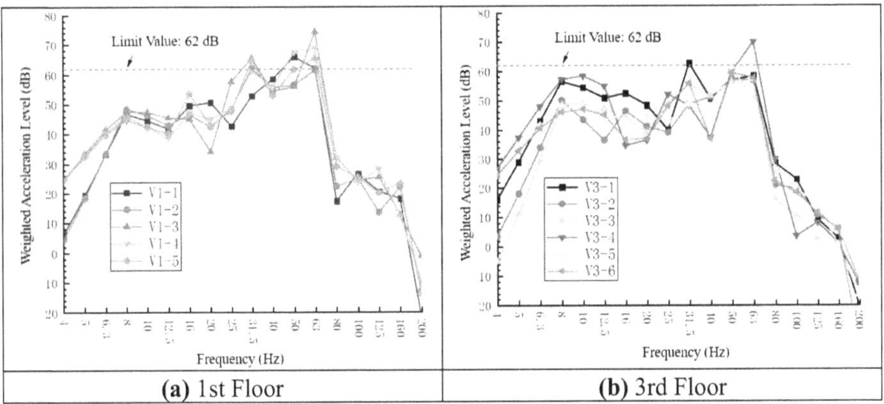

| **(a)** 1st Floor | **(b)** 3rd Floor |

Fig. 3. Frequency Response Level at Each Measurement Point on Different Floors Before Vibration Isolation

As shown in Figs. 3(a)–3(b), without vibration isolation measures, under the influence of subway train operations, the maximum frequency response levels on the 1st floor of the teaching building range from 62.0 dB to 69.4 dB; on the 2nd floor, the range is 60.6 dB to 65.9 dB; on the 3rd floor, the range is 56.9 dB to 67.9 dB; on the 4th floor, the range is 52.2 dB to 58.7 dB; and on the 5th floor, the range is 52.4 dB to 56.4 dB. Vibration levels exceed the limits on the 1st to 3rd floors, with the largest exceedance occurring on the 1st floor, where the exceedance is 7.4 dB.

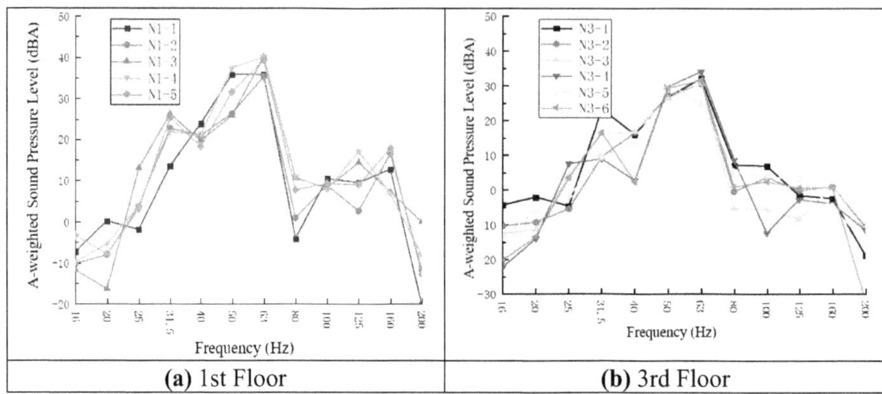

(a) 1st Floor	(b) 3rd Floor

Fig. 4. Indoor Secondary Radiation Noise at Each Floor Before Vibration Isolation (1/3 Octave Band)

As shown in Figs. 4(a)–4(b), without vibration isolation measures, under the influence of subway train operations, the indoor secondary radiation noise on the 1st floor of the teaching building ranges from 36.2 dBA to 41.2 dBA; on the 2nd floor, it ranges from 32.6 dBA to 40.1 dBA; on the 3rd floor, it ranges from 32.2 dBA to 40.1 dBA; on the 4th floor, it ranges from 31.9 dBA to 33.7 dBA; and on the 5th floor, it ranges from 25.7 dBA to 29.7 dBA. It can be observed that indoor secondary radiation noise exceeds the limit on the 1st and 2nd floors, with the largest exceedance of 6.2 dBA occurring on the 1st floor.

4 Comparison of Subway Vibration Isolation and Damping Treatment Solutions

As discussed above, the vibrations induced by subway movements and the associated secondary structural noise exceed the allowable limits and may negatively impact the usage of the teaching building. Therefore, it is necessary to address the environmental pollution caused by these vibrations. There are three primary solutions to this issue, as shown in Table 1: track vibration isolation, transmission path vibration isolation, and building vibration isolation. The suitability of each method will be compared and analyzed based on the actual conditions of the project.

Based on the actual conditions of the project, the subway vibration and isolation treatments for the teaching building can be further subdivided into three specific options, as shown in Table 2.

Table 1. Comparison of Subway Vibration Mitigation Solutions

Solution Method	Treatment and Project Context	Suitability
Track Vibration Isolation	Treatment: Floating slab track technology Project Context: Line 9 has already been constructed without the use of floating slab track technology	Not applicable
Transmission Path Isolation	Treatment: Installing a vibration isolation trench between the subway excitation and the building structure. The trench depth needs to be at least 0.6 times the wavelength (usually requiring several meters of depth) Project Context: Located in the eastern financial district, the site is small and does not have the conditions to dig a vibration isolation trench	Not applicable
Building Vibration Isolation	Treatment: Vibration isolation devices at the building's foundation Project Context: The conditions are suitable for implementation	Applicable

Table 2. Comparison of Subway Vibration Isolation and Damping Treatment Options

Solution Type	Treatment and Project Context
Base Isolation + Upper Structure Damping	Treatment: The base is equipped with vibration isolators, which can only address the vibrations induced by the subway. The upper structure uses viscous dampers for vibration reduction Project Context: The foundation consists of 5 m of fill soil. As the piles can transmit subway-induced vibrations, composite foundation treatment is adopted Cost: 6.5 million Construction Time: 3 months
Steel Spring Bearing Isolation + Upper Structure Damping	Treatment: The steel spring bearing isolation can only address the vibrations induced by the subway. The upper structure uses viscous dampers for vibration reduction Project Context: The foundation consists of 5 m of fill soil. Pile foundations can be used, with steel spring bearings installed at the top of the basement columns Cost: 10 million Construction Time: 1.5 months

(continued)

Table 2. (continued)

Solution Type	Treatment and Project Context
Three-Dimensional Isolation (Vibration and Shock Control) Bearings	Treatment: Three-dimensional isolation bearings not only address the vibrations induced by the subway but also solve the upper structure's isolation and damping problems Project Context: The foundation consists of 5 m of fill soil. Pile foundations can be used, with three-dimensional isolation bearings installed at the top of the basement columns Cost: 3 million Construction Time: 1.5 months

Note: The three-dimensional isolation (vibration) bearings are designed to control both vibration and shock.

5 Application of Three-Dimensional Seismic Isolation (Vibration Control) Technology in This Project

As shown in Table 2, after comparing various factors such as technical feasibility, cost, and construction duration, three-dimensional seismic isolation (vibration control) bearings have been selected for this project. Due to the functional requirements of the building (the basement serves as a cafeteria and the first floor contains classrooms), the bearings are arranged in the basement. The height of the lower support pier is 3.6 m, the height of the upper support pier ranges from 1.2 to 1.25 m, and the bearing height is between 0.5 and 0.55 m. The cross-section of the upper support pier is 1.2 m × 1.2 m, while the cross-section of the lower support pier is 1.0 m × 1.0 m. The thickness of the waterproofing plate is 0.6 m, the pile diameter is 1.0 m, and the size of the foundation slab is 2.2 m (length) × 2.2 m (width) × 1.0 m (height). The structure of the three-dimensional seismic isolation (vibration control) bearing is shown in Fig. 5.

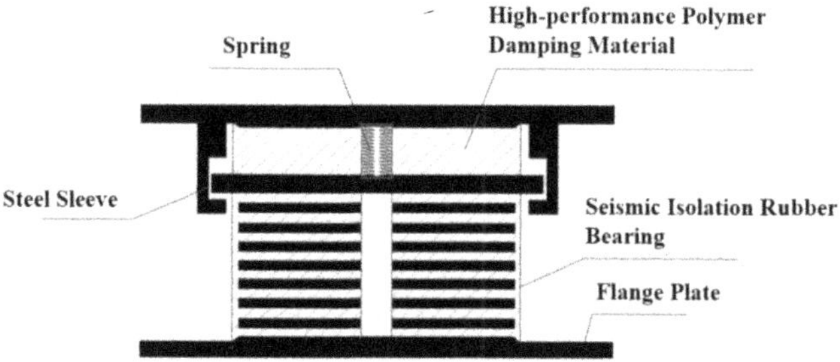

Fig. 5. Structure of Three-Dimensional Seismic Isolation (Vibration Control) Bearing

5.1   Evaluation of the Vibration Control Performance of the Three-Dimensional Seismic Isolation Bearings for Subway Vibration Mitigation

A finite element model of the train-track-tunnel-soil-building system was established. After applying vibration isolation measures, the acceleration levels at various interior measurement points on each floor of the teaching building were calculated under the influence of subway traffic loads. The weighted acceleration levels are shown in Fig. 6, and the indoor secondary radiated noise in each room of the building, in 1/3 octave bands, is shown in Fig. 7.

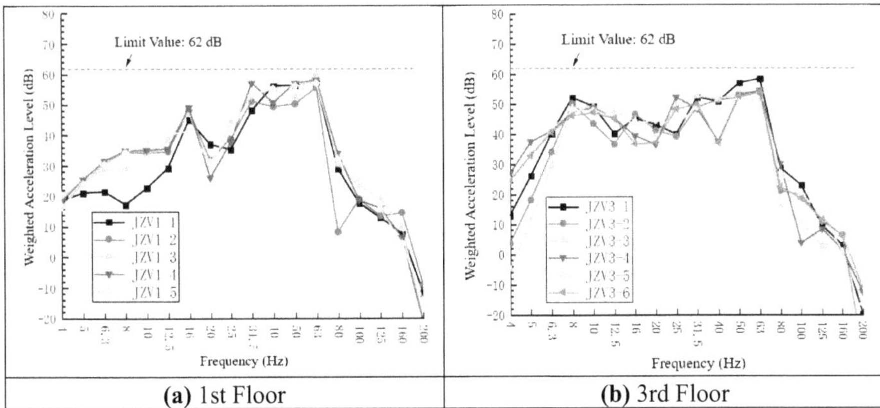

<table>
<tr><td>(a) 1st Floor</td><td>(b) 3rd Floor</td></tr>
</table>

Fig.6. Frequency Band Vibration Levels at Measurement Points on Each Floor After Vibration Isolation

From Fig. 6(a) to Fig. 6(b), it can be observed that after the installation of vibration isolation bearings, under the influence of subway train operation, the maximum frequency band vibration levels on the first floor of the teaching building range from 57.0 to 60.1 dB; on the second floor, from 51.1 to 55.0 dB; on the third floor, from 51.6 to 58.3 dB; on the fourth floor, from 50.0 to 54.6 dB; and on the fifth floor, from 46.5 to 50.6 dB. These results demonstrate that the vibration isolation bearings effectively reduce indoor vibrations, with the frequency band vibration levels at all measurement points falling below the vibration limits for "residential, educational, and commercial areas" as specified in the "Standards for Vibration and Secondary Radiated Noise in Buildings Caused by Urban Rail Transit and Measurement Methods" (JGJ/T170-2009).

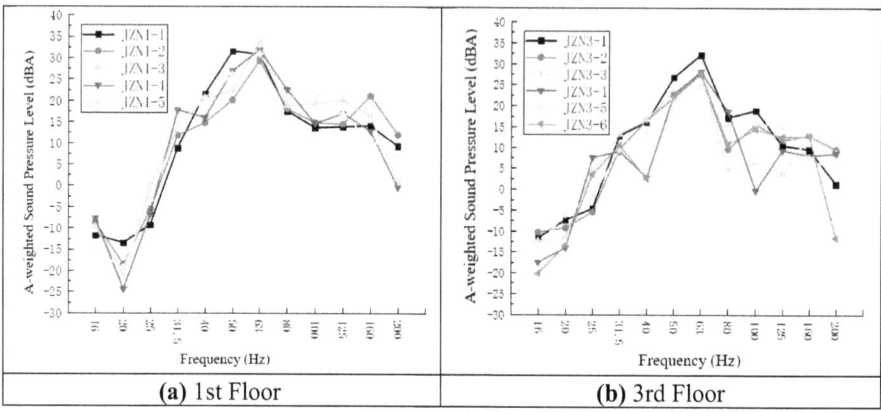

<table>
<tr><td align="center">(a) 1st Floor</td><td align="center">(b) 3rd Floor</td></tr>
</table>

Fig. 7. Indoor Secondary Radiation Noise at Each Floor After Vibration Isolation (1/3 Octave Band)

From Figs. 7(a) to 7(b), it can be seen that after the installation of vibration isolation bearings, under the influence of metro train operation, the indoor secondary radiated noise in the teaching building ranges from 30.0 to 34.4 dBA on the 1st floor, from 23.7 to 30.2 dBA on the 2nd floor, from 26.7 to 33.3 dBA on the 3rd floor, from 21.9 to 25.2 dBA on the 4th floor, and from 17.9 to 21.2 dBA on the 5th floor. It is evident that the installation of vibration isolation bearings effectively reduces indoor secondary radiated noise. The equivalent continuous sound levels of secondary radiated noise at all measurement points are below the limits specified in the "Standard for Limits of Vibration and Secondary Radiated Noise Induced by Urban Rail Transit on Buildings and Its Measurement Methods" (JGJ/T170-2009), which sets the secondary radiated noise limits for "residential and educational-cultural commercial zones."

5.2 Evaluation of the Seismic Isolation Performance of Three-Dimensional Seismic Isolation (Vibration Control) Bearings

A comparison of the shear forces on each structural floor before and after the implementation of seismic isolation is shown in Table 3. According to Article 6.1.3 of the Building Seismic Isolation Design Standard, if the shear force ratio at the base of a seismic isolated structure does not exceed 0.5, the seismic measures for the upper structure can be determined by reducing the seismic design level by one degree relative to the local seismic hazard. This project involves a frame structure located in a seismic zone of intensity 7 (0.10 g). The seismic grade of the frame structure is Level III. Considering that the building's function is educational, the seismic measures should be considered with an increase in one seismic grade. Since the maximum base shear ratio is 0.42, which is less than 0.50, the seismic measures can be reduced by one grade. Therefore, the seismic grade for this project is still taken as 7.

Table 3. Comparison of Structural Shear Forces on Each Floor Before and After Seismic Isolation

Floor	Shear Force in X-direction (Main Direction)			Shear Force in Y-direction (Main Direction)		
	Non-isolated (kN)	Isolated (kN)	Story Shear Force Ratio	Non-isolated (kN)	Isolated (kN)	Story Shear Force Ratio
6	101	23	0.22	106	34	0.33
5	3825	990	0.26	3509	1052	0.30
4	6018	1824	0.30	5398	1851	0.34
3	7695	2646	0.34	6629	2605	0.39
2	9039	3308	0.37	7838	3301	0.42
1	10371	3810	0.37	9102	3805	0.42

Through calculations and analysis, the eccentricity of the isolation layer, the wind load bearing capacity of the isolation layer, the contact pressure on the bearing surface under gravity load, the restoring force of the isolation bearings, and the displacement angle have all been verified to meet the relevant design codes and standards. The analysis results indicate that under the rare earthquake scenario, the performance levels of the upper support pier and its associated frame beams, the lower support pier, ordinary vertical components, and ordinary horizontal components all satisfy the performance objectives.

6 Conclusion

Based on a real engineering case, this study combines theoretical analysis and numerical simulation methods to investigate building vibration reduction and seismic isolation. The main conclusions are as follows:

(1) There are three main integrated solutions for building response to subway-induced environmental vibrations: track isolation, propagation path isolation, and building isolation. The appropriate vibration reduction scheme for subway projects should be selected based on the geological conditions of the site. For buildings requiring both vibration and seismic control, the impact of factors such as the superstructure should also be considered.

(2) The use of three-dimensional seismic isolation bearings can significantly reduce vibrations in the teaching building caused by subway movement, as well as prevent excessive noise from secondary structures. Under rare three-dimensional earthquake loading, the horizontal peak acceleration of the superstructure decreases by approximately 60%, demonstrating good horizontal isolation performance.

(3) The application of three-dimensional seismic isolation bearings to address both vibration and seismic control issues can greatly reduce costs and shorten construction timelines.

Acknowledgements. This work was supported by the Science and Technology Project of Power China Chengdu Engineering Corporation Limited [No. P62824]. The financial support is greatly appreciated.

References

1. Wang, H., Tang, Z., Song, L., Li, L., Lin, H., Hu, X.: Simulation study on ground vibration reduction measures of the elevated subway line. Appl. Sci. **14**(15), 6706 (2024)
2. Mei, C., Wang, D., Zhang, Y.: Vibration control and transmission mechanism of super high-rise building located on subway based on spring vibration isolation system. Adv. Struct. Eng. **27**(12), 2167–2189 (2024)
3. Xiao, P., Miao, L., Zheng, H., Lei, L.: Application and vibration reduction properties of prefabricated and cast-in-place phononic-like crystal polymer concrete track bed in subway engineering. J. Mater. Civ. Eng. **36**(9), 04024252 (2024)
4. Chen, J., Zeng, X., Umar, H.A., Xie, Y., Long, G.: Study of the vibration reduction performance of rubberized self-compacting concrete filling layer in prefabricated slab track. J. Mater. Civ. Eng. **35**(6), 04023150 (2023)
5. Wang, Q., Miao, L., Zheng, H., Xiao, P., Zhang, B.: Design of elastic metamaterial plate and application in subway vibration isolation. Appl. Phys. A **130**(8), 557 (2024)
6. Li, Z., Ma, M., Liu, K., Jiang, B.: Performance of rubber-concrete composite periodic barriers applied in attenuating ground vibrations induced by metro trains. Eng. Struct. **285**, 116027 (2023)
7. Li, X., Chen, Y., Zou, C., Chen, Y.: Train-induced vibration mitigation based on foundation improvement. J. Build. Eng. **76**, 107106 (2023)
8. Forcellini, D., Kalfas, K.N.: Inter-story seismic isolation for high-rise buildings. Eng. Struct. **275**, 115175 (2023)
9. Miao, L., Lei, L., Li, C., Wang, J., Qian, Z.: Vibration reduction of low frequency of phononic-like crystal structures for subways. J. Mech. Mater. Struct. **17**(3), 193–205 (2023)
10. Cardone, D., et al.: Modelling and seismic response analysis of existing Italian residential RC buildings retrofitted by seismic isolation. J. Earthq. Eng. **27**(4), 1069–1093 (2023)
11. Xu, H., He, W., Zhang, L., Liu, W.: Shaking table test of a novel three-dimensional seismic isolation system with inclined rubber bearings. Eng. Struct. **293**, 116609 (2023)
12. Ghorbi, E., Toopchi-Nezhad, H.: Annular fiber-reinforced elastomeric bearings for seismic isolation of lightweight structures. Soil Dyn. Earthq. Eng. **166**, 107764 (2023)
13. Zhao, Z., Wang, Y., Chen, Q., Qiang, H., Hong, N.: Enhanced seismic isolation and energy dissipation approach for the aboveground negative-stiffness-based isolated structure with an underground structure. Tunn. Undergr. Space Technol. **134**, 105019 (2023)
14. Geng, D., Dai, N., Guo, P., Zhou, S., Di, H.: Implicit numerical integration of highly nonlinear plasticity models. Comput. Geotech. **132**, 103961 (2021)

Preliminary Study on the Mechanism of Influence of Smart On-Street Parking Upgrading on Vehicle Owners' Parking Behavior: Taking Pudong New Area of Shanghai as an Example

Yang Ke[✉]

Shanghai Puhui Zhitu Transportation Technology Co., Ltd., Pudong New Area,
Shanghai 200120, China
yangke1@puhuizhitu.com

Abstract. With the continuous growth in the number of motor vehicles in cities, "parking difficulty" has become a major issue restricting urban development. Promoting intelligent management and refined operation of on-street parking resources is a key path to improving public space utilization efficiency. Taking Pudong New Area of Shanghai as a case study, this paper systematically analyzes the mechanism of influence of three core factors—price, technology, and management—on vehicle owners' parking behavior during the smart upgrading of on-street parking. The study finds that the smart upgrade significantly enhances the standardization of parking behavior and data transparency through means such as accurate charging, full-time supervision, and efficient overdue payment collection. However, in core areas with highly concentrated demand, the regulatory effect of the price leverage is relatively limited, and the demand factor remains dominant. This research provides empirical evidence and decision-making reference for optimizing urban parking management policies.

Keywords: On-Street Parking · Smart upgrading · Parking Behavior · Price Elasticity · Technology Empowerment · Pudong New Area

1 Relevant Research Review

Domestic and international studies indicate that on-street parking management is a vital component of urban traffic governance. Traditional manual management models suffer from issues such as low efficiency and frequent charging loopholes. With the development of technologies like the Internet of Things and big data, smart parking offers new avenues for optimizing resource allocation and guiding rational parking demand through accurate sensing and data analysis.

Tang Pengcheng (2011) used system dynamics to construct a price linkage model for urban parking charges and road congestion charges. Through simulation using Haidian

A. Razminia et al. (Eds.): ITFT 2025, CCIS 2876, pp. 203–214, 2026.
https://doi.org/10.1007/978-3-032-20592-6_19

District in Beijing as an example, the study pointed out a clear substitute and complementary relationship between the two, suggesting that implementing linked pricing can more effectively curb traffic demand and optimize social benefits. Cheng Yang (2021), based on a big data analysis environment, constructed a TMLR-ARMA model combining multivariate linear regression and autoregressive moving average for parking demand prediction, and used a feature-weighted clustering method to zone urban parking lots, providing data-driven decision support for optimizing parking resource management. Liu Jianbin (2022) improved the cruise parking model to reveal that on-street parking choice is a decision process where travelers seek a balance between time cost and monetary cost. Using a delay model and cellular automaton, the study verified the significant effect of optimizing parking choices (such as regulating price) on reducing road segment traffic delay and enhancing passage efficiency, offering theoretical basis for on-street parking management.

Existing research mostly focuses on technical solutions or the evaluation of a single policy effect, lacking a systematic mechanism analysis of how smart upgrading impacts vehicle owners' parking behavior. This paper aims to fill this gap by constructing a comprehensive analytical framework of "Price-Technology-Management" and conducting empirical testing using the practice in Pudong New Area as a sample.

2 Current Status of Smart On-Street Parking at the Municipal and District Levels

2.1 Current Status of Smart On-Street Parking Management in Shanghai

In 2022, the Shanghai Municipal traffic management department issued the Notice on Accelerating the Promotion of Smart Parking Lot (Garage) Construction in the City, clearly proposing to advance the smart upgrading of on-street and off-street parking lots during the "14th Five-Year Plan" period. It established corresponding construction plans and technical standards, aiming to build a networked smart parking management system covering the entire city with unified charging and payment.

According to the unified requirements of the Shanghai Municipal traffic management department, users are encouraged to prioritize online payment through the "Shanghai Parking" client for on-street parking fees, while retaining the offline payment channel collected by on-site fee collectors via POS machines. For parking spots that have completed smart upgrading and are officially operational, the district platform system will send overdue payment reminder text messages to vehicle owners within 48 to 72 h after a debt is incurred. Furthermore, fee collectors still support on-site reminders and supplementary payments for historical debts.

2.2 Current Status of Smart On-Street Parking in Pudong New Area

Pudong New Area is one of the regions in Shanghai with the most concentrated road parking resources. It currently has over 310 chargeable road sections, including temporary support sections for large events and permanently marked chargeable sections, totaling approximately 22,000 on-street parking spots. Since 2023, Pudong New Area has been gradually implementing smart upgrading. As of March 2024, the smart transformation of 97 roads and approximately 4,680 permanently marked chargeable parking spots has been completed and put into operation in four batches.

In the initial phase of the smart parking system's launch, on-site fee collectors are, in principle, retained during the first year of operation. This is to gradually cultivate vehicle owners' usage habits, strengthen parking regulation management, and effectively carry out historical overdue payment collection. The current personnel configuration standard in Pudong New Area is about 1 administrator for every 30 parking spots. The plan is to gradually optimize and reduce on-site manpower after operations stabilize, based on actual conditions.

3 Factors Influencing Smart Upgrading of On-Street Parking

3.1 Price Factor

Based on the fee standards and charging regulations for smart road parking lots in the city, which were approved by the municipal price and finance departments, the on-street parking fee standards and charging regulations in all districts of Shanghai are executed as follows:

Table 1. Fee Standards and Charging Regulations for Smart Road Parking Lots

Area	Day				Night (per time)	Residential peak-sharing monthly fee (Workday night, weekend, and statutory holidays all day)
	First hour charged by actual parking duration			After 1 h, cumulative increase every 30 min		
	0–15 min	15–30 min	30–60 min			
Key Areas within Inner Ring	4 RMB	8 RMB	15 RMB	10 RMB	10 RMB	400 RMB
Other Areas within Inner Ring	3 RMB	6 RMB	10 RMB	6 RMB	6 RMB	300 RMB
Between Inner & Outer Ring (incl. Outskirts)	2 RMB	4 RMB	7 RMB	4 RMB	5 RMB	200 RMB

Zoned Pricing. According to regulations, the city's road parking lots are divided into three tiers from core to periphery based on geographical location, implementing differentiated charging (See Table 1). The price level decreases stepwise as the regional tier decreases. This zoned pricing strategy adheres to the economic principle that higher prices suppress demand. By setting higher prices in core areas with high parking demand, non-essential parking demand can be effectively filtered, thereby optimizing the allocation efficiency of on-street parking spots (a scarce public resource) to ensure they serve higher-priority short-term parking.

Precise Time Segmentation. Smart charging supports refined time-slot division. Daytime temporary parking fees are segmented into 15-min, 15-min, 30-min units, and subsequent 30-min units, with dynamically adjusted unit prices. This is intended to implement the parking management principle of "primarily off-street, supplemented by on-street". Subdividing the first 30 min into two 15-min billing units aims to encourage short-term parking, reduce the actual cost of super-short parking (e.g., <15 min), thereby guiding "stop-and-go" behavior, and increasing parking spot turnover rate.

Off-Peak Monthly Pass. To alleviate night parking conflicts in some older residential communities, the off-peak monthly pass mode is allowed for application in specific road parking lots. Users parking during regulated off-peak hours (night, weekends, and statutory holidays) have a monthly maximum charge. If the total charge based on per-use billing is lower than this maximum, the actual incurred amount is settled. This mode provides price predictability through bundled pricing, aiming to guide nearby residents' vehicles to use on-street resources orderly during low-demand periods, achieving "peak-shaving and valley-filling" and enhancing the overall utilization efficiency of road facilities in terms of space and time.

3.2 Technical Factors

Based on the Notice on Accelerating the Promotion of Smart Parking Lot (Garage) Construction in the City and relevant standards, on-street parking charging modes in Shanghai are categorized into three levels—G0, G1, and G2—based on the degree of smartness, with increasing technical configuration and management effectiveness.

G0 Model: Pure Manual Fee Collection
Vehicle entry/exit recognition, timing, charging, and fee collection all rely on the fee collector's handheld terminal. Key characteristics include:

Limited timing accuracy, only supporting a minimum billing unit of 1 h, unable to achieve fine segmentation.

Parking and departure rely on manual patrol, lacking night supervision, leading to frequent order omissions.

Lack of equipment-assisted supervision, making on-site bargaining and charging loopholes common.

Does not support "Shanghai Parking" online payment and does not perform text message reminders.

G1 Model: Geomagnetic Detection + Manual Assistance

Geomagnetic sensors are deployed in each parking spot to automatically detect vehicle entry/exit, and the fee collector photographs and registers the license plate information. Characteristics:

Supports precise time segmentation charging (e.g., 15 min, 30 min).

Vehicle entry/exit is automatically prompted by the system, reducing manual patrol pressure, but some night orders are still missed due to incomplete evidence collection.

Technical means assist supervision, effectively curbing bargaining and charging loopholes.

Supports both "Shanghai Parking" online payment and offline collection channels, and includes a text message reminder function.

G2 Model: High-Position Video + Manual Assistance

This is the highest level of smartness, achieving full automation of vehicle entry/exit and license plate recognition via high-position video equipment, with manual staff mainly responsible for auxiliary management and payment collection. Advantages include:

Full support for precise time segmentation charging.

24-h uninterrupted capture of parking records, essentially achieving supervision without omissions.

Further reduces reliance on manual operations, enhancing management efficiency and data accuracy.

Supports both "Shanghai Parking" online payment and offline collection channels, and includes a text message reminder function.

3.3 Management Factors

Manual On-Site Collection: Fee collectors can query historical overdue parking records in real-time via handheld terminals and conduct targeted on-site reminders and supplementary payment operations for vehicles present. This mode is direct and effective, particularly for collecting historical debts or assisting vehicle owners unfamiliar with online operation.

System Text Message Collection: For G1 and G2 overdue orders, the district platform automatically sends a reminder text message to the vehicle owner within 48 to 72 h, guiding them to complete the supplementary payment through online channels like the "Shanghai Parking" APP. This achieves efficient, standardized remote reminder, effectively expanding the collection coverage.

4 Analysis of the Mechanism of Influence on Parking Behavior

4.1 Analysis of Parking Behavior Under Current Pricing

Analysis of Zoned Pricing and Precise Time Segmentation

Based on G2 road section parking data in Pudong New Area from April 1 to October 1, 2025, this study selected time-based charging orders spanning days and which were non-zero as the analysis sample. The distribution of the Parking Propensity Index (average parking duration in minutes) per parking spot per day for different parking duration intervals in various areas was shown in Fig. 1.

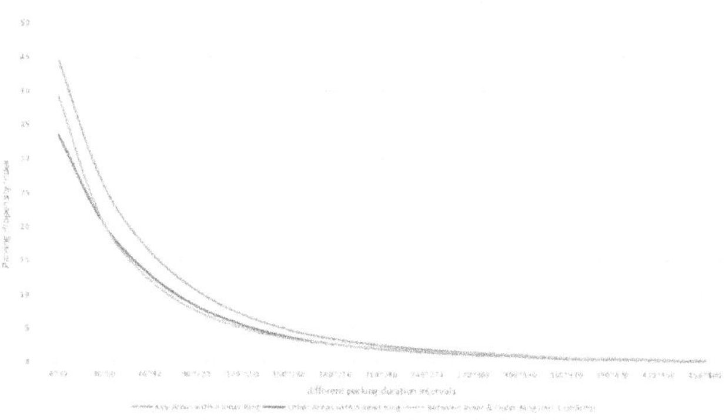

Fig. 1. Zoned Pricing and Precise Time Segmentation Parking Propensity Trend

From Fig. 1, although the overall trend of parking duration distribution for Class I areas (highest price, corresponding to Key Areas within Inner Ring in Table 1) is generally consistent with Class II and III areas—all decreasing as parking duration increases—the frequency in the short-term parking interval (e.g., 0–60 min) is notably higher for Class I areas. Conversely, in longer parking duration periods (e.g., above 210 min), the frequency in Class III areas is slightly higher. This phenomenon suggests that in Class I areas with highly concentrated parking demand, despite the higher price level, short-term parking behavior remains quite active. This indicates that the current regional differentiated pricing has a limited regulatory effect on parking behavior. In core areas with tight supply, the influence of demand factors on parking behavior is significantly greater than the price factor, and the existing pricing mechanism struggles to effectively curb rigid parking demand.

To more accurately identify the influence of parking duration and time-slot unit price on parking behavior, a quantitative analysis model was further constructed. Parking duration (x_1) and time-slot unit price (x_2) were used as independent variables, and the Parking Propensity Index (y) was used as the dependent variable. A sample data set was established (with partial examples shown in Table 2) and fitted using a non-linear regression method.

Through comparison of goodness-of-fit, the exponential model Eq. (1) was finally selected:

$$y = 78.38 \times e^{(-0.01768x_1 - 0.03574x_2)} + 0.8732 \tag{1}$$

The model's coefficient of determination (R^2) is approximately 0.98, indicating high explanatory power. It reflects the relationship between the variables well and can serve as a baseline model for subsequent prediction of smart on-street parking behavior.

Analysis of Off-Peak Shared Parking

To further evaluate the actual effect of the off-peak shared parking policy in regulating residents' parking behavior, non-zero parking orders generated during workday nights, weekends, and statutory holidays were selected as the analysis sample from G1 and G2 road section parking data in Pudong New Area from April 1 to October 1, 2025. The study

Table 2. Sample dataset example

Parking Duration (x_1)	Time-Based Price (x_2)	Parking Preference Indicator (y)
450	6	0.28637316
450	10	0.36400544
420	6	0.36411427
450	4	0.37805636
420	10	0.44687764
390	6	0.45504466
420	4	0.46853102
390	10	0.55190314
360	6	0.56366935
390	4	0.56646309
360	10	0.68234680
360	4	0.69218901
330	6	0.89036230
…	…	…

focused on the parking behavior trends of users who applied for the off-peak monthly pass and ordinary temporary parking users. The sample data was divided into two categories: parking records of users who had applied for the off-peak monthly package, and records of temporary parking users who had not applied for the policy. A trend comparison chart was plotted by counting the number of parking occurrences for both types of users in the same off-peak hours (workday night, weekend, and holidays) across different months, to visually reflect the policy's guiding effect on parking behavior.

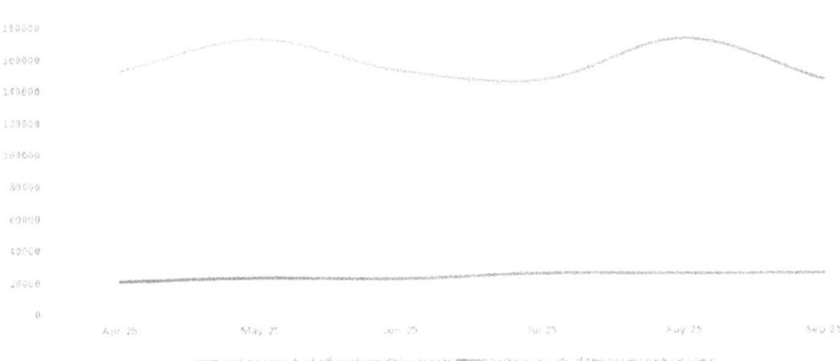

Fig. 2. Trend Chart of Parking Occurrences for Applicants and Non-Applicants of Off-Peak Pass during Off-Peak Hours

Figure 2 shows that the parking occurrences for off-peak monthly pass users are lower than those for temporary parking users across all months. The overall fluctuation is relatively smooth and slightly increasing, suggesting that the policy has successfully attracted a stable group of residents who use on-street parking spots. During the summer period of June-August, the parking occurrences of non-off-peak users show a slight upward trend, possibly related to an increase in summer activities. The trends indicate that the off-peak monthly pass policy enhances residents' willingness to use on-street parking spots through providing price predictability and a monthly cost ceiling mechanism. Crucially, it improves the utilization rate of parking spots during low-demand periods such as nights and holidays.

4.2   Analysis of the Impact of Technology Upgrading on Parking Occurrences

To systematically evaluate the impact of smart technology upgrading on on-street parking behavior, parking data from Pudong New Area between October 1, 2024, and October 1, 2025, was analyzed. G2 and G1 sections were selected as analysis objects, focusing on the change trend in the number of parking orders to reveal the influence mechanism of different technical paths on parking frequency.

Analysis of G2 Upgrade Impact

Three batches of road sections that completed the G2 upgrade and started operation in January, February, and March 2025 were selected. Non-zero orders were used as valid samples, and the change trend in the number of parking orders before and after the upgrade was plotted.

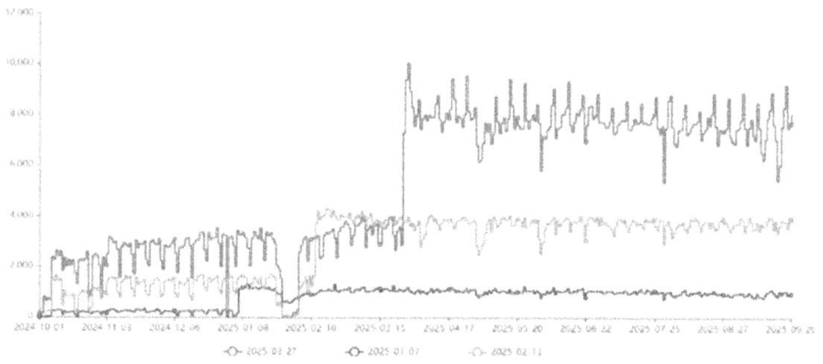

Fig. 3. G2 Road Section Order Volume Trend Chart Before and After Launch

Figure 3 shows a significant increase in the number of parking orders after the G2 upgrade, approximately 2.5–3 times the quantity during the pre-upgrade manual management period. A clear peak appeared in the initial period after the upgrade, possibly due to vehicle owners' unfamiliarity with the automated charging method and exploratory parking behavior. Over time, the number of orders gradually declined and stabilized, reflecting the process of vehicle owners adapting to the smart charging model. The G2 mode, utilizing high-position video equipment for fully automated recognition and timing, effectively eliminated issues such as missed orders and bargaining prevalent in manual management, improving the completeness and accuracy of order capture. This is the main reason for the significant increase in the statistics of parking occurrences.

Analysis of G1 Upgrade Impact

To further compare the differences between various technical paths, two batches of road sections that completed the G1 upgrade in January and February 2025 were selected as samples, and the change in the number of parking orders was plotted.

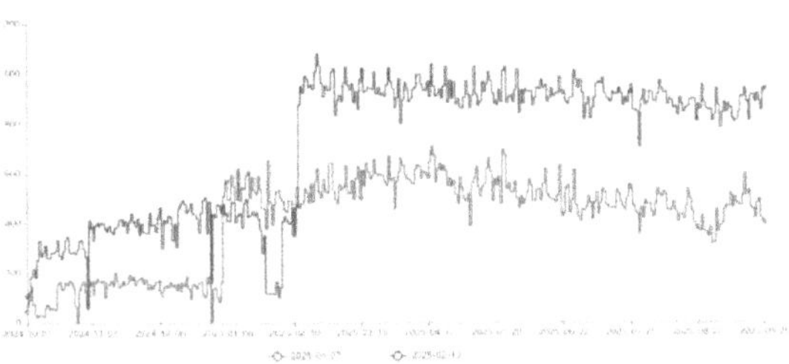

Fig. 4. G1 Road Section Order Volume Trend Chart Before and After Launch

Figure 4 demonstrates that the number of parking orders also increased significantly after the G1 mode upgrade. The increase is similar to the G2 mode, approximately 2.5–3 times the original manual management stage. However, unlike G2, the G1 sections did not show the significant initial peak after the upgrade; the overall trend was relatively smoother. This difference primarily stems from the G1 mode's continued reliance on manual input of license plates and limited night supervision capability. Vehicle owners' perception of the change in charging method is less intense than in the G2 mode, leading to a more gradual behavioral adaptation process.

4.3   Analysis of the Impact of Payment Collection Methods on Payment

To systematically evaluate the actual effect of different payment collection management methods on vehicle owners' payment behavior, this study focused on the first batch of G2 high-position video road section parking data in Pudong New Area that was operational from September 2023 to October 2025. It analyzed the mechanism and phased characteristics of text message collection and manual on-site collection in enhancing payment compliance.

According to operational records, the text message collection function was officially launched in October 2023. Figure 5 shows that during the period without any collection measures, the payment rate was below 30%. After the implementation of text message collection, the payment rate significantly increased to about 60% in a short time. This indicates that the system's automatic overdue payment reminders had a clear positive guiding effect on vehicle owners' payment behavior. Simultaneously, as the collection mechanism was strictly enforced, some non-rigid demand vehicle owners gradually reduced their on-street parking behavior, leading to a monthly decreasing trend in the payable amount, with the payment rate stabilizing at around 60%.

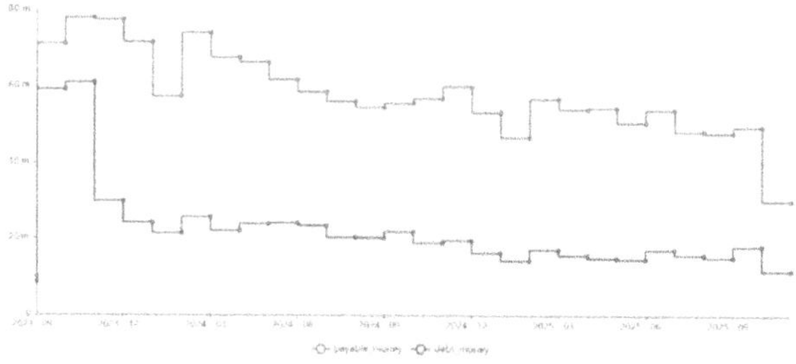

Fig. 5. Trend Chart of Fee Collection Status for the First Batch of G2 Road Sections

In October 2024, the management unit further implemented an enhanced mechanism for offline manual collection. Fee collectors provided on-site reminders and supplementary payment guidance for vehicles with overdue payments. This action further boosted the payment rate to over 70%. Although the total parking demand decreased further, payment compliance significantly improved. This illustrates that the "human-machine combination" collection model has better adaptability in complex scenarios, particularly in enhancing the willingness to pay for vehicle owners who are less sensitive to online notifications or adhere to traditional operating habits.

From an effectiveness perspective, the two collection methods are complementary: text message collection has wide coverage and low cost, suitable for most vehicle owners; manual collection, on the other hand, provides strong on-site deterrence and assistance, effectively compensating for the shortcomings of pure online reminders. The combination of the two forms an "online + offline" closed-loop management, which is key to achieving a continuous increase in the payment rate. It is suggested that the dual-track collection mechanism should be maintained in future smart parking management. Furthermore, reminder strategies and personnel configuration should be further optimized based on vehicle owner behavior data to create a more efficient and user-friendly parking payment environment.

5   Comprehensive Discussion and Research Insights

5.1   Key Research Findings

Based on the multi-dimensional analysis of smart parking data in Pudong New Area, this study draws the following core findings:

Limited Regulatory Effect of Price Signals: In Class I areas with prominent supply-demand conflicts, despite the implementation of higher zoned pricing, short-term parking demand remains strong. This suggests that rigid demand has low price sensitivity.

Technology Upgrading is the Foundation for Enhancing Management Efficiency: The G2 (high-position video) mode demonstrates clear advantages in accuracy and full-time supervision compared to the G1 (geomagnetic + manual) mode. It more thoroughly eliminates management blind spots, but its initial launch has a greater impact on vehicle owner behavior and requires a transition period for guidance.

Synergy of Management Methods is Key to Policy Implementation: The composite management model, comprising "text message collection + manual on-site collection," achieves a combination of broad coverage and precise intervention. It is the core mechanism for the steady increase in the payment rate.

5.2 Policy Optimization Recommendations

Based on the above findings, this paper proposes the following policy recommendations:

Implement More Refined Dynamic Pricing Strategies: It is suggested to explore the introduction of a floating pricing mechanism based on real-time occupancy, rather than a fixed high unit price, in areas with extremely high demand (Class I). This would allow for more sensitive regulation of instantaneous demand.

Adopt Differentiated Technology Promotion Paths: Prioritize the promotion of the G2 mode in core and traffic-sensitive areas to maximize management effectiveness. In non-core areas or during the transition phase, the lower-cost G1 mode can be adopted to achieve steady improvement.

Construct a Smart Vehicle Owner Service System: Beyond payment collection, proactive service functions like "parking bill prediction" and "discount time-slot push" could be added. This shifts the focus from "management" to "guidance," enhancing vehicle owner experience and compliance willingness.

5.3 Limitations and Future Outlook

This study still has some limitations. First, the analysis is mainly based on operational data, lacking questionnaire evidence regarding vehicle owners' subjective willingness (such as price acceptance, perception of technology usability). Second, the research time span is limited, preventing observation of the long-term effects of smart upgrading. Future research could combine multi-source data (e.g., mobile signaling data, vehicle owner interviews) for deeper causal inference and track the sustainability of policy effects.

6 Conclusion

The smart upgrading of on-street parking is a systematic project involving technology, management, and policy. The practice in Pudong New Area demonstrates that achieving accurate charging, comprehensive sensing, and efficient management through smart means can effectively standardize parking behavior and enhance resource utilization efficiency. However, smart transformation is not achieved overnight. Its success depends on the precision of the pricing strategy, the suitability of the technical solution, and the synergy of the management measures. Moving forward, the focus should remain on data-driven decision-making to continuously optimize management strategies, ultimately achieving the sustainable development goal of on-street parking characterized by "efficient management, friendly experience, and resource conservation."

References

Tang, P.: Research on Price Linkage of Urban Parking Fees and Congestion Charging. Harbin Institute of Technology (2011)

Chen, Z., Yang, J.: Research on the formation mechanism and guiding strategies for the shortage of urban parking space. J. Chongqing Univ. Technol. (Nat. Sci.) **38**(9), 236–245 (2024)

Chen, P.: Urban Center Curbside Parking and Garage Parking combined Pricing Model. Chongqing Jiaotong University (2019)

Cheng, Y.: Research on intelligent parking model based on big data analysis. Master's thesis. Chongqing University of Posts and Telecommunications (2021)

Liu, J.B.: Analysis and modeling of on-street parking choice and parking behavior. Master's thesis. Jilin University (2022)

Jia, Z.X.: Optimization and engineering verification of on-street parking management technology in Shenzhen. Traff. Transp. **40** (2024)

Li, K.: Research on governance countermeasures for on-street parking problems in Zhengzhou central urban area. Sci. Technol. Vis. **16** (2017)

Jiang, Y., Rong, J., Yin, J.M.: On-street parking management and practice in small and medium-sized cities: a case study of Hailing District, Taizhou. Traff. Eng. **21** (2021)

Chen, G., Shen, J., He, J., et al.: An overall analysis method of urban road parking lots based on data mining. Int. J. Secur. Netw. **16**, 105–111 (2021). https://doi.org/10.1504/ijsn.2021.100 39838

Owota, K.M., Aprioku, I.M.: Urban road and on-street parking in Niger Delta Region of Yenagoa, Bayelsa State, Nigeria. J. Geogr. Reg. Plann. **2018**(11) (2018). https://doi.org/10.5897/JGR P2018.0706

Transportation Electrification, Energy Systems, and Grid Integration

Optimization and Application of Urban Rail Transit Energy Storage Systems Utilizing Rolling Dynamic Programming

Yajie Zhao$^{(\boxtimes)}$, Chuanfei Diao, and Fei Lin

Beijing Jiaotong University, Beijing 100044, China
`20117021@bjtu.edu.cn`

Abstract. The application of supercapacitor energy storage systems (SCESS) in urban rail transit facilitates the recovery and reuse of regenerative braking energy, thereby reducing traction energy consumption and supporting the transition toward low-carbon urban transit systems. Based on an analysis of the structural of urban rail transit networks, this paper proposes an energy management strategy (EMS) founded on dynamic programming, which enables effective matching between the SCESS and traction load demands. To validate the effectiveness and advanced performance of the proposed EMS, a 1.5 MW SCESS prototype was developed and deployed on an operational metro line in China for field testing. Experimental results demonstrate that, compared to conventional fixed-threshold strategy, the proposed approach improves the average energy saving rate by 5.49%. These findings confirm the strategy's superior energy-saving performance and technological advancement, highlighting its practical value for real-world applications in sustainable urban rail systems.

Keywords: Urban Rail Transit · Supercapacitor Energy Storage Systems · Energy Management Strategy · Dynamic Programming

1 Background

Currently, the global urban rail transit sector is undergoing a significant transformation, characterized by simultaneous infrastructure expansion and technological innovation. Market analyses indicate that the public transportation industry, which includes rail transit, is expected to maintain robust growth in the coming years, with a compound annual growth rate (CAGR) of approximately 8.90%, reflecting substantial development potential. In China, urban rail transit has evolved into a large-scale, networked system. By August 2025, operations had been launched in 54 cities across the country, with a total track length exceeding 11,200 km and a monthly passenger volume of 2.88 billion trips. This extensive network plays a vital role in urban mobility. In response, the industry is actively advancing toward the strategic goal of "green and intelligent urban rail," promoting sustainability and digitalization across the entire lifecycle. As a backbone of public transportation, the green transition of urban rail is critical to supporting China's

A. Razminia et al. (Eds.): ITFT 2025, CCIS 2876, pp. 217–227, 2026.
https://doi.org/10.1007/978-3-032-20592-6_20

national objectives of carbon peaking and carbon neutrality. Consequently, initiatives such as eco-friendly construction and maintenance, optimized power supply systems, and enhanced energy recovery have become essential measures for the sector to fulfill its social responsibilities and contribute to sustainable development.

Urban rail transit systems typically use DC power supply with uncontrolled diode rectifiers in traction substations, resulting in unidirectional power flow. This prevents regenerative braking energy from being fed back to the grid. When such energy is not absorbed by nearby trains, the DC network voltage rises. If it exceeds a set threshold, trains must switch to mechanical braking, dissipating kinetic energy as heat and causing energy waste, brake wear, and tunnel dust. Studies indicate that regenerative braking accounts for 30%–40% of traction energy, making its recovery crucial for reducing energy consumption and operational impacts in urban rail systems. Ground-based regenerative energy absorption technology primarily follows two approaches: energy feedback and energy storage. Energy feedback employs PWM rectification technology by connecting a DC–AC converter and a step-up transformer to the DC and AC sides of the urban rail traction power supply system, respectively. This method offers benefits such as low cost and a compact footprint. However, since it interfaces with the AC bus, its implementation may significantly affect the power quality of the AC grid. In contrast, energy storage technology leverages the spatiotemporal transfer characteristics of energy storage systems to store regenerative braking energy in devices such as supercapacitors or batteries. The stored energy is later released during train traction, enabling the recycling of regenerative energy. Energy storage systems involve fewer interfaces with the power supply infrastructure, allow for simpler retrofitting of existing lines, and can enhance the power supply capacity. As a result, this approach has gained widespread adoption in international practice.

The effectiveness of the supercapacitor energy storage systems (SCESS) relies heavily on its advanced energy management system (EMS). Early research, such as [1–5], established traditional logic-based control strategies founded on closed-loop regulation of key electrical parameters—voltage, current, power, and state of charge (SOC)—to govern regenerative energy recovery. While these studies demonstrated fundamental energy-saving potential, they lacked a systematic framework for optimizing critical parameters. To address these limitations, subsequent innovations introduced adaptive control strategies. Wang et al. [6] developed a threshold optimization framework that accounts for the no-load voltage of traction substations, substantially enhancing EMS adaptability to evolving power infrastructure. Lin et al. [7] extended this approach by implementing a dynamic threshold adjustment mechanism responsive to real-time voltage fluctuations. Recognizing the interplay between traction network dynamics and vehicle operation, Yang et al. [8] proposed a braking voltage synchronization strategy and empirically validated its significant improvement in dynamic response performance. Since then, the field has shifted toward a smart control paradigm. For instance, Liu et al. [9] implemented a fuzzy logic controller to monitor real-time power flow from both the UCESS and traction substations, demonstrating superior adaptability in metro simulation studies. Meanwhile, advances in machine learning algorithms have enabled further sophistication. Yang et al. [10] proposed a reinforcement learning framework for autonomous parameter tuning and optimization, while Yoshida et al. [11] introduced similar methodologies for battery-integrated systems. Despite these advances, current EMS designs and control strategies remain heavily dependent on local state variables, such as traction network voltage and braking voltage curves. However, the emergence of Automatic Train Operation (ATO) and enhanced railway communication networks has created transformative opportunities. Recent research has proposed innovative integrated EMS architectures that combine predictive train scheduling with power system telemetry, enabling proactive and demand-oriented energy management. This paradigm shift aims to overcome the limitations of localized control strategies and achieve system-wide energy optimization in urban rail transit systems (URTS).

This paper proposes a dynamic programming-based EMS for SCESS. The strategy integrates offline design planning with online adjustment to ensure that the power and energy states of the SCESS align in real time with load demand, thereby effectively enhancing operational energy efficiency. Section 2 establishes a model of the integrated SCESS. Section 3 provides a detailed analysis of the proposed EMS optimization methodology. A case study along with experimental validation is presented in Sect. 4. Finally, Sect. 5 summarizes the main conclusions of the paper.

2 Urban Rail Transit Modeling with SCESS

Figure 1 illustrates the URTS integrated with an SCESS. The overall system consists of three primary subsystems: the power supply system, the vehicle unit, and the SCESS. The power supply system fulfills a dual role by delivering power to traction loads, such as vehicle propulsion, as well as to non-traction loads, including lighting, escalators, ventilation, and station auxiliary equipment. The vehicle unit is responsible for passenger transportation, operating on fixed routes and schedules while adhering to predefined speed and timing requirements. The SCESS is strategically deployed within the traction substation, where it captures regenerative braking energy as trains decelerate into stations and releases stored energy during train acceleration, thereby enhancing energy recovery and lowering the overall energy consumption of the system.

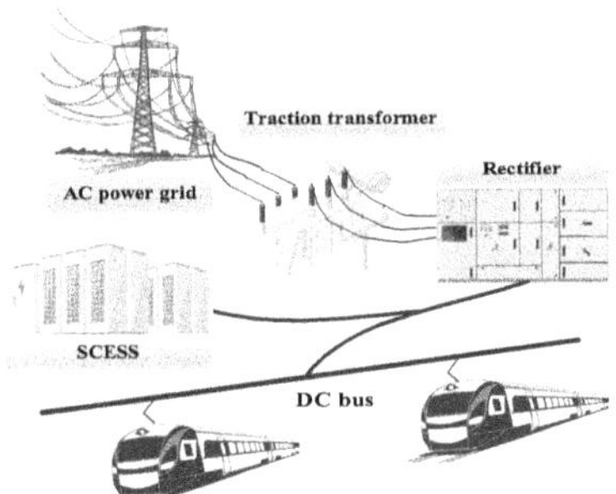

Fig. 1. Urban rail transit modeling with SCESS

The architecture of the SCESS, depicted in Fig. 2, comprises two main functional layers: the device layer and the control layer. The device layer includes DC/DC converters and SC units connected in parallel to the URTS DC bus network. This configuration enables bidirectional power flow between the traction network and the SCESS. The control layer monitors key system parameters—such as DC bus voltage, state of charge (SOC), and current—in real time, and employs pulse width modulation (PWM) control to regulate the charging and discharging processes of the SCESS.

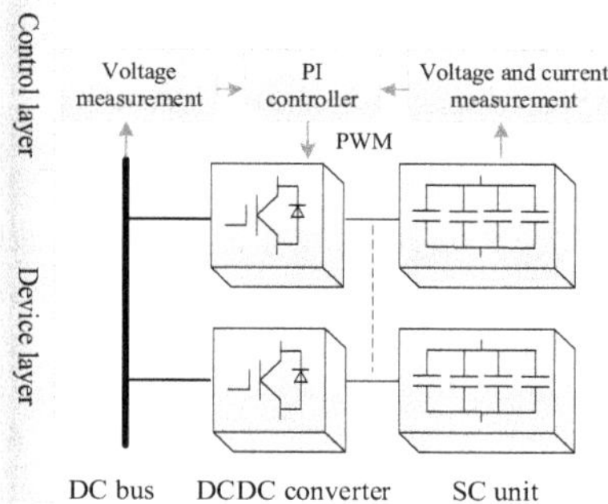

Fig. 2. Architecture of SCESS

In addition, the energy storage unit in the device layer is composed of multiple modules connected in both series and parallel configurations, and satisfies Eq. (1).

$$\begin{cases} C_{uc} = N_p \cdot C_m / N_s \\ u_{uc}(t) = u_{uc}^{ini} + \int_{ini}^{t} i_{uc}(t)/C_{uc}\,dt \\ soc(t) = \left[u_{uc}(t)/u_{uc}^{max} \right]^2 \\ E_{uc}(t) = \frac{1}{2}C_{uc} \cdot u_{uc}^2(t) \end{cases} \tag{1}$$

where N_p denotes the number of parallel branches in the SC bank, N_s represents the number of series connections in the SC bank, C_m is the nominal capacitance of a single SC module, C_{uc} is the total capacitance of the SC energy storage unit, $u_{uc}(t)$ and $u_{uc}(t)$ are the real-time voltage and initial voltage of the SC energy storage unit, respectively, $soc(t)$ denotes the state of charge, u_{uc}^{max} denotes the maximum operating voltage, and $E_{uc}(t)$ represents the real-time energy storage capacity of the SC energy storage unit.

3   EMS Based on Rolling Dynamic Programming (RDP-EMS)

The effective operation and management of SCESS in URTS are critical to overall system performance. Currently, the most widely adopted strategy is a threshold-based low-level control architecture, which identifies real-time operating conditions along the line and regulates SCESS power flow by stabilizing the DC bus voltage. However, the efficacy of this method heavily relies on the optimal design of threshold parameters. The implementation of ATO in URTS has improved the predictability of traction and braking power, as well as overall energy consumption. This progress creates new opportunities for more refined SCESS operation and control strategies.

This paper proposes a dynamic programming-based operational scheme for SCESS. The scheme determines the optimal operational trajectory to maximize energy efficiency by performing rolling optimization of the SCESS State of Energy (SOE). Dynamic programming, originally introduced by Richard Bellman, is an optimization technique that decomposes complex decision-making problems into interrelated stages and recursively determines the optimal sequence of decisions based on the principle of optimality. The SCESS SOE optimization problem satisfies two key prerequisites of dynamic programming—optimal substructure and the Markov property (non-aftereffect)—thus rendering it well-suited for this approach. The fundamental principle of dynamic programming is defined as follows:

$$\begin{cases} x(k+1) = f[x(k), u(k), k] \\ x(0) = x_0 \end{cases} \tag{2}$$

where $x(k)$ represents the state variable at the k-th stage, with $x(k) \in X \in R^n$, $u(k)$ denotes the control variable at the same stage, with $u(k) \in U(x(k), k) \in R^m$, k is the stage index, f denotes the transfer function, and x_0 is the initial state of the system.

It is worth noting here that the goal of the dynamic programming process is to identify the optimal control sequence $u^*(k)$ that minimizes the total cost function $J[x(0), u]$.

$$J[x(0), u] = \sum_{k=0}^{N-1} L[x(k), u(k), k] \tag{3}$$

The total cost function $J[x(0), u]$ is the sum of stage-wise cost functions L, and the cost at each stage k is given by:

$$J^*[x(k), k] = \min_{u(k)\in U} \left\{ J^*[x(k-1), u(k-1), k-1] + L_k[x(k), u(k)] \right\} \tag{4}$$

where $J^*[x(k), k]$ is the total cost of transitioning from the initial state $x(0)$ to state $x(k)$ along the optimal control sequence when the optimization process reaches stage k, and L_k represents the cost of transitioning from state $x(k-1)$ to state $x(k)$.

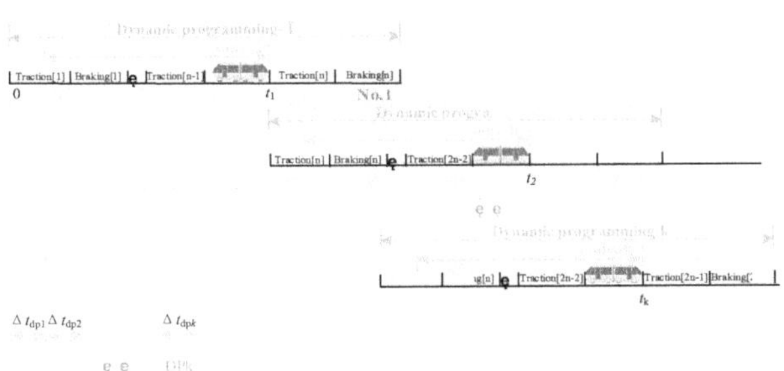

Fig. 3. Rolling dynamic programming process (RDP-EMS)

Figures 3 illustrate the rolling SOE planning process of SCESS using dynamic programming. The associated state and control variables are expressed in Eq. (5):

$$\begin{cases} x(t) = SOE(t) \\ u(t) = \Delta u(t) \end{cases} \tag{5}$$

where $\Delta u(t)$ is the threshold adjustment amount for the SCESS.

To maximize the energy-saving effect of the UCESS, the unabsorbed braking energy is selected as the objective function for optimization.

$$J = \min \int_0^t L\left(p_b^{veh} - p_c^{ess}\right) dt \tag{6}$$

where L is the stage cost function, comprising the vehicle braking power p_b^{veh} and the UCEES charging power p_c^{ess}.

The vehicle braking power is calculated by:

$$p_b^{veh} = \sum_1^n p_b^{veh,i}, p_b^{veh} < 0 \tag{7}$$

The objective function must be optimized within the feasible region defined by the state and decision variables, along with all operational constraints.

$$\begin{cases} SOE_{\min} \leq SOE(k) \leq SOE_{\max} \\ \Delta u_{\min} \leq \Delta u(k) \leq \Delta u_{\max} \\ u_{uc}^{\min} \leq u_{uc}(k) \leq u_{uc}^{\max} \\ 0 \leq i_{uc}(k) \leq i_{uc}^{\max} \end{cases} \tag{8}$$

where $u_{uc}(k)$ and $i_{uc}(k)$ denote the respective voltage and current on the low-voltage side of the SCESS, and $i_{uc}^{\max}$ represent the maximum allowable current.

According to Bellman's theory, this problem can be reformulated as a multi-stage decision model, targeting the minimization of total braking loss from the initial state to stage k. This yields the following recursive equation:

$$J^*[SOE(k), k] = \min_{u(k) \in U} \left\{ \begin{array}{l} J^*[SOE(k-1), \Delta u(k-1), k-1] \\ +L_k[SOE(k), \Delta u(k)] \end{array} \right\} \tag{9}$$

where $J^*[SOE(k), k]$ is the minimum total braking energy loss from the initial state to stage k.

On this basis, the corresponding optimal decision sequences for the energy storage decision are then given by:

$$u^*(k) = \arg \min J_k[SOE(k)] \tag{10}$$

4   Case Study

This study involves the development and field testing of a 1.5 MW SCESS prototype deployed in a subway station. The parameters of the power supply system and the SCESS are presented in Table 1 and Table 2, respectively. The substation is equipped with two rectifiers and employs a third-rail power supply system to deliver power to the trains. The SCESS is connected to the DC traction bus through dedicated positive and negative switch cabinets. The SC cabinet is installed on the low-voltage side of the DC/DC converter cabinet, while the control cabinet is placed on the high-voltage side. Figure 4 presents the prototype and its field installation layout. The system comprises three key components: a control cabinet, a converter cabinet, and an supercapacitor cabinet. The control cabinet is tasked with executing the RDP-EMS strategy proposed in this study. The converter cabinet employs a half-bridge topology for power distribution and voltage conversion, while the SC cabinet stores and delivers the energy recovered from regenerative braking.

Table 1. Parameters of the power supply system

Component	Parameter	Unit	Value
Power Supply System	External power supply voltage	kV	10
	DC supply voltage	V	750
	Supply capacity	kVA	2 * 2000

Table 2. Parameters of the SCESS

Component	Parameter	Unit	Value
SCESS	Rated power	kW	1500
	Energy storage	kWh	9.7
	Input voltage	V	500–1000
	SC voltage range	V	330–700

Experimental studies were carried out during normal subway operation to assess the reliability of the SCESS and the accuracy and effectiveness of its control system. Throughout the tests, key parameters including DC traction network voltage, SC voltage, and SC current were recorded using an oscilloscope. This paper compares the proposed RDP-EMS with the traditional fixed threshold energy management strategy (FT-EMS). Figures 5 and 6 present the oscilloscope waveforms of the SCESS over a 360-s period. The DC traction network voltage (200 V/div) is shown by the green curve, the SC voltage (100 V/div) by the pink curve, and the SC current (100 A/div) by the blue curve. Positive current values denote charging, while negative values indicate discharging.

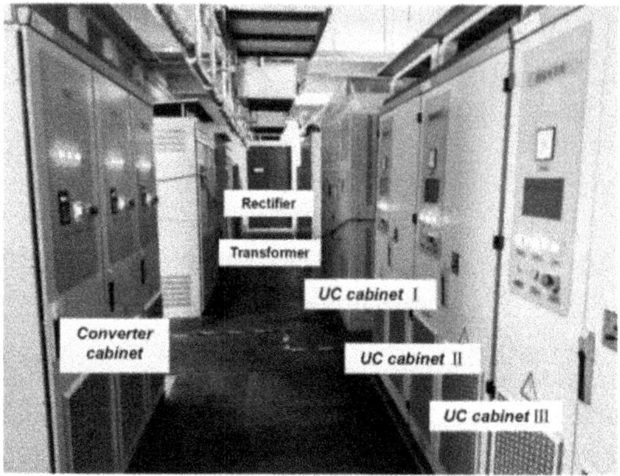

Fig. 4. Photograph of the 1.5 MW prototype and its on-site installation

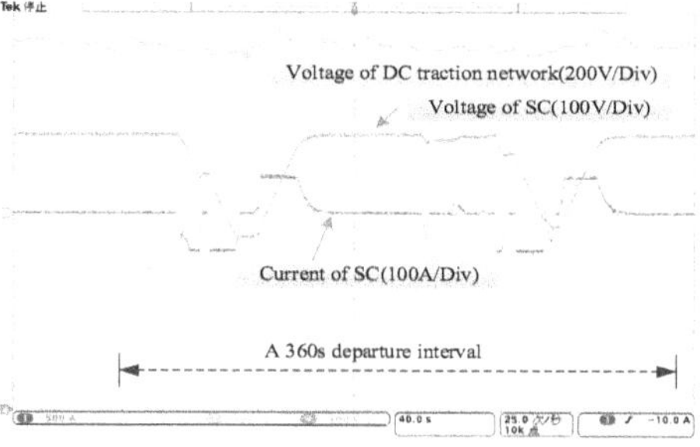

Fig. 5. Operation data recording of UCESS under FT-EMS

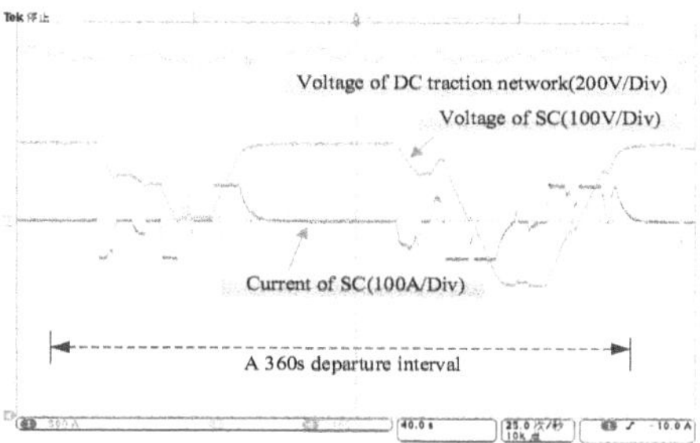

Fig. 6. Operation data recording of UCESS under RDP-EMS

For a comparative analysis of the performance between the two strategies, this study further examines the real-time power and power constraint limits of the SCESS under each approach. The real-time power was obtained by multiplying the measured voltage and current, whereas the power constraint limit was calculated as the product of the maximum allowable current and the real-time voltage. As shown in Fig. 7, the red dashed box indicates the charging phase. Owing to its more relaxed power constraint, the RDP-EMS captures a larger amount of regenerative braking energy than the FT-EMS, as evidenced by the yellow shaded area in the figure.

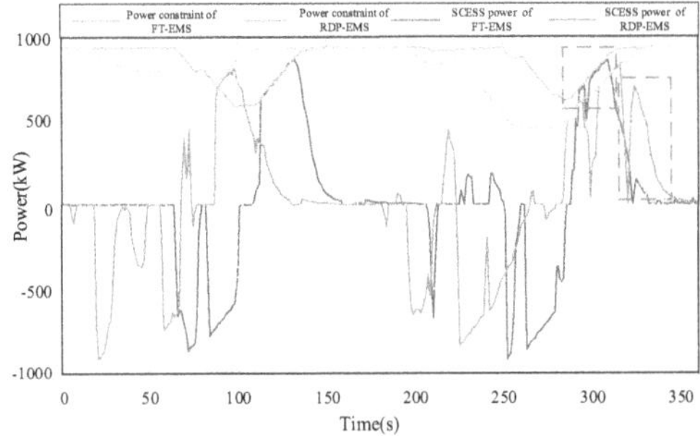

Fig. 7. Real-time operating power and constraint statistics

Table3 summarizes the traction substation output energy and the SCESS charging/discharging energy under three operating conditions. Under a 360-s departure interval, the substation consumes 64.70 kWh without UCESS. With the FT-EMS strategy, this value decreases to 55.04 kWh, corresponding to an energy saving of 14.93%. The proposed RDP-EMS strategy further reduces the output energy to 51.82 kWh, yielding a saving rate of 19.91%.

Table 3. Energy saving effect statistics and comparison

Strategy	Substation Output of (kWh)	Charging Energy of SCESS (kWh)	Discharging Energy of SCESS (kWh)	Energy saving rate (%)
Without SCESS	64.70	/	/	/
FT-EMS	55.04	12.75	11.84	14.93
RDP-EMS	51.82	14.28	13.13	19.91

Finally, comparative experiments were conducted under different departure intervals, as summarized in Fig. 8. During peak hours with a 150-s departure interval, the energy saving rate achieved by RDP-EMS was 5.51% higher than that of FT-EMS. Under off-peak conditions with a 600-s interval, this performance gap increased to 5.88%, further demonstrating the superior adaptability and efficiency of the proposed RDP-EMS strategy.

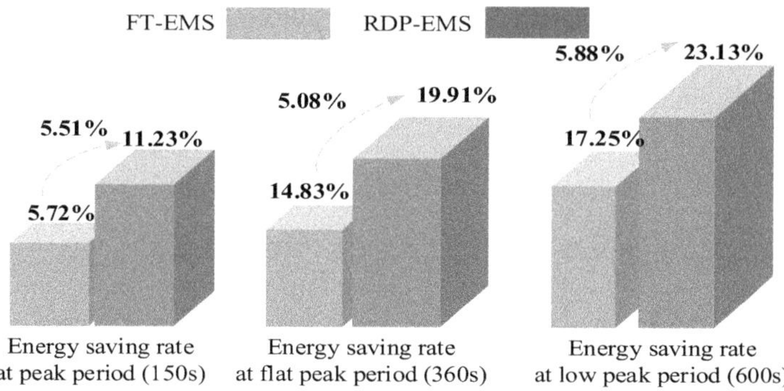

Fig. 8. Comparison of energy-saving rate under different departure intervals

5   Conclusion

To enhance the efficiency of supercapacitor energy storage systems (SCESS) in urban rail transit systems (URTS), this paper proposes an energy management strategy based on rolling dynamic programming. A prototype system was developed and deployed in a URTS traction substation to validate its practical feasibility. Experimental results demonstrate the effectiveness of the proposed RDP-EMS, which achieved energy savings of 5.51%, 5.08%, and 5.88% at departure intervals of 150, 360, and 600 s, respectively— consistently outperforming the FT-EMS strategy. By successfully implementing this strategy in engineering practice, significant energy savings can be achieved in URTS operations. This advancement plays a pivotal role in promoting green development within the transportation sector by reducing its carbon footprint and enhancing its operational sustainability.

References

1. Gao, Z., Fang, J., Zhang, Y., et al.: Control strategy for wayside supercapacitor energy storage system in railway transit network. J. Mod. Power Syst. Clean Energy **2**(2), 181–190 (2014)
2. Hayashiya, H., Abe, S., Iino, Y., et al.: Proposal of a novel control method of Li-ion battery system for regenerative energy utilization in traction power supply system. In: Power Electronics & Motion Control Conference. IEEE (2016)
3. Ciccarelli, F., Iannuzzi, D.: A novel energy management control of wayside Li-Ion capacitors-based energy storage for urban mass transit systems. In: International Symposium on Power Electronics Power Electronics, Electrical Drives, Automation and Motion. IEEE (2012)
4. Ciccarelli, F., Pizzo, D., et al.: Improvement of energy efficiency in light railway vehicles based on power management control of wayside lithium-ion capacitor storage. IEEE Trans. Power Electron. **29**(1), 275–286 (2013)
5. Grbovic, P.J., Delarue, P., Moigne, P.L., et al.: Modeling and control of the ultracapacitor-based regenerative controlled electric drives. IEEE Trans. Industr. Electron. **58**(8), 3471–3484 (2011)
6. Wang, J., Yang, Z., Lin, F., et al.: Thresholds modification strategy of wayside supercapacitor storage considering DC substation characteristics. In: IECON 2015 - 41st Annual Conference of the IEEE Industrial Electronics Society. IEEE (2016)

7. Lin, F., Li, X., Zhao, Y., et al.: Control strategies with dynamic threshold adjustment for supercapacitor energy storage system considering the train and substation characteristics in urban rail transit. Energies **9**(4), 257 (2016)
8. Yang, Z., Yang, Z., Xia, H., et al.: Brake voltage following control of supercapacitor-based energy storage systems in metro considering train operation state. IEEE Trans. Ind. Electron. (2018)
9. Liu, Y., Yang, Z., Wu, X., et al.: Adaptive threshold adjustment strategy based on fuzzy logic control for ground energy storage system in urban rail transit. IEEE Trans. Veh. Technol. **70**(10) (2021)
10. Yang, Z., Zhu, F., Lin, F.: Deep-reinforcement-learning-based energy management strategy for supercapacitor energy storage systems in urban rail transit. IEEE Trans. Intell. Transp. Syst. (2020)
11. Yoshida, Y., Arai, S., Kobayashi, H., et al.: Charge/discharge control of wayside batteries via reinforcement learning for energy-conservation in electrified railway systems. Electric. Eng. Japan (2021)

Capacity Optimization of Supercapacitor Energy Storage in Urban Rail Transit: A Cheetah Algorithm-Based Approach

Yajie Zhao$^{(\boxtimes)}$, Chuanfei Diao, and Fei Lin

Beijing Jiaotong University, Beijing 100044, China
`20117021@bjtu.edu.cn`

Abstract. Supercapacitor Energy Storage Systems (SCESS) are widely used in urban rail transit for recovering regenerative braking energy from trains. With the expansion of their applications, optimizing the economic benefits of SCESS has become an important research topic. This paper focuses on the capacity configuration of SCESS and proposes a joint optimization approach that integrates train dwell time and storage capacity. Based on a system model of urban rail transit and modular configuration principles, the proposed method uses the payback period as the optimization objective and employs a Cheetah-based swarm intelligence algorithm to determine the optimal configuration. The approach is validated using operational data from a real-world urban rail line in China. Case study results show that the joint optimization strategy reduces the payback period from 6.75 years to 5.01 years, compared to optimizing SCESS capacity alone, demonstrating a significant improvement in economic performance. Furthermore, when compared with other metaheuristic algorithms such as the Genetic Algorithm and Particle Swarm Optimization, the proposed method achieves better optimization efficiency and effectiveness.

Keywords: Supercapacitor Energy Storage Systems · Capacity Configuration · Payback Period · Cheetah Optimization

1 Background

With the widespread adoption of AC drive technology, regenerative braking has been increasingly implemented in urban rail transit trains. Unlike air braking, regenerative braking avoids brake shoe wear, thereby reducing maintenance costs and enabling the reuse of generated regenerative energy. The operational characteristics of urban rail systems—such as short inter-station distances, frequent starts and stops, and high train density—result in considerable regenerative braking energy. However, most traction substations in urban rail networks employ diode-based unidirectional rectifiers, which prevent the feedback of regenerative energy into the AC grid. In the absence of nearby traction trains capable of absorbing this energy, the DC bus voltage of the braking train rises sharply. To prevent overvoltage, the train resorts to resistor braking or regenerative current limiting, converting the braking energy into waste heat through braking resistors or shoes. This approach not only fails to utilize regenerative energy efficiently but also raises tunnel temperatures due to excessive heat dissipation.

Advances in energy storage technology have led to the application of various energy storage devices in urban rail transit. Currently, the main energy storage technologies include flywheels, supercapacitors, and batteries, each differing in cost, energy density, power density, and cycle life due to their distinct energy storage mechanisms. Among these, supercapacitors—also known as electric double-layer capacitors—are high-power storage devices composed of polarized electrodes, current collectors, a separator, and an electrolyte. The electrodes are typically made of porous activated carbon, which provides a large surface area and minimal charge separation distance, endowing supercapacitors with high capacitance. When voltage is applied, supercapacitors can charge and discharge rapidly. Throughout this process, ions move without undergoing chemical reactions with the electrodes. As a result, supercapacitors offer high efficiency, long cycle life, and high power density, making them well-suited to the high-power and frequent cycling demands of urban rail traction systems.

The development of supercapacitor energy storage systems (SCESS) capacity configuration methods can be divided into three distinct phases. In the initial phase, researchers established fundamental principles using basic analytical techniques. For example, Teymourfar et al. [1] proposed a method based on instantaneous power boundary conditions; however, this early approach was later found to result in equipment redundancy in practical investment scenarios. The second phase saw the introduction of optimization algorithms into SCESS capacity design. Lee et al. [2] applied Lagrangian optimization combined with gradient search iteration and validated their method through simulation based on Seoul Metro Line 7. Building on this, Wang et al. [3] improved computational efficiency and simulation speed using an enhanced genetic algorithm. Chen et al. [4] further advanced the field by proposing an integrated optimization framework that simultaneously considered control parameters and capacity planning in system design. Other innovations included Pang et al.'s [5] non-dominated sorting genetic algorithm (NSGA) based on a simplified model, and Liu et al.'s [6] weighted optimization model that balanced investment costs and substation-level energy consumption in a hybrid energy storage system. Although these second-phase studies effectively utilized heuristic algorithms to optimize SCESS capacity through multi-objective approaches, several key limitations emerged. Most notably, the optimization results were highly system-specific, meaning the corresponding methods and processes were tailored to particular use cases and lacked reproducibility. This characteristic significantly restricted their practical application in large-scale industrial and mass production scenarios, highlighting the need for more universal and scalable optimization frameworks.

The current forefront of SCESS capacity optimization—constituting the third phase—emphasizes system-level coordination across multiple dimensions, which has become a major focus of contemporary research. Notably, Kampeerawat et al. [7] proposed a weighted multi-objective optimization approach that effectively balances substation-level energy consumption and energy storage system capacity. References [8, 9] designed and established a multi-objective optimization framework integrating vehicle time parameters (e.g., running/dwelling duration) with onboard SCESS configuration, employing a genetic algorithm validated using operational data from metro systems in Bangkok and Jinan. Further advancing this direction, Wang et al. [10] introduced a hybrid optimization strategy combining an artificial bee colony algorithm with differential methods for onboard energy storage deployment. They conducted a comparative performance analysis using operational data from the Beijing Metro. However, their approach has inherent limitations, as onboard energy storage systems are subject to operational constraints different from those of stationary storage installations. Moreover, Zhu et al. [11] made notable progress in this phase by developing an integrated optimization model that coupled no-load voltage of traction substations, braking resistor activation thresholds, vehicle parameters, and SCESS capacity. Although this model demonstrated theoretical performance improvements via genetic algorithm optimization, its practical application still faces significant obstacles. In particular, key infrastructure variables such as substation no-load voltage are typically fixed in operational railway networks, making real-time adjustments impractical. Despite the model's theoretical robustness, this fundamentally limits its real-world applicability, underscoring the persistent challenge of aligning theoretical optimization formulations with practical engineering applications and constraints.

This paper presents a joint optimization method based on the Cheetah Optimization Algorithm to enhance the economic performance of SCESS. Section 2 outlines the urban rail transit modeling framework. Section 3 details the principles and framework of the proposed algorithm, followed by a case study in Sect. 4. The paper concludes with the findings and conclusions in Sect. 5.

2 Modeling of Urban Rail Transit Systems

The traction power supply system comprises substations, SCESS, trains, overhead contact lines, running rails, and return lines. As illustrated in Fig. 1, the DC traction power supply system forms a complex nodal network topology. Due to the real-time operation of trains on both upward and downward tracks, this topology exhibits time-varying behavior and parallel multi-conductor characteristics.

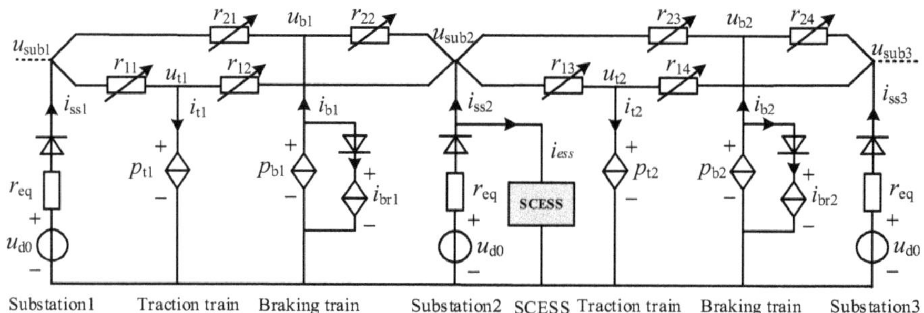

Fig. 1. Circuit topology diagram of traction power supply system with SCESS

By applying Kirchhoff's Current Law (KCL) to the circuit topology shown in Fig. 1, the nodal voltage equations for the traction power supply system can be derived as given in Eq. (1).

$$
\begin{bmatrix}
\frac{1}{r_{11}}+\frac{1}{r_{21}} & -\frac{1}{r_{11}} & -\frac{1}{r_{21}} & 0 & 0 & 0 & 0 \\
-\frac{1}{r_{11}} & \frac{1}{r_{11}}+\frac{1}{r_{12}} & 0 & -\frac{1}{r_{12}} & 0 & 0 & 0 \\
-\frac{1}{r_{21}} & 0 & \frac{1}{r_{21}}+\frac{1}{r_{22}} & -\frac{1}{r_{22}} & 0 & 0 & 0 \\
0 & -\frac{1}{r_{12}} & -\frac{1}{r_{22}} & \frac{1}{r_{12}}+\frac{1}{r_{22}}+\frac{1}{r_{13}}+\frac{1}{r_{23}} & -\frac{1}{r_{13}} & -\frac{1}{r_{23}} & 0 \\
0 & 0 & 0 & -\frac{1}{r_{13}} & \frac{1}{r_{13}}+\frac{1}{r_{14}} & 0 & -\frac{1}{r_{14}} \\
0 & 0 & 0 & -\frac{1}{r_{23}} & 0 & \frac{1}{r_{23}}+\frac{1}{r_{24}} & -\frac{1}{r_{24}} \\
0 & 0 & 0 & 0 & -\frac{1}{r_{14}} & -\frac{1}{r_{24}} & \frac{1}{r_{14}}+\frac{1}{r_{24}}
\end{bmatrix}
\begin{bmatrix}
u_{\text{sub1}} \\ u_{\text{t1}} \\ u_{\text{b1}} \\ u_{\text{sub2}} \\ u_{\text{t2}} \\ u_{\text{b2}} \\ u_{\text{sub3}}
\end{bmatrix}
=
\begin{bmatrix}
i_{\text{ss1}} \\ i_{\text{t1}} \\ i_{\text{b1}} \\ i_{\text{ss2}} \\ i_{\text{t2}} \\ i_{\text{b1}} \\ i_{\text{ss3}}
\end{bmatrix}
\tag{1}
$$

In the formula, $r_{11}, r_{12}, r_{13}, r_{14}, r_{21}, r_{22}, r_{23}$, and r_{24} are the line resistances, and the value of the line resistance varies depending on the position of the train on the line. U_{sub1}, $u_{\text{sub2}}, u_{\text{sub3}}, i_{\text{ss1}}, i_{\text{ss2}}$, and i_{ss3} are the output voltages and output currents of substation 1, substation 2 and substation 3, respectively. $u_{\text{t1}}, u_{\text{b1}}, u_{\text{t2}}, u_{\text{b2}}, i_{\text{t1}}, i_{\text{b1}}, i_{\text{t2}}$, and i_{b2} are the contact wire side voltage and current values of traction train 1, braking train 1, traction train 2, and braking train 2, respectively.

2.1 Substation Modeling

As shown in Fig. 2, the equivalent circuit of a substation can be represented by an ideal voltage source in series with an equivalent internal resistance, and its output characteristics are also provided.

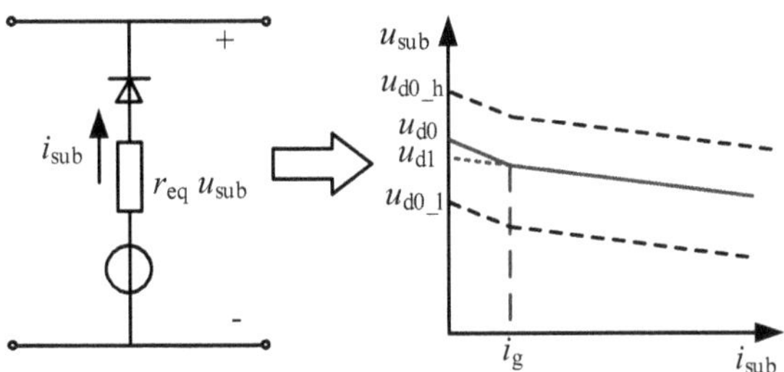

Fig. 2. Equivalent circuit and voltage and current output characteristics of the substation

$$
u_{\text{sub}} =
\begin{cases}
u_{\text{d0}} - i_{\text{sub}} \cdot r_{\text{eq0}} & 0 < i_{\text{sub}} \leq i_{\text{g}} \\
u_{\text{d1}} - i_{\text{sub}} \cdot r_{\text{eq1}} & i_{\text{sub}} > i_{\text{g}}
\end{cases}
\tag{2}
$$

In the formula, u_{d0} is the no-load voltage of the substation, u_{d1} is the equivalent voltage of the substation characteristic curve when $i_{sub} > i_g$; r_{eq0} and r_{eq1} are the equivalent resistance of the substation, i_g is the critical current value, and u_{sub} and i_{sub} are the substation output voltage and output current, respectively. As shown in the figure, since the no-load voltage will fluctuate within the range of u_{d0_l} and u_{d0_h}, the substation characteristic curve will also shift up and down with the change of the no-load voltage.

2.2 Train Modeling

During traction, the train's energy demand is supplied by the traction substation, nearby braking trains, and the SCESS, resulting in a voltage drop across the contact network. During braking, part of the regenerative braking energy is used to power the train's auxiliary systems, while the remainder is fed back into the contact network and absorbed by nearby traction trains and the energy storage system, leading to a rise in the network voltage. Due to the current-limiting nature of regenerative braking, an onboard braking resistor is activated when the voltage exceeds the allowable range to suppress overvoltage. The train model, depicted in Fig. 3, represents both the traction system and the braking resistor using controlled current sources.

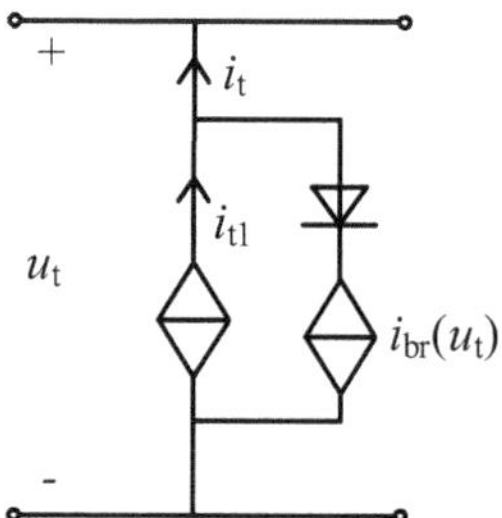

Fig. 3. Train equivalent circuit model

During braking, the onboard braking resistor dissipates regenerative energy by regulating the duty cycle of the braking chopper based on the DC-link capacitor voltage. The resulting current is governed by Eq. (3), while the permissible feeder current for the train is given by Eq. (4).

$$i_{br} = \begin{cases} 0, u_t \leq u_{brst} \\ \frac{u_t - u_{brst}}{u_{brlim} - u_{brst}} \cdot \frac{u_t}{R_b}, u_t > u_{brst} \end{cases} \tag{3}$$

$$i_t = i_{t1} - i_{br} \tag{4}$$

In the formula, u_t is the train voltage, R_b is the resistance value of the on-board braking resistor, u_{brst} is the starting voltage of the braking resistor, u_{brlim} is the limiting voltage of the braking resistor; i_{t1} is the train current, i_{br} is the current consumed by the braking resistor, and i_t is the train feeder current.

2.3 SCESS Modeling

The equivalent circuit models for the low-voltage and overhead contact line sides of the SCESS are depicted in Fig. 4. For the low-voltage side, a first-order supercapacitor model is introduced. This model accurately represents the variations in voltage, current, and stored energy at the energy storage terminal, rendering it appropriate for steady-state system analysis.

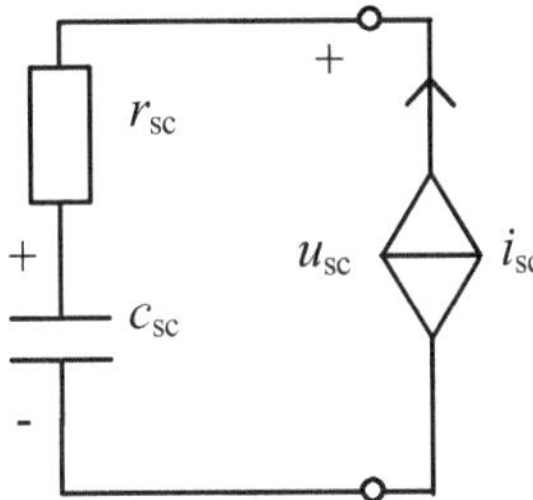

Fig. 4. Supercapactior equivalent circuit model

$$u_{sc}(t) = v_{osc}(t) + i_{sc}(t) \cdot r_{sc} \tag{5}$$

In the formula, $u_{sc}(t)$ is the real-time voltage of the supercapacitor, $v_{osc}(t)$ is the voltage across the equivalent capacitor of the supercapacitor, and $i_{sc}(t)$ is the current of the supercapacitor.

3 The Proposed Joint Optimization Allocation Strategy

To improve economic returns, a novel method is proposed that co-optimizes SCESS capacity and train dwell time. The optimization aims to minimize the investment payback period, as formalized below:

$$\min f(T_w, M_e) = \frac{C_{uc}}{365 \cdot E_{save} \cdot C_{ele}} \tag{6}$$

where T_w is the dwell time sequence at each station, M_e is the number of the UCESS installation sequence, E_{save} represents the single-day energy savings, and C_{uc} is the investment cost of the SCESS. C_{ele} is the electricity price.

The calculation of energy savings is defined as:

$$\begin{cases} E_{save} = E_{sub}^{bef} - E_{sub}^{opt} \\ E_{sub}^{bef} = w_1 \cdot E_{sub,t_1}^{bef} + w_2 \cdot E_{sub,t_2}^{bef} + ... + w_i \cdot E_{sub,t_i}^{bef} \\ E_{sub}^{opt} = w_1 \cdot E_{sub,t_1}^{opt} + w_2 \cdot E_{sub,t_2}^{opt} + ... + w_i \cdot E_{sub,t_i}^{opt} \end{cases} \tag{7}$$

where E_{sub}^{bef} and E_{sub}^{opt} denote the total output of the traction substation in one day before and after optimization, respectively, and variables w_1, w_2, and w_i correspond to the respective frequencies of departure intervals t_1, t_2, and t_i within a single day.

The cost of the SCESS is determined by its power and capacity specifications. A modular design approach is adopted to comply with industry standards. As such, the total investment cost for the SCESS is calculated as follows:

$$C_{uc} = \sum_{1}^{n} m_e^i \cdot C_{uc}^{\mathrm{mod}} \tag{8}$$

where m_e^i is the number of SCESS units installed at the i-th traction substation, and C_{uc}^{mod} is the cost of a single standardized unit.

In addition to meeting the basic needs of passengers and maintaining proper service quality, dwell times must also meet the following constraints:

$$t_w^{i\,\min} \leq t_w^i \leq t_w^{i\,\max} \tag{9}$$

where $t_w^{i\,\min}$ and $t_w^{i\,\max}$ represent the minimum and maximum allowable dwell times at the i-th station, respectively.

This paper presents an algorithm framework, depicted in Fig. 5, for the holistic optimization of capacity configuration and dwell time, considering the nonlinear energy

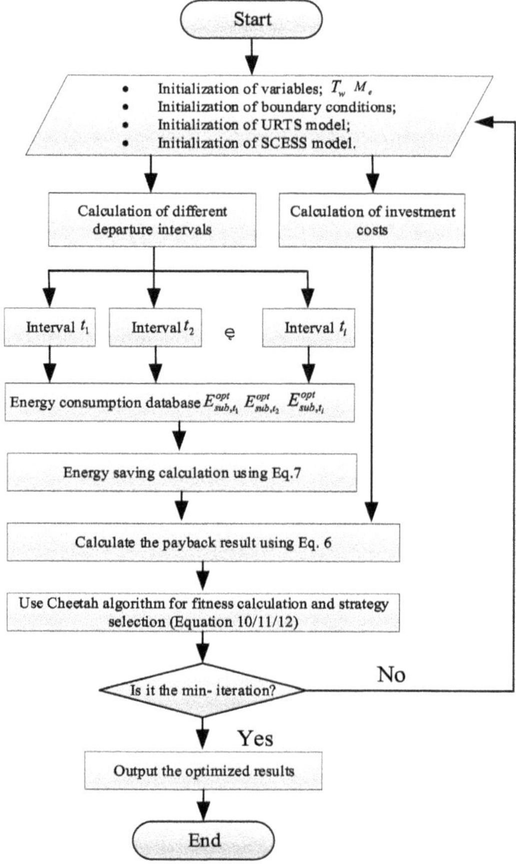

Fig. 5. Design optimization process based on CA

coupling between the URTS and SCESS. The framework employs a heuristic swarm intelligence technique based on the Cheetah Algorithm (Akbari et al., 2022), which emulates the search, wait, and attack hunting tactics of cheetahs to iteratively refine solutions. A key feature of this algorithm is its robust optimization capability coupled with rapid convergence.

The iterative mechanisms of the algorithm are described as follows:

- Search strategy:

$$X_{i,j}^{t+1} = X_{i,j}^t + r_{i,j}^{-1} \cdot \alpha_{i,j}^t \tag{10}$$

- Wait strategy:

$$X_{i,j}^{t+1} = X_{i,j}^t \tag{11}$$

- Attack strategy:

$$X_{i,j}^{t+1} = X_{B,j}^t + \theta_{i,j} \cdot \beta_{i,j}^t \tag{12}$$

where $r_{i,j}^{-1}$ represents the random factor, $\alpha_{i,j}^t$ denotes the search step length, $X_{B,j}^t$ is the current optimal position, and $\theta_{i,j}$ and $\beta_{i,j}^t$ denote the steering factor and interaction factor, respectively.

4   Case Study

A case study is conducted using operational data from a metro line in China. The line comprises 13 stations and 10 traction substations. A schematic diagram of the line is provided in Fig. 6, which includes key parameters such as inter-station distances and dwell times. The line operates with 6-car Type B trains, with detailed specifications provided in Table 1. In consideration of the significant advantages of modular design for large-scale SCESS deployment, the module shown in Table 2 is adopted as the minimal configuration unit.

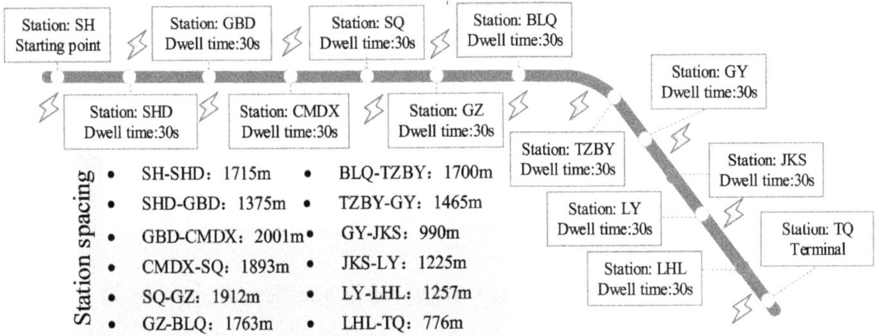

Fig. 6. Schematic diagram of the case study line

Table 1. Parameters of the vehicle

Component	Parameter	Unit	Value
Vehicle	Rated voltage	V	750
	Vehicle load	t	AW0: 200 AW2: 288.08 AW3: 312.8
	Maximum speed	km/h	80
	Maximum dwell time	s	25
	Minimum dwell time	s	35

Table 2. Parameters of the modular SCESS

Component	Parameter	Unit	Value
Modular UCESS	Rated power	kW	500
	Energy storage	kWh	2.52
	Input voltage	V	500–1000
	UC voltage range	V	330–700
	Investment cost	yuan	600,000

As illustrated in Fig. 7, a simulation platform has been developed in this study to support the design optimization process. The platform consists of three core components: DC Power Flow Analysis (DC-PFA), Multi-Train Traction Calculation (MTTC), and Design Optimization based on the Cheetah Algorithm (DO-CA). The DC-PFA module models traction substations and line impedances, capturing energy outputs as well as voltage and current dynamics within the traction power supply system. It transmits real-time voltage and current data via an information bus. The MTTC module simulates the traction and braking processes of multiple trains, accounting for energy consumption and various interactions among them. It also feeds train position, voltage, and current data into the information bus. Integrated with the system, the SCESS incorporates a modular SCESS energy storage model to reflect its power and energy fluctuations under different configurations, and transmits corresponding power and energy data to the information bus. Finally, the DO-CA module executes the proposed optimization algorithm, leveraging the Cheetah Algorithm to handle system design and performance computations.

The optimization process and corresponding results are presented in Fig. 8 and Table 3, respectively. Implementation results show that the DO-CA algorithm converges after 600 iterations, whereas the Genetic Algorithm (GA) and Particle Swarm Optimization (PSO) require 655 and 690 iterations, respectively, indicating higher computational efficiency of the proposed method. Moreover, the final solution obtained by DO-CA outperforms those of GA and PSO, highlighting its stronger capability in global exploration and optimization.

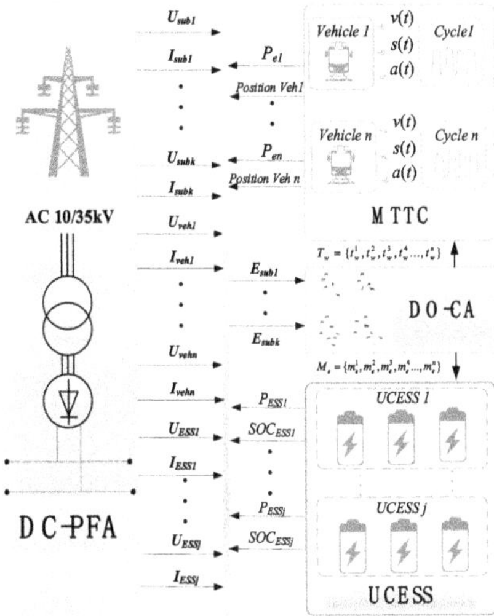

Fig. 7. Simulation platform for design optimization phase

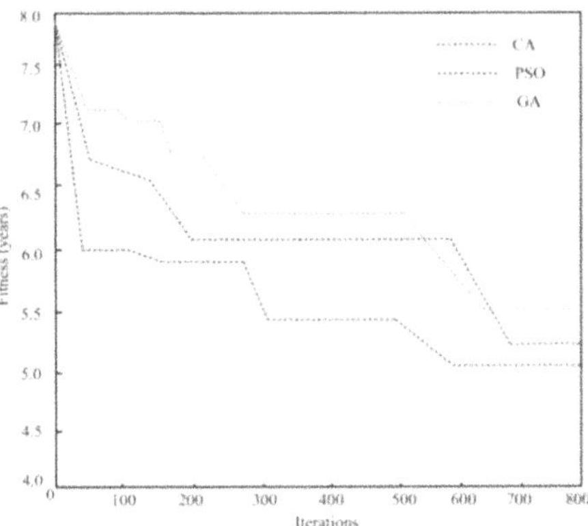

Fig. 8. Optimization process and comparison with conventional methods

The payback period comparison between different optimization methods is shown in Table 4. It is shown that the joint optimization approach reduces total investment by 25.7% and shortens the payback period from 6.75 years to 5.01 years compared to the SCEES-only optimization scenario.

Table 3. Design optimization results and comparison

Station	SCESS-only Optimization		Joint SCESS Optimization	
	Dwell time (s)	SCESS (unit)	Dwell time (s)	SCESS (unit)
SH	30	3	35	2
SHD	30	3	28	2
GBD	30	4	30	3
CMDX	30	4	35	2
SQ	30	3	26	3
GZ	30	3	28	2
BLQ	30	3	31	2
TZBY	30	4	30	3
GY	30	3	25	3
JKS*	30	/	25	/
LY	30	2	32	2
LHL*	30	/	34	/
TQ	30	3	35	2
Total	390	35	394	26

Table 4. Comparison of investment payback period

Approach	Investment (yuan)	Payback period (year)
SCESS-only Optimization	21,000,000	6.75
Joint SCESS Optimization	15,600,000	5.01

5 Conclusion

This study proposes a co-optimization strategy based on the Cheetah Algorithm to enhance the economic performance of supercapacitor energy storage systems (SCESS) in urban rail transit. By simultaneously optimizing train dwell time and SCESS capacity, the strategy effectively reduces the investment payback period. Simulation results demonstrate that the proposed approach shortens the payback period from 6.75 years to 5.01 years, a reduction of 25.7%, indicating significant economic improvement. The strategy contributes to the development of low-carbon transportation and supports energy conservation and emission reduction in urban rail systems. Due to length constraints, future work will involve field validation through practical engineering projects to further verify the operational effectiveness of the proposed method.

References

1. Teymourfar, R., Asaei, B., Iman-Eini, H.: Stationary super-capacitor energy storage system to save regenerative braking energy in a metro line. Energy Convers. Manage. **56**, 206–214 (2012)
2. Lee, H., et al.: Capacity optimization of the supercapacitor energy storages on DC railway system using a railway powerflow algorithm. Int. J. Innovative Comput. Inf. Control, 2739–2753 (2011)
3. Wang, B., Yang, Z., Lin, F., et al.: An improved genetic algorithm for optimal stationary energy storage system locating and sizing. Energies **7**(10), 6434–6458 (2014)
4. Chen, H., Yang, Z., Lin, F., et al.: Research on energy management and capacity configuration optimization of supercapacitor energy storage devices for urban rail transit based on genetic algorithm. J. China Railway Soc. **41**(09), 59–66 (2019)
5. Pang, T., Zhao, R., Jiang, L., et al.: Capacity configuration method of urban rail energy storage system based on NSGA-II and simplified energy storage model. In: 2023 IEEE 3rd International Conference on Industrial Electronics for Sustainable Energy Systems (IESES), pp. 1–6. IEEE (2023)
6. Liu, Y., Yang, Z., Lin, F., et al.: Research on adaptive energy management and capacity optimization configuration of urban rail ground hybrid energy storage system. Trans. Chin. Soc. Electrotech. Eng. **36**(23), 4874–4884 (2021)
7. Kampeerawat, W., Koseki, T.: A strategy for utilization of regenerative energy in urban railway system by application of smart train scheduling and wayside energy storage system. Energy Procedia **138**, 795–800 (2017)
8. Kampeerawat, W., Koseki, T.: Efficient urban railway design integrating train scheduling, wayside energy storage, and traction power management. IEEJ J. Ind. Appl. **8**(6), 915–925 (2019)
9. Wang, X., Sun, P., Wang, Q., et al.: Joint optimization combining the capacity of subway on-board energy storage device and timetable. IET Intell. Transp. Syst. **17**(1), 193–210 (2023)
10. Zhu, F., Yang, Z., Zhao, Z., et al.: Two-stage synthetic optimization of supercapacitor-based energy storage systems, traction power parameters and train operation in urban rail transit. IEEE Trans. Veh. Technol. **70**(9), 8590–8605 (2021)
11. Gao, Z., Fang, J., Zhang, Y., et al.: Control strategy for wayside supercapacitor energy storage system in railway transit network. J. Mod. Power Syst. Clean Energy **2**(2), 181–190 (2014)

A Coordinated Optimization Strategy for Electric Vehicle Charging Guidance Under Urban Road Network Constraints

Lingyu Guo[1], Yang Du[1], Zhongguang Yang[1], and Yun Zhou[2]([✉])

[1] Electric Power Research Institute, State Grid Shanghai Electric Power Company, Shanghai 200437, China
[2] School of Electrical Engineering, Shanghai Jiao Tong University, Shanghai 200240, China
`weekcloud@126.com`

Abstract. The growing penetration of electric vehicles (EVs) in urban road networks has brought the problem of EV charging to the forefront. To tackle the EV charging guidance issue in urban road networks, this paper presents an EV guidance strategy based on Mixed Integer Linear Programming (MILP), taking the road network structure of the Dalinghao bay area as the research basis. First, a vehicle-road-network information model is constructed, incorporating the road network structure of the Dalinghao bay area, as well as information regarding local EV fleets and charging station clusters. Second, an EV charging guidance model for urban road networks is formulated using the MILP model, with input data obtained from the vehicle-road-network information model. Finally, practical computational examples are utilized to elaborate on the fundamental characteristics of the proposed method and validate its effectiveness and feasibility. Results from the computational experiments demonstrate that the proposed strategy effectively reduces EV queuing time and improves the utilization balance of charging infrastructure.

Keywords: Electric Vehicle Charging Guidance · Urban Road Network Modeling · Mixed-Integer Linear Programming · Spatiotemporal Optimization

1 Introduction

China's new energy vehicle (NEV) penetration rate hit 31.6% in 2023, and by May 2024, it had risen to a high level of 47.8%. Fueled by ongoing technological innovations, electric vehicle (EV) sales have surged, and their proportion of the overall automotive market has continued to expand. Nevertheless, this rapid development trend has posed challenges in terms of charging guidance [1, 2]. Within complex urban road network environments, EV charging guidance presents substantial hurdles. If a large number of urban EVs engage in uncoordinated charging at a given moment, it is highly likely to result in massive charging queues, greatly prolonging the waiting time for EV users and thereby disrupting their travel plans. More critically, it may lead to congestion in both road networks and charging stations, thereby impairing the operational efficiency of urban

A. Razminia et al. (Eds.): ITFT 2025, CCIS 2876, pp. 240–251, 2026.
https://doi.org/10.1007/978-3-032-20592-6_22

transportation and charging infrastructures. Existing strategies do not fully account for EV charging guidance in complex urban road networks, which may significantly increase EV users' waiting times and reduce the operational efficiency of charging stations.

Recent research on EV guidance strategies in urban road networks primarily focuses on temporal optimization [3]. Temporal guidance seeks to make EV users charge at more economical times with lighter grid loads, achieving load balancing and cost optimization. Literature [4] proposes a V2G-based real-time EV dispatching strategy to reduce charging and grid loss costs. Literature [5] uses a fuzzy control algorithm to optimize EV charging plans, meeting charging demands while realizing grid peak shaving and valley filling. Literature [6] develops a spatiotemporal EV guidance strategy considering charging decision conflicts and TOU service fees. It reduces user charging costs, improves operator revenues, eases distribution network load fluctuations, and promotes rational spatiotemporal distribution of charging loads via bilateral matching and TOU pricing. Literature [7] introduces a CSMS based on an improved TD3 deep reinforcement learning algorithm. Its core is to maximize EVCS operational revenue; by optimizing electricity procurement, photovoltaic utilization, and energy storage dispatching, it enhances charging station economic benefits, promoting infrastructure expansion and EV popularization to support climate change mitigation.

The second research focus lies in spatial guidance. Spatial guidance works by merging traffic road network and charging station information, then guiding EVs according to geographic data. Literature [8] builds a multi-objective optimization model that includes "vehicle-station-road-network" factors; it uses a graph reinforcement learning algorithm to capture information from irregular environments and learn strategies for fast EV charging guidance. Literature [9] puts forward a method for simulating urban charging loads and a corresponding spatial guidance strategy that accounts for user preferences in hot weather. This solution boosts the accuracy of simulating the spatiotemporal distribution of charging loads when faced with conditions like high temperatures or traffic congestion. Spatiotemporal dual-scale guidance seeks to guide EV charging by jointly considering the time and space dimensions in a comprehensive manner.

At the same time, several studies have also been conducted regarding spatiotemporal coordination. Literature [10] puts forward a charging strategy that integrates EV spatiotemporal coordination. Its utility lies in effectively mitigating power grid congestion, enhancing the utilization efficiency of charging stations, and cutting down user waiting time and charging costs through the integration of spatiotemporal dimension optimization and dispatching.

Many existing studies have paid limited attention to the impact of urban road network characteristics. As a result, when EVs submit charging requests within complex urban environments, it may be challenging for cloud platforms to obtain timely and accurate real-time vehicle data. This can hinder the ability to estimate EV arrival times and travel distances to charging stations, potentially reducing the effectiveness of charging guidance and leading to increased queuing times. To address these limitations, this paper proposes a charging guidance strategy that incorporates urban road network factors. First, a digital model of the Dalinghao Bay area's road network is constructed using geographic data and an open digital map API. Then, vehicle-road-network information is integrated into a Mixed-Integer Linear Programming (MILP) framework to optimize the charging guidance process. Finally, simulation experiments conducted on the Dalinghao Bay road network in Shanghai demonstrate that the proposed strategy can help reduce user queuing times and improve the operational efficiency of charging stations.

2 Multi-dimensional EV Charging Guidance Architecture for Urban Road Networks

To reduce the waiting time of EV users queuing for charging services at stations, this study develops a charging guidance framework tailored to urban traffic network features (see Fig. 1). The framework is structured into three interactive components: the road network execution layer, the charging station-vehicle communication layer, and the cloud-based decision layer. Upon initiating a charging request, EV users transmit relevant vehicle data to both the cloud platform and the real-time traffic network. Through data synchronization between the real-time traffic network and the cloud, critical vehicle attributes, including real-time position, vehicle energy parameters, and current state of charge (SOC), are accurately computed. The cloud system then integrates this data with real-time road conditions to establish a dynamic digital map. Based on this modeled network, optimal charging stations are assigned to users, enabling streamlined and effective charging guidance.

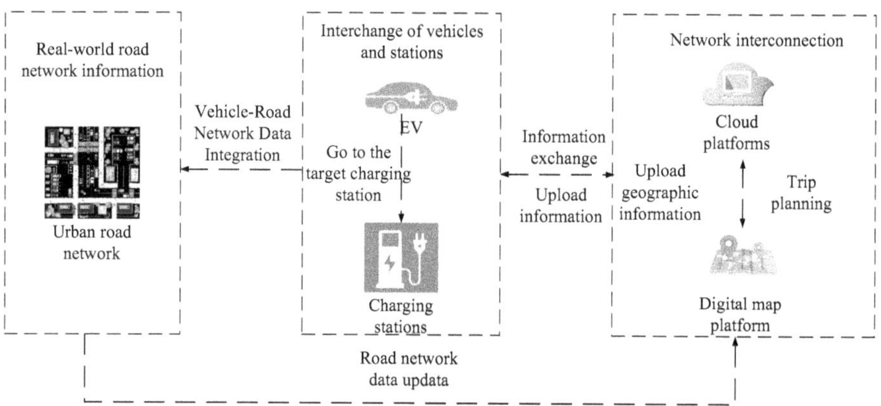

Fig. 1. Urban road network EV charging guidance framework.

The specific workflow of the EV optimized guidance strategy proposed in this paper is as follows:

1) Upon submitting a charging application, an EV user first uploads to the cloud a set of data: their real-time position on the road network (expressed as latitude-longitude coordinates), road network attributes, EV specifications, and information about charging stations within the dispatching area. Additionally, the user provides real-time vehicle data, such as the EV's current SOC. Concurrently, charging stations in the dispatching zone transmit their operational status to the cloud, including charger occupancy status, electricity pricing for charging, and reservation availability. After

aggregating this data, the cloud collaborates with the digital map system to build a dynamic real-time model of the urban road network, which is used to compute necessary EV-related data.

2) Utilizing the dynamic real-time urban road network model, the cloud and digital map system calculate parameters for each EV's trip to every charging station in the dispatching zone—including estimated arrival time, travel distance, and charging time. Based on the MILP model, the cloud platform determines the optimal charging station and formulates a charging plan for each EV. Subsequently, the digital map system generates corresponding route guidance based on these decisions.

3) In cases where certain EVs remain unguided in the current dispatch round, these unguided users are prioritized for guidance in the subsequent round to maintain user satisfaction. During this process, charging stations in the dispatching zone upload their charger data and the arrival rate of EVs. The cloud proceeds to compute the service intensity of each station, assessing two key factors: whether the charging stations are utilized optimally and whether EV users have the shortest possible queuing time.

3   Establishment of Urban Road Network Model

3.1   Definition of Fundamental Parameters

Prior to introducing the strategy proposed in this paper, the basic parameters utilized herein need to be defined first. In (1)–(4), S_{St} refers to the set of charging stations in the dispatch area; S_{EV} refers to the set of EVs that have made charging applications within the dispatch area; S_j^P refers to the set of charging piles in the j-th charging station within the dispatch area; S_T refers to the discrete time window of the dispatch cycle.

$$S_{St} = \{1, 2, 3, ..., N_{St}\} \tag{1}$$

$$S_{EV} = \{1, 2, 3, ..., N_{EV}\} \tag{2}$$

$$S_j^P = \{N_1^P, N_2^P, N_3^P, ..., N_j^P\}, j \in S_{St} \tag{3}$$

$$S_T = \{1, 2, 3, ..., N_T\} \tag{4}$$

Among the defined parameters, N_{St} stands for the total number of charging stations in the dispatch area; N_{EV} stands for the number of EVs requiring charging service within the dispatch area; N_j^P stands for the number of charging piles in the j-th charging station; N_T refers to the discretization of the dispatch cycle T, where $N_T = T / \Delta t$ and Δt is the time step size.

3.2   Construction of Urban Road Network Models

Modeling of urban road networks is performed using data uploaded from road networks to the cloud and digital platforms, intended to compute parameters like EV arrival time at each charging station in the dispatch area, charging time, and distance traveled after a charging request is initiated. Initially, the cloud and digital map platforms delineate the boundaries of the physical urban road network and reconstruct its structure within the digital map environment. Subsequently, the delineate digital road network undergoes re-division into segments at 100 m × 100 m intervals, as shown in Fig. 2(b).

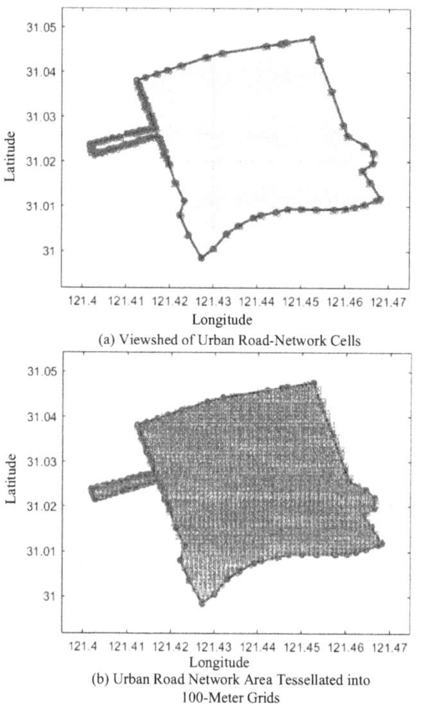

Fig. 2. Digital modeling of urban road networks.

3.3 Calculation of Vehicle-Road Network Data

Based on the discretized urban road network model, key parameters such as EV arrival time and travel distance to each charging station can be computed when the EV submits a charging application at any coordinate in the dispatch area. The arrival distance from EV i to charging station j is defined as D_{ij}; using the average speed V_i of each road segment, the arrival time $T_{i,j}^{S}$ from EV i to charging station j can be derived. The charging time $T_{i,j}^{C}$ is also computable, as illustrated in (5)–(6).

$$T_{i,j}^{S} = D_{ij}/V_i \tag{5}$$

$$T_{i,j}^{C} = \frac{(\mathrm{Soc}_i^{\mathrm{tar}} - \mathrm{Soc}_{i,j}^{D}) \times E_i}{P_{\mathrm{ch},j}} \ i \in S_{\mathrm{EV}}, j \in S_{\mathrm{St}} \tag{6}$$

In (5)–(6), $Soc_{i,j}^D$ indicates the state of charge (SOC) of EV i upon arrival at charging station j; $P_{ch,j}$ refers to the amount of electricity that the EV's battery receives per unit time; E_i is the battery capacity of EV i. The EV arrival time and charging time computed using the digital urban road network model can offer data support for subsequent charging guidance, which helps effectively mitigate the impact of complex road networks on EV charging guidance.

4 A Mixed-Integer Linear Programming Framework for Optimal EV Charging Guidance

4.1 Definitions of Three Categories of 0-1 Variables

1) EV charging station selection variable

When an EV initiates a charging request, it can be guided to a charging station that lies within its remaining driving distance. Define the 0–1 variable $x_{i,j}$ for the EV's charging station selection:

$$x_{i,j} = \{0, 1\}\, i \in S_{EV}, j \in S_{St} \tag{7}$$

In (7), $x_{i,j} = 1$ when EV k is successfully guided to charging station i; in all other cases $x_{i,j} = 0$.

2) Charging initiation variable for EV

Once an EV is directed to a charging station, it concludes the waiting phase and proceeds to the charging phase, which corresponds to one specific charging start time window. Thus, define the 0–1 variable $y_{i,t}$ for the EV's charging start time window:

$$y_{i,t} = \{0, 1\}\, i \in S_{EV}, t \in S_T \tag{8}$$

$$\sum_{t \in S_T} y_{i,t} = 1 \tag{9}$$

In (8), $y_{i,t} = 1$ signifies that EV i begins charging in the t-th time window; otherwise, $y_{i,t} = 0$. Meanwhile, EVs are allowed to remain uncharged within the dispatch horizon, as represented in (9).

3) EV Continuous Charging State Variable

Once an EV enters the charging process, it typically remains in the charging state within consecutive time windows. Define the 0–1 variable $u_{i,t}$ for the EV's charging state:

$$u_{i,t} = \{0, 1\}\, i \in S_{EV}, t \in S_T \tag{10}$$

In (10), $u_{i,t} = 1$ when EV i is in the charging process during the t-th time window; correspondingly, $u_{i,t} = 0$ when the EV is in states of addressing, waiting, or completion.

4.2 Objective Function

For the purpose of minimizing the total time spent by EV users on charging addressing and charging waiting, the objective function is defined as presented in (11).

$$\min \sum_{i \in S_{EV}} \left(\sum_{t \in S_T} y_{i,t} Axu_t + (1 - \sum_{t \in S_T} y_{i,t}) M_p \right) \tag{11}$$

$$Axu_t = t \tag{12}$$

In (11), Axu_t is an auxiliary time parameter, which is defined in (12) in detail; M_p is a penalty coefficient large enough, and it can take the value of N_T. The first part of the objective function aims to prioritize an earlier charging start time window for EVs, which in turn reduces the total time users spend on charging addressing and waiting. The second component encourages EVs to initiate charging within the current dispatch cycle to maximize resource utilization and user satisfaction.

4.3 Constraints

1) EV charging station selection constraints

Within a single EV charging guidance dispatch cycle, an electric vehicle is either successfully directed to a charging station or remains unassigned in this cycle, with no station selected. The selectivity constraints for EV charging include:

$$\sum_{j \in S_{St}} x_{i,j} \le 1 \ i \in S_{EV} \tag{13}$$

$$\sum_{t \in S_T} y_{i,t} \le 1 \ i \in S_{EV} \tag{14}$$

Equation (13) restricts a vehicle to being guided to a maximum of one target charging station within the guidance dispatch cycle; Eq. (14) indicates that a vehicle can enter the charging state only once within the guidance dispatch cycle.

2) EV charging initiation time constraints

Only after an EV travels to and arrives at the charging station can it begin charging. The constraints on the EV's charging start time are as follows:

$$y_{i,t} Axu_t \ge T_{i,j}^{S} x_{i,j} \ i \in S_{EV}, j \in S_{St}, t \in S_T \tag{15}$$

3) EV charging continuous constraints

After an EV reaches the target charging station and begins charging, it should be in the charging state during consecutive time windows until it attains the target SOC. The EV continuous charging constraints are as follows:

$$u_{i,t} \ge \sum_{t'=(t-\min(t,T_{i,j}^{C})+1)}^{t} y_{i,t} \ i \in S_{EV}, j \in S_{St}, t \in S_T \tag{16}$$

4) Charging station operational constraints

Parameter $N_{i,j}^{\mathrm{pile}}$ represents the number of occupied charging piles at station j during time window t, where this value is determined by the number of piles allocated to and used by EVs in the prior guidance cycle. The corresponding charging station constraint is:

$$\sum_{i\in S_{\mathrm{EV}}} x_{i,j}u_{i,t} + N_{i,j}^{\mathrm{pile}} \leq N_j^{\mathrm{P}}\ i \in S_{\mathrm{EV}}, j \in S_{\mathrm{T}}, t \in S_{\mathrm{T}}\triangleright \tag{17}$$

Equation (17) enforces that, for any time window, the number of EVs in the process of charging at a specific charging station cannot exceed the total number of charging piles at that station. This constraint guarantees that the station's charging resources are not overused, maintaining the consistency between the number of charging EVs and the actual available pile quantity.

5 Case Study

5.1 Background of the Case Study

For the purpose of validating the effectiveness and feasibility of the proposed strategy, this paper employs real-world data from charging stations within the road network of Shanghai's Dalinghao bay area to conduct a practical case simulation. The study focuses on 100 EVs as the research subjects. As illustrated in Fig. 3, the Dalinghao bay area road network comprises 11 charging stations, with detailed specifications of these charging stations listed in Table 1.

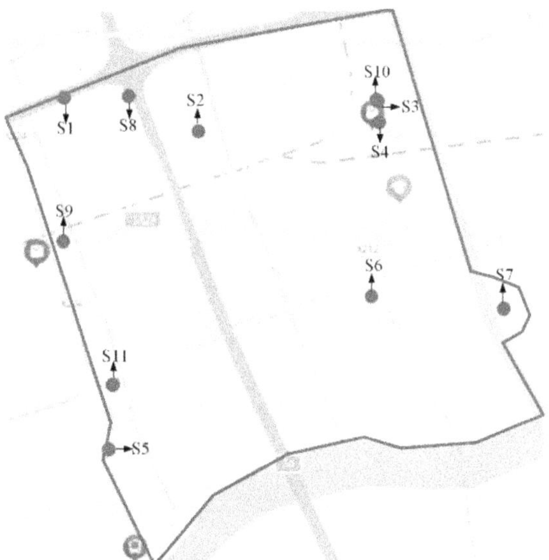

Fig. 3. Charging station distribution in Dalinghao bay area road network.

Table 1. Charging station data in Dalinghao bay area

NO	Longitude	Latitude	Pile Quantity	Charging Power
S1	121.418	31.0398	24	120 kW
S2	121.432	31.0367	30	150 kW
S3	121.451	31.0392	9	20 kW
S4	121.451	31.0374	12	200 kW
S5	121.423	31.0088	6	20 kW
S6	121.45	31.0221	32	120 kW
S7	121.464	31.0211	9	150 kW

5.2 Main Case Study Results

Table 2. Main case study results

Charging guidance results	Proximity guidance strategy	Proposed strategy
Average arrival time of EVs	6.63 min	8.91 min
Average arrival distance of EVs	2.19 km	3.20 km
Average charging time of EVs	22.73 min	22.14 min
Average queuing time of EVs	21.06 min	10.30 min
Regional charging station service intensity variance	1.1096	0.7023

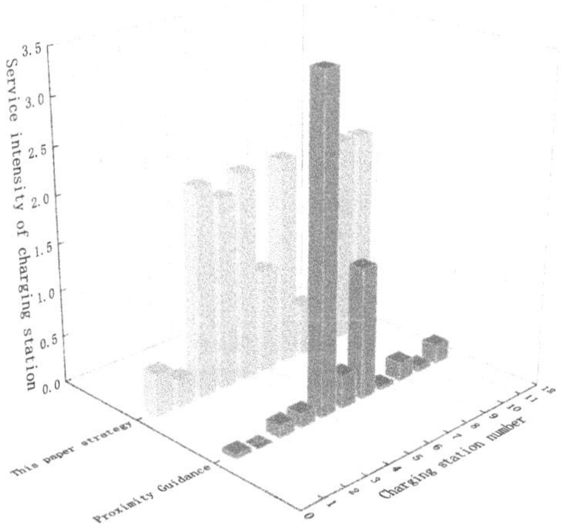

Fig. 4. Charging station service intensity comparison in the main case.

Within the dispatch cycle, the specific guidance optimization outcomes for EVs are illustrated in Table 2 and Fig. 4. Table 2 contrasts the methodology proposed in this paper with the proximity guidance strategy for charging stations. The simulation results indicate that the proposed method reduces the average queuing time of EV users by 51.1%, and the service variance among charging stations is also smaller compared to the proximity guidance strategy. Based on these findings, the proposed methodology in this paper can more effectively meet user charging needs while promoting a more balanced and efficient use of charging infrastructure.

5.3 Comparative Case Study Results

This section extends the analysis by introducing an additional comparative case that considers varying EV penetration levels. The comparative evaluation is conducted between the proposed strategy and the conventional proximity guidance strategy.

Table 3. Guidance outcomes under varying EV penetration levels

Charging guidance result	Average queuing time of EVs (min)		Regional charging station service intensity variance (min)	
	Proximity guidance strategy	Proposed strategy	Proximity guidance strategy	Proposed strategy
100 EVs	21.06	10.3	1.1096	0.7023
110 EVs	20.96	8.99	0.9802	0.6079
120 EVs	26.44	9.17	1.1040	0.4596
130 EVs	27.34	9.53	1.0390	0.4607

Four sets of comparative cases are designed for EV quantities of 100, 110, 120, and 130, respectively. All core experimental conditions remain consistent with those described in Sect. 5.2, ensuring that the comparative evaluation between the proposed strategy and the proximity guidance strategy under different EV penetration levels is both accurate and reliable.

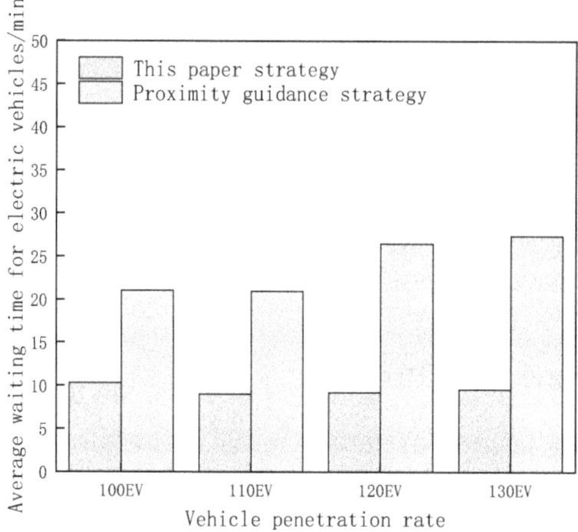

Fig. 5. Average waiting time in queue of EV users across different vehicle penetration scenarios.

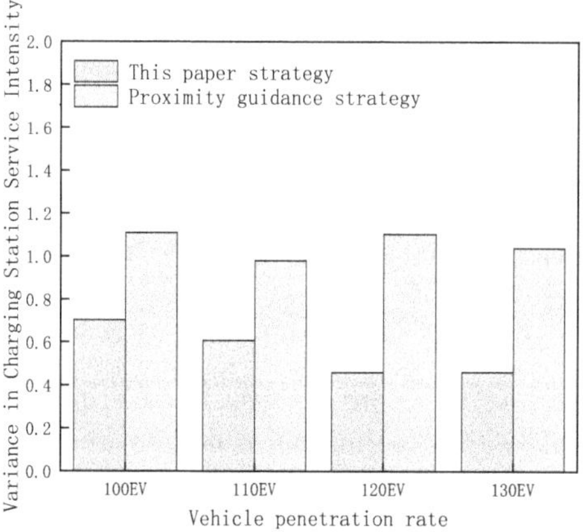

Fig. 6. Variance in service intensity among charging stations.

From the results shown in Table 3 and Fig. 5, it can be observed that across all vehicle penetration scenarios, the proposed strategy consistently yields a lower average queuing time compared to the proximity guidance strategy. As the EV penetration level increases, both the average queuing time and the variance of charging station service intensity exhibit a decreasing trend. This suggests that under the given road network conditions, the system's ability to accommodate EVs improves with higher penetration levels. Moreover, as illustrated in Fig. 6, the proposed strategy effectively reduces disparities in service intensity among charging stations, resulting in a more balanced utilization of charging infrastructure. This mitigates the overloading and underutilization issues that commonly occur with proximity guidance strategy.

6 Summary

This study proposes an electric vehicle (EV) charging guidance strategy that incorporates urban road network data and leverages a MILP model. Simulations are conducted using the road network of Shanghai's Dalinghao bay area. The main findings are summarized as follows:

1) A detailed urban road network model for the Dalinghao bay area is established, and comprehensive data on charging stations within the region are organized, forming the foundation for effective EV charging guidance.
2) By integrating road network characteristics into the MILP framework, the proposed strategy significantly reduces average user queuing times and achieves a more balanced utilization of charging infrastructure across the network.
3) Simulation results across different EV penetration scenarios demonstrate that the proposed strategy consistently achieves shorter queuing times and lower variance in charging station service intensity. These results suggest that the urban road network, when supported by the proposed strategy, can better accommodate growing EV demand while ensuring more balanced infrastructure utilization.

Acknowledgment. This work was sponsored by the Science and Technology Project from the State Grid Shanghai Municipal Electric Power Company of China (52094024002R).

References

1. Su, S., Sun, J., Lin, X., et al.: Intelligent charging navigation for electric vehicles. Proc. CSEE **33**(S1), 59–67 (2013)
2. Tian, L., Zhang, M., Wang, H., et al.: Evaluation and solutions to the impact of electric vehicles on power grid. Proc. CSEE **32**(31), 43–49 (2012)
3. Zhao, Y., Xu, T., Li, Y., et al.: Study on electric vehicle dispatching strategy based on time-of-use electricity price. Power Syst. Prot. Control **48**(11), 92–101 (2020)
4. Chen, K., Niu, Y.: Real-time dispatching strategy for electric vehicles based on V2G technology. Power Syst. Prot. Control **47**(14), 1–9 (2019)
5. Chen, M., Gao, J., Chang, G., et al.: Study on orderly charging strategy of electric vehicles in microgrid under V2G mode. Power Syst. Prot. Control **48**(08), 141–148 (2020)
6. Xia, Q., Li, H., Shi, Y., et al.: Electric vehicle charging guidance strategy considering charging decision conflicts and time-of-use service fees. Electr. Power Autom. Equip. **42**(5), 68–74 (2022)
7. Li, H., Zhang, J., Zhang, Y., et al.: Charging station management strategy for returns maximization via improved TD3 deep reinforcement learning. Int. Trans. Electr. Energy Syst. **2022** (2022)
8. Yuan, H., Zhang, J., Xu, P., et al.: Research on rapid charging demand guidance of power-transportation coupled network based on graph reinforcement learning. Power Syst. Technol. **45**(3), 979–986 (2021)
9. Han, L., Ye, C., Zhu, C., et al.: Spatial guidance strategy for urban charging load considering user willingness under high-temperature weather. Autom. Electr. Power Syst. **48**(10), 139–150 (2024)
10. Zhang, J., Pei, Y., Shen, J., et al.: Charging strategy unifying spatial-temporal coordination of electric vehicles. IEEE Access **8**, 74853–74863 (2020)

Comprehensive Operational Analysis of a Typical PV–Storage–Charging–Swapping Integrated Station

Haojing Wang[✉], Chen Fang, Yu Zhang, and Huawei Huang

East China Electric Power Test & Research Institute Co., Ltd, Shanghai 200437, China
`wanghj_sg@126.com`

Abstract. Against the backdrop of global energy transition and the rapid popularization of electric vehicles (EVs), traditional single-function charging facilities can no longer meet the demands for efficient energy supply, low-carbon operation, and grid-friendly interaction. Integrated PV–storage–charging–swapping stations, which integrate photovoltaic (PV) power generation, energy storage systems (ESS), EV charging, and battery swapping services, have emerged as a critical solution for optimizing urban energy infrastructure. This study focuses on a typical PV–storage–charging–swapping demonstration station in East China, China, and conducts a comprehensive operational analysis based on on-site survey data collected from March 10 to March 16, 2025. The research details the station's system architecture, hardware configuration parameters, and temporal operational characteristics of each subsystem (PV, ESS, charging, battery swapping, and load). Key findings indicate that the station achieves efficient clean energy utilization through a "PV priority, ESS regulation, and grid backup" strategy: the 352 kW PV system contributes approximately 20% of the station's annual electricity demand; the 100 kW/215 kWh ESS effectively smooths PV power fluctuations and realizes peak-valley load regulation; and the diversified charging/swapping facilities (including ultra-fast charging piles, fast charging piles, V2G piles, bus charging station and a battery swapping station) meet the daily energy supply needs of over 300 EVs. Furthermore, the critical role of the flexible interconnection device in managing power distribution between two transformers is highlighted. This study, grounded in real-world operational data, provides detailed empirical references for the design, construction, and operational management of similar integrated stations, supporting the low-carbon and intelligent upgrading of urban transportation energy systems.

Keywords: PV–storage–charging–swapping integrated station · operational analysis · on-site survey data · subsystem performance · energy balance

1 Introduction

The global transition to low-carbon transportation has accelerated the deployment of EVs, driving the demand for efficient and sustainable charging infrastructure. Traditional charging stations, relying solely on grid power, face challenges such as peak load pressure

A. Razminia et al. (Eds.): ITFT 2025, CCIS 2876, pp. 252–262, 2026.
https://doi.org/10.1007/978-3-032-20592-6_23

and high electricity costs. PV-storage-charging-swapping integrated stations, integrating renewable energy generation, energy storage, and multi-mode EV services, have become a promising solution to balance energy supply and demand. China has taken the lead in promoting such integrated stations, with the charging and swapping industry experiencing rapid growth in recent years. The "light-storage-charging-swapping-discharging" integrated operation model has been recognized as a key direction for future EV infrastructure development. However, most existing studies focus on optimization strategies or theoretical design, lacking comprehensive operational analysis based on field-measured data. Empirical research on the actual performance of such stations, including PV generation characteristics, load fluctuation rules, and equipment operation patterns, remains insufficient.

Existing studies on PV-storage-charging systems and battery swapping technology cover multiple aspects. References [1] reviews the development stages of China's NEV charging and swapping industry, presents achievements and challenges, and predicts trends with EU/US experiences. References [2] explores the application of PV-storage-charging integrated technology, introduces its core logic, analyzes key technologies. References [3] proposes an optimal operation method for integrated solar energy storage and charging power stations by constructing a cost-benefit model. References [4] develops a bi-objective optimization model for PV-storage EV charging stations focusing on storage capacity impacts. References [5] studies the planning and operation optimization of building-integrated PV-storage systems, proposing a comprehensive optimization method to enhance renewable energy consumption and system economy. References [6] conducts an early review of battery swapping station design, establishing a battery state transition model and analyzing constraints like charger quantity, but lacks recent empirical data. References [7] addresses capacity configuration and comprehensive benefits of PV-storage-charging EV charging stations, using Monte Carlo simulation for EV load modeling and particle swarm optimization for multi-objective solving. References [8] proposes an optimal operation strategy for PV-storage-charging stations considering decision-dependent uncertainty, constructing a robust optimization framework but lacking extensive field validation. References [9] discusses the industrial application trend of "PV-storage-charging-swapping-discharging" integrated operation in high-speed EV charging scenarios, introducing practical cases but with limited theoretical depth. References [10] focuses on the electrical design of PV-storage-charging integrated charging stations, covering system topology, equipment parameter selection and protection configuration, but lacking long-term operational stability analysis.

However, most existing studies rely on simulation data or theoretical models, lacking in-depth analysis based on real-world operational data from integrated stations. Few have systematically documented detailed hardware configurations, high-resolution temporal performance (e.g., 15-min interval power data). This gap limits the practical applicability of research findings, as station operators require empirical insights into subsystem interactions, load distributions, and energy balance to inform daily management. To address this, our study conducts a comprehensive operational analysis of a typical PV–storage–charging–swapping demonstration station in East China, utilizing field-collected data. Key contributions include: documenting the station's architecture and component parameters through on-site investigation to provide a reference for similar projects; analyzing operational characteristics—such as PV generation profiles, charging load patterns, and ESS charge–discharge behavior—using 15-min interval data from March 10–16, 2025, and evaluating energy flow dynamics to quantify PV self-consumption, ESS regulation capability, and grid dependency, thereby validating the effectiveness of the "PV priority, ESS regulation, and grid backup" strategy in enhancing energy self-sufficiency. Notably, the study focuses on operational analysis rather than optimization, aiming to objectively interpret real-world data and offer empirical support for the practical deployment of integrated stations.

2   System Architecture of the PV–Storage–Charging–Swapping Integrated Station

The studied demonstration station is located in a high-traffic area adjacent to major highways in East China, covering an area of approximately 5900 m2. It was constructed in two phases: Phase I was commissioned in December 2022, and Phase II was expanded in January 2025 to enhance its service capacity. The station integrates five core subsystems—PV power generation, ESS, charging, battery swapping, and energy management—which operate collaboratively to achieve efficient energy conversion and intelligent control. The station's actual scene and topology diagrams are shown in Figs. 1 and 2, respectively.

Fig. 1. The Actual Scene of the PV–Storage–Charging–Swapping Integrated Station

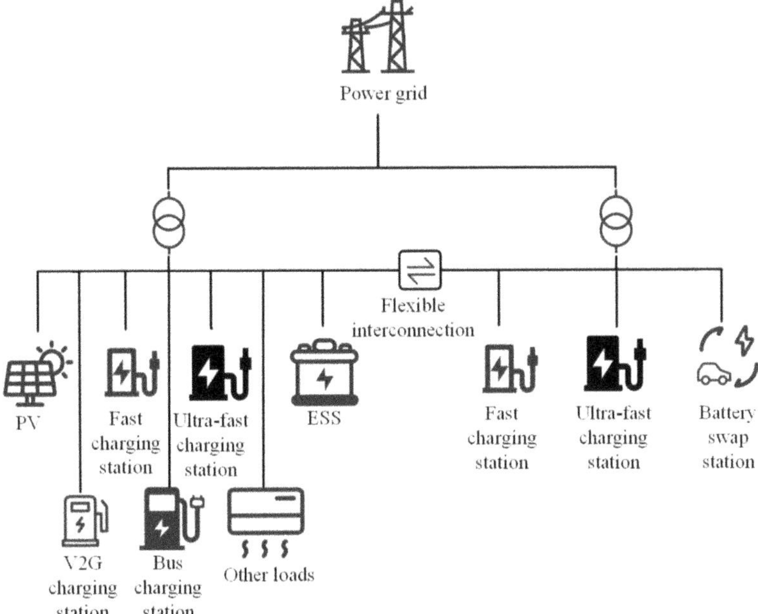

Fig. 2. The topological diagram of the PV–Storage–Charging–Swapping Integrated Station

2.1 PV Power Generation System

The PV system is designed to maximize the use of available space, with modules installed on rooftops, charging canopies, and station walls. Based on on-site inspections, the system has a total installed capacity of 352 kW, both using monocrystalline silicon modules.

The PV system converts solar energy into direct current (DC) via the photovoltaic effect. After DC confluence (using a 4-in-1 combiner box), the electricity is inverted to alternating current (AC) by a 350 kW grid-tied inverter and connected to the station's 0.4 kV AC bus. According to operational rules, PV power is prioritized for on-site load supply; surplus electricity is either stored in the ESS or fed into the grid (if the ESS is fully charged).

2.2 Energy Storage System (ESS)

The ESS is deployed to address PV power volatility and grid peak load pressure. Based on on-site measurements and equipment specifications, the system uses lithium iron phosphate (LFP) batteries with a rated capacity of 215 kWh and a rated charge/discharge power of 100 kW. Key components include battery packs, a bidirectional power converter (PCS), and a battery management system (BMS).

The PCS enables bidirectional power flow: during periods of excess PV power or low electricity tariffs (valley periods), it charges the battery packs; during peak load periods or insufficient PV generation, it discharges to support on-site loads.

The BMS monitors battery voltage, current, and temperature in real time to prevent overcharging/overdischarging and ensure system safety.

2.3 Charging System

The charging system is designed to meet diverse EV needs, including private cars, buses, and V2G-enabled vehicles. It consists of four types of charging facilities, with parameters verified through on-site equipment checks and operational logs (Table 1).

Table 1. Key Configuration Parameters of Charging Facilities

Facility category	Technical parameters	Quantity
Fast charging piles	60–120 kW, 50–1000 V	18
Ultra-fast charging piles	60–250 kW, 50–1000 V	10
V2G charging piles	50–60 kW, 200–950 V	2
Bus-specific charging	200 kW,300–1000 V	2

2.4 Battery Swapping System

The battery swapping system is a third-generation facility developed by a leading EV manufacturer, providing standardized swapping services for specific EV models. Based on on-site observations and operational records, The system includes 12 backup battery packs, of which nine are 75 kWh standard-range packs and three are 100 kWh long-range packs, an automated swapping robot, and a battery maintenance platform.

The automated robot uses laser positioning to complete battery removal, inspection, and installation, ensuring high accuracy and efficiency. After swapping, used batteries are charged and tested on the maintenance platform (including SOC calibration and safety checks) before being put back into service. This system significantly reduces user waiting time compared to traditional charging.

2.5 Flexible Interconnection Device

The station is equipped with a 250 kW low-voltage flexible interconnection device connecting its two 1250 kVA transformers. This device enables bidirectional power mutual assistance between the two transformers, addressing uneven load distribution issues. When one transformer faces high load (e.g., peak charging hours), the other can supply supplementary power to prevent overload, enhancing power supply stability. It aligns with the integrated station's collaborative operation logic (as referenced in the study) by optimizing transformer utilization and ensuring reliable subsystem operation.

2.6 Energy Management System (EMS)

The EMS serves as the "brain" of the integrated station, coordinating all subsystems and collecting real-time data—such as power, voltage, and state of charge—via a system with a 15-min sampling interval. It executes a hierarchical control strategy based on preset rules. At the basic control layer, PV power is prioritized for on-site loads. Surplus PV generation charges the ESS up to 90% SOC, with any excess fed into the grid; when PV generation falls short, the ESS discharges if SOC exceeds 20%, otherwise the grid supplements the load.

In the load regulation layer, the EMS adjusts ESS charging and discharging according to time-of-use electricity tariffs: charging from the grid during valley periods (0:00–7:45) and discharging during peak periods to reduce grid electricity purchases. The safety control layer monitors transformer load (two 1250 kVA units) and grid voltage, curtailing non-critical charging loads when transformer load exceeds 80% of rated capacity. Additionally, the EMS generates daily operational reports covering PV generation, ESS cycles, charging/swapping services, and grid power consumption, which served as key data sources for this study.

3 On-Site Operational Data and Subsystem Performance Analysis

To analyze the station's operational characteristics, on-site data were collected from March 10 to March 16, 2025 (a typical spring week with no public holidays), including 15-min interval power data for all subsystems. All data are obtained through field research to ensure authenticity and accuracy.in the rare event of a data point loss (e.g., communication interruption), linear interpolation was applied to maintain data continuity.

3.1 PV Power Generation Performance

From the perspective of the daily power generation characteristics of photovoltaics, the PV system only generates power during daylight hours (6:00–18:00), with generation peaks aligned with solar irradiance. Figure 3 shows the average PV power curve (March 10–16).

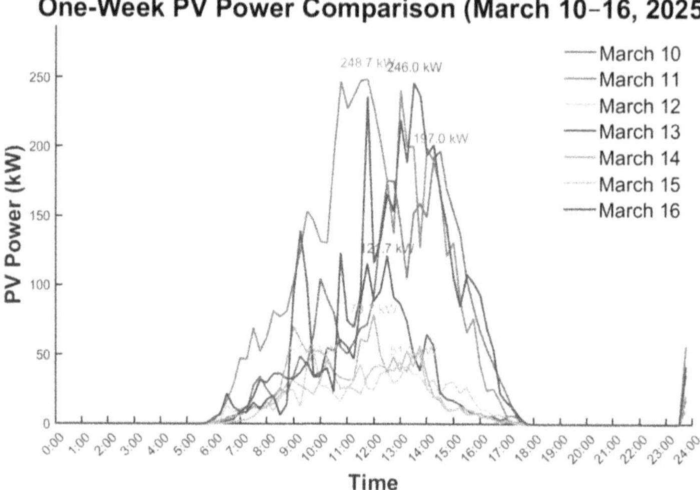

Fig. 3. Average PV Power Curve (March 10–16, 2025)

The highest daily power generation was recorded on March 11, reaching 248.7 kWh under clear skies and strong solar irradiance, whereas the lowest output occurred on March 15 at only 39.28 kWh due to overcast conditions—highlighting the system's considerable sensitivity to weather. Peak generation generally takes place between 9:00 and 13:00, aligning with solar noon, with an average peak power of 58.7 kW observed from March 10 to 16. Beyond 15:00, generation declines rapidly as solar irradiance diminishes.

3.2 ESS Operational Performance

The ESS operates in two main modes: PV surplus absorption and peak-valley arbitrage. Table 2 shows the average daily ESS data from March 10 to 16.

Table 2. Average daily ESS data

Date	Charge Volume (kWh)	Discharge Volume (kWh)	Average SOC (%)
3.10	89.25	76.42	58.2
3.11	95.70	82.35	61.5
3.12	78.40	69.15	56.8
3.13	67.30	60.57	54.3
3.14	70.60	63.54	55.1
3.15	92.10	82.89	59.7
3.16	94.20	84.78	60.2

From March 10 to 16, the ESS operated stably. Its daily charge volume ranged 67.30–95.70 kWh (peak on 3.11) and discharge volume 60.57–84.78 kWh, with slight net charges daily. Average SOC stayed 54.3%–61.5%, well within the 20%–90% safe range, avoiding overcharge/overdischarge. This stability let it effectively absorb surplus PV power and conduct peak-valley arbitrage, supporting the station's energy balance.

3.3 Charging System Performance

BasedThis station is a demonstration site integrating photovoltaic, energy storage, charging, and battery swapping capabilities. This station features four types of charging piles: fast-charging piles, super-charging piles (60–250 kW), V2G piles, and bus-dedicated piles. These facilities support efficient and sustainable transportation by leveraging renewable energy. To evaluate their performance, we analyzed data from March 10 to March 16, 2025, including total energy generation and power metrics. Energy generation reflects the total output, while power indicates instantaneous charging rates. For assessing daily operational efficiency, energy generation is more relevant as it captures the overall energy supplied to electric vehicles, directly related to user demand and station utilization.

The daily energy generation for the week is summarized in Table 3. The values were derived from the total energy data, calculated as the sum of 15-min intervals over each day.

Table 3. Daily Energy Generation of Charging Piles (March 10–16, 2025)

Date	Energy Generation (kWh)
3.10	7895.90
3.11	6660.62
3.12	7377.38
3.13	7256.74
3.14	8037.17
3.15	8293.32
3.16	8377.51

Analysis of Table 3 reveals fluctuations in daily energy generation. March 11 shows the lowest output, possibly due to reduced demand on a weekday or external factors like weather conditions affecting solar energy input. In contrast, March 15 and 16 exhibit higher generation, indicating peak usage, potentially linked to weekend charging patterns or increased bus fleet activity. The overall trend shows a gradual increase from March 10 to 16, suggesting rising station adoption or optimal charging scheduling. This variability highlights the importance of energy management strategies, such as leveraging storage systems to balance supply and demand.

To analyze the operational characteristics of the four charging piles, I selected March 10 as a typical day for analysis. The power comparison chart of each charging pile is shown in Fig. 4.

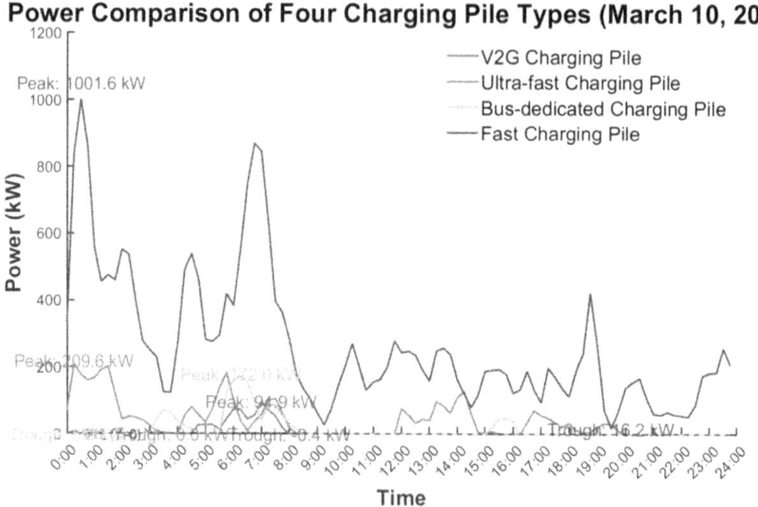

Fig. 4. Power Comparison of Four Charging Types (March 10, 2025)

On March 10, the power distribution across the four types of charging piles at this Station demonstrated clear functional differentiation: fast-charging piles dominated the base load with high and sustained power, averaging 266.23 kW and peaking sharply during early morning and evening commuting hours; super-charging piles provided intermittent high-power boosts, averaging 40.50 kW with notable activity at dawn and late afternoon, serving users requiring rapid energy replenishment; V2G piles played a flexible role in grid interaction, averaging 7.33 kW and showing clear discharge peaks to support grid stability during morning demand surges; while bus-dedicated piles operated on a scheduled, low-average-power pattern, concentrating usage between 03:00 and 08:00 to prepare the public transport fleet for daily service, collectively forming a balanced and efficient charging ecosystem that meets diverse user needs and supports grid stability.

In summary, This station's charging facilities demonstrate robust performance, with energy generation analysis providing insights into usage trends. The power curve for March 10 emphasizes the role of different pile types in managing demand, underscoring the station's capability as a model for sustainable transportation solutions. Future work could involve disaggregating data by pile type for granular optimization.

3.4 Battery Swapping System Performance

The battery swap station at the demonstration site provides efficient energy replenishment for electric vehicles, complementing the charging infrastructure. The table below summarizes the daily swap statistics from March 10 to March 16, 2025, based on 15-min interval data:

Table 4. Key Indicators of Battery Swap Stations

Date	Number of Vehicles	Total Swap Energy (kWh)	Average Swap Time (min)
3.10	12	878.7	4.8
3.11	16	1140.8	5.1
3.12	11	840.5	4.9
3.13	14	879.2	5.0
3.14	18	1231.7	5.2
3.15	13	845.3	4.7
3.16	15	1128.6	5.0

Analysis of the data reveals consistent daily swap operations with notable demand fluctuations. March 14 recorded the highest swap energy (1231.7 kWh) and vehicle count (18), indicating peak usage potentially linked to increased commercial fleet activity or weekend travel preparation. The relatively stable average swap time of approximately 5 min demonstrates the operational efficiency and standardization of the swap process. The station maintained robust performance throughout the week, with swap events distributed across daytime and evening hours, showing particular concentration during morning (07:00–09:00) and afternoon (14:00–17:00) periods. This pattern suggests the station effectively serves both private EV users and commercial fleets, with the battery swap system providing a rapid alternative to conventional charging, significantly reducing vehicle downtime and enhancing the overall efficiency of the transportation energy ecosystem at the demonstration site (see Table 4).

4 Conclusion

When this study conducted a comprehensive operational analysis of a typical PV–storage–charging–swapping demonstration station in East China, using on-site survey data from March 10 to March 16, 2025, and seasonal typical day data. The key conclusions are as follows:

System Architecture and Configuration: The station's five-core subsystems (PV, ESS, charging, swapping, EMS) are rationally designed to meet diverse user needs and low-carbon operation goals. The 352 kW PV system, 100 kW/215 kWh ESS, and diversified charging/swapping facilities (ultra-fast piles, fast piles, V2G piles, BSS) form a flexible and efficient energy system.

This study provides detailed empirical data and operational insights for the design and management of PV–storage–charging–swapping integrated stations. Future research could focus on long-term performance degradation of PV/ESS equipment and user behavior analysis to further improve station operation.

Acknowledgment. This work is supported by the Shanghai Rising Star Program (23QB1400500).

References

1. Wang, F., Zhang, Q.: The development of China's new energy vehicle charging and swapping industry: review and prospect. Preprints, 202507.2011 (2025)
2. Yan, P.: Research on the application of integrated technology of photovoltaic power generation, energy storage and charging. J. Power Eng. **03**, 2025 (2025)
3. Yang, J., Ye, L., Li, N., Sun, B., Zhang, Z.: The Optimal operation method of integrated solar energy storage and charging power station considering multiple benefits of energy storage. Energy Proc. **01**, 2024 (2024)
4. Guo, W., et al.: Bi-objective collaborative optimization of a photovoltaic-energy storage EV charging station with consideration of storage capacity impacts. Front. Energy Res. **12**, 1517011 (2024)
5. Chen, K., Xiao, X., Tian, P., et al.: A comprehensive optimization method for planning and operation of building-integrated photovoltaic energy storage system. Proc. CSEE **43**(13), 5001–5012 (2023)
6. Mahour, M., Hosseini, Z.S., Khodaei, A., Kushner, D.: Electric vehicle battery swapping station. arXiv (2017)
7. Yang, M.: Research on capacity configuration and comprehensive benefits of integrated PV-storage-charging EV charging station. M.S. thesis, North China Electric Power University, Beijing, China (2020)
8. Lin, Y., Yang, J., Wang, H., et al.: Optimal operation strategy for integrated PV-storage-charging station considering decision-dependent uncertainty. Zhejiang Electr. Power **44**(10), 91–101 (2025)
9. Qi, X.: New energy vehicle high-speed charging moves towards "PV-storage-charging-swapping-discharging" integrated operation. China Ind. News, 010 (2025)
10. Chen, D., Yu, Y., Liao, W., et al.: Research on electrical design of charging station based on PV-storage-charging integration technology. Commun. World **32**(09), 118–120 (2025)

Construction of Charging Load Profiles and Analysis of Complementary Characteristics for Regions with Complex Traffic and Weak Power Grids

Lingyu Guo[1], Yang Du[1], Shuze Du[1], and Yun Zhou[2]($\boxtimes$)

[1] Electric Power Research Institute, State Grid Shanghai Electric Power Company, Shanghai 200437, China
[2] School of Electrical Engineering, Shanghai Jiao Tong University, Shanghai 200240, China
`weekcloud@126.com`

Abstract. As a key link in the transportation low-carbon transition, electric vehicle (EV) charging behavior challenges urban power grid operation, especially in areas with complex traffic and weak grids where charging load volatility intensifies pressure. This study took Dalinghao Bay as the research area, collected 15-min granularity charging load data from 6 typical blocks, and analyzed data from a workday and a non-workday. By constructing load characteristic profiles and calculating complementary indicators (Pearson Correlation Coefficient, Load Overlap Index, Peak-Valley Shift Degree), it revealed distinct temporal rules of charging loads across block types and confirmed significant complementary potential between different functional areas.

Keywords: Areas with Complex Traffic · Areas with Weak Power Grids · Charging Load Profiles · Complementary Characteristics · Pearson Correlation Coefficient

1 Introduction

As a key transportation low-carbon transition pathway, EV charging behavior poses new challenges to urban power grids, with extensive research conducted on its charging load modeling and analysis. For instance, Reference [1] proposed a modeling method for residential EV charging load considering parking behavior and state of charge (SOC). Reference [2] analyzed EV charging characteristics using measured data, highlighting the correlations between charging parameters. Reference [3] and [4] further identified typical charging load profiles and explored the spatial-temporal distribution of charging demands across different areas and seasons, revealing significant differences. Reference [5] investigated the distribution network supportability under EV integration, defining key parameters like coincidence factors. To mitigate the adverse impacts of random charging, strategies such as optimal allocation of charging facilities and distributed generation [6], and demand response mechanisms [7, 8] have been proposed. Additionally, studies like [9] and [10] have utilized measured data to analyze EV load profiles and their impacts on grid operation, emphasizing the need for realistic modeling.

© The Author(s), under exclusive license to Springer Nature Switzerland AG 2026
A. Razminia et al. (Eds.): ITFT 2025, CCIS 2876, pp. 263–274, 2026.
https://doi.org/10.1007/978-3-032-20592-6_24

In urban areas with complex traffic and weak power grids, the temporal-spatial concentration and volatility of charging loads further aggravate grid operational pressure. Thus, deeply depicting EV charging load profiles and exploring their complementary potential are crucial for improving charging facility utilization, easing grid peak pressure, and advancing vehicle-grid interaction (V2G). This study focuses on these load and complementary characteristics in such contexts: it analyzes charging facility usage in these areas, clarifies load features across regions and times, develops detailed load profiles, and examines complementarity via metrics like Pearson correlation coefficient. It provides data support for optimizing charging facility layout and improving efficiency, aiding the development of resilient, intelligent urban charging service systems.

2   Research Area and Data Overview

2.1   Research Area

Figure 1 is a schematic diagram showing the location of the Dalinghao Bay Science and Technology Innovation Source Function Area in Shanghai. As a functional area designated for sourcing scientific and technological innovation in Shanghai, this region features a complex spatial structure and dense transportation nodes, exhibiting typical characteristics of a "complex traffic" area. Within the area, elevated expressways (e.g., S32, S4) and rail transit (e.g., Jianchuan Road Station on Metro Line 5) intersect, forming a multi-level, multi-modal transportation network.

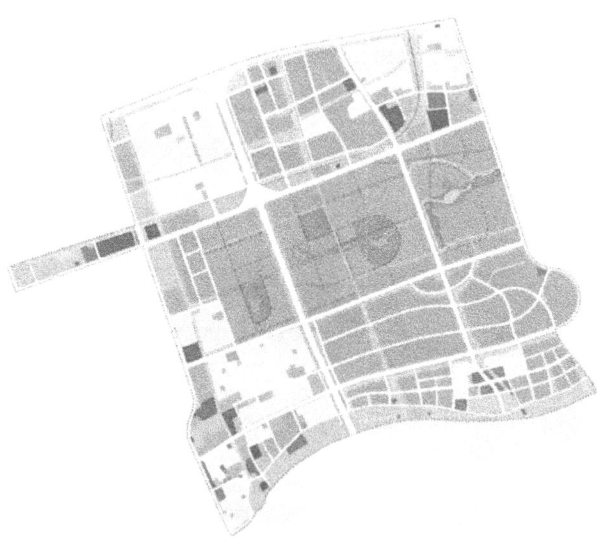

Fig. 1. Typical study area with complex traffic and weak grid conditions.

As a rapidly developing hub for technology and industry aggregation, "Dalinghao Bay" faces significant power load challenges amid its transition from an "old industrial base" to an innovation park. Meanwhile, it also features a complex traffic network and variable travel patterns. This combination of complex traffic and high grid load pressure makes it an ideal subject for researching charging load profiles, optimizing charging facility layout, and identifying vehicle-grid interaction regulation needs: it supports analyzing charging load fluctuations across time and transportation scenarios, truly reflects key issues, and ultimately helps construct engineering-valuable and policy-referential charging load characteristic profiles and complementary analyses.

2.2 Data Sources and Block Division

To deeply characterize and extract EV charging behavior, this study takes Dalinghao Bay as a typical case, selecting 6 representative block types for charging load data collection and analysis. Each block is confirmed via on-site surveys, Geographic Information System (GIS) boundary demarcation, and charging data aggregation, as detailed in Table 1. The core data is the January 2024 historical operating load, including 96 daily 15-min interval charging power records. A typical workday (January 2, Tuesday) and non-workday (January 6, Saturday) are chosen to identify block-specific charging load characteristics. Collected by charging operators and the distribution network side, the data has been cleaned and structured, containing daily load curves and hourly power distribution to support load characteristic profile construction and inter-regional complementarity analysis.

The boundaries of the blocks are standardized using latitude and longitude coordinates and visually presented on a map in Fig. 2. Temporal analysis of charging loads and construction of characteristic profiles for different types of blocks are then conducted, focusing on two main aspects: analysis of charging load characteristic profiles for different block types, and analysis of the complementary characteristics of charging loads between different block types.

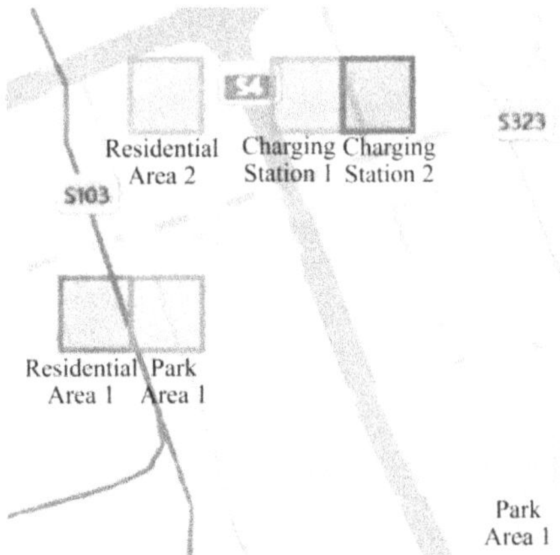

Fig. 2. Schematic diagram of geographic locations of different types of blocks.

Table 1. Information of Different Types of Blocks

No	Block Type	Block Name	Boundaries of the Block
1	Residential Area	Residential Area 1	North Latitude 31.025756, South Latitude 31.021261, East Longitude 121.418245, West Longitude 121.413002
2	Residential Area	Residential Area 2	North Latitude 31.039232, South Latitude 31.034736, East Longitude 121.423487, West Longitude 121.418246
3	Park Area	Park Area 1	North Latitude 31.025754, South Latitude 31.021258, East Longitude 121.423486, West Longitude 121.418244
4	Park Area	Park Area 2	North Latitude 31.016740, South Latitude 31.012238, East Longitude 121.449669, West Longitude 121.444435
5	Charging Station	Charging Station 1	North Latitude 31.039224, South Latitude 31.034726, East Longitude 121.433965, West Longitude 121.428726
6	Charging Station	Charging Station 2	North Latitude 31.039218, South Latitude 31.034719, East Longitude 121.439201, West Longitude 121.433964

3 Analysis of Charging Load Characteristic Profiles

To gain an in-depth understanding of the charging behavior characteristics of different types of functional blocks on typical days, this section constructs charging load characteristic profiles for six typical blocks based on the actual charging power data from two days—January 2, 2024 (workday) and January 6, 2024 (non-workday). It also conducts a horizontal comparative analysis to reveal the differences and regularities in the charging load timing among different types of areas.

3.1 Charging Load Characteristics of Residential Areas

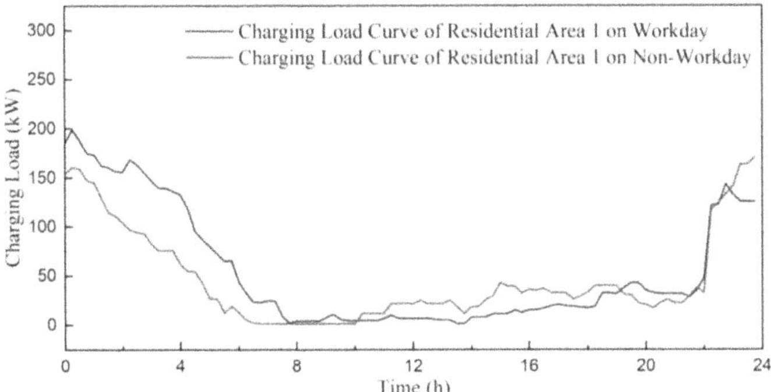

Fig. 3. Charging load curve of Residential Area 1.

As the most concentrated activity space for urban EV users, the charging behavior of residential areas is significantly influenced by residents' daily schedules, commuting trips, and family life rhythms. As shown in Figs. 3 and 4, both residential areas show an obvious "evening charging peak": Residential Area 2 has a peak power over 300 kW, higher than Residential Area 1; they also maintain a baseline load from 00:00 to 6:00, indicating off-peak night charging. Load curves are flatter with lower peaks on non-workday. This "weaker concentration, stronger dispersion" enables more regulation. Overall, residential EV charging has regular intraday fluctuations and clear differences; while load concentration brings short-term grid pressure, its regularity and user guidance potential support future "demand response" and peak-valley regulation.

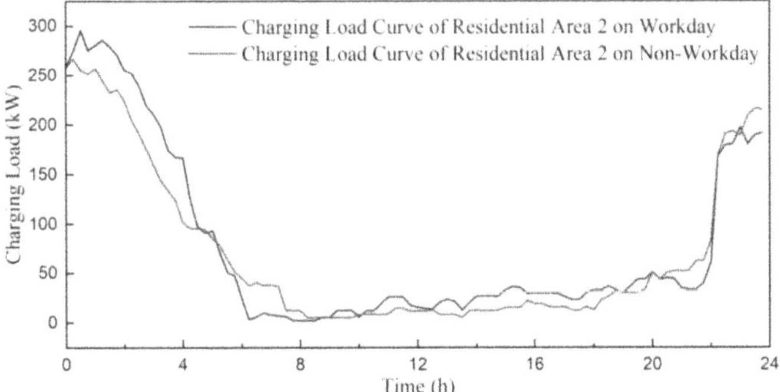

Fig. 4. Charging load curve of Residential Area 2.

3.2   Charging Load Characteristics of Park Areas

Park areas, which host office, R&D, and industrial functions, show distinct charging load characteristics on workday and non-workday. As shown in Figs. 5 and 6, both parks exhibit a "single-peak concentration" pattern: charging load rises rapidly after 8:00 a.m., peaks between 10:00 a.m. and 12:00 p.m., stays relatively stable, then drops to a trough after 16:00–17:00 on workday; Park Area 1's peak is about 10 kW, slightly lower than Park Area 2's ~ 14 kW. This aligns with staff arrival times and lunchtime vehicle use, showing charging is concentrated during daytime working hours, especially mornings and lunch breaks. The charging load remains at an extremely low level throughout non-workday, with the overall load curve approximating a "baseline state". This indicates that the vehicle utilization rate in the parks during weekends is extremely low, the operational activities of enterprises within the parks are significantly reduced, and both the parking space utilization rate and the charging pile activation rate have decreased noticeably, presenting a typical characteristic of "low-load idleness".

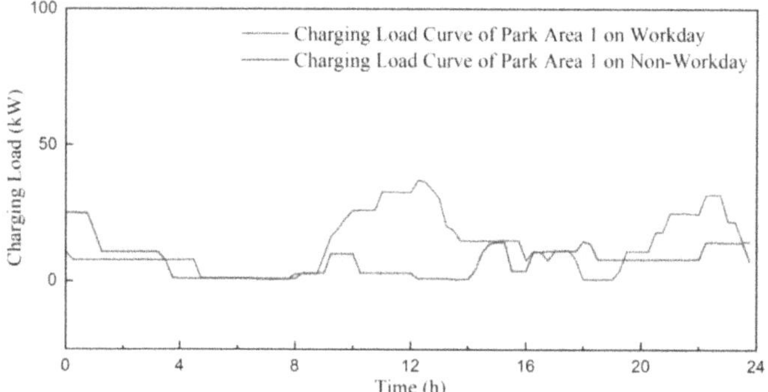

Fig. 5. Charging load curve of Park Area 1.

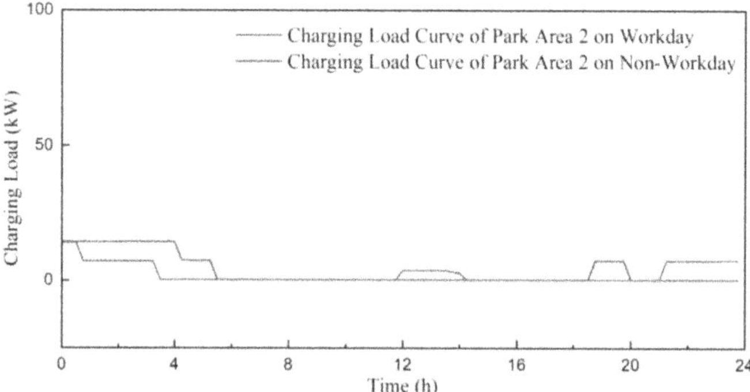

Fig. 6. Charging load curve of Park Area 2.

3.3 Charging Load Characteristics of Charging Stations

As key urban EV energy-supplement nodes, charging stations have more complex, diverse, and high-frequency charging loads than residential areas and parks. As shown in Figs. 7 and 8, Charging Station 1 runs at a high load all day on workday: rising after 7:00 a.m., peaking 9:00–11:00 a.m., 12:00–14:00 p.m., and 18:00–20:00 p.m., showing "alternating multi-period peaks". Charging Station 2 has lower overall power but also multi-peaks, with more balanced peak power and higher nighttime charging. On non-workday, both stations see a slight load drop but run all day, with peak times similar to workday (notable noon/evening peaks). This phenomenon indicates that the service objects of charging station facilities are more diverse, covering noncommuting demand vehicles such as shared vehicles, weekend travel vehicles, and urban logistics and distribution vehicles, with small load elasticity and high rigidity. Unlike the sharp non-workday load decline in residential areas/parks, charging stations' stable operation makes them critical for urban transportation system stability.

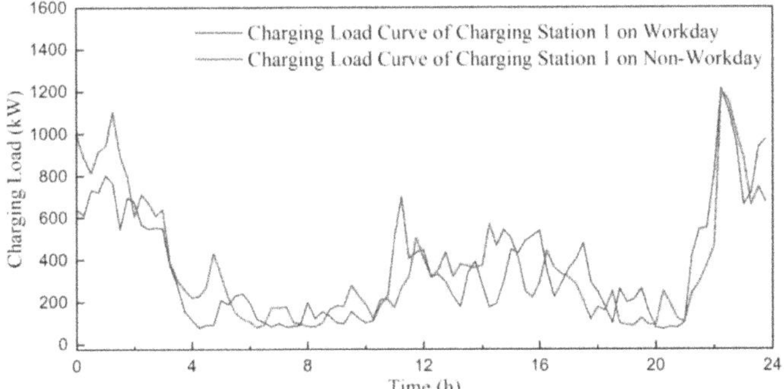

Fig. 7. Charging load curve of Charging Station 1.

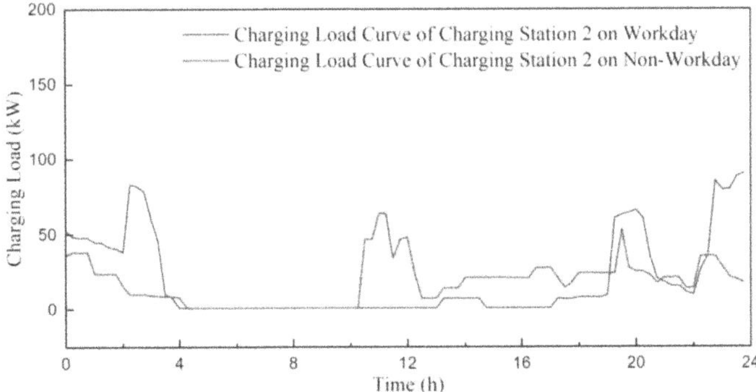

Fig. 8. Charging load curve of Charging Station 2.

4 Analysis of Charging Load Complementarity Characteristics

4.1 Summary of Characteristic Profiles

Table 2. Results of Charging Load Characteristic Profiles for Different Types of Areas

No	Block Type	Charging Load Characteristic Profiles
1	Residential Area	Charging behavior is highly dependent on residents' commuting rules. It shows an obvious evening peak on workdays, while the peak declines and time periods are scattered on non-workdays. The load concentration is strong, with good predictability and regulation potential
2	Park Area	A single-peak load is formed during the daytime on workdays, mainly concentrated in the morning and noon. The vehicle usage rule is stable, and the load drops significantly on non-workdays with small fluctuations. It has obvious controllability and time-shifting space
3	Charging Station	It operates with multi-peaks throughout the day, featuring high load and strong volatility. There is no significant difference in load between workday and non-workday, and the operation continuity is strong. It serves as a high-frequency energy supplement hub in the region and is suitable as a key node for load regulation

As summarized in Table 2, the charging load characteristic profiles in different types of areas show significant differences and regularities. Based on the full-month data of the above six typical areas in January 2024, this section constructs and calculates three types of complementarity indicators from the aspects of temporal coordination of load operation and peak-valley differences, so as to systematically evaluate the load complementarity potential between different areas.

4.2 Theories and Methods for Complementarity Characteristics Analysis

1) Pearson Correlation Coefficient

$$r_{xy} = \frac{\sum_{n}^{t=1}(x_t - \overline{x})(y_t - \overline{y})}{\sqrt{\sum_{n}^{t=1}(x_t - \overline{x})^2}.\sqrt{\sum_{n}^{t=1}(y_t - \overline{y})^2}} \tag{1}$$

Pearson Correlation Coefficient (PCC) measures the overall correlation between two areas' charging load curves, with values ranging from [-1, 1]. A value closer to 1 means higher load synchronization and weaker complementarity; a value closer to -1 indicates negative correlation and good complementarity potential. Its calculation formula is shown in (1), where x_t and y_t are the two areas' load values at the t-th time point, $\overline{x}$ and $\overline{y}$ respective mean values, and n = 96. This method is suitable for macro-evaluating the similarity of daily average load curves or monthly load sequences.

2) Load Overlap Index

$$LOI_{xy} = \frac{1}{n} \sum_{n}^{t=1} \frac{min(x_t, y_t)}{max(x_t, y_t)} \tag{2}$$

Load Overlap Index (LOI) reflects the time-period overlap degree of charging loads between two areas; a lower value means more staggered load distribution and stronger complementarity. The Peak-Valley Shift Degree (PVSD) describes the time difference of main peaks/valleys between two load curves; a larger value indicates greater peak-shaving/valley-filling space. The LOI calculation formula is shown in (2), which quantifies the extent to which the two areas are in a high-load state simultaneously.

3) Peak-Valley Shift Degree

$$PVSD_{i,j} = \frac{1}{2n} \left(\left| t_i^{peak} - t_j^{peak} \right| + \left| t_i^{valley} - t_j^{valley} \right| \right) \tag{3}$$

PVSD characterizes the temporal difference between the peak and valley moments of two areas' charging load curves. It reflects their peak-valley stagger degree and serves as a key indicator for identifying load peak-shifting potential. Its calculation formula is shown in (3), where t_i^{peak} and t_j^{peak} are the main peak times of Area i and j's daily average load curves, t_i^{valley} and t_j^{valley} are the occurrence time of the principal valley in the areas, and n = 96. A larger PVSD means more temporal stagger of main peaks/valleys between the two areas, indicating greater peak-shifting dispatching space and load complementarity; a smaller value signals overlapping peaks/valleys and poor complementarity.

4.3 Results of Charging Load Complementarity Characteristics

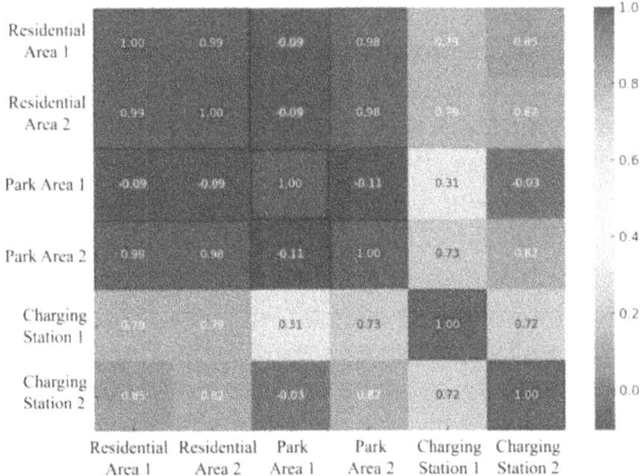

Fig. 9. Calculation results of Pearson correlation coefficient.

The calculation results of the three complementarity evaluation indicators for the six typical areas in Fig. 2 are shown in Fig. 9 and Table 3. The results indicate that the three typical functional areas exhibit significant differences in the temporal distribution of charging behaviors, operational rules, and peak periods, thereby forming a solid foundation for load complementarity.

Table 3. Calculation Results of Load Overlap Index and Peak-Valley Shift Degree

No	Scenario	LOI	PVSD
1	Residential Area 1 - Residential Area 2	0.571128	0.958333
2	Residential Area 1 - Park Area 1	0.176311	0.583333
3	Residential Area 1 - Park Area 2	0.040148	0.03125
4	Residential Area 1 - Charging Station 1	0.129692	0.541667
5	Residential Area 1 - Charging Station 2	0.351329	0.010417
6	Residential Area 2 - Park Area 1	0.112296	0.479167
7	Residential Area 2 - Park Area 2	0.02293	0.989583
8	Residential Area 2 - Charging Station 1	0.227081	1.4375
9	Residential Area 2 - Charging Station 2	0.200654	0.947917
10	Park Area 1 - Park Area 2	0.188756	0.59375
11	Park Area 1 - Charging Station 1	0.027586	1.0625
12	Park Area 1 - Charging Station 2	0.361274	0.572917
13	Park Area 2 - Charging Station 1	0.005207	0.572917
14	Park Area 2 - Charging Station 2	0.114276	0.041667
15	Charging Station 1 - Charging Station 2	0.045565	0.53125

As shown in Fig. 9, residential areas have the highest load curve correlation, reflecting synchronized resident commuting and living schedules. However, this high correlation means strong load synchronization, weak complementarity, and difficulty achieving peak shaving within the same area type. By contrast, PCC between residential areas and other areas is generally low, indicating good temporal complementarity potential. Further analysis of LOI and PVSD shows the average LOI between parks and residences is only ~0.09, indicating a good foundation for coordinated regulation. In terms of PVSD, values between parks and residences are generally over 0.5, reflecting obvious peak-valley stagger and peak-shifting advantages, which helps coordinate multi-source loads and ease peak pressure. Notably, LOI between stations and other areas is generally low and PVSD over 0.5, further showing stations have highly staggered charging with other areas and act as natural load buffers.

Table 4. Direct Complementarity Analysis Results of Different Types of Areas

No	Complementary Scenario	Complementarity Analysis Result
1	Residential Area & Park Area	Peaks are obviously staggered with low overlap, suitable for implementing load transfer based on day-night time division or strategic electricity price guidance
2	Park Area & Charging Station	Daytime operations are staggered, which can be used for zoned charging of high-frequency operating and office vehicles
3	Residential Area & Charging Station	Possesses bidirectional complementarity potential. Especially during nighttime charging periods, V2G technology can guide the coordinated management of household and public loads

Based on systematic calculations and analyses of three indicators, different functional areas show significant differences in charging behavior timing, operational rhythms, and load peak-valley structures. As shown in Table 4, these differences form a solid foundation for temporal complementarity. Utilizing such complementarity can realize efficient infrastructure allocation, alleviate concentrated peak pressure, improve charging efficiency and grid flexibility, and help build a more resilient and intelligent urban charging service system.

5 Conclusion

This study establishes a comprehensive charging load profiling methodology and conducts an in-depth analysis of complementary characteristics in EV charging behavior within challenging urban environments featuring complex transportation networks and vulnerable grid infrastructure. By integrating multi-source spatiotemporal data from residential districts, industrial parks, and public charging stations in Shanghai's Dalinghao Bay area, this study uncovers distinctive temporal load patterns and reveals remarkable complementarity across different urban functional blocks. The innovative evaluation framework, which systematically incorporates Pearson correlation coefficients, load overlap indices, and peak-valley shift degrees, provides robust quantitative evidence for significant coordination potential in charging scheduling and grid-load interaction. Particularly noteworthy is the strong temporal complementarity between residential and industrial zones, as well as the consistent load buffering capacity demonstrated by public charging stations. These findings establish a pioneering data-driven foundation for optimizing charging infrastructure deployment, enhancing grid operational flexibility, and facilitating the transition toward resilient and intelligent urban energy ecosystems in rapidly electrifying metropolitan regions.

While the findings are derived from January data reflecting winter conditions, the proposed charging load profiling methodology and identified inter-block complementarity patterns still offer valuable references for other metropolitan areas facing complex traffic and weak grid constraints. To further enhance the generalizability of the observed charging behaviors and complementarity characteristics across different seasonal climates, future research could incorporate multi-seasonal data to verify and refine the conclusions.

Acknowledgment. This work was sponsored by the Science and Technology Project from the State Grid Shanghai Municipal Electric Power Company of China (52094024002R).

References

1. Guo, C., Liu, D., Zhu, C., et al.: Modeling and analysis of charging load of electric vehicles in residential areas. Elect. Power Autom. Equipment **40**(1), 1–9 (2020)
2. Chen, Z., Zhang, Z., Zhao, J., et al.: An analysis of the charging characteristics of electric vehicles based on measured data and its application. IEEE Access **6**, 24475–24487 (2018)
3. Huang, W., Wang, J., Wang, J., et al.: EV charging load profile identification and seasonal difference analysis via charging sessions data of charging stations. Energy **288**, 129771 (2024)
4. Yi, T., Zhang, C., Lin, T., et al.: Research on the spatial-temporal distribution of electric vehicle charging load demand: a case study in China. J. Clean. Prod. **242**, 118457 (2020)
5. Tong,X., Guo, C., Yang, X., et al.: Research on characteristics of electric vehicle charging load and distribution network supportability. In: IEEE PES Asia-Pacific Power and Energy Engineering Conference, pp. 1539–1542 (2016)
6. Liu, L., Wu, T., Chen, X., et al.: Multi-objective optimal configuration of DG and EV charging stations based on spatiotemporal characteristics and demand response. Electr. Power Autom. Equipment **41**(11), 48–56 (2021)
7. Zhao, H., Yan, X., Ren, H.: Quantifying flexibility of residential electric vehicle charging loads using non-intrusive load extracting algorithm in demand response. Sustain. Cities Soc. **50**, 101664 (2019)
8. Gong, C., Yao, Z., Chen, H., et al.: An optimal coordinated planning strategy for distributed energy station based on characteristics of electric vehicle charging behavior under carbon trading mechanism. Int. J. Electr. Power Energy Syst. **147**, 108884 (2023)
9. Hasan,K.N., Muttaqi, K.M., Borboa, P., et al.: "Measurement-based electric vehicle load profile and its impact on power system operation. In: 2019 9th International Conference on Power and Energy Systems (ICPES), pp. 1–6 (2019)
10. Akil,M., Kilic, E., Bayindir, R., et al.: Uncoordinated charging profile of EVs based on an actual charging session data. In: 2021 10th International Conference on Renewable Energy Research and Application (ICRERA), pp. 459–462 (2021)

From Time Series to Feature Matrix: A Novel PSO-SVM Framework for Self-discharge Diagnosis of Lithium-Ion Batteries

Chenghao Liu[1,2]($\boxtimes$), Xinyu Zhang[1], Zhenyu Wang[1], and Yuhao Zhang[1]($\boxtimes$)

[1] China Automotive Engineering Research Institute Co., Ltd., Chongqing 401122, China
{liuchenghao,zhangyuhao01}@caeri.com.cn
[2] School of Big Data and Software Engineering, Chongqing University, Chongqing 400044, China

Abstract. Lithium-ion power batteries are currently the most widely used energy storage devices in electric vehicles. Rapid and accurate diagnosis of battery faults is crucial for the safe operation of vehicles. This paper proposes a method for diagnosing self-discharge faults in power batteries based on individual adaptive voltage thresholds and Particle Swarm Optimization-Support Vector Machine (PSO-SVM). The research focuses on the voltage signals of power batteries, combines the boxplot method with expert review to label samples of self-discharge faults. Through the sliding window method, 16 features in the time domain and frequency domain are extracted. Principal component analysis is then used to further reduce the dimensionality of voltage features, obtaining the first five principal components with a cumulative variance contribution of 95% as inputs for the PSO-SVM model. The aim of this method is to improve the accuracy of self-discharge fault identification in batteries. The final results show that the proposed method has high recognition accuracy, strong reliability, and potential value in practical electric vehicle applications. It provides theoretical support for enhancing the safety performance of electric vehicles.

Keywords: power battery · Voltage signal · Self-discharge · Support Vector Machine · Principal Component Analysis

1 Introduction

Confronted with the increasingly severe energy crisis and environmental challenges, electric vehicles (EVs) have gained widespread global recognition as a pivotal sustainable solution [1]. As their core power source, lithium-ion power batteries hold an irreplaceable position due to advantages such as high energy density, high power density, and long cycle life [2]. However, battery safety issues, particularly the risk of thermal runaway, remain a critical bottleneck constraining their large-scale adoption; such incidents not only directly threaten driving safety but also severely undermine public confidence in EVs [3–5]. Statistics indicate that in the first half of 2025 alone, over 1.52 million new energy vehicles were recalled in the Chinese market, with more than 52% of these

A. Razminia et al. (Eds.): ITFT 2025, CCIS 2876, pp. 275–287, 2026.
https://doi.org/10.1007/978-3-032-20592-6_25

faults originating from the battery system. This highlights the paramount importance of developing real-time and accurate battery fault diagnosis technologies for ensuring the healthy development of the industry.

Battery faults often manifest as anomalies in sensor data, such as voltage and current. For instance, sudden voltage drops or persistent deviations from the normal range often indicate internal short circuits, connection faults, and other failures [6, 7]. Consequently, real-time monitoring and diagnosis of voltage signals have become the frontline for ensuring battery safety. Nonetheless, battery voltage signals exhibit complex characteristics, including being typically time-varying, nonlinear, and inconsistent across individual cells, making it challenging to accurately extract weak early signs of faults from them [8, 9].

To address this challenge, existing research has primarily formed two diagnostic paradigms: threshold-based methods and model-based methods. Threshold-based methods are intuitive in principle, identifying faults by comparing real-time data with preset thresholds [10]. Due to their simplicity and ease of implementation, they are widely integrated into Battery Management Systems (BMS) [11, 12]. For instance, Duan et al. [13] established a dynamic threshold based on information entropy to evaluate battery inconsistency. Liao et al. [14] utilized open-circuit voltage to rapidly detect the self-discharge rate and set thresholds accordingly. However, the performance of such methods highly depends on the selection of thresholds: excessively high thresholds lead to insufficient sensitivity and increased missed alarms, while overly low thresholds are prone to false alarms. More importantly, the nonlinear nature of battery voltage makes it difficult for fixed thresholds to reliably distinguish between normal and abnormal states under complex operating conditions.

In contrast to threshold-based methods, model-based approaches focus on constructing mathematical models of the battery and diagnose faults by comparing the residuals between the model outputs and actual measurements. For example, scholars like Sidhu [15], Wang [16], and Liu [17] employed nonlinear models with Extended Kalman Filtering, Recursive Least Squares, and Adaptive Extended Kalman Filtering, respectively, for state estimation and residual evaluation. Ouyang [18], Gao [19], and Feng [20] developed average-difference models, mean-difference models, and chemistry-based models using voltage and temperature for detecting internal short circuit faults in lithium-ion batteries. Although effective in specific scenarios, the generalization capability of these methods is often limited. They require complex model identification and parameter tuning for different fault modes, resulting in complicated implementation and insufficient robustness under unforeseen operating conditions.

In recent years, data-driven methods have emerged as a new path to overcome the above bottlenecks. These methods bypass complex mechanistic modeling and directly learn the nonlinear mapping between faults and features from historical EV operational data. Related research has extensively explored various machine learning and deep learning techniques, such as the improved Radial Basis Function neural network approach proposed by Wang et al. [21], the wavelet neural network algorithm by Yao et al.[22], the correlation analysis method by Xia et al. [23], the Random Forest model and three-step diagnostic algorithm by Yang et al. [24], the Unscented Particle Filter algorithm established by Liu et al. [25], the neural network algorithm utilized by Zhao et al. [26], and the Long Short-Term Memory neural network approach used by Jorge et al. [27], among other data-driven methods. Despite their promise, current data-driven methods still face two inherent bottlenecks in practical deployment: First, the curse of dimensionality: Battery systems typically consist of dozens to hundreds of cells connected in series. Using the raw time-series data from all cells directly as model input leads to a severe curse of dimensionality, causing a sharp decline in computational efficiency and a surge in memory usage. Second, non-standardized input: The complex and variable operating conditions of vehicles result in voltage sequences of varying lengths. This characteristic of indefinite-length input poses significant challenges for standardized data processing and model generalization.

To simultaneously address the challenges of "exploding data dimensionality" and "indefinite-length data input," this study constructs a hybrid diagnostic framework that integrates adaptive thresholds with an improved PSO-SVM model based on a feature matrix. The contributions of this paper are mainly reflected in:

1) Proposing a time-frequency feature matrix construction method that converts original indefinite-length time-series data into structured features of fixed dimensions, achieving standardization of model input and fundamentally resolving the non-standardized input challenge;
2) Introducing Principal Component Analysis (PCA) to compress and denoise the feature matrix, significantly enhancing model efficiency and generalization capability while retaining most information (cumulative variance contribution rate 95%), thereby effectively mitigating the curse of dimensionality;
3) We introduced an improved Particle Swarm Optimization (PSO) algorithm and integrated it with SVM to construct an intelligent parameter optimization model. By incorporating an adaptive mutation mechanism, this enhanced PSO algorithm significantly improves its ability to escape local optima, thereby enabling precise identification of the globally optimal parameter combination for SVM in complex fault diagnosis scenarios.

The remainder of this paper is organized as follows: Sect. 2 introduces the data sources, Sect. 3 details the fault definition and preprocessing methods, Sect. 4 presents the model experiments and result analysis, and Sect. 5 concludes the paper and outlines future work.

2 Data Source

This chapter details the dataset employed in this study, covering its fundamental overview, compositional characteristics, and the specific meanings of its data fields. This dataset serves as the foundational data source and validation basis for the subsequent self-discharge fault diagnosis model presented in this thesis.

2.1 Dataset Overview

The "New Energy Vehicle Power Battery Generative Dataset" used in this research is a comprehensive battery dataset generated via advanced AI simulation techniques, based on real-world vehicle operating environments. The dataset is constructed to provide high-quality, large-scale foundational data for research areas such as battery performance evaluation, fault diagnosis, and lifespan prediction.

Key information regarding the dataset is as follows:

1) Battery Types: It encompasses two mainstream power battery chemistries: Lithium Nickel Manganese Cobalt Oxide (NMC) and Lithium Iron Phosphate (LFP).
2) Data Scale and Source: The dataset originates from operational data of 1,000 new energy vehicles operating in real-world environments. This foundational data is expanded and enriched through simulation, ensuring it possesses both the complexity of real-world conditions and the scale/completeness required for research.
3) Fault Types: The dataset is labeled with four critical battery states: Normal, High Internal Resistance, Capacity Anomaly, and Self-Discharge. This provides the necessary conditions for supervised training and testing of fault diagnosis models.

2.2 Dataset Composition and Characteristics

The dataset comprehensively records multi-dimensional time-series data during both vehicle charging and operation. It covers key parameters from the whole-pack level (e.g., total voltage, total current) down to the individual cell level (e.g., cell voltages, extreme temperatures), fully capturing the real-time operational status of the power battery system.

The fault modes contained within the dataset, particularly the self-discharge fault, are the primary focus of this study. Self-discharge faults typically manifest as abnormal decay of individual cell voltages or an increase in voltage inconsistency. These signatures can be accurately captured by fields within the dataset such as VOLT_N, MAX_CELL_VOLT, and MIN_CELL_VOLT. This refined data labeling establishes a crucial foundation for achieving high-accuracy fault identification in this paper. To more intuitively demonstrate the fundamental characteristics and charge-discharge behaviors of the batteries represented in this dataset, typical samples were extracted from both the LFP and NMC battery data. Their voltage-time and SOC-time profiles under charge/discharge conditions are plotted, as shown in Figs. 1 and 2, respectively.

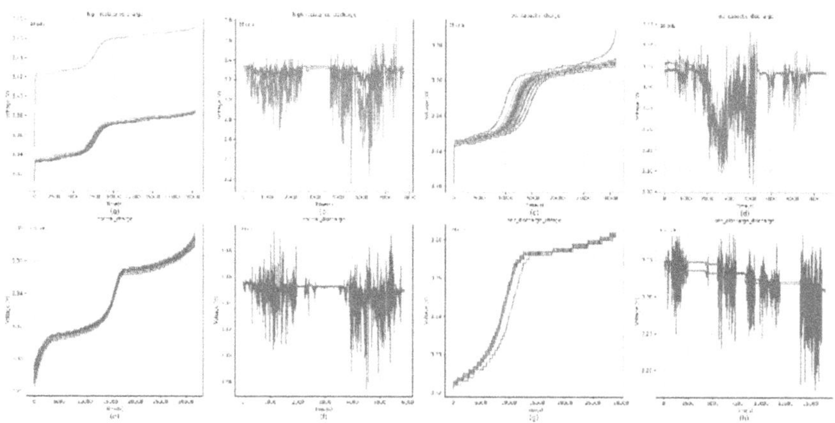

Fig. 1. Typical data profiles of LFP battery.

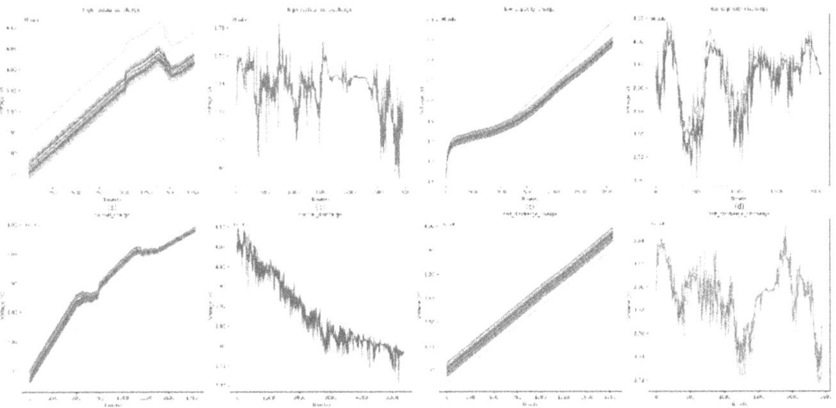

Fig. 2. Typical data profiles of NMC battery.

3 Fault Location Based on Adaptive Thresholds

3.1 Fault Type

This study primarily focuses on the self-discharge fault in electric vehicle power batteries. The self-discharge fault is often persistent, leading to a gradual increase in the State of Charge (SOC) divergence among cells. This results in a reduction of the battery system's actual available capacity, inaccurate SOC estimation, and limitation of power performance. Consequently, it can cause the battery to operate beyond its safe boundaries. In severe cases, it may induce an internal short circuit, triggering rapid temperature rise. This can initiate chain reactions within the battery's internal materials, leading to continuous heat release, thermal runaway, and potentially thermal propagation, ultimately resulting in the ignition of the battery pack and the vehicle.

3.2 Data Preprocessing

The New Energy Vehicle Power Battery Generative Dataset contains data from 800 normal vehicles and 200 faulty vehicles. Eight categories of data were selected: timestamp, total voltage, total current, total number of cells, list of cell voltage values, maximum cell voltage, minimum cell voltage, and charge status. The subsequent data cleaning process followed the methodology of Zeng et al. [28]:

1) Rows containing missing or invalid values in the data list were removed.
2) Data points where the minimum cell voltage was less than 2.0 V or the maximum cell voltage exceeded 5.0 V were discarded.
3) Rows where the SOC was less than 10 or greater than 95 were excluded.
4) Data corresponding to the static charging state were filtered and retained.

For the cleaned data, the list of cell voltage values was separated according to the cell identifier, yielding the original voltage data matrix

$$U = \{u_1'', u_2'', u_3'', \cdots, u_k''\}$$

where k denotes the cell identifier and $u_k^{''}$ represents the cell voltage sequence.

Considering that voltage exhibits a certain degree of fluctuation when a self-discharge fault occurs, the voltage median x_k was calculated for each cell voltage sequence u_k. The difference between each sampling point in u_k and the median x_k was then computed, resulting in the median difference matrix $U\prime = \{u_1\prime, u_2\prime, u_3\prime, \cdots, u_k\prime\}$. This matrix represents the fluctuation amplitude of each cell's voltage signal relative to a stable voltage reference. Subsequently, for the median difference sequence $u_k\prime$ of each cell, a moving average with a window length of 300 was applied to smooth the voltage data, ultimately yielding the feature matrix $U_f = \{u_1, u_2, u_3, \cdots, u_k\}$ of the original voltages.

3.3 Threshold Identification fo r Faulty Vehicles

To determine the thresholds for the preliminary diagnosis of self-discharge faults, this paper employs the boxplot method. This method is a non-parametric approach for outlier detection that does not require the data to conform to a normal distribution and is robust against the influence of outliers. First, for the feature matrix U_f, the first quartile Q_1 and the third quartile Q_3 for each individual cell are obtained, followed by the calculation of the Interquartile Range:

$$IQR = Q_3 - Q_1$$
$$Q_1 - m \cdot IQR \le x \le Q_3 + m \cdot IQR$$

The normal range for a data point x is defined as falling within the condition $[Q_1 - m \cdot IQR, Q_3 + m \cdot IQR]$ below, where $m = 3$. Values outside this range are identified as potential outliers. Since there are k cells, a corresponding set of k fault diagnosis thresholds is established. Crucially, as these diagnostic thresholds are derived from the data of individual cells, each vehicle is assigned a unique set of voltage thresholds specific to its own condition. This inherent adaptability underscores the robustness of the proposed self-discharge fault diagnostic methodology.

4 Self-discharge Fault Diagnosis Based on PSO-SVM

4.1 Feature Extraction

Section 3 of this paper identified the location and timing of self-discharge fault occurrences. However, in the initial stage of a self-discharge fault, the characteristic values tend to fluctuate around the decision threshold, leading to a degree of sparsity in the initial fault labels. Consequently, a stable self-discharge fault is confirmed only when faults are detected consecutively for 5 min, corresponding to 30 sampling points.

For the original voltage data identified with a stable self-discharge fault, a sliding window approach is employed. A window length of 300 is used to segment the data from left to right with a 50% overlap, producing raw voltage sequences $F(n)$ of length $n = 300$. . A Fast Fourier Transform (FFT) is then applied to each $F(n)$ to obtain its frequency spectrum function

$$f_{FFT}(s) = \begin{cases} \sum_{n=0}^{N-1} F(n)W_N^{kn}, 0 \le k \le N-1 \\ \qquad\quad 0, \; others \end{cases}$$

in the frequency domain.

Subsequently, a total of 16 features are extracted from each $F(n)$ sequence across both the time and frequency domains.

Time-domain features: Mean, Variance, Skewness, Kurtosis, 2nd-order Autocorrelation Coefficient, Total Signal Energy, Slope, Peak-to-Peak Distance, Mean Absolute Deviation, Root Mean Square Value, and Mean Absolute Difference.

Frequency-domain features: Spectral Distance, Maximum Power Spectral Density, Power Spectral Density Bandwidth, Spectral Roll-off, and Spectral Entropy.

4.2 Data Dimensionality Reduction via PCA

Among the 16 extracted time and frequency-domain features, potential correlations between some variables may lead to feature redundancy. Principal Component Analysis (PCA) is therefore utilized to synthesize the original multi-dimensional, correlated variables into a smaller set of representative components. The objective of PCA is to project the high-dimensional data onto a lower-dimensional space via linear transformation, maximizing the variance retained in the projected dimensions. This achieves dimensionality reduction without significant loss of information contained within the original dataset.

For the normalized sample set, the Kaiser-Meyer-Olkin (KMO) Measure of Sampling Adequacy exceeds 0.9, and Bartlett's Test of Sphericity shows significance. These results indicate a high degree of inter-correlation among the voltage feature indicators across different dimensions, validating the suitability of PCA for further dimensionality reduction. The cumulative variance contribution rate of the first five principal components exceeds 95%. Consequently, these five components are selected as composite variables for subsequent analysis. These principal components are primarily represented by the original features: Mean, Variance, Skewness, Kurtosis, and Spectral Distance.

4.3 Identification Model Construction and Optimization

This study employs a Support Vector Machine (SVM) to construct the identification model for power battery self-discharge faults, as the feasibility of SVM for this task has been demonstrated in previous research. Let the power battery state sample set be denoted as: $\{x_i,\ y_i,\ i = 1,\ 2, \cdots, I\}$, $y_i \in \{0, 1\}$, $I = 1, 2, \cdots, 2022$, with samples belonging to either the normal state or the fault state. Finding the optimal separating hyperplane for the SVM is transformed into solving the following convex quadratic programming problem:

$$\min_{\omega,b} \frac{1}{2}||\omega||^2$$
$$s.t.\ y_i(\omega^T \cdot x_i + b) - 1 \geq 0,\ i = 1, 2, \cdots, I$$

where ω is an I-dimensional weight vector and b is a scalar bias term.

However, the data labels might not be linearly separable, which can hinder the model's ability to find the optimal hyperplane. To address this, slack variables $\xi_i \geq 0$

are introduced, each incurring a cost of ξ_i. Consequently, the learning problem is reformulated as the following convex quadratic programming problem:

$$\min_{\omega,b,\zeta} \frac{1}{2}||\omega||^2 + c \cdot \sum_{i=1}^{I} \xi_i$$

$$s.t.\, y_i(\omega^T \cdot x_i + b) \geq 1 - \xi_i,\, \xi_i \geq 0,\, i = 1, 2, \cdots, I$$

where $c > 0$ is a penalty parameter, a positive constant specified by the user. Next, Lagrange multiplier vectors $\alpha = (\alpha_1, \alpha_2, \cdots, \alpha_I)^T$ are introduced for each inequality constraint, defining the Lagrangian function:

$$L(\omega, b, \xi, \alpha, \mu) = \frac{1}{2}||\omega||^2 + c \cdot \sum_{i=1}^{I} \xi_i$$

$$-\sum_{i=1}^{I} \alpha_i(y_i(\omega^T \cdot x_i + b) - 1 + \xi_i) - \sum_{i=1}^{I} \mu_i \xi_i$$

where $\alpha_i \geq 0$, $\mu_i \geq 0$.

The dual form of this problem is obtained as:

$$\max_{\alpha} \frac{1}{2} \sum_{i=1}^{I} \sum_{i=1}^{I} \alpha_i \alpha_j y_i y_j (x_i \cdot x_j) + \sum_{i=1}^{I} \alpha_i$$

$$s.t. \sum_{i=1}^{I} \alpha_i y_i = 0,\, 0 < \alpha_i < c$$

Given the optimal solution $\alpha_i^* = (\alpha_1^*, \alpha_2^*, \cdots, \alpha_I^*)^T$ to the dual problem, the optimal solutions ω^* and b^* for the primal problem can be expressed as:

$$\omega^* = \sum_{i=1}^{I} \alpha_i^* y_i x_i$$

$$b^* = y_i - \sum_{i=1}^{I} y_i \alpha_i^* (x_i \cdot x_j)$$

From the above results, the separating hyperplane and the classification decision function are derived:

$$\sum_{i=1}^{I} y_i \alpha_i^* (x \cdot x_i) + b^* = 0$$

$$f(x) = sign(\sum_{i=1}^{I} y_i \alpha_i^* (x \cdot x_i) + b^*)$$

The SVM can map linearly inseparable data from the original space to another high-dimensional feature space H by applying a kernel function, thereby seeking the optimal separating hyperplane. The classification decision function of the SVM model based on the Radial Basis Function (RBF) kernel is given below, which demonstrates robust performance against noise in complex data:

$$K(x, x_i) = exp(-\frac{||x - x_i||^2}{2\sigma^2})$$

In this equation, $\frac{1}{2\sigma^2} > 0$ represents the kernel function bandwidth, denoted here as g.

Substituting Equation yields the classification decision function for this case:

$$f(x) = sign(\sum_{i=1}^{I} y_i \alpha_i^* exp(-g||x - x_i||^2) + b^*)$$

Here, x, x_i, α_i^*, b^* are the optimized parameters from the model solution are incorporated.

During the modeling process, the Particle Swarm Optimization (PSO) algorithm is introduced to optimize the kernel bandwidth g of the RBF kernel and the penalty parameter c. The initial particle population size is set to 10, and the number of optimization iterations is set to 100.

When a battery sample x_i of unknown status is input into the classification decision function, the output result $f(x_i)$ is obtained. If $f(x_i) = 0$, the sample x_i is classified as being in a normal state. If $f(x_i) = 1$, the sample x_i is identified as having a self-discharge fault.

5   Experiments and Results Analysis

5.1   Experimental Setup

This chapter validates the effectiveness of the proposed adaptive PSO-SVM model for power battery self-discharge diagnosis through three sets of experiments. The experimental data originates from an generated power battery dataset. The raw data for each vehicle includes voltage readings from 96 individual cells. Sixteen time-domain and frequency-domain features (e.g., mean, variance, skewness, kurtosis, spectral distance) were extracted from this data. Subsequently, Principal Component Analysis (PCA) was employed to select the top five most contributing features as input for the PSO-SVM model. The dataset was randomly split into training and testing sets in a 7:3 ratio. The model training and testing process was repeated 50 times, and the results were averaged. All experiments were conducted under identical hardware and software environments (Python 3.8, Scikit-learn library). Evaluation metrics included Accuracy, Precision, Recall, F1-Score, and AUC value. Training time was also recorded for efficiency analysis.

5.2 Model Comparison Experiments

To evaluate the performance of the PSO-SVM model, this study compared it against several classic machine learning models, including SVM, Random Forest, XGBoost, and Logistic Regression. For this comparison, the PSO-SVM model utilized the 5 PCA-reduced features (denoted as PSO-SVM-5), while the other models were trained using the same feature set. The experimental results are shown in Fig. 3 and Table 1. PSO-SVM-5 significantly outperformed all comparative models across all evaluation metrics. Specifically, from the performance metric bar charts in Fig. 3(a), PSO-SVM-5 achieved an accuracy of 96.60%, a precision of 95.85%, a recall of 97.20%, an F1-Score of 0.9652, and an AUC value of 0.9760. All these metrics are substantially higher than those of the other models.

Figure 3(b) further highlights the comparative advantage in F1-Score, clearly demonstrating the superior comprehensive performance of PSO-SVM-5. In contrast, the performance of the other models was comparatively poorer: Random Forest achieved an accuracy of only 67.80%, Logistic Regression 88.89%, XGBoost 75.96%, and the standard SVM model was the lowest at 63.95%. These results indicate that the PSO-SVM model possesses higher classification capability and robustness for the task of power battery self-discharge fault diagnosis.

Table 1. Comparative Experimental Results of Machine Learning Models.

Model	Accuracy	Precision	Recall	F1-Score	AUC
PSO-SVM	96.60%	95.85%	97.20%	0.9652	0.9760
Random Forest	67.80%	68.37%	62.62%	0.6537	0.7508
Logistic Regression	88.89%	93.65%	82.71%	0.8784	0.9503
XGBoost	75.96%	77.55%	71.03%	0.7415	0.8356
SVM	63.95%	68.97%	46.73%	0.5571	0.6715

From the perspective of training efficiency, Fig. 3(c) shows the comparison of training times for different models. The training time for PSO-SVM was 6.52 s, which falls within the mid-range among the compared models. Random Forest was the fastest to train (3.01 s) but exhibited lower performance. XGBoost required the longest training time (50.71 s), yet its performance was still inferior to PSO-SVM. The training times for Logistic Regression and the standard SVM were 11.80 s and 4.03 s, respectively. Overall, PSO-SVM achieves the best diagnostic performance while maintaining relatively high training efficiency.

Furthermore, Fig. 3(d) presents the ROC curves of the different models. The ROC curve of PSO-SVM is the closest to the top-left corner, with an AUC value of 0.9760, significantly higher than the other models. This further validates the superior performance of PSO-SVM in the binary classification task.

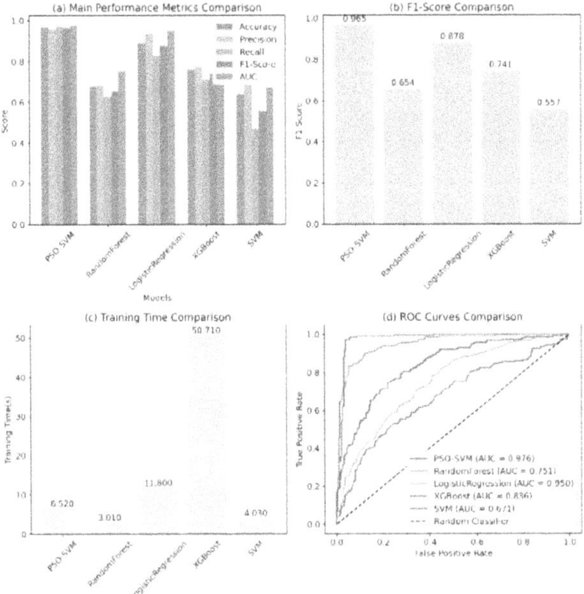

Fig. 3. Comparative Experimental Results of the Models.

6   Conclusion

To enhance the safety performance of electric vehicle power batteries, this paper proposed a self-discharge fault diagnosis method based on adaptive thresholds and PSO-SVM. This method can accurately and in real-time locate individual battery cells with potential self-discharge risks, enabling early diagnosis before faults escalate. This helps prevent further degradation of safety performance and ultimately avoids thermal runaway incidents.

The process begins with preliminary feature extraction from the individual cell voltage sequences. The boxplot method is used to set cell-specific adaptive fault diagnosis thresholds. These thresholds, combined with manual review, are employed to label the location and timing of self-discharge fault occurrences, which subsequently serve as the fault labels for the identification model. Subsequently, the sliding window method is applied to extract both normal and abnormal voltage samples. From each sample, a total of 16 time-domain and frequency-domain features are extracted. Principal Component Analysis (PCA) is then utilized for further dimensionality reduction, resulting in five principal components with a cumulative variance contribution of 95%, which are used as the input for the PSO-SVM model. The final results demonstrate that the proposed method achieves high recognition accuracy. It is suitable for monitoring self-discharge faults in electric vehicle power batteries and provides theoretical support for improving the driving safety performance of electric vehicles.

In future research, unsupervised learning methods could be considered. These would train the identification model using normal samples, potentially mitigating the impact of inaccurate labeling. Furthermore, this study focused solely on the self-discharge phenomenon during the battery charging state. In reality, voltage signals during vehicle operation may also contain crucial information related to self-discharge. Therefore, the next step will involve integrating real-world electric vehicle operational scenarios to fully leverage battery data across its entire life cycle, aiming to achieve more accurate identification of self-discharge faults.

References

1. Wang, C.Y., et al.: Lithium-ion battery structure that self-heats at low temperatures. Nature **529**(7587), 515–518 (2016)
2. Li, W.A.N.G., Leqiong, X.I.E., Guangyu, T.I.A.N., Xiangming, H.E.: Safety accidents of Li-ion batteries: reliability issues or safety issues. Energy Storage Sci. Technol. **10**(1), 1 (2021)
3. Ma, M., Li, X., Gao, W., Sun, J., Wang, Q., Mi, C.: Multi-fault diagnosis for series-connected lithium-ion battery pack with reconstruction-based contribution based on parallel PCA-KPCA. Appl. Energy **324**, 119678 (2022)
4. Shang, Y., Lu, G., Kang, Y., Zhou, Z., Duan, B., Zhang, C.: A multi-fault diagnosis method based on modified sample entropy for lithium-ion battery strings. J. Power Sources **446**, 227275 (2020)
5. Feng, X., Weng, C., Ouyang, M., Sun, J.: Online internal short circuit detection for a large format lithium ion battery. Appl. Energy **161**, 168–180 (2016)
6. Feng, X., He, X., Lu, L., Ouyang, M.: Analysis on the fault features for internal short circuit detection using an electrochemical-thermal coupled model. J. Electrochem. Soc. **165**(2), A155 (2018)
7. Hannan, M.A., Lipu, M.H., Hussain, A., Mohamed, A.: A review of lithium-ion battery state of charge estimation and management system in electric vehicle applications: challenges and recommendations. Renew. Sustain. Energy Rev. **78**, 834–854 (2017)
8. Xiong, R., Yu, Q., Shen, W., Lin, C., Sun, F.: A sensor fault diagnosis method for a lithium-ion battery pack in electric vehicles. IEEE Trans. Power Electron. **34**(10), 9709–9718 (2019)
9. Zhang, C., Jiang, Y., Jiang, J., Cheng, G., Diao, W., Zhang, W.: Study on battery pack consistency evolutions and equilibrium diagnosis for serial-connected lithium-ion batteries. Appl. Energy **207**, 510–519 (2017)
10. El Mejdoubi, A., Chaoui, H., Gualous, H., Van Den Bossche, P., Omar, N., Van Mierlo, J.: Lithium-ion batteries health prognosis considering aging conditions. IEEE Trans. Power Electron. **34**(7), 6834–6844 (2018)
11. Zhao, R., Liu, J., Gu, J.: Simulation and experimental study on lithium ion battery short circuit. Appl. Energy **173**, 29–39 (2016)
12. Xia, B., Chen, Z., Mi, C., Robert, B.: External short circuit fault diagnosis for lithium-ion batteries. In: 2014 IEEE Transportation Electrification Conference and Expo (ITEC), pp. 1–7. IEEE (2014)
13. Duan, B., Li, Z., Gu, P., Zhou, Z., Zhang, C.: Evaluation of battery inconsistency based on information entropy. J Energy Storage **16**, 160–166 (2018)
14. Liao, H., Huang, B., Cui, Y., et al.: Research on a fast detection method of self-discharge of lithium battery. J. Energy Storage **55**(PA), 105431 (2022)
15. Sidhu, A., Izadian, A., Anwar, S.: Adaptive nonlinear model-based fault diagnosis of Li-ion batteries. IEEE Trans. Industr. Electron. **62**(2), 1002–1011 (2014)
16. Wang, Y., Tian, J., Chen, Z., et al.: Model based insulation fault diagnosis for lithium-ion battery pack in electric vehicles. Measurement, 443–451 (2018)
17. Liu, Z., He, H.: Sensor fault detection and isolation for a lithium-ion battery pack in electric vehicles using adaptive extended Kalman filter. Appl. Energy **185**, 2033–2044 (2017)

18. Ouyang, M., et al.: Internal short circuit detection for battery pack using equivalent parameter and consistency method. J. Power Sources **294**, 272–283 (2015)
19. Gao, W., Zheng, Y., Ouyang, M., Li, J., Lai, X., Hu, X.: Micro-short-circuit diagnosis for series-connected lithium-ion battery packs using mean-difference model. IEEE Trans. Industr. Electron. **66**(3), 2132–2142 (2018)
20. Xuning, F., Yue, P., Xiangming, H., et al.: Detecting the internal short circuit in large-format lithium-ion battery using model-based fault-diagnosis algorithm. J. Energy Storage **18**, 26–39 (2018)
21. Wang, J., Zhang, S., Hu, X.: A fault diagnosis method for lithium-ion battery packs using improved RBF neural network. Front. Energy Res. **9**, 702139 (2021)
22. Yao, L., Xiao, Y., Gong, X., Hou, J., Chen, X.: A novel intelligent method for fault diagnosis of electric vehicle battery system based on wavelet neural network. J. Power Sources **453**, 227870 (2020)
23. Xia, B., Shang, Y., Nguyen, T., Mi, C.: A correlation based fault detection method for short circuits in battery packs. J. Power Sources **337**, 1–10 (2017)
24. Ruixin, Y., Rui, X., et al.: A fractional-order model-based battery external short circuit fault diagnosis approach for all-climate electric vehicles application. J. Clean. Prod. **35**, 950–959 (2018)
25. Datong, L., Xuehao, Y., et al.: An on-line state of health estimation of lithium-ion battery using unscented particle filter. IEEE Access **6**, 40990–41001 (2018)
26. Yang, Z., Peng, L., et al.: Fault and defect diagnosis of battery for electric vehicles based on big data analysis methods. Appl. Energy **207**, 354–362 (2017)
27. Jorge, I., Mesbahi, T., Samet, A., et al.: Time Series Feature extraction for lithium-ion batteries state-of-health prediction. J. Energy Storage **59**, 106436 (2023)
28. Zeng, J.B., Zhang, Y.Y., Zhang, Z., et al.: Identification of power battery voltage inconsistency faults in electric vehicles based on K-means++ clustering with dynamic k-values (in Chinese). SCIENTIA SINICA Technologica **53**, 28–40 (2023)

Lightweight Multiclass Intrusion Detection on Electric Vehicle Infrastructure

Mehmet Bozdal[1,2] iD, Ali Özkahraman[3(✉)] iD, Alper Savaşçı[1] iD, and Zoya Pourmirza[2] iD

[1] Abdullah Gül University, Kayseri, Türkiye
[2] University of Birmingham, Birmingham, UK
[3] Iskenderun Technical University, Iskenderun, Türkiye
`ali.ozkahraman@iste.edu.tr`

Abstract. Electric vehicle (EV) charging infrastructures are increasingly networked, making them susceptible to cyber-physical attacks that can disrupt service and damage assets. This paper proposes a lightweight, host-based intrusion detection system (IDS) using a depth-wise separable convolutional neural network (CNN) for multiclass classification of anomalies in EV charging systems. We utilize the CICEVSE2024 dataset, applying Mutual Information (MI) for feature selection to identify the top 40 most relevant host-level kernel events. The proposed model is assessed with accuracy, precision, recall, and F1-score. Results demonstrate that the depth-wise separable CNN model achieves an F1-score of 0.9077 and an Accuracy of 0.9092 for 17-class classification, proving its effectiveness in identifying specific attack types using a reduced feature set.

Keywords: EV Charging Security · Anomaly Detection

1 Introduction

Electric vehicles (EVs) have a key role in decarbonizing the transportation sector. As of 2024, EVs accounted for over 20% of global new car sales, bringing the total number of EVs on the roads to approximately 58 million [1]. The electrification of transportation is reshaping the power grid landscape, as EV charging infrastructure has become a critical component of the modernizing energy ecosystem. Besides supplying high-quality charging power through power conversion equipment, EV charging stations are cyber-physical components that include a high level of digital technologies for interacting with different entities such as EV owners, grid operators, and financial services. Figure 1 illustrates an EV charging station operating within a power distribution grid in three-level hierarchy where the grid energy management system (EMS) carries out the grid operations such as voltage regulation, congestion management and protective relaying; the charging station level coordinates its charging service provided to EV owners under physical capacity constraint of the charging station and the dynamic hosting capacity of the distribution feeder where the station is connected, the EV level represents the customer behaviors regarding when to connect/disconnect their vehicles.

A. Razminia et al. (Eds.): ITFT 2025, CCIS 2876, pp. 288–296, 2026.
https://doi.org/10.1007/978-3-032-20592-6_26

EV charging stations communicate with vehicles, cloud servers, utility grids, and user applications using protocols such as the Open Charge Point Protocol (OCPP) and ISO 15118. This high level of connectivity enhances operational efficiency and improves user experience. However, it also introduces significant cybersecurity vulnerabilities that can compromise both the charging infrastructure and the broader power system.

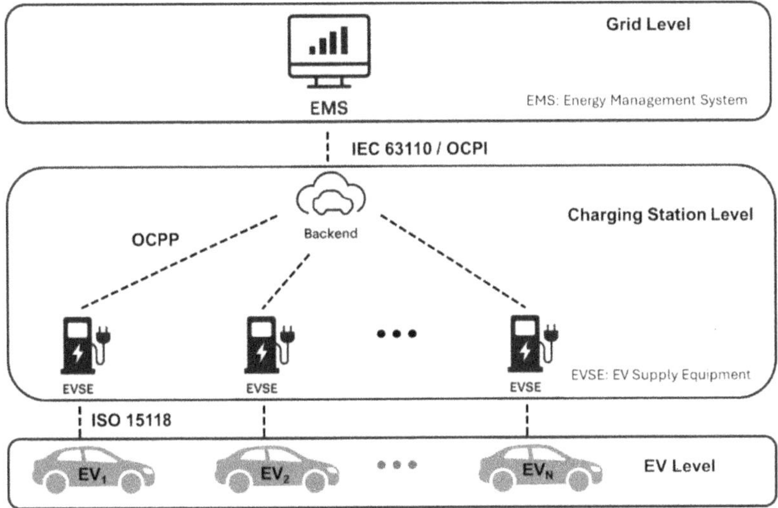

Fig. 1. Cyber-physical EV charging infrastructure.

Research in [2] and [3] shows the vulnerabilities of the ISO 15118 and OCPP protocols, respectively. Attackers may exploit these weaknesses by intercepting vehicle-to-charger communications, particularly where unencrypted channels are used, or by targeting firmware updates, backend network traffic, user credentials, payment information, or internal hardware communications through physical access [4]. Attacks targeting the EV charging infrastructure can impact the stability and reliability of the power grid. By manipulating the aggregated charging load profiles, adversaries can induce severe operational disturbances, including frequency and voltage instabilities, power quality degradation, and unbalanced phase loading [5]. To safeguard critical electric power infrastructure, appropriate protection mechanisms must be implemented. These mechanisms should ensure the confidentiality, integrity, and availability of communication and control systems across the EV charging ecosystem. Strong encryption and authentication mechanisms should be in place to harden against attacks. Furthermore, continuous monitoring should be deployed for those attacks that pass security barriers.

Various intrusion detection systems have been deployed to detect attacks. Machine learning and deep learning methods are highly used as these methods can understand the system behavior, and some may detect unseen attacks. Implementing these methods requires a benchmarking dataset such as the Canadian Institute for Cybersecurity EV charger attack dataset 2024 (CICEVSE2024) [6]. Multi-view graph contrastive representative learning [7], random forest [8], Temporal Convolutional Network [9], Federated Learning-based Anomaly Detection System [10] have utilized the CICEVSE2024 dataset for benchmarking. This work focuses on balancing the model's performance and computational complexity by selecting important features. Therefore, this work presents an anomaly detection system to protect EV charging stations. The main contributions of this paper are summarized as follows:

- We propose a lightweight intrusion detection model using a depth-wise separable CNN, an architecture well-suited for on-device deployment in resource-constrained EV chargers.
- We demonstrate the effectiveness of using host-based kernel-level events for fine-grained, multiclass classification of 17 distinct anomaly types, moving beyond simple binary detection.
- We introduce a robust feature selection pipeline, using Mutual Information (MI) to systematically reduce the feature space from 911 raw system features down to the top 40 most informative kernel events.

The remainder of the paper is organized as follows. Section 2 provides the methodology of the paper, where Mutual Information and the proposed depth-wise CNN model are presented. Section 3 describes the experimental setup, followed by Sect. 4, which concludes the paper.

2 Methodology

2.1 Mutual Information (MI)

Filtering-based feature selection techniques evaluate features using statistical criteria that are independent of the learning algorithm. These methods are computationally efficient since they do not require repeated model training, making them suitable for high-dimensional datasets where wrapper-based approaches would be computationally expensive. Additionally, they mitigate overfitting risks because the selection process is not tied to any specific model.

Among these methods, Mutual Information (MI) quantifies the dependency between each feature and the target variable, identifying those that share the most information with the output. It is mathematically defined as:

$$I(X;Y) = \sum_{x,y} p(x,y) log \frac{p(x,y)}{p(x)p(y)} \tag{1}$$

where X is the input variable, Y is the output variable, $p(x,y)$ is the joint probability distribution of X and Y, and $p(x)$ and $p(y)$ are their respective marginal probabilities. A higher value of $I(X;Y)$ indicates that feature X carries more information about the target Y.

Unlike correlation-based techniques that capture only linear relationships, MI effectively identifies both linear and non-linear dependencies without assuming any particular data distribution. This property enhances its robustness and suitability for complex, real-world datasets.

In feature selection, MI is employed to rank features according to the amount of information they provide about the target. Features with higher MI scores are considered more relevant, while those with lower scores can be excluded. This process yields a compact and informative feature subset, reducing model complexity, improving generalization, and decreasing training time without compromising predictive accuracy.

2.2 Proposed Model

The core component of the proposed architecture is the depth-wise separable convolution, an efficient convolutional operation that decomposes a standard convolution into two sequential processes: a depth-wise convolution followed by a pointwise convolution, as illustrated in Fig. 2. This decomposition substantially reduces computational cost and parameter count while maintaining comparable representational capacity to conventional convolutions.

In a standard convolution, a single operation simultaneously filters input features across all channels and combines them to form new output features. A standard convolutional layer with K filters applied to an input of C_{in} channels requires $K * C_{in} * F * F$ parameters per kernel (where F is the kernel size), leading to substantial computational complexity.

In contrast, the depth-wise separable convolution factorizes this single operation into two distinct, specialized layers:

- The depth-wise convolution applies separate filters, one per input channel, to perform spatial filtering. This requires only $C_{in} * F * F$ parameters.
- The pointwise convolution (a 1x1 convolution) then projects the channel-wise features into a new, higher-dimensional space by linearly combining them. This requires $C_{in} * C_{out} * 1 * 1$ parameters.

By decoupling spatial filtering from channel-wise combination, the total number of parameters becomes $(C_{in} * F * F) + (C_{in} * C_{out})$, which is drastically lower than the $(C_{in} * F * F * C_{out})$ of the standard convolution. This factorization typically results in a theoretical reduction in computational cost by a factor of nearly F^2, making it exceptionally suitable for applications where efficiency is paramount.

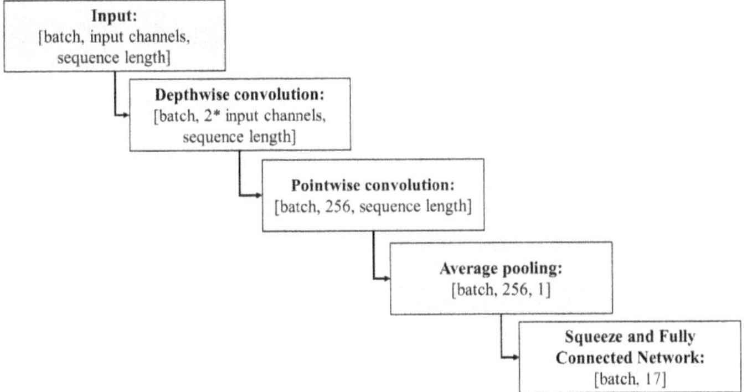

Fig. 2. Building block of the proposed depth-wise 1D-CNN model.

The specific implementation of our depth-wise separable convolution block, as defined in the Fig. 2, introduces several key design choices to enhance feature representation. First, in the depth-wise convolution layer, we deliberately set the output channels to $2*C_{in}$ rather than maintaining the same number. This expansion effectively doubles the feature maps after spatial filtering, allowing the model to capture a richer set of spatial characteristics from each input channel before the pointwise combination. The subsequent pointwise convolution then performs channel fusion on these expanded features, projecting them to a desired dimensionality specified by point-wise output. Following these convolutional operations, we apply an Adaptive Average Pooling layer to aggregate the temporal information globally. This operation reduces each feature map to a single value by taking the mean across the entire sequence length, effectively making the model invariant to the input sequence length and preventing overfitting by reducing the number of parameters in the final fully connected layer. The combination of channel expansion in depth-wise convolution and global temporal pooling creates a robust feature extractor that is both computationally efficient and effective for classification tasks.

3 Experimental Results and Performance Analysis

3.1 Dataset and Experimental Setup

The Canadian Institute for Cybersecurity EV charger attack dataset 2024 (CICEVSE2024) [6] is used in this research. CICEVSE2024 simultaneously captures three complementary data streams from an experimental EVSE testbed: (i) power consumption data from the main board, measured via wattmeter and the I2C protocol to reflect workload variations; (ii) network traffic from ISO 15118 and OCPP communication interfaces, recorded using Wireshark and TCPdump; and (iii) host activities, encompassing kernel and Hardware Performance Counter (HPC) events from the SECC/main board (Raspberry Pi 4 Model B) using the Linux Perf tool.

The "EVSE-B-HPC-Kernel-Events" subset was selected, which originally contained 911 features. This subset focuses on kernel and Hardware Performance Counter (HPC) events captured from the device's main board. The dataset is imbalanced and contains 17 classes, including benign traffic and attacks spanning Denial-of-Service (DoS), reconnaissance, and cryptojacking.

A multi-stage preprocessing pipeline was applied to refine the feature set. First, columns with constant values and rows with missing data were removed, which reduced the feature set to 226. Then, as described in Sect. 2.1, Mutual Information (MI) scores were calculated, and the top 40 most informative features were selected for model training.

All experiments were conducted on a workstation equipped with an NVIDIA GeForce GTX 3060 GPU, and models were implemented using the PyTorch framework. The data was partitioned into an 80% training set and a 20% testing set. All 40 selected features were normalized using Standard Scaler before being input to the model. The proposed method was trained for 100 epochs using the Adam optimizer with a learning rate of 0.01 and a Cross Entropy Loss function.

3.2 Results and Discussion

The performance of the proposed 1D-CNN is detailed in the confusion matrix in Fig. 3. The model demonstrates high precision and recall for the two largest classes, achieving perfect classification for both cryptojacking (384 correct instances) and none (456 correct instances). This indicates a strong ability to distinguish the most common attack type and benign traffic. However, significant confusion is observed among reconnaissance-type attacks. For instance, os-fingerprinting is frequently misclassified as port-scan (3 instances) and service-detection (3 instances). Similarly, os-scan is misclassified as port-scan (1 instance) and vuln-scan (3 instances). This suggests that while the model effectively detects malicious activity, it struggles to differentiate between these semantically similar scanning behaviors.

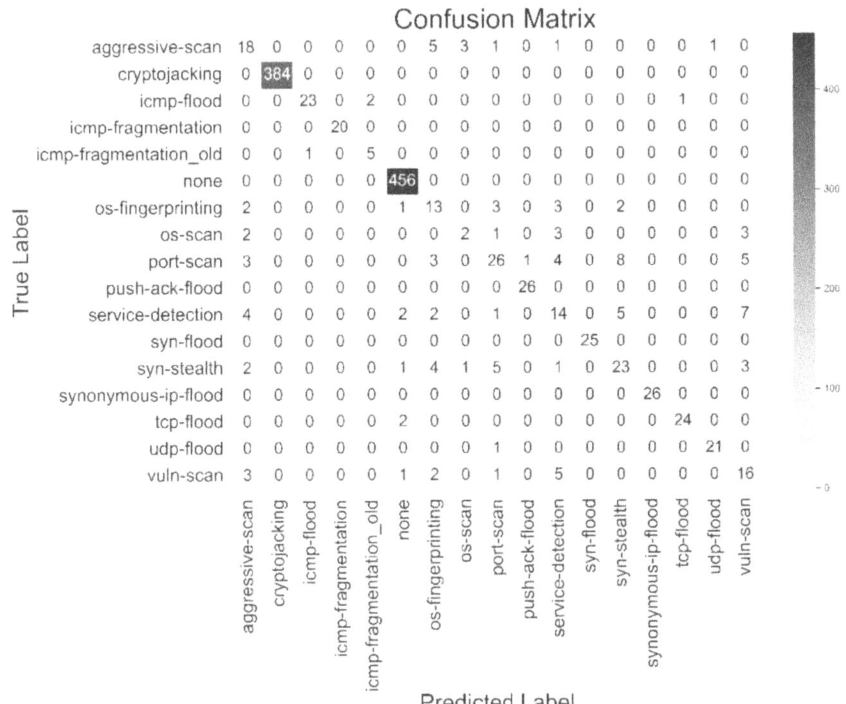

Fig. 3. Confusion matrix of the proposed depth-wise 1D-CNN model on the 17-class CICEVSE2024 test set.

Training loss and test accuracy in Fig. 4. The solid red line (left y-axis) shows the model's training loss converging towards a low value. The dashed blue line (right y-axis) shows the test accuracy stabilizing around 89–91%, indicating the model has learned generalizable features.

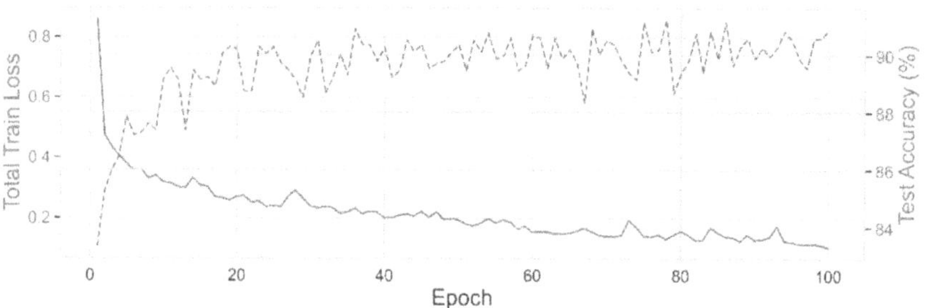

Fig. 4. Training loss and test accuracy of the proposed depth-wise 1D-CNN over 100 epochs.

Table 1. Comparison with existing methods.

Model	Number of Classes	Number of Channels	Accuracy	Precision	Recall	F1-Score
MVGCRL [7]	2	47	–	0.9771	0.9679	0.9711
Explainable DL [11]	2	12	0.9754	0.9757	0.9754	0.9754
TCN [9]	2	193	0.9980	0.9960	1.0	0.9980
Proposed Depth-wise CNN	2	40	0.9943	0.9924	0.9955	0.9939
TCN [9]	17	193	0.93	–	–	–
Proposed Depth-wise CNN	17	40	0.9092	0.9081	0.9092	0.9077

Table 1 presents a comparative performance analysis between the proposed CNN model and several existing approaches, including the Multi-View Graph Contrastive Representation Learning (MVGCRL) [7], and Temporal Convolutional Network (TCN) [9] architectures. The comparison considers the number of classes, the number of input channels, and four key performance metrics: Accuracy, Precision, Recall, and F1-Score.

In the multiclass classification task involving 17 classes, the TCN model achieved an accuracy of 0.93 with 193 input channels, demonstrating that a deeper temporal convolutional structure can handle a larger class set effectively, though at the expense of high input dimensionality. In contrast, the proposed depth-wise CNN achieved a comparable accuracy of 0.9092 with only 40 channels. TCN has a model size of 1.04 MB, while the proposed method decreased the size significantly to 0.097 MB. This indicates a substantial reduction in feature dimensionality and model size while maintaining competitive performance. TCN has 1.298 MFLOPs, while our proposed method has significantly less computational requirements with 0.05322 MFLOPs. Furthermore, the proposed CNN obtained balanced Precision (0.9081), Recall (0.9092), and F1-Score (0.9077), reflecting stable classification performance across all classes.

Overall, the proposed CNN demonstrates an advantageous trade-off between computational efficiency and detection accuracy. Its ability to perform reliably with fewer input channels underscores its potential suitability for real-time or resource-constrained environments, such as edge-deployed intrusion detection systems.

4   Conclusion and Future Work

This paper proposed a lightweight, host-based IDS for multiclass anomaly detection in EV charging infrastructure. By applying MI for feature selection, we identified the 40 most critical kernel-level events from the CICEVSE2024 dataset. Our proposed 1D-CNN model, which utilizes efficient depth-wise separable convolutions, achieved an overall accuracy of 0.9092 and an F1-score of 0.9077 in classifying 17 distinct attack types. Analysis of the confusion matrix and t-SNE plots confirmed the model's strong ability to separate benign traffic and cryptojacking attacks, while also highlighting the challenge of distinguishing between similar reconnaissance attack types.

Future work will focus on a multi-modal IDS where the model is fed by all three complementary data streams (power, network, host) to explore generalization capabilities across attack classes.

Acknowledgement. The authors gratefully acknowledge the financial support of the Scientific and Technological Research Council of Türkiye (TÜBİTAK) through the travel grant awarded under application number 1919B022509674.

References

1. IEA, Global EV Outlook 2025 Expanding sales in diverse markets (2025). https://www.iea.org/. Accessed 04 Oct 2025
2. Bao, K., Valev, H., Wagner, M., Schmeck, H.: A threat analysis of the vehicle-to-grid charging protocol ISO 15118. Comput. Sci. Res. Dev. **33**(1–2), 3–12 (2018). https://doi.org/10.1007/S00450-017-0342-Y/FIGURES/2
3. Hamdare, S., et al.: Cyber defense in OCPP for EV charging security risks. Int. J. Inf. Secur. **24**(3), 1–25 (2025). https://doi.org/10.1007/S10207-025-01055-7/FIGURES/14
4. Johnson, J., Berg, T., Anderson, B., Wright, B.: Review of electric vehicle charger cybersecurity vulnerabilities, potential impacts, and defences. Energies **15**, 3931 (2022). https://doi.org/10.3390/EN15113931
5. Acharya, S., Dvorkin, Y., Pandzic, H., Karri, R.: Cybersecurity of smart electric vehicle charging: a power grid perspective. IEEE Access **8**, 214434–214453 (2020). https://doi.org/10.1109/ACCESS.2020.3041074
6. Buedi, E.D., Ghorbani, A.A., Dadkhah, S., Ferreira, R.L.: Enhancing EV charging station security using a multi-dimensional dataset: CICEVSE2024. In: Lecture Notes in Computer Science (including subseries Lecture Notes in Artificial Intelligence and Lecture Notes in Bioinformatics), vol. 14901 LNCS, pp. 171–190 (2024). https://doi.org/10.1007/978-3-031-65172-4_11/FIGURES/8

7. Li, Y., Chen, G., Dong, Z.: Multi-view graph contrastive representative learning for intrusion detection in EV charging station. Appl. Energy **385**, 125439 (2025). https://doi.org/10.1016/J.APENERGY.2025.125439

8. Makhmudov, F., Kilichev, D., Giyosov, U., Akhmedov, F.: Online machine learning for intrusion detection in electric vehicle charging systems. Mathematics **13**(5), 712 (2025). https://doi.org/10.3390/MATH13050712

9. Benfarhat, I., Goh, V.T., Lim Siow, C., Sheraz, M., Chee Chuah, T.: Temporal convolutional network approach to secure open charge point protocol (OCPP) in electric vehicle charging. IEEE Access **13**, 15272–15289 (2025). https://doi.org/10.1109/ACCESS.2025.3529526

10. Purohit, S., Govindarasu, M.: FL-EVCS: federated learning based anomaly detection for EV charging ecosystem. In: Proceedings - International Conference on Computer Communications and Networks, ICCCN (2024). https://doi.org/10.1109/ICCCN61486.2024.10637543

11. Rahman, M.M., Hossain Chayan, M.M., Mehrin, K., Sultana, A., Hamed, M.M.: Explainable deep learning for cyber attack detection in electric vehicle charging stations. In: Proceedings of the 2024 11th International Conference on Networking, Systems and Security, NSysS 2024, vol. 24, pp. 1–7 (2025). https://doi.org/10.1145/3704522.3704534

Author Index

GPSR Compliance
The European Union's (EU) General Product Safety Regulation (GPSR) is a set
of rules that requires consumer products to be safe and our obligations to
ensure this.

If you have any concerns about our products, you can contact us on

ProductSafety@springernature.com

In case Publisher is established outside the EU, the EU authorized
representative is:

Springer Nature Customer Service Center GmbH
Europaplatz 3
69115 Heidelberg, Germany